A Teaching Artist's Companion

A Teaching Artist's Companion

HOW TO DEFINE AND DEVELOP YOUR PRACTICE

Daniel Levy

OXFORD

UNIVERSITY PRESS

Oxford University Press is a department of the University of Oxford. It furthers
the University's objective of excellence in research, scholarship, and education
by publishing worldwide. Oxford is a registered trade mark of Oxford University
Press in the UK and certain other countries.

Published in the United States of America by Oxford University Press
198 Madison Avenue, New York, NY 10016, United States of America.

Library of Congress Cataloging-in-Publication Data
Names: Levy, Daniel, 1961– author.
Title: A teaching artist's companion : how to define
and develop your practice / Daniel Levy.
Description: New York, NY : Oxford University Press, [2019] |
Includes bibliographical references and index.
Identifiers: LCCN 2018057507 | ISBN 9780190926168 (pbk.) |
ISBN 9780190926151 (hardcover)
Subjects: LCSH: Music—Instruction and study. |
Arts—Study and teaching | Artists as teachers.
Classification: LCC MT1 .L578 2019 | DDC 780.71— dc23
LC record available at https://lccn.loc.gov/2018057507

for my mother

CONTENTS

ACKNOWLEDGMENTS

In the Hindustani tradition it is considered a bit disrespectful to say the name of one's teachers, or *gurus*, aloud. But on those occasions when you need to do so, as Falu Shah once explained to me, you reach up and tug on your right earlobe as you do, which means "please forgive me for saying your name out loud, honored teacher." I would like to thank some of my honored teachers, who have touched my life with their generosity and erudition. With one hand on my earlobe, thank you Mr. McNeill, Cornell Wiley, William D. Burton, David Wheeler, and Jim Sheppard for teaching me how to make music; Jocko Cummings and Pam Fox for teaching me what joyful rigor could mean; Elsie Chan and John Lee for giving me room to run at Lower East Side Prep; Cathryn Williams for opening the door at LCE; Tom Cabaniss, Hilary Easton, Jean Taylor, John Toth, Patricia Chilsen, Jerry James, Salla Saarikangas, and Barbara Ellman for showing me the artistry in teaching artistry; Amy Powers for suggesting that I write this book, and for sharing her dream of my felling a sequoia with a pocket knife; Judith St. Croix for warning me of the perils of know-it-all-ness; Ann Gregg for her unremitting drive to improve all projects; Manuel Bagorro for being the best thought partner a teaching artist could have; Robbie, Kenyatta, Daniel, Hakim, and the men at Sing Sing for giving me every chance to get it right; JoAnne Bernstein and Anthony Ball for making LOS such a beautiful place to work and create; the teaching artists and staff of the 92nd Street Y for their inspiring zeal and insistence on excellence; Misty Tolle for believing in and supporting my approach; Larisa Gelman for inviting me to be her partner in creating programs that we both love; Sarah Johnson for her vision, her tolerance for my questions, and for always knowing the best places to deploy me. The classroom teachers and correctional facility and shelter staff I have worked with have also been my teachers, influencing my practice in so many positive ways; I especially want to thank my colleagues at PS114, PS24x, PS36, PS130Q, Paterson School 4, Sing Sing, Rikers Island, Siena House, and HELP Bronx Morris for their dedication and generosity. Many individuals helped this book take shape. I am happily indebted to Glenna Avila, Cynthia Campoy Brophy, Heather Bryce, Maggie Costigan, Derek Fenner, Jean Johnstone, Barry Stewart Mann, Tongo Eisen-Martin, Jeff Mather, James Miles, Jennifer Oliver, Margaret Peot, Carol Ponder, Sebastian Ruth, Greg Thornton, and Aysha Upchurch, who all generously contributed their Views and anecdotes to the book; it was a joy to talk shop with them. I am also grateful to Jessica, Jason and Margaret from the Northern

Manhattan Writers Co-op and Daniel Bernstein for reading and encouraging when I needed a boost, Bruce Murray for pointing out the lay of the land, Eric Booth for his steady friendship and targeted guidance, Ava Lehrer for her keen eye and happy spirit, Barbara Clark for her notes on the early drafts and cool, clear insight as an agent. I will always be grateful for editor Suzanne Ryan's seeing the potential of this book in those gnarly early drafts, and for the incisive critique that she and the OUP peer reviewers provided. Finally, thank you Sam Levy for your discernment and high standards regarding teaching and learning, and thank you always Margaret Peot, this teaching artist's companion: tireless reader, beloved partner, the still point in a turning world.

CONTRIBUTING WRITERS

Glenna Avila is an artist, educator, and arts administrator, dedicated to the arts, young people, and communities. She is currently the Wallis Annenberg artistic director of the CalArts Community Arts Partnership (CAP) program and has been with CAP since 1991. Before CalArts, she directed community art centers for the City of Los Angeles Department of Cultural Affairs for fourteen years. She has painted more than seventy-five community murals throughout Los Angeles, the majority of which are collaborations with youth and their communities. As a teaching artist, she has taught in public schools, in museums, in after-school mental health programs, and with incarcerated youth in juvenile detention centers and probation camps since 1985. She was one of ten artists commissioned by the Olympic Organizing Committee to paint a mural on the freeway in downtown Los Angeles for the 1984 Olympic Arts Festival. www.calarts.edu/cap

Cynthia Campoy Brophy is the executive director and founder of artworxLA (formerly the HeArt Project). She was previously the publicist for the Los Angeles Museum of Contemporary Art, a Coro Southern California Arts Leadership fellow, a Vision Award recipient recognizing social entrepreneurial leaders, and a Eureka Foundation fellow. She is currently on the national steering committee for the Creative Youth Development Partnership, and has served on numerous committees and panels for the National Guild for Community Arts Education, Los Angeles County Arts Commission, Los Angeles Unified School District Options Task Force, and the City of Los Angeles's Department of Cultural Affairs. She was appointed by the speaker of the California State Assembly to serve on the California Cultural and Historical Endowment. She was board chair for Arts for LA, and a Durfee Sabbatical recipient, and participates in Harvard Graduate School of Education's "Scaling for Impact" program. www.artworxla.org

Heather Bryce is the artistic director and founder of Bryce Dance Company and has won awards and national attention for her innovative choreography and community engagement work. Bryce explores timely and relevant themes through intricate choreography and interdisciplinary collaboration. Her work has been presented at venues including: Flynn Center for the Performing Arts, Mark Morris Dance Center, Gibney Dance, Dixon Place, the Tank, Town Hall Theater (VT), the Dance Complex, and Spruce Peak Performing Arts Center.

Bryce currently works as a teaching artist for Alvin Ailey American Dance Theater, Lincoln Center Education, the Performing Arts Center at SUNY Purchase, and the Center for Arts Education. She holds her MFA in interdisciplinary arts from Goddard College. www.brycedancecompany.com

Maggie Costigan has been a teaching artist in Hawaii public schools since 1989, providing curriculum integrated dance residencies to over seventy-five kindergarten through eighth grade classrooms annually. She is part of the Artistic Teaching Partner Roster for the Hawaii State Foundation on Culture and the Arts' Artist in the Schools Program, and has been a frequent participant in Honolulu Theatre for Youth's Collaborative Residency Project, working with classroom teachers to design and implement arts curriculum for the classroom. As the executive director of the Maui Dance Council, Maggie has expanded the organization's Chance to Dance program to service fifteen public schools and over five thousand youth annually. She currently resides on the island of Maui, where she continues to study and choreograph dance, while enjoying the Pacific Ocean in her spare time.

Derek Fenner is an artist, educator, and researcher living on Ohlone land in Oakland, California. He earned his MFA in writing and poetics from the Jack Kerouac School of Disembodied Poetics at Naropa University. He has an MA in educational leadership from Mills College. After a decade of experience as an art educator and administrator in the Massachusetts juvenile justice system, he is completing his doctorate in education at Mills College. His research interests include youth participatory action research as pedagogy, juvenile justice education, decolonizing methodologies, and arts-based research. He is the arts learning program manager for the Alameda County Office of Education, where he also serves as a faculty member for the Integrated Learning Specialist Program. LinkedIn Profile: www.linkedin.com/in/derek-fenner-04898757/

Jean Johnstone is the executive director of Teaching Artists Guild, a national organization dedicated to strengthening the field of teaching artistry. She was the founding director of Applied Theater Action Initiative, and developed and ran international multimedia programs for youth, programs for artists transitioning from homelessness, and incarcerated youth. Jean studied at the Moscow Art Theatre and spent several years teaching dramaand directing in Hong Kong. She sits on the policy council for the California Alliance for Arts Education, and is a board member of the Francophone School. She holds a graduate certificate and bachelor's degree in theater arts from University of California, Santa Cruz, and certificates from the Moscow Art Theatre and Eugene O'Neill Theater Center. www.teachingartistsguild.org

Barry Stewart Mann is a professional storyteller, educator, actor, and writer based in Atlanta. A graduate of Harvard University with an MFA in Theater from the University of San Diego, Barry has performed on dozens of stages; told tales to thousands in schools, libraries, festivals, camps, and beyond; and led classes, workshops, and residencies with groups of all ages and backgrounds, from nursery schools to nursing homes. Barry has been a roster performer or teaching artist with the Alliance Theatre, Georgia Wolf Trap, Young Audiences, Georgia Council for the Arts, Fulton County Teaching Museum, Atlanta Partnership for Arts in Learning, Old Globe Theatre, California Playwrights Project, and San Diego Institute for Arts in Education. He was named National Storyteller of the Year, was heard as a regular contributor to the public radio program "Recess!," and tells stories internationally with Dream On Productions of Buenos Aires, Argentina. www.barrystewartmann.com

Originally from San Francisco, **Tongo Eisen-Martin** is a poet, movement worker, and educator. His latest curriculum on extrajudicial killing of black people, *We Charge Genocide Again!*, has been used as an educational and organizing tool throughout the country. His book *Someone's Dead Already* was nominated for a California Book Award. His latest book, *Heaven Is All Goodbyes*, was published by the City Lights Pocket Poets series, shortlisted for the Griffin Poetry Prize, and won a California Book Award and an American Book Award.

Jeff Mather is a community-based public artist and environmental sculptor and teaching artist based in Atlanta. He is a lead artist, cofounder, and board president for the Atlanta Partnership for Arts in Learning. He coaches the designing and building of large-scale architectural sculptures. He is a member of Alternate ROOTS and several of his community-based public art projects have been funded by ROOTS' Community/Artist Partnership Program. He has also been the lead artist for the Onsite/Insight Program, coaching multi-school environmental art partnerships in Atlanta Public Schools. www.facebook.com/MatherSiteArt/

Originally from Chicago, **James Miles** is the executive director of Arts Corps. Before joining Arts Corps, he was the director of education at Urban Arts Partnership in New York City. James has also facilitated workshops and designed curriculum for the New Victory Theater, Roundabout Theatre, Disney Theatrical Group, and others. Previously a professor at NYU, James shared his expertise as an advisory board member of SXSW EDU and Catalyst Arts. A graduate of Morehouse College and Brandeis University, James has presented at SXSW EDU, ITAC, EdTechXEurope, Google, and has provided professional development to teachers across the world. His work has been covered by Complex Magazine, NPR, National Guild, CBS, U.S. Department of Education, and ASCD. He can be frequently found on Twitter, as @fresh_professor, writing about arts, education, educational policy, and academic inequity. www.artscorps.org

Jennifer Oliver is a dance teaching artist and the artistic director of A Step Beyond. Oliver holds a BA in dance from University of California, Irvine, and an MA in expressive arts therapy from the European Graduate School. She is an active dance artist, performing both locally and internationally. As an educator and therapist, Oliver has provided creative dance education and artful practices for students and adults for twenty years. From 2005 to 2015 Jennifer served as the associate director for Young Audiences of San Diego where she cofounded and directed the Arts Education Resource Organization (AERO), Title 1 through the Arts, Arts Empower, and the Teaching Artist Institute of San Diego. Oliver was the San Diego representative for the statewide initiative, Teaching Artist Support Collaborative, and served on the National Arts Education Council for Americans for the Arts. www.a-step-beyond.org

Margaret Peot is an artist, writer, and teacher, and for over twenty years a professional costume painter, working on Broadway shows (such as *Wicked, Frozen, The Lion King*), ice shows, circuses, and arena events. She has written and illustrated several books to help readers realize their artistic potential, including two coloring books in the series *Let's Color Together: A Shareable Coloring Book for Parents and Kids* (Sourcebooks 2015–16). Believing that "art-making can be for everyone," Peot presents art workshops to children and adults, including Creative Aging Training at the Creative Center at University Settlement. Margaret's book *Inkblot: Drip, Splat, and Squish Your Way to Creativity* (Boyds Mills, 2011) was awarded a Eureka! Silver Medal for nonfiction children's books and was an Orbis Pictus Honor Book, and her early reader picture book, *Crow Made a Friend* (Holiday House 2014) was an Ohioana Awards finalist. www.margaretpeot.com

Carol Ponder, an award-winning performing and teaching artist, has worked for over forty years as an actress, singer, and musician. She and her husband Robert Kiefer performed *My Father's War*—their two-person storytelling and song performance with workshop—for the 2018 International Teaching Artist Conference (ITAC4) at Carnegie Hall. In her thirty years as a teaching artist, consultant, and researcher, Carol has partnered with classroom teachers, administrators, and clinical therapists to develop and facilitate arts-based projects and professional development. Her clients include: International Storytelling Center in Jonesborough, Tennessee; TPAC Education (1987–2016), Nashville, Tennessee; the Veterans Administration and other veterans organizations in ten states (2010–ongoing); seven Lincoln Center–style aesthetic education institutes (1988–ongoing); the Empire State Partnership Project, New York (1999–2009); VSA Arts International; and Borderless Arts Tennessee (2003–ongoing). www.myfatherswar.org

Sebastian Ruth is a professional musician and educator committed to exploring connections between the arts and social change. He graduated from Brown University in 1997, where he worked closely with education scholars Theodore Sizer, Mary Ann Clark, and Reginald Archambault on a project exploring the relationship between moral education and music, and with members of the Charleston String Quartet in Brown's chamber music program. Sebastian is the founder and artistic director of Community MusicWorks, a nationally recognized organization that connects professional musicians with urban youth and families in Providence, Rhode Island. As a member of the Providence String Quartet, the organization's resident ensemble, he has performed in recent seasons in Providence, Boston, Los Angeles, Banff, and New York, and with members of the Borromeo, Muir, Miro, Orion, and Turtle Island String Quartets, with pianist Jonathan Biss, and violist Kim Kashkashian. Sebastian serves on the board of the International Musical Arts Institute, and on the advisory boards of the Sphinx Organization. In 2012, Sebastian received an honorary doctorate from Brown University, and was named by *Strings Magazine* as among the twenty-five most influential people in the string music world. www.communitymusicworks.org

Artist-activist **Greg Thornton** lives in Seattle, Washington. He has worked as a teaching artist for the past six years in collaboration with Arts Corps, Seattle Public Schools, Center for Children and Youth Justice, and the Vera Project, among other local schools and organizations. Greg's visual arts lesson plans encourage and inspire his students to engage in self-expression and allow a space for his students to telltheir truth through art. Greg's classrooms provide a safe, nonjudgmental setting for students to focus on their own growth and identity. In addition to being a full-time teaching artist, Greg runs a small business called Black Iconic T-Shirts, which produces T-shirts that celebrate important individuals in black culture and history and invite the viewer into each person's life and accomplishments. www.blackiconictshirts.com

Aysha Upchurch is an artist, instructor, and education consultant who is committed to youth advocacy, social inclusion, artistry development, and transformative education. Whether on stage or in the classroom, hip-hop is a thread throughout her work. Aysha holds an MA in International Peace and Conflict Resolution from American University, and combines this knowledge with hip-hop to design and facilitate conflict resolution workshops for youth. She has been on faculty at George Mason University, Howard Community College, Harvard University, and Salem State University. She received her EdM from the Harvard Graduate School of Education (HGSE), and as a visiting practitioner in education there, she served as the inaugural artist-in-residence with the Arts in Education program, exploring the pedagogical implications of cross-disciplinary artistic collaboration, community dance cyphers, and hip-hop pedagogy. Aysha joined the faculty at HGSE in fall 2018, teaching courses on hip-hop education and embodied learning, as well as launching and directing HipHopEX—a collaborative lab for high school and graduate students to experience, explore, and experiment with hip-hop arts in education. www.ayshaupchurch.com

A Teaching Artist's Companion

Introduction

What Teaching Artists Do

I was a young artist, composing and performing in New York City, a recent arrival from the Midwest. To make ends meet, I taught music at an alternative high school for high-risk dropouts and Chinese immigrants on the Lower East Side: guitar orchestra and song-based ESL, English as a Second Language. After two years of full-time work, I swore off teaching. I did not feel like an artist while teaching, and did not have any real teaching technique. I was burned out. But a few years later when Lincoln Center Institute invited me to become a music teaching artist, I discovered an approach to teaching (à la Dewey, Greene, and Vygotsky) that made sense. Over thirteen part-time years, I designed and taught my own workshops, emulating master teachers and teaching artists. Through this work I awoke to a sense of service and social justice, and came to see teaching artistry as social activism. Obsessed with being truly *effective*, I wanted to reach and empower students as deeply and consistently as possible, in spite of all the given constraints on time and resources. After Lincoln Center, 92Y hired me to write curriculum for their K–3 music teaching artists, as did Carnegie Hall, where I rewrote all of the high school and K–5 curriculum. I kept experimenting, tweaking and road-testing various models of engagement and activity in classrooms, concert halls, homeless shelters, and correctional programs. I went from being the burnt-out guy who was never going to teach again to the guy who loves to teach.

I'm drawn to teaching artist work again and again by a sense of *possibilities*. It's strongest at the beginning of a workshop, when I'm making eye contact with students for the first time: an intense awareness of the wonderful potential of each human being there to create, grow, question, challenge, feel, and connect. Freedom and possibility are in the air. *What will these students make and do during our time together? What surprising insights or questions will they have? What do they already know, and what do they wonder? What discoveries will they make? What paradoxes will they uncover, metaphors invent, ideas and energies release?* And right alongside that energized sense of possibility comes a sense of responsibility. *I may be able to be of benefit to the people gathered here.* During those first moments of eye contact, a relationship is already forming, living and immediate. Maybe you've been there, too: an artist-educator face to face with new students, their amazing potential, and your desire to make the most of every moment you'll share with them.

Where you find art, artists, and the potential for teaching and learning—in after-school workshops, ateliers, YMCAs, educational outreach programs, community centers, libraries, homeless shelters, health care and correctional facilities, K–12 and all types and levels of schools (including undergraduate and graduate-level universities)—you will find teaching artists and their students at work.

Teaching artists (TAs) are poets, dancers, musicians, actors, painters, writers, composers, theater directors—professional arts practitioners who sometimes teach. The Association of Teaching Artists defines a teaching artist as *a practicing professional artist with the complementary skills and sensibilities of an educator, who engages people in learning experiences in, through, and about the arts.* In this book, the term *teaching artist* broadly refers to artists who guide a group's creation of or engagement with works of art, in any educational setting. Any group that teaching artists serve will be called *students* (who, in other contexts, might be considered learners, co-learners, or artists, to name but a few roles that workshop participants play). Any place teaching artists and students might meet will be called a workshop or class.

Artists become teaching artists when they leave their art-making space and enter a community in order to educate (from the Latin *educare*, "to draw out") or teach (from the ancient Greek root δείκνυμι [*deíknumi*] meaning "to show or point out"). Teaching artists *draw out* and *point out* aspects of their students' experiences as they make and explore works of art together. Our students form communities of learners who make and do, reflect and revise, express their ideas and bring beauty into the world. The resulting enhancement of students' ability to listen, engage, imagine, and problem-solve can change their lives, and our shared world, for the better.

History shows us that artists have always taught, either to pass on a craft (Medieval guilds, Renaissance ateliers) or to support their own art-making (from dance, music, and drawing masters to university professors). Beginning with Chicago's Hull House (1889), through Louis Armstrong's transformative experience at the Colored Waifs' Home for Boys (1914), to Young Audiences (1952), right up to the present moment's Arts-in-Education and Creative Youth Development movements, the teaching artist lineage has been inspired by a sense of service.

Our Craft

During the forty years since the term was invented at Lincoln Center, *teaching artist* has become a recognized vocation. During the second half of the twentieth century, a number of factors made the invention of teaching artists necessary. In broad strokes: large arts presenters were looking to build future audiences, while smaller companies and studios established educational outreach programs that helped identify them as robust and community-minded. At the same time, many schools faced funding cuts in the 1970s, and urban schools often trimmed their dance, visual art, theater, and music programs, or relegated them to after-school status. By the 1980s, arts organizations were providing services directly to schools, and artists were delivering the services. The relationship grew through (and was shaped by) the implementation of national and local academic standards in the 1990s, the Arts Integration movement in the 2000s, and the current social justice arts education movement.

Today, teaching artists have become integral to education and Arts-in-Education. Hundreds of state and local Arts-in-Education organizations, a growing number of teaching artist organizations (the San Francisco-based Teaching Artists Guild, the Association of Teaching Artists), and at least one national association (the National Guild for Community Arts Education) are serving the needs of arts program administrators and teaching artists. The training programs available to teaching artists are still mostly organization-based (arts presenters professionally developing their own teaching artists) and discipline-based (art schools training and certifying visual art teaching artists). But more generalized and career-oriented programs for teaching artists in multiple disciplines are also becoming available: Community-Word Project's Teaching Artist Project (New York), a training and internship program; University of the Arts' Teaching Artist Certificate program (Philadelphia), Young Audiences Teaching Artist Studios and Programs (in Oregon, California, Texas, Louisiana, Indiana, Maryland, and more), Teachers College at Columbia University's Teaching Artist Community Certificate Program. Kadenze Academy, partnered with Lincoln Center Education and the Queensland Performing Arts Centre (Brisbane, Australia), offer four open-enrollment online courses, an "entry-level program for those wishing to develop their practice as teaching artists." The current "Big List" on the Teaching Artists Guild website lists more than fifty open-enrollment teaching artist training opportunities, from two-hour workshops to four-year degree programs. The United Federation of Teachers recognizes, supports, and represents teaching artists (in New York City), although the national teachers union, the American Federation of Teachers, does not. Higher education programs are embracing the field (Columbia College Chicago, Harvard Graduate School of Education, Sebastian Ruth's Music and Social Action course at Yale and Coursera). A quarterly professional journal, *The Teaching*

Artist Journal, began publication in 2009. The biannual International Teaching Artist Conference (ITAC) began meeting in 2012. This loose association of institutions and organizations supports the expanding range of opportunities available to teaching artists.

Despite these developments, the teaching artist field remains a do-it-yourself, work-in-progress affair. As we progressed past the early invent-and-innovate stage of practice, a specific craft of teaching artistry took shape—but that craft has yet to be defined or, rather, the current definition of a teaching artist's craft is remarkably diffuse, a collection of lists and anecdotes. We are dependent on an artist-to-artist oral tradition for technique, clarification, and insight. The resulting ambiguity serves us in some positive ways. It is healthy and appropriately responsive to keep inventing our individual practice. Artists see teaching as a creative act, the making of a thing not seen before; the more it is so, the more we can wholeheartedly engage as artist-educators. Tolerance for ambiguity is one of the capacities we hope to embody; because learning outcomes are often hard to track, there is ambiguity built into what we do. Our undefined craft does reflect some of the reality of our experience.

But as workaday teaching artists in the classroom, we have to decide which practices to emphasize and which to avoid. For that, ambiguity does not serve us well. We're doing our best to be *crafty* without defining our craft. Even though the challenges of the work have remained unchanged, conscientious practitioners in the twenty-first century are still asking each other the same basic questions teaching artists were asking forty years ago.

Those same questions are at the heart of *A Teaching Artist's Companion*:

How is a teaching artist's craft defined?

What approaches or practices allow us to improve our craft?

Our institutional partners and teaching artist colleagues generously offer workshops and publications to help us define and improve our craft. In these shared spaces, we get a sense of common purpose. But in the end we are still independently self-defining and self-improving. We reflect on our successes and struggles, and we cultivate insight based on that observed experience. Our honest self-evaluation is key to establishing and maintaining high standards for our work. To the extent that we can match our actions to our aspirations, our practice improves, and we evolve. Happily, a willingness to self-reflect is something that comes naturally to artists and therefore to teaching artists. This dynamic is likely already ingrained in your teaching practice: invent and innovate, then observe and reflect, and improve over time by applying the lessons you learn. In my own classroom practice, I've experienced many moments when I've failed to serve my students with a skillful response, or failed to design well. The moments in which my work with students appeared to be falling apart were ultimately important teachers of craft, invaluable opportunities to reconnect with students and redefine my teaching practice. Reflection makes it possible for a failing or weakness to become an insight or strength. Over time, successful approaches develop into skillful means and positive habits. Given the important place self-reflection holds in our process, *A Teaching Artist's Companion* also asks:

How effective is our self-reflection?

What structures might serve to make it more effective?

To invent our craft, we invent or borrow the structures we need: warm-ups, activities, lesson and unit plans. We rarely walk into a class and wing it; if we are to serve our students, we know we can do better than that. Instead, we shape our workshops on paper in advance, structure our use of time and materials: we plan. We know that projects and events rarely go according to plan. We can't be sure how the plan will play out in real time, especially in an atmosphere that encourages creative freedom, risk-taking, and improvisation, but we plan nonetheless. *How much of what happens in our workshops is planned, and how much is spontaneous? What kind of planning is needed to build spontaneity and responsiveness into the process?* Mastering the planning aspect of your craft means being able to design structures that engender maximum engagement, growth, and joy for everyone in the community you serve. Your planning and preparation are grounded in your belief system, so to round out the *Teaching Artist's Companion* inquiry:

What are your values and beliefs as an artist/educator?

How connected are your beliefs, plans, and actions in the classroom?

I've been asking myself these questions since 1993, when I began working for Lincoln Center as a music teaching artist. Since then I've taught hundreds of music-making workshops and pre-concert classes. As detailed in Chapter 1, "The Evolution of a Teaching Artist," I was inclined by nature as well as nurture to view the work as an ongoing experiment. Each classroom session was a chance to explore and pursue the perfection of the practice. I documented my process, reflected a lot, and gathered evidence to support my craft. Over time, and in collaboration with accomplished artists and teachers, my students and I came to experience less *trial and error* and more *trial and success*. Observing other teaching artists at work, I saw that we were all grappling with the same basic questions, regardless of specific arts discipline. I started wondering how we could access each other's expertise and share knowledge. In partnerships with the 92nd Street Y, the Little Orchestra Society, and Carnegie Hall's Weill Music Institute, I created new programs, as well as written curricula and professional development workshops for other artists. This process made me even more aware of the challenges facing curriculum designers. In 2003, I resolved to try to be of service to other teaching artists and began drafting what would become *A Teaching Artist's Companion.*

View, Design, Respond

Teaching artist work falls into three parts or phases: View, Design, and Respond. *A Teaching Artist's Companion* makes use of this framework throughout the book. *View* is your personal take on how teaching and learning happen, your values and beliefs. It includes your overall point of view (such as your definition of your roles as a teaching artist and the overlapping communities where these roles play out) as well as your ideas about how to apply what you know. *Design* and *Respond* are the phases of teaching artist work where *View* manifests in real time and space. To *Design* is to plan a teaching and learning experience before entering the classroom. *Respond* refers to our actions in the company of students as we actually teach a workshop. Of these three, View, Design, and Respond, View is primary, since it is the point of origin that determines what we Design and how we Respond.

View is also primary as the first of three terms—View, Meditation, and Action—that are used to frame Tibetan Buddhism's Dzogchen teachings. To directly see the nature of mind is the *View*; the way of stabilizing that View and making it an unbroken experience is *Meditation*; and integrating that View into our daily life is what is meant by *Action*.

Whether or not you are a Buddhist, you can observe View, Meditation, and Action functioning in your life, because the sequence encompasses what is arguably the most common of human experiences. You already have a set of beliefs that grow and change over time, a developing understanding of the nature of mind (your View). You spontaneously reflect and compare your View with your specific experiences, mature as you reflect, and plan your future actions (your Meditation). You apply what you have learned during Meditation in daily life (your Action). Some of us are more reflective than others, but we all engage in these three practices to some extent.

View, Design, and Respond similarly encompass the teaching artist's experience. You already have personal beliefs and understandings about art, teaching, and learning (your View). You plan what you do before you enter a classroom or workshop space (your Design phase). You apply what you know as you interact on your feet in the classroom or workshop space (your Respond phase). For our purposes, View, Design, and Respond are separated and presented in this order. But in practice, the three easily overlap and share common concerns and focal points. And all three are far from static; View informs Design and Respond, but also grows and changes over time according to what we experience during Design and Respond.

A Teaching Artist's Companion invites you to delineate your craft in terms of View, Design, and Respond. The text encourages you to develop your own View, and offers a range of models as a resource to help you clarify the Design and Respond phases of your work. Within this framework, I won't espouse a single methodology or posit any hard and fast rules (*One must always . . ., One must never . . .*). Instead you'll find stories and detailed observations on the mechanics and mysteries of our practice. I'll invite you to think of yourself as a craftsperson, and provide field-tested examples of teaching artist craft for your consideration. I'll raise questions with the intention of helping you to hone the questions you are already asking. When I provide answers, they are meant to be *provisional*, a step on the way to your mastery of teaching artist practice.

You'll also be invited to consider your practice as a collection of discrete skills, each worthy of your scrutiny and development. These skills are the *essential practices of all TAs working in all art forms and workshop types*. Staying within the View, Design, Respond framework, I'll separate them out as Design Practices and Respond Principles:

Design Practices of Teaching Artist Craft

establishing safe space—how we build trust and supportive, creative communities of learners

accessing prior knowledge—how we work with and build on what our students already know

using open questions—how to formulate and make the most of open and closed questions

constructing analogies—approaching unfamiliar works of art or processes via more familiar analogous processes

modeling—how demonstrating a process can invite and facilitate student work

exploiting multiple modalities—how students' different learning styles affect the way we design activities

placing contextual information—the role of context in creative work

reflecting—different techniques for and approaches to reflection

describe/analyze/interpret—examples of reflective prompt types and alternative models of reflection

Respond Principles of Teaching Artist Craft

the container—seeing the workshop space as a container for teaching and learning, with its own boundaries and dynamics

the community of learners—how we as coaches and facilitators can support, challenge, and guide our students *honor every response*—how to work with the range of positive and negative responses that students offer when we invite their work, ideas, and questions

the art of the follow-up—eight response strategies that can help us draw out students' ideas and insights, while modeling engagement, curiosity, and community-mindedness

thriving and struggling—how arts education students thrive, and the many ways they can struggle, with a look at classroom management and the effects of social toxicity, and emotional and developmental disabilities

How You Might Use This Book

If you are new to teaching artistry, you might best use *A Teaching Artist's Companion* the way you would use a map to help you spend a day in an unfamiliar city, as a reference that supports an immersive journey. At the start of the day, before you dive in and walk the streets, you refer to the map to help you decide where to begin and what a good sequence of sites might be. During the day, you use it to reorient yourself (even if you are not quite lost) or get a sense of scale, distance, and place. At the end of the day, you use the map to reflect on where you went, and your reflection shapes your plan for the next day's exploring. City maps are not designed with you and you alone in mind. But their design allows you to customize, according to your personal interests, how you use them. Customize your own use of *A Teaching Artist's Companion* as you plan, support, and reflect on your immersion in teaching artistry. I suggest spending some time exploring the book in a spirit of serendipity in order to get a sense of the scope and details, then returning to the beginning to read through the chapters in order. Absorb what is here, choose the ideas and techniques you want to try out, and shape your own work.

If you are an experienced practitioner, please bring your expertise to a virtual conversation with me as you read. Compare your experience and experience-based beliefs with the ones I offer here. Examine them "as a goldsmith examines gold," question, dissect, analyze, and please do judge. You'll know what to do. I hope you have fun using this book as a tool for focused reflection on your practice. We spend most of our teaching time alone (with our students); we're rarely observed and too rarely have a chance to talk shop with other experienced practitioners. Let's talk shop.

For arts administrators who hire, train, or professional develop teaching artists, *A Teaching Artist's Companion* is a field report: here is what's happening out there, from a working teaching artist's perspective. I am still working in the field, continuing to experiment, and making sure I can practice what I preach. I've tried to emphasize the practical, as opposed to theoretical, in ways that I hope you will appreciate and find ways to put to use. With practicality in mind, the book might be used as a toolkit during your professional development and curriculum writing processes. With your help, teaching artists will come to do their best work sooner rather than later in their careers.

Visual artists, dancers, and theater or other artists may notice that while the framing thesis of the book (View, Design, Respond) and the way that thesis is broken out (Design Practices and Respond Principles) address practices that teaching artists in all disciplines recognize as vital, many of the work samples (lesson plans and program outlines) in *A Teaching Artist's Companion* are music-based. I hope you'll find that your discipline-specific lesson- and program-planning needs are addressed in a number of ways. The lesson plans and program outlines are presented as concrete and *translatable* examples. I've tried to make it as easy as possible for you to sift out each activity's essence for your own art-form-specific purposes. The book is organized, and each section written, with this quality in mind. My faith in the translation dynamic comes from my own teaching artist training. A great deal of my View and Design practice originated with visual arts and dance teaching artists whose work I experienced, admired, translated, and put to musical uses. You'll find comments and contributions from veteran theater, dance, and visual arts teaching artists throughout the book.

When a teaching artist's intention, art, and craft align, wonderful things happen. We're able to serve our workshop participants with skill and ease. They are able to imagine, create, observe, and interact with energy, sophistication, and satisfaction with their work. We find that we really can tap our students' amazing potentials and make the most of the short time we spend with them. The View, Design, Respond framework is meant to empower teaching artists to more *deliberately reflect on and cultivate* the causes and conditions that lead to this quality of experience. It is also an invitation to broaden our perspective as practitioners of teaching artistry. As we become more aware of our craft, we can develop a panoramic view of each teaching and learning situation. The broader our perspective, the more aware we are of the connection between mindfulness of our actions and the liberation that we experience (as well as engender) when leading our workshops. In *The Myth of Freedom and the Way of Meditation*, Chogyam Trungpa Rinpoche describes this connection by pointing out that mindfulness creates space:

> *Right mindfulness does not simply mean being aware; it is like creating a work of art. If you are drinking a cup of tea with right mindfulness, you are aware of the whole environment as well as the cup of tea. You can therefore trust what you are doing; you are not threatened by anything. You have room to dance in the space, and this makes it a creative situation. The space is open to you.*[1]

Once we develop the habit of staying aware of the whole picture, we can become fearless in our teaching artist practice. There won't be a circumstance that we are not prepared to work with. We'll have a realistic sense of what the relationships are, what our goals are, and the limits of our own means. The workshop space will be open to us, and the ease that we feel can radiate out to our students. This responsive freedom is the ultimate empowerment for a teaching artist.

I hope this book entices you to observe the View, Design, and Respond frame at work in your own practice. Examine your own experience to see if these ideas don't ring true in thought, and also work well in the field. Once you do, I hope you find yourself leading your workshops in an increasingly joyful and effective manner. I hope you'll enjoy the fruits of your encounters, as the hero of your own teaching artist story, for the benefit of the children, adults, and communities we serve.

1

The Evolution of a Teaching Artist

I am sitting in vice principal John Chen's office as he reviews my music class lesson plans. From where I sit, the light from the window shines through John's bangs and eyelashes, and I realize that his black hair is undeniably blue, not black. I wonder if this is true of all people with Chinese ancestry, or if John dyes his normally black hair blue. John is in the unenviable position of trying to help someone who is enthusiastic, has little idea what he is doing, and doesn't want to be helped. I'm a first-year teacher at Lower East Side Prep, an alternative high school on Manhattan's Lower East Side. The school specializes in serving a mix of recent Chinese-speaking immigrants and students who the system labels, not without reason, high-risk dropouts, teenagers who have failed to thrive in larger schools all across the city. Most of the Taiwanese-, Cantonese-, and Mandarin-speaking students have lied about their age on their immigration forms in order to take advantage of New York City's policy of offering a free public education to anyone under the age of twenty-one. They are mature young adults, working nights in sweatshops, stores, and factories, improving their English by day in the public schools. The African-American and Spanish-speaking kids at the school are in the minority. It is pretty orderly, as far as high schools go. One day a boy carrying a black duffel bag is pulled from my class and arrested; there is a loaded Uzi in the bag. But such episodes are exceptional.

John's blue eyebrows seem to be permanently raised for the duration of our meeting. My lesson plans are a mixture of formal-sounding bullshit scripted out to satisfy the Board of Education's requirements and unrealistic, hyper-ambitious teaching goals. The fact is I don't know how to teach. John may be wondering if I might really be able to coordinate an ongoing review of the major philosophies of the world within my beginning guitar curriculum. Part of me wants to ask for help, but I'm too guarded, uniformed, and immature to do so. As a full-time teacher three months into my first year, I am struggling, out of my depth, already on the way to burning out.

Every Design and Respond example and activity presented in this book is grounded in this View: *a community of learners / making & doing / in an atelier setting.* In practice, one's View isn't static. View evolves, as influenced by the evidence of our senses as we teach. My own View evolved slowly, from humble and dysfunctional beginnings. The story of how I arrived at this particular View, which is proving to be robust and practical across a wide variety of teaching opportunities, may be of interest, if you'll kindly permit me a little autobiography.

We'll begin the evolution of this teaching artist in 1988, there in John's office. The job had started out well enough and looked promising. I was happy to be employed full-time at a job I had never before imagined myself doing: teaching English as a second language and running a guitar orchestra at an inner city alternative high school. Principal Elsie Chan watched me teach a test class as a kind of audition (I think I had the second year ESL students singing the chorus of Don McLean's "American Pie") and decided I had what it took, or at least enough of what it took to begin. She told me I had a talent for teaching and offered me a job on the spot. The Board of Education's base pay of $35,000 a year with health benefits was more salary than I had ever seen. I could start paying off my student loans. I became a school teacher with a classroom and attendance sheets and grades. I had no idea what I was getting into, but I felt sure it would be an improvement on doing au pair work and construction while scrambling for music gigs. This was my View: start at 8:05 a.m. and finish at 2:30 in the afternoon. How hard could it be?

It was hard, and I was bad at it. I had no real teaching technique or craft, so I based my classes on what I had learned from marching band and wind ensemble rehearsals at a rural Midwestern high school. Not a great fit for an experimental inner-city school with older, street-savvy students. In the beginning I filled out what looked like reasonable and proper lesson plan sheets, as required by the Board of Education, and nursed things along. And that seemed, as my father used to say, *good enough for government work.* I was idealistic, as well as overconfident about my ability to pull off some big plans. One such plan was to devote the first ten minutes of every class to a survey of world philosophies that in my vivid fantasy would impress, engage, and inspire my students. The Chinese kids would love me because I knew more about Chinese philosophy than they did (*Hey kids, let me tell you about the watercourse way of the Tao . . .*). The Latino and African-American kids would love me because I was cool (even though I hadn't even known a single non-white person until I started college some five years before) (see Figure 1.1). None of this self-aggrandized fantasy manifested in the real world. My students remained unimpressed, although some of them befriended me, and many of them did learn to play a bit of guitar. While ambitious, I was also deeply ambivalent about the work, inspired but unable to follow through on the basis of inspiration.

FIGURE 1.1 The author at Lower East Side Prep High School, 1988

On one hand, I couldn't help fantasizing about what a great teacher I might be, bringing the students to a passion for music-making, leading them as they sang and played with enthusiasm and mastery. On the other hand, I wasn't at all keen on defining myself as a teacher. I knew I was an artist, a composer in teacher's clothing. Real artists don't teach, right? When it became evident that my students were not progressing as planned, instead of reaching out to the experienced teachers and administrators around me for help, I tried to tough it out alone. My music program stumbled along, neither thriving nor failing. I did have a connection with some of my students and the ability to, at times, successfully lead a class. I managed to present proper holiday concerts and even established and directed New York's first city-wide all-alternative high school talent shows. But there was an emotional weight to the work that

I wasn't prepared for. As I grew closer to my students, they told me of the crime, violence, and poverty in their lives. One young man calmly explained the link between his better performance in school, sleeping well at night, and keeping a loaded gun handy. The brightest and most promising students became pregnant or homeless and dropped out of school. They were disaffected and stressed in ways I could not even think how to address. My own ignorance of social injustice embarrassed me, and I was troubled by my inability to do anything to help.

As I started my second year of teaching, I was already exhausted by the daily grind. Instead of writing music after school, as I imagined I would be doing, I found myself stressed and increasingly depressed. I did not like the work I was doing, or where it seemed to lead, away from my own music-making. I was becoming less of an artist and not showing evidence of being much of a teacher. Self-image and reality were at odds with each other. I found excuses to take every possible sick and vacation day. An after-school alcohol abuse pattern developed. On the night before the final concert of my second year of full-time teaching, I went out drinking in Hell's Kitchen and to this day have no idea how or when I got back to my Washington Heights apartment. The next morning my girlfriend stuck me in the shower, and I made it to the concert. We agreed that this episode was a wake-up call. Something was going terribly wrong, and I needed to change before it got any worse.

Fast forward four years and eighty therapy sessions later. I was happily married to my then-girlfriend-now-wife, practicing Buddhist meditation, and engaging in more wholesome after-hours pursuits. Based in a tiny flat in the West Village, I was an artist again, finishing an MFA at New York University, and playing gigs on bass and guitar, forming collaborations, recording. My wife and I were both living the New York artist's life. When I reached out to my undergraduate jazz bass teacher Cornell Wiley back in Columbus, Ohio, to tell him what I was up to and thank him for all the ways I was benefitting from his tuition, he said, "Well, I'm proud of you. You went to New York and you not only took the tiger by the tail, you also swung him around and bit him on the ass."

Some colleagues at NYU suggested that while my composing career was taking shape I might try teaching. Really? No thanks. I had sworn that off. The antipathy was still there. I was sure that teaching would destroy my chances of succeeding as a working artist, a sacrifice I was unwilling to make. I believed in the power of the arts to change peoples lives. I was still intrigued by the puzzle of how people learn and grow. As a Buddhist, I was preparing to take formal vows to work for the benefit of all beings. The idea that I might be helpful to someone through the realms of music and teaching, on some level, I had to admit, appealed to me. Just who might be involved or where or how that might happen, I didn't know.

A few weeks before graduation, NYU professor Mel Marvin invited me to stroll around the East Village with him. Mel, an accomplished theater composer and great teacher, was encouraging me to continue my work as a composer. We talked about his composing and teaching, and Mel kindly offered to introduce me to the folks at Lincoln Center Institute (now Lincoln Center Education). Mel thought that LCI and I would be a good fit and imagined I would find both the work and the underlying philosophy interesting. I followed up on his advice and, thanks to his entrée, was soon scheduled for a job interview as a potential teaching artist, a job title I had never heard before. I read some Maxine Greene to prepare for the interview. Her terms were unfamiliar, but the teaching and learning dynamics she described rang true.

For my teaching artist audition, LCI deputy director Cathryn Williams presented me with an in-office desktop teaching artist test. The work of art: composer H. K. Gruber's anarchic multi-genre 1976 comic opera *Frankenstein*, a "pan-demonium for chansonnier and orchestra after children's rhymes by H. C. Artmann." How would I teach to this work, Cathryn asked. The poetry in the text was wild, fragmented, and playfully set to music. I'd recently been reading Tristan Tzara's *Seven Dada Manifestos and Lampisteries*, which included an exercise in Dada poetry-making, which I connected with the sensibility of the Gruber/Artmann work. Borrowing from Tzara, I told Cathryn I'd have children take a newspaper, cut out individual sentence fragments, place them in a bag, shake the bag, and pull out three fragments that they had to combine and set to a rhythm that pleased them. Apparently not bad for an aesthetic education first-timer. I ran the gauntlet of the LCI three-week teaching artist training program, joined the LCI roster, and begin work as a teaching artist.

For the next thirteen years I learned what I needed to know on the job. The Institute's model of aesthetic education and collaboration between teaching artists and classroom teachers afforded me opportunities to do so, and was, in fact, designed to have me do so. The work included leading summer session teacher training, administrators' workshops, family workshops, higher education workshops and one-off professional development sessions, and developing contextual support materials (the Window on the Work). But most of the work took place in urban and suburban elementary school classrooms. During this time, I worked in some sixty different school settings, teaching to some thirty diverse works of art: the tango music of Astor Piazzola, the traditional Irish *sean-nós* singing of Cathie Ryan, the jazz drumming of Lewis Nash, Mozart's solo piano music, David Tudor's *Rainforest* installation, Babatunde Olantunji's kora songs, Guy Klucevsek's virtuoso accordion.

I saw every classroom session or workshop as a kind of lab where I could try out different approaches: what works better, more often, for more students? LCI asked (required, really) classroom teachers and teaching artists to codesign their own units of study, preparation workshops leading to encounters with high-quality works of art. This setup was ideal for my laboratory approach. I was able to teach essentially the same material or process to different classes many times during a unit of study, sometimes teaching the same basic lesson to as many as ten or twelve classes in the same grade or within a small range of grade levels. This meant I could observe, reflect on results, and tweak activities again and again as I went. If parts of my Design failed, I could alter them and try again. If my Response work was working well, I could examine the kind of wording I was using in my prompts and open questions and confirm the types of words and structures that yielded consistently better results. Over time and hundreds of classroom sessions, I was able to piece together a picture of how people—children and adults—respond to different invitations and prompts, when they thrive, when they hold back. My View took shape as I saw my beliefs proven true or false in the classroom. Every teaching idea was road-tested. Every workshop was a chance to hone my craft, and to alter my View according to what I discovered.

As I worked, reading Maxine Greene led to John Dewey. Their ideas made eminent sense, and led me to see teaching as a way to change the world. Not that I would be the world changer, but that I might play a role in enabling others to do so. Maxine said that before an individual can change their world, they first have to be able to *see* what it is, and then *imagine* it being different. I believed that engagement with the arts could help make this happen. I'd seen the truth of this in my own life and in the lives of others. Teaching suddenly looked subversive and challenging on a new level.

The classroom laboratory situation was energized. I needed information and technique *right away*, so that I could use it *right away*. In many of these on-the-spot situations, there were master classroom teachers at work who already seemed to know much of what I needed to know. I observed and emulated them where I saw fit. I might have been happy to work out my teaching artist practice on my own, flying solo as I did before in the full-time public school classroom setting. Not asking for help was an old habit that was hard to break. But the LCI model created a kind of enforced professional development. I was required to collaborate, whether or not that was in my plan. What I experienced in collaborations had such a positive effect on my work that observation and analysis of classroom teachers at work became a choice. Master teachers were there to be discovered, in every school. They were not difficult to find, since they were happy and confident in their work and their classrooms functioned so well. Nearly every teacher I met and observed was competent and professional. About one out of ten were masterful. I saw them at work at every level of teaching. Some were passionate generalists. Others felt called to teach special education or junior high kids. Many of the master teachers I worked with were in grade school classrooms. Their mastery comprised what I came to believe were the essentials of teaching craft: *building community, anticipating students' needs and removing impediments, using prior knowledge,* and *modeling*. If all teaching artists were to master these four skills for a specific age group, that (in combination with our artistic expertise) would probably be enough to qualify us to teach anyone, anywhere.

What made these teachers of young children especially good at creating community, working with prior knowledge, removing impediments, and modeling? They were specialists in the business of introducing new ideas to less experienced beings. This was and is their day-to-day work. One might argue that all teachers introduce unfamiliar ideas to less experienced individuals, which is not untrue, but in those early grades, teachers are working with *much* less experienced individuals. The students are fully formed human beings, yes, but they also operate within some predictable developmental limits: a limited ability to work with abstraction and metaphor, to collaborate, to delay gratification, to tolerate ambiguity. Early grade teachers have to be good at forming communities because their students' developmental potential for participating in community is still emergent. They can't count on students knowing the drill of how to function within a community of learners, so they have to be good at defining and maintaining the boundaries of the classroom container for teaching and learning. Their students need to connect prior knowledge to new ideas for learning to feel meaningful; they are too young to sit politely and patiently with ideas with which they do not feel connected. Impediments are not so much removed as skillfully avoided, when classroom teachers design activities that honor the students' present capabilities, and work within students' cognitive and motor limitations. Modeling is key to success with these students because they take it in better than written or oral instructions.

Watching talented grade school teachers at work was a joy. Having them comment on or change what I was doing, molding my teaching when we were in the classroom together, was humbling. The best of them made use of any number of skills and techniques, while remaining spontaneous and peaceful as students embraced or struggled with the work at hand. I paid attention, literally took notes, and my View developed. I wanted to be more like these teachers in my teaching artist work. I sensed how their techniques could be adapted for my own art-centric uses, without my becoming *teacherly*.

These teachers' mastery of creating community, working with prior knowledge, removing impediments, and modeling was also made possible by their solid and practical understanding of child development. They knew their students' developmental needs, anticipated where they might falter or soar. They created flexible pedagogical structures and allowed scope for excellence. I came to see their teaching activity as a well-informed mitigation of any circumstances that would impede learning. The teachers could not exactly predict their students' learning process, but they did draw on theory and experience to remove obstacles to learning, clearing the field so that more students could succeed more often. Observing this dynamic shaped my current View of the teaching artist's role as predictor and remover of impediments.

During this time with Lincoln Center Institute my artist-colleagues were the dance, visual arts, music, and theater teaching artists there. Those of us in the LCI Teaching Artist Collaborative, an on-your-feet, walk-the-talk think tank for working teaching artists, met to reflect on our classroom practice. We held regular meetings to observe and discuss craft, share successes, evaluate artifacts and evidence of student learning, and troubleshoot practical issues in the schools. We invented documentation and assessment techniques, shared demonstration activities, and dissected our personal applications of what we came to see as a shared idea of what constitutes teaching artistry. We were an independent and opinionated bunch, as you might expect, some of us seasoned, some new, some erudite, some a little wild. There was a determined sense of openness. Anyone who had the temerity to say "this is how things are" in the context of the Collaborative was obviously spoiling for a fight. At that time the View we embraced was that of aesthetic education, and the aesthetic education world's foremost authority, the formidable Maxine Greene, was LCI's philosopher-in-residence. That the teaching branch of Lincoln Center found it important to have a philosopher-in-residence says a lot about their opinion of the importance of *View*.

As the Collaborative examined teaching artist practice, any Design that did not have the work of art at its center was rejected as inferior, a nonstarter. If an activity did not clearly connect with the work of art under study, we admonished each other to either alter the activity and the connective thread until it did connect, or simply start over. This rigor became ingrained in my thinking. Connection to the work of art (or art-making process) is the first gate any idea has to pass through in order to make it into a Design. Making & Doing was absolutely essential, as inspired by Dewey and confirmed by our own experience as professional makers and doers in our fields; *experiential learning* was the watchword at the time. Equally important, and sort of symbiotically linked to both the centrality of the work of art and the primacy of Making & Doing, was the *de facto* View of *art-making* as *choice-making*. This View almost always resulted in activities that illuminated different focal artists' processes by asking students to engage in the same or closely parallel choice-making processes—choosing materials, levels, colors, gestures, sounds—and being aware of making those choices. I took part in dance, theater, and visual arts activities that invited me in to choice-making processes in those art forms. The activities were almost always well designed and well connected to the work of art under study. I experienced genuine engagement and personal connections with works of art along the same lines that my aesthetic preparation had indicated were possible. I came to believe in the work we were doing not only because it was reported to work for others, but because it worked so well for me as a learner. Twenty years later, the connections continue, in that the works of art we studied are still vivid in my memory and still influencing how I see and experience other works of art. Also, the habits of openness and inquiry that the LCI Teaching Artists Collaborative encouraged are foundational in my teaching artist practice. Many artists naturally tend toward openness and inquiry. My colleagues and I transformed artistic habits of mind into a living, breathing, rewarding teaching practice.

Cultivating each individual's engagement with a work of art by guiding them to make choices (during Making & Doing) that connect directly to the work of art was the Greene-and-Dewey-inspired View that Lincoln Center Institute espoused and encouraged teaching artists to embody. This was not a View that was ever stated explicitly. And I don't believe the artists and artist-administrators who made up the Institute would ever have countenanced making such a statement, let alone agreed with my phrasing of it. At LCI, View remained implicit, to be continually discovered and refined rather than stated outright. LCI asked all of us, as individuals in partnership with our classroom teachers, to work out for ourselves just how an aesthetic education View would manifest in units of study. As an institution, LCI would standardize planning session forms, or other aspects of the work they saw as mechanical or less creative. But they avoided even suggesting using, repeating, or defining any particular approaches or specific teaching artist techniques beyond warm-ups, active learning, and reflection. This seemed right to me as I worked with four or five schools exploring two or three works of art every year, in units of study lasting from three to seven visits, while I was finding my practice.

Then a number of things happened at more or less the same time. I had been working as a teaching artist for twelve years. My workshops were steadily becoming more and more successful. My self-reflective questions about teaching practice had proven useful. I felt I was beginning to have some idea as to what I was doing and started imagining ways to share my ideas with other teaching artists. More than one friend suggested writing a book, so I started outlining one. But I lacked clarity about the role of child development and the dynamics of classroom communities, and had a View that was still amorphous. I sensed there were some big chunks missing from my model, but I didn't know what they were. I approached LCI about incorporating some field-tested approaches to teaching artistry into Lincoln Center Institute teaching artist training, basic practices that all of us needed to master: working in multiple modalities, modeling, working with contextual information and students' prior knowledge. But, at the time, the LCI administration was clear: *This is not a part of our model, not what we do.* So after years of good work together, I decided to leave a supportive and progressive institution and move on.

Teaching artist freelancing away from LCI started slowly. I worked one-off projects with Young Audiences, New Jersey Performing Arts Center, the Park Avenue Armory, and Symphony Space. I did some adjunct teaching at New York University and Marymount Manhattan College, working through variations on the same essential practices I had used in grade schools. I experimented, kept reading. I completed a first draft of this book, but was unable to find a guiding metaphor or frame to keep it from being anything but a long list of practices or a collection of highly specialized lesson plans, which I did not imagine anyone needed or wanted. I designed a one-year curriculum for Musicians for Harmony, and a three-year program for the Harmony Program, New York's El Sistema-style project. But none of these projects led to continued teaching artist work or ongoing working relationships.

With teaching work coming in at a trickle, I worked part-time at a Madison Avenue art gallery for owner Dorothy Carus, and under her tutelage developed a good eye for early-twentieth-century Russian and German avant-garde works on paper. When money got especially tight, I'd call cellist and contractor Mark Cupkovic. He hired me on to do light construction for his company, and I learned to sling mud (joint compound, the stuff that goes over the screw holes in drywall) and paint walls and trim without holidays (little patches of thin paint where the previous wall color shows through) or ropes (lines of paint that look like little strings). Mark knew that New Yorkers liked a really smooth wall. I was also writing scores for plays and films and having some success in the music theater world. At the same time, I was in the same spot so many New York–based artists find themselves: making art, but not making enough money to cover the bills.

When Sarah Johnson and Jessica Balboni at the 92nd Street Y's educational outreach department invited me to join their teaching artist roster, I happily accepted. They had a pre-written curriculum for teaching artists to use. I did not care for it. The teaching ideas seemed out of order, or misdirected, or just not much fun, considering the K–3 crowd they were meant to reach. I went into East Harlem schools and did the work, but I altered the program's scripted lessons and taught the workshops according to my own lights. Sara and Jessica came to observe me teach, then took me out to lunch. They noticed that I did not follow the written curriculum. They asked, "Why did you change it?"

My turkey sandwich seemed suddenly dry as I considered the possibility that I was about to lose my job. I chewed, swallowed, sipped some water, opened the printed curriculum and started working through what I saw there, activity by activity, point by point, one alteration at a time: what connected and did not connect with the work of art, what was fun or not fun for the students, what followed a consistent through-line of inquiry and what did not. Sarah and Jessica liked what I was doing, and asked me to work as 92Y's curriculum writer. The following summer, I began writing and editing for their *Music in the Schools* program. (Since then, retained by subsequent directors Misty Tolle, Larisa Gelman, and Ava Lehrer, I have continued to do so, and continued to road-test the quality of the curriculum writing by teaching it in Harlem and the South Bronx, and coaching other 92Y teaching artists. The 92Y Center for Arts Learning & Leadership's Discovery Series: Music has grown and gained recognition for ongoing excellence). In terms of evolution, curriculum writing began to look like a wonderful avenue to reach many students and in an oblique way help train teaching artists—and I enjoyed doing it.

Curriculum writing work proliferated. 92Y artistic director Bob Gilson asked me to design a new early childhood music program. With the help of Fretta Reitzes and the outstanding teachers in 92Y's Goldman Center for Youth and Family, I received an informal crash course in early childhood education. This led me to discover the Reggio Emilia atelier approach referred to in my View, which formed the basis for 92Y's SoundGarden classes. Carnegie Hall's Weill Music Institute, now headed by Sarah Johnson, asked me to create new curriculum for their K–2 Musical Explorers program, as well as their international high school programs (Global Encounters), and their grades 3–5 LinkUp program for orchestral music. At around the same time I started doing teaching artist work for the Little Orchestra Society, which has been my atelier, my Design and practice lab, for the last eleven years. Through some forty half-day visits each year with Little Orchestra and forty full days teaching for 92Y's Center for Arts Learning and Leadership, I'm still in the classroom, actively assessing and developing my curriculum writing and teaching artistry, keeping what I write grounded in reality.

As for the most recent stage of the evolution of this teaching artist, I find my ideas about the nature of our work opening up, especially as regards service and social justice. The collaborations at Carnegie led to being invited into their Musical Connections program, where I now work in health care, homeless shelter, and correctional settings (including Sing Sing, Rikers Island, see Fig. 1.2, and in a separate partnership with the Solera String Quartet's Project Music Heals Us, the Danbury Federal Correctional Facility). Whether in these settings or in the schools, I'm increasingly aware of our work as service to

FIGURE 1.2 The author at Sing Sing Correctional Facility, 2012. Still from the Carnegie Hall video "Behind Bars: Music at Sing Sing."

the individuals whose lives we touch, and service to the communities we live within and affect by our actions, and more impressed by and grateful to the professionals who work full-time serving in these venues.

As I write this in the spring of 2018, artists are questioning what *service* means in the context of social justice. Some teaching artists are identifying as social justice teaching artists, rather than dance or visual arts TAs, and teaching to social justice rather than to works of art or art-making processes. Other artists are keeping the work of art as their primary focus, but addressing social justice issues when they find these issues are a natural or salient aspect of that work. Sarah Johnson at the Weill Music Institute assures me that the divergence is not a problem; that there is room for many different approaches in the Arts-in-Education world, and that each organization and each artist need to be doing the work that they believe in. I recently applied for a position training teaching artists. For my audition, I was asked to teach a social justice workshop. I balked. While I am actively working to deconstruct my own white male privilege, studying black history and culture, and taking part in professional development workshops on racial and cultural sensitivity and anti-oppression practices, my expertise is in teaching artistry, not social justice. I'm unwilling to teach outside of my expertise. Also I prefer my social justice/service orientation to be personal and internal, rather than explicit or part of my job title. I didn't get the TA training job. That particular door closed when I questioned my auditioners about the necessity of teaching to social justice, and made my preferred View of *a community of learners / making & doing / in an atelier setting* clear. For the moment, my pursuit of social justice will come through art-driven processes.

That said, the professional development on social toxicity and classroom dynamics I've received over the past three years is making my work with students—especially black and brown boys and teens—more successful. I'm not sure if the changes would be subtle or obvious to an observer, but they feel profound to me. I'm more aware of what my students may be experiencing in and out of school, and what they may at first see when they look at me. My responses to these young men have shifted. I'm warmer, more trusting of their interest, good will, and ability to do excellent work, readier to ask them to bring their ideas to the table, faster to praise and celebrate their contributions. We're more deeply engaged with each other. Perhaps most importantly, inspired by the words of George Yancy (see "Dear White America," *New York Times*, December 24, 2015, or for a deeper dive, his book *On Race*), I find myself ready to "begin, right now, to practice being vulnerable." This has been transformative for me personally, and it is an easy fit with my Buddhist practice. I really like what vulnerability is doing to my teaching.

The Association of Teaching Artists surveys our community about once a year. For a sobering look at what two hundred and seventy respondents from all over the United States have to say about our field, visit the ATA website and read the results from the fall 2015 survey "Challenges Faced by Teaching Artists." For their spring 2018 survey, I listed these "questions I have about my practice": *What is the relationship between teaching to a work of art or art-making process, and teaching to social justice? How can I address race- and system-based inequities in the settings where I work? Where are there unnoticed opportunities to empower students, and how can I make the most of them? How can I set healthy limits for myself so that I don't overwork or burn out? How can I empower non-arts classroom teachers to be excellent Arts-in-Education collaborators?*

As my practice opens up, I'm aware of my debt to and gratitude toward the classroom teachers, teaching artists, and arts administrators who have taught me that any response, action, creation, conundrum, missed opportunity, false start, work of art, classroom experience, collaboration, surprising research, View shift, Design flaw, Design triumph, failure to Respond, or mastery of Response that transpires can be embraced and made useful as I attempt to master my craft. This book is my attempt to bring the many threads of their teaching together into a form that is useful to anyone interested in teaching artistry. I hope it helps you find your own mastery, and that your practice brings you, your students, and your colleagues every satisfaction and joy that can come out of our work.

2

View

to look at, see, or watch in a particular way

to scrutinize, observe

to look on in a particular light

to survey or examine mentally

an opinion or way of thinking about something

the things that can be seen from a particular place

extent or range of vision

a mode or manner of looking at or regarding something

an opinion or judgment colored by the feeling or bias of its holder

the foreseeable future

Love/Loathe

In October 2013, thirty of New York City's best and brightest teaching artists and arts-in-education administrators gathered at the DiMenna Center on West 37th Street for a professional development session titled "Making the Most of Your Creative Sessions." As part of a warm-up, we approached a twenty-foot-long sheet of blank paper on the wall. On the far left was the word LOVE. On the far right, LOATHE. As facilitator of the workshop, I asked each participant to think of some of the roles they play in workshop settings, to give each role a name or title, and write each of those somewhere on the continuum between LOVE and LOATHE, depending on how they felt about playing that role. If they were deeply ambivalent about a role, it would go smack in the middle, and so on. They were also invited to add to or otherwise comment on what others had written once the process got going. (Some items appeared more than once, when different individuals felt differently about the same role.) In less than five minutes, amidst a lot of nodding and laughing, we had a Love/Loathe map that looked like this (Figure 2.1):

performer	songwriter	ignorer of the energy of	asshole-manager	record-keeper
developer of content	learn & grow in my art	dominant	arranger	warm-fuzzy-ist
creative designer	teacher	cool kids	orchestrator	initial teeth-puller
conversation sparker	healer	team member	logistics manager	bullshit caller-outer
connector	student for life	1-on-1 conduit	uncomfortable	fixer of unrealistic time constraints
riddler	praiser	liaison	silence manager	musical part printer
artist	person-meter	interrogator	cat herder	herder
orchestrator	secret mirror	summarizer	time keeper	sayer of the same thing over and over
inspirer	organizer	collaborator	photo-copier	planner
space-holder	instigator	encourager	time manager	homework giver
content-provider	rhythm-holder	therapist	detail manager	inter-group mediator
composer	notator	facilitator		inter-group translator
engager	motivator	entertainment		opener of closed minds
harmonizer	translator	coordinator of details		attendance taker
silent sounding board	interlocutor			last minute detail finder-outer
logistics person	planner			poopy-pants accommodator
humorist	listener			instant responder
pathway	engineer of safe space			materials printer
therapist	person who has to hear "no"			inflexible expectations negotiator
collaborator	mentor			bullshit denier
listening/feeling companion				organizer of the unorganized
				implementer
				not-knower of important content
				bad cop
				crowd controller

FIGURE 2.1 Love/Loathe Continuum

By identifying their many roles on the Love/Loathe map, the teaching artists and arts-in-education administrators articulated one aspect of their *View*, described in the introduction to this book: *Teaching artist work falls into three parts or phases:* View, Design, *and* Respond. View *is your personal take on how teaching and learning happen, what you believe in and value.* Design *and* Respond *are where* View *manifests in real time and space. Your* Design *is the planning you do before entering the classroom.* Respond *refers to your actions in the company of students as you teach a workshop.*

View is global and foundational: global in that it encompasses macro- and micro- aspects of teaching and learning, philosophy and practice, and foundational in that it determines what we Design and how we Respond. Let's look at these global and foundational qualities in three hypothetical Views of a specific art-making process (songwriting) and how these Views might manifest as three different Designs for a songwriting workshop.

You already have a View of what songwriting means, even if you are not an experienced songwriter. Your View includes any craft related to the process (lyric writing, harmony, song forms), as well as any direct or indirect experience of the songwriting process (songs you've written, songs you know that were written by others, and anecdotal evidence of how the songs came about, such as the story of young Julian Lennon's drawing of a school chum named Lucy providing the genesis of John Lennon and Paul McCartney's "Lucy in the Sky with Diamonds"). You might believe songwriting is a predictable process, or that lyric first is always easier than music first, or that rhyme is less important than people make it out to be. Whether you (the holder of the View) are aware of it or not, View becomes the basis of your Designing (the songwriting workshop on paper, the means by which you intend to equip your participants to succeed as songwriters within given constraints of time, space, and resources) and Responding (the songwriting workshop as students actually experience it).

One View of songwriting might be:

Songwriting is a way to have fun playing with combinations of words and music.

This View might lead a teaching artist to design a process that emphasizes playfulness, perhaps incorporates improvisation, and explores the pleasures of rhythmic and lyric craft as an inspiration and model. The Respond phase of this workshop will reward and encourage inventiveness.

Another View of songwriting:

Songwriting is a form of poetry where music supports the form of the poem.

This View might lead to a workshop Design that deals more directly with lyrics and structure, as well as an examination of how song form and other musical elements interact with text to make meaning.

Another View of songwriting (coincidentally, my own, so I can elaborate happily):

Songwriting is the act of telling a truth to an audience using lyrics and tune & accompaniment.

This View emphasizes personal artistry and craft. The individual student/artist is responsible for defining what constitutes *truth*. Theirs may be a funny truth, a sad truth, a terrible truth, or a liberating truth. Each student has a story to tell. Since this View holds the musical structure of *tune & accompaniment* important (a single melody in the foreground, instruments in the background, as in popular songs), students will be invited to consciously manipulate tune & accompaniment to serve and support the truth stated in their lyric. In the songwriting process implied by this View, inspiration and insight (some knowledge of and a desire to express a truth) meet with a specific craft (dealing with how the musical and lyric materials are structured). Once a draft of a song is complete, the View shapes our self-reflection and rewriting process: *Have we succeeded in communicating our truth to each other* (within the workshop) *and ultimately to our audience* (the outside world)?

All three Views assume that each participant possesses enough prior knowledge to make the process possible. All three workshops would benefit from being run by a songwriting-crafty facilitator, an experienced artist with knowledge of musical and lyric structures, who could offer support to the less experienced artists on an as-needed basis.

These three Views of songwriting use compressed language to imply the details of a larger vision. We can extrapolate activities based on each View, almost as if it were one of those diligently parsed mission statements that committees are required to produce. Thankfully, the process of articulating your View is internal—you probably won't have to answer to a committee. But since each word ultimately spins out into all the elements of your Design and Respond phases, each word is important. Clean, clear statements of View are easier to spin out into detailed nuts-and-bolts Designs. This applies to both situational Views (your view of songwriting), as well as to your broader, overall View.

Surprisingly, because View is global and foundational, it can go unexamined; you may not even be aware of your View until circumstance prompts you to self-reflect. Before reading any further, please build a quick draft of your View by finishing as many of the prompts as you can on the My View Worksheet (Figure 2.2).

Your View

How consciously do you connect your View with your activity Designs and the ways you Respond during workshops? I've come to believe that our success as teaching artists—including our effectiveness serving students, happiness in

My View

The social contract of my workshops is that we see ourselves as…

The best practice of my workshops is that we…

My favorite model or metaphor for a workshop is…

My role as teaching artist is…

My students' role is…

My approach, attitude or philosophy is…

The strategy I use to bring all this together is…

FIGURE 2.2 My View Worksheet

the job, and satisfaction with our work—depends on the strength of that connection. This belief is the thesis that underlies *A Teaching Artist's Companion*. Defining and developing the connection is an ongoing, perhaps life-long process. The connection needs to be established and revisited, because your View will evolve as you gather experience. The polarities of theory and practice, studio and classroom, clarity and confusion, confidence and hesitancy that teaching artists move through as they work are all grist for the mill. (For a look at how my own View developed over time, please see Chapter 1, "The Evolution of a Teaching Artist.")

The Design and Respond activities presented in these pages are grounded in my own View:

> *a community of learners*
>
> *making & doing*
>
> *in an atelier setting*

Such compressed language calls for unpacking. "Community of Learners" refers to a constructivist social contract that I use in classrooms or workshops, as inspired by the work of pioneering psychologist Lev Vygotsky. "Make and Do" is shorthand for the tenets of aesthetic education, which emphasizes the primacy of making, doing, and reflecting as the basis of learning, as observed in and inspired by the philosophy of Maxine Greene and John Dewey, and the dance, visual arts, theater, and music teaching artists of Lincoln Center Education, Carnegie Hall, and the 92nd Street Y. "Atelier setting" is shorthand for my adaptation of the student-centered Reggio Emilia school/studio practice I have long admired. *Atelier* (French for *workshop*, from the Middle French for a carpenter's workshop or pile of wood chips) more commonly refers to a room where an artist or artisan works: a dance studio, a milliner's workroom, a blacksmith's forge. In my View, the atelier is a shared creative space, a container for teaching and learning.

To introduce constructivism, Patti Saraniero and Lisa Resnick write on the Kennedy Center's ARTSEDGE website that

> *in constructivism, learning occurs through experiencing the world. This twentieth-century theory is built on the work of psychologist Jean Piaget, who believed that children build their own knowledge through play and their experiences. Constructivism also takes cues from psychologist Lev Vygotsky and his understanding that learning is a social activity. Arts education lends itself very naturally to constructivism, and constructivist learning is described much like arts learning . . . (both emphasize) thinking, analyzing, understanding, and applying.*[1]

The path that led me to a constructivist View was experiential, not academic. I first encountered the workaday truth of these ideas in my own classroom practice. When I was introduced to the cogent writings of Vygotsky, Dewey, Greene, and the Reggio Emilia approach in professional development sessions, I found I was already on the same path, fully invested in structuring *experiential make-and-do learning* for *communities of learners*. It was exhilarating to find my own discoveries reflected in the writings of these great twentieth-century educational theorists. Their written observations had more shape and clarity than mine, which enabled me to observe their theories at work in the world. As I embraced and tried to embody these ideas, I felt more a part of the community of educators: apparently what I recognized and valued was also recognized and valued by other, more experienced practitioners.

In the longer term, encountering these theories helped me distinguish a hierarchy of ideas; some ideas were so resonant that they suggested whole sets of subsequent practices. The three ideas in my View are of this order. Each of these is really a deep and rich View unto itself, a body of theory and practice from which I freely borrowed: a *community of learners* from Vygotsky, *making & doing* from Dewey and Greene, *in an atelier setting* from the Reggio Emilia approach. If these Views appeal to you, I hope you'll let the thinkers, artists, and teachers who originated them speak to you directly by going to the primary sources.

Here is a decompressed version of my Vygotsky, aesthetic education, and Reggio Emilia–informed View, restated using the View-eliciting prompts you saw earlier.

The social contract of my workshops . . .
is that we see ourselves as a community of learners (as per Vygotsky).
The main best practice of my workshop . . .
is that we Make and Do (as per Dewey and Greene).
My favorite model or metaphor for a workshop is . . .
an atelier (as per Reggio Emilia).
My role as teaching artist . . .
is that of instigator, coach, partner, co-learner, modeler of processes and
*   practices, artist, responsive listener, predictor, and remover of impediments.*
My students' and partners' role is . . .
that of explorers, listeners, doers, makers, wonderers, players, challengers,
*   questioners, partners (as per the TAs of Lincoln Center, Carnegie Hall,*
*   and the 92nd Street Y).*
My approach, attitude, or philosophy is . . .
a willingness to serve, and tolerance for ambiguity (as per my own values).
The strategy I use to bring all this together is . . .
to work within a View, Design, and Respond framework in a manner that
*   supports spontaneity, connectedness, and joy in the classroom.*

Your strengths as an artist and educator play a role in determining your View. Or perhaps View is based in our natural tendency to operate from our strengths. Take a moment to respond to these four prompts on the My Strengths Worksheet (Figure 2.3).

Now that you've defined some of your strengths, look for connections between your strengths and your View. To model making that kind of connection,

My Strengths

I have a clear sense of...

The most important personal qualities I bring to my work are...

In my work, I sincerely and especially enjoy...

I possess an unquestioning belief ...

FIGURE 2.3 My Strengths Worksheet

I'll track my own Strength/View connection: *I have a clear sense* of what to value, notice, and praise in the classroom. This strength makes me trust my ability to respond in the moment, according to the needs of both individuals and larger groups. If I am clear on what to value, notice, and praise, it is harder for any response or situation to throw me too far off balance. My View will tend to favor situations where this kind of responsiveness is most valuable (ateliers and communities of learners). Since I feel that *the most important personal qualities I bring to my work* are patience and openness, and because *I sincerely and especially enjoy* having sympathetic joy in my students' process and discoveries, my View will favor situations where students do generative work (Making & Doing). And if I really *possess an unquestioning belief* in less experienced individuals' creative potential, then my strong belief will match well with my workshop Designs.

Now extend your answers to the previous "My Strength" prompts to follow your strengths to their corresponding roles in defining what your View favors, tends to, matches, emphasizes, or includes on the My Strength/View Connection Worksheet (Figure 2.4).

My Strength / View Connection

I have a clear sense of (your answer),

so my View (favors, tends to, matches, emphasizes, includes)…

The most important personal qualities I bring to my work are (your answer),

so my View…

In my work, I sincerely and especially enjoy (your answer),

so my View…

I possess an unquestioning belief (your answer),

so my View…

FIGURE 2.4 My Strength/View Connection worksheet

Were you able to easily connect your strengths with your View? Were some connections stronger than others? Were there any surprises? If making the connection wasn't an easy process, that might be a cue to either restate or re-evaluate your strengths, or to redefine your View. Both are pretty plastic to begin with. Even experienced practitioners can benefit from a Strength/View tune-up: *Am I developing in my craft? Where am I strongest now? Does my View reflect these strengths?*

Once your View and strengths are articulated, the connections between View, Design, and Respond become more apparent.

The View–Design–Respond Cycle

At first glance, View, Design, and Respond seem straightforwardly sequential: we possess a View, then we Design a workshop, then we Respond once we are in that workshop space with students. But during Respond (as we observe students' attending, making & doing, and reflecting) the efficacy of our Design becomes apparent in real, interactive time, as we self-reflect: *Is this working, or not?* The observations we make in that moment loop back to connect with one or more of the three phases of the work. To illustrate this, the following flow chart (Figure 2.5) begins with View–Design–Respond (1, 2, 3), then indicates the pathways by which the initial sequence becomes a cycle (4, 5, 6):

1   View determines Design and Respond
2   Design affects Respond
3   Respond means . . .
4   Loop back to Respond
5   Loop back to Design
6   Loop back to View

1—VIEW DETERMINES DESIGN AND RESPOND

Your values and the beliefs you hold regarding the arts and teaching and learning are your View. These fundamental assumptions function as the basis for all of your subsequent choices and actions. Your View directly informs any Design you create. It also determines the style and substance of your in-classroom responses, aka the Respond phase of your work. View exists without reference to a specific time, place, or activity (in contrast to Design and Respond). View determines Design and Respond in the same way that content dictates form.

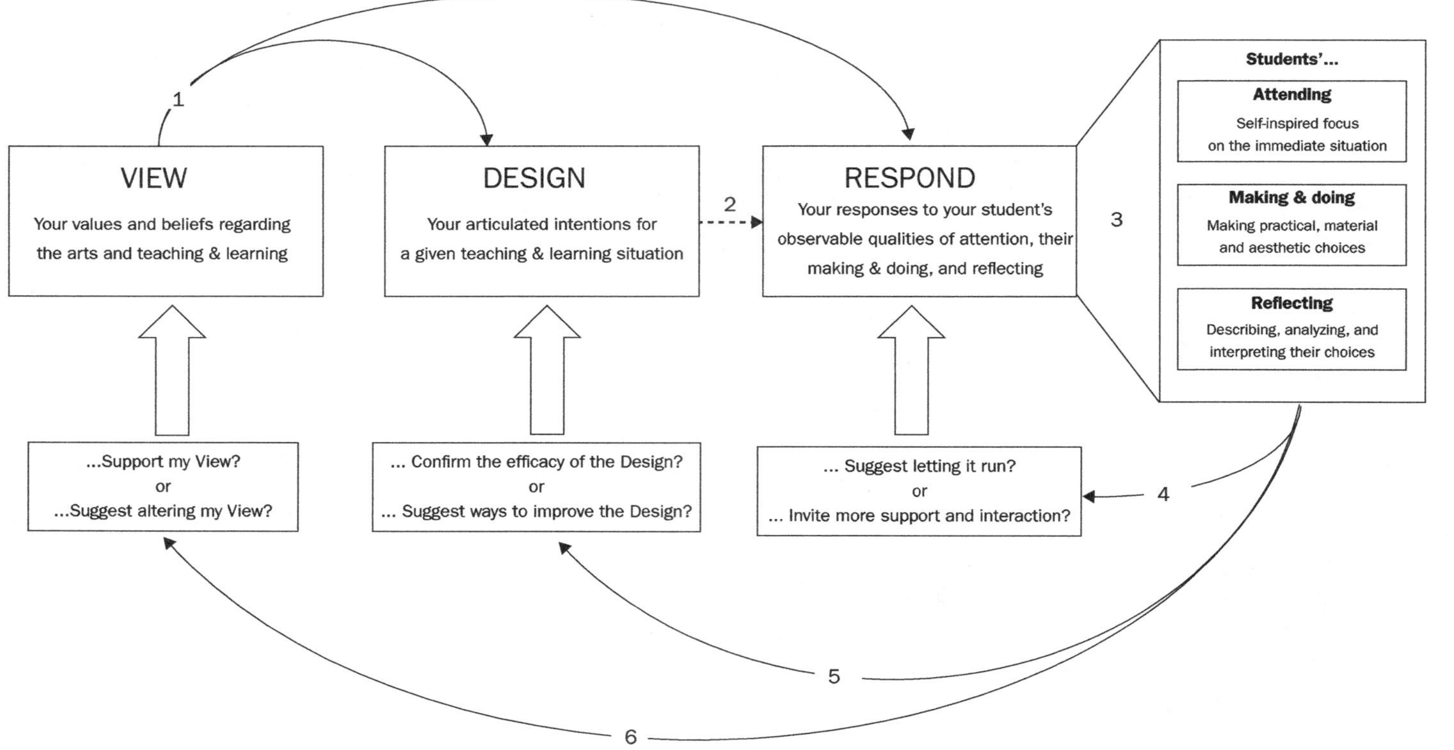

FIGURE 2.5 The View–Design–Respond Cycle

2—DESIGN AFFECTS RESPOND

Design *affects* Respond, rather than directly determining what you do there; the dotted line ┄┄┄➤ on the flowchart indicates the lesser effect. Design takes place before you are in the presence of your students, but you *imagine* being in their presence as you Design. The Respond phase takes place in the presence of students. How you Respond is an element of your Design, implicitly if you Design without considering any of your responses, explicitly to the extent that you consciously predict and shape the style and content of your responses.

3—RESPOND MEANS . . .

Respond begins when you initiate an activity in the presence of your students. As the activity unfolds, you observe the qualities of your students' Attending (their focus on the immediate situation), their Making & Doing (the processes that involve students' practical, material, and aesthetic choices) and their Reflecting (as they describe, analyze, or interpret their choices).

The possible pathways in the View, Design, Respond cycle multiply as soon as Respond begins, during any instance of students' Attending, Making & Doing, and Reflecting that you observe. Responding to what your students are showing you means adjusting the activity on the spot. Depending on what you see—and as always depending on your original View regarding what your role is and what you should do about what you see—you'll either a) feel your choices are working well and stay the course, or b) loop back to amend either your View, Design, or your Respond phase. Altering View, Design, and Respond on the basis of your direct experience might happen in the moment or well after the fact, depending on the speed and clarity of your self-reflection.

4—LOOP BACK TO RESPOND

When your students' Attending, Making & Doing, or Reflecting are less than optimal, your help is needed. The situation invites more of your support and interaction, and you Respond accordingly. If, however, student work is going well, the best response may be to let it run without intervention, and continue to watch and listen. It probably won't be long before someone has a question or some work to share, a new possibility to which you can respond.

5—LOOP BACK TO DESIGN

When your students' Attending, Making & Doing, or Reflecting are less than optimal, your Design may be at fault. Diagnose the situation. What you discover will suggest ways to improve your Design, either in the moment or the next time you do the same activity. If you observe a consistently high quality of

Attention, Making & Doing, and Reflecting with different groups of students (not just with the gifted and talented all-stars), the efficacy of your Design is being confirmed by the evidence of your own senses. After the workshop, it is worth taking the time to note which aspects of your Design worked particularly well, with the goal of incorporating those ideas into future Designs. I keep two sets of lesson plans: my original Design, and an after-the-fact annotated version called "what really happened."

6—LOOP BACK TO VIEW

When your students' Attention, Making & Doing, and Reflecting are less than optimal, your Design and Respond practices may be inefficient or ineffective. Address any deficiencies by tracing the problems back to their roots in your View, and adjusting it accordingly. If you observe a high quality of Attention, Making & Doing, and Reflecting, your View is confirmed and reinforced: you have evidence that your View results in effective Design and Respond practices.

You don't need to strive to follow the View–Design–Respond flow chart, or impose it on your work: the sequence is already there. As a caring, observant teaching artist, you already naturally allow what you observe to cycle back and change what you believe, plan, and practice in the classroom (believe = View, plan = Design, and practice = Respond). You question an activity that doesn't go well, and you consider it validated if it does. The View–Design–Respond Cycle is a handy schematic of how the information derived from direct experience in the classroom often flows. What makes the chart useful is that it makes us more explicitly aware of the possibility of making informed alterations, helps us see what we are doing so that we can decide for ourselves how to do it better.

Your growth as a teaching artist depends on your ability to reflect on your work. Whatever your discipline, your art form, or your View, Design, and Respond practices, the flow chart invites you to observe and reconsider how you use the information that your students present to you. *What is their Attention, Making & Doing, and Reflecting telling you about your own View, Design, and Respond practice? How does what you observe confirm your insight or intuition? Where does what you observe suggest that you need to alter your ideas?*

Try using the View–Design–Respond Cycle to connect your on-the-ground experience with your at-your-desk reflection. If it works for you, you'll be able to reflect more precisely, and apply what you learn from your classroom experiences more deliberately, and perhaps sooner than you might otherwise have done.

One complete loop through a View–Design–Respond Cycle might take any amount of time. Realizations can happen on the spot, in micro-seconds.

Other observations and alterations take a long time to articulate and work through. Here are two case studies that offer examples of the View, Design, and Respond cycle at work. Each deals with some detail of how my overall View of *a community of learners / making & doing / in an atelier setting* has played out in a classroom. Both examples are drawn from recent experience with *Hello, Composers,* a hybrid preparation and art-making workshop for public school grade-schoolers. The program has for eleven years been a laboratory for trying out various Design ideas, and for attempting to perfect my Respond practices. The program's success depends on the encouragement and support of the accomplished teachers who kindly welcome me into their classrooms. For a detailed look, see the *Hello, Composers* section in "Four View, Design, and Respond Based Programs" on page 185.

CASE STUDY 1: IN WHICH DESIGN REPEATEDLY FAILS UNTIL I GET A
NEW VIEW

During the first couple of years of the *Hello, Composers* program, I held on to the *View* that I would be able to develop written materials that would help my young charges be better equipped, craftier composers. So many basic and useful structural ideas might be observed in songs students already knew; I would find ways to reveal these structures (song form, melodic sequencing, motivic development) and place those particular tools in my students' hands. I cringe to say it now, but I believed in worksheets. In a spirit of experimentation, my *Design* included lessons where worksheets guided the work. I was sure my students could learn music composition techniques from the materials, in part because I took pains to distill and recast the ideas into kid-friendly formats.

But none of my worksheets worked. I'd print out a stack of what I thought were attractive, easy-to-follow step-by-step exercises, model their use, then watch as a bored class doodled on them, or ignored them and searched for something else to do. (If you don't believe that second graders are capable of brutal honesty, try submitting your ego to some experiment similar to mine). Eight or ten worksheets in a row failed. If a worksheet did not fly in my first *and* second *and* third period classes, I would admit defeat and revert to a non-worksheeted Design for the remaining iterations of that lesson. The Respond phase evidence was that my worksheet failed to elicit much *attending,* let alone any *making & doing.* I felt confident about the wording of the various instructions, since it was the same type and density of language I used in class when I was actively guiding similar exercises (an ill-founded confidence, given the difference between an instruction one reads and an instruction one hears). I knew from experience that helpful, functional worksheets were possible because I was already using one for our Box Melodies project. But on reflection I saw that the Box Melody document was a simple graphic organizer. It didn't try to guide process or thinking; the boxes merely made it easier for composers to capture, notate, organize, and share their ideas.

I don't use worksheets anymore.

In terms of the View–Design–Respond cycle: an untested View yielded a Design that tried to foist the use of a written guide on a group of young students who had no real use for such a guide. In the classroom, the Design failed so consistently and so often that it was abandoned, and View was amended to eliminate using any worksheet that was not immediately useful. Subsequent Designs would favor direct experience and avoid worksheet-guided processes. A more global *note to self* also made its way into my View: *During Design, even careful, thoughtful imagining of how students will react to an invitation may be wrong. Don't be so surprised when the work does not go as planned. Be less attached to seeing your Design succeed, and more flexible and responsive in the moments when it does not.*

CASE STUDY 2: IN WHICH DIRECT EXPERIENCE DURING RESPOND ALTERS
BOTH VIEW AND DESIGN

My *View* in this art-making workshop included the belief that all the artwork we created should come from the students. With parents and family members attending a final celebration concert, I wanted to be able to say in all truthfulness that I had not written a note of the music they were about to hear: it was all students, all the time. I had avenues of expression and venues for my own work and didn't need the classroom to be one of them. My own music teachers only occasionally demonstrated their abilities or offered themselves as exemplars when teaching me, and I accepted this as a kind of tradition. Based on these factors, I was sure I should carefully avoid having a hand in composing any of the music we made in class.

My *Design* reflected this belief. In the atelier, I acted as musical amanuensis for my students. I set up prompts and supportive exercises that made it possible for students to successfully compose. Whenever their musical choice was unclear, I would ask them to clarify, rather than filling in information or changing it myself.

During *Respond,* I observed that students' *attention* was excellent, that their *making & doing* was energized and yielded individualized and interesting results. Their *reflections* on process and product seemed insightful in a way that told me the workshop was a success. (One assessment I used for this was to ask students at the end of the year to give advice to composers of the future: *What should they care about? What were the best ways to work? What should they be sure to remember?* The sincerity and concern in their answers was heartwarming, but also confirmed that they strongly self-identified as composers and believed in their own capabilities and skills enough to confidently share them).

During the first three years of teaching and tweaking the program, which included nearly three hundred individual classroom sessions, I continually questioned my Design. In the Respond phase, most students were thriving. But I wondered what else we could try that might yield stronger, more detailed work from more students. I was still seeing students struggle with the composing process, more struggle than I thought was good. Also we were working with musical layers (several patterns of sound happening at the same time), but I was avoiding a solid exploration of tune & accompaniment structure (a single melody in the foreground, supporting instruments in the background, as in popular songs), even though that structure was a feature of almost all the layered music students were familiar with and loved. Was I getting perhaps too tight, too staid in my Design, perhaps the result of a too-complacent View? I started questioning my belief in not co-composing with students. I already improvised, played guitar and piano, and sang with them; the interaction was in fact a cornerstone of our work. Why not co-composing? I was careful to model any process we entered into; why not model a tune & accompaniment structure that invited them in?

Once my View loosened up, it prompted a change in Design. I recorded and notated three contrasting accompaniment loops and gave them what I hoped would be attractive names: "Funky E Minor" (which was simple) and "Spooky D Minor" (which was silly), and "Shimmering World," which was quite close to my professional work in terms of harmony and an emotionally richer affect. Students listened to all three accompaniment loops and voted on which they wanted to work with first. Then they played glockenspiels along with the agreed-on four-measure loop until they created a tune that they liked, and notated their ideas with the letter names of the notes in the patterns they created (which appeared on each metal key of their instruments: a, b, c . . .).

As they played along with the recording, experimenting, and improvising, I walked around, encouraging and praising. I put small, colorful stickers on the hands of students whose work I thought was interesting, patterns that were especially musical and made for a good model, or chose work from a student who didn't often volunteer or have recognized success experiences. After I had a few examples to draw from, we all stopped playing and turned our attention to the classroom Smart Board. There I input the sticker-handed composers' melodic layers into our digital playback system, with their names attached to their melodies. We experimented with the new layers, re-ordering, re-combining, fragmenting. The work was done when we ran out of time. If we finished one tune & accompaniment piece and still had time, we voted again and worked on another.

Students' response to the new invitation was passionate. Almost every class jumped to work on "Shimmering World," which surprised me. It was less pop music than the other two, longer and more sophisticated. From the first I observed a pleasant, intense attending as well as making & doing, which confirmed that the instructions and modeling were well-tuned to their needs. There was a clear willingness to keep working, keep experimenting and playing and listening—no one wanted to stop; everyone wanted to contribute. I often forgot to bring up tune & accompaniment, but the basis for doing so was experientially established. Students who were not the class stars had a chance to shine and receive public praise. To my personal delight, the work opened up new dissonances and syncopations. In contrast to the other projects in the program, not every student had a chunk of melody or a layer in this piece—less than ideal, but acceptable, since the other projects guaranteed that all students' work would be represented in the final celebration concert. The spirit of this experiment spread into other aspects of my Design. Inspired by the students' success with writing melody to a predetermined accompaniment, we created truly co-composed drum layers to help unify the accompaniments in a text-setting project, to everyone's approval.

In terms of the View–Design–Respond cycle: after a well-established View yielded a useful Design, observed qualities of students' work during Respond suggested making alterations in both Design and View. Once View was changed (*co-composing is OK*), Design changes followed, resulting in more fun, better music, and a looser, more responsive teaching artist. From those new Respond phase observations, one final perpetually View-altering loop continues to play out, an admonition to self: *stay loose—have fun.*

In this chapter, we've looked at View in general, as well as its dynamic relationship with Design and Respond. All of the remaining materials in *A Teaching Artist's Companion* are grounded in the View I introduced a few pages back: *a community of learners / making & doing / in an atelier setting.* The next two chapters present and detail the specific Design practices and Respond principles that are every teaching artist's bread and butter.

A Compendium of Views

I invited teaching artists from across the United States to define their Views using the same "My View" prompts you completed earlier. Dancers, actors, sculptors, poets, and musicians kindly responded. When these Views are placed side by side, strong resonances and some gentle dissonances come up. If your own View aligns with these, most of which come from experienced practitioners, take it as a sign that you're in the right line of work. The Views appear twice, the first time grouped according the author (one teaching artist's View all in one place), and a second time organized by prompt (all the different teaching artist responses to a single question in one place). I hope you enjoy reading and comparing these as much as I did.

A COMPENDIUM OF VIEWS (ORGANIZED BY ART FORM/AUTHOR)

The social contract of my workshops is that we see ourselves as . . . co-creators of the learning, as innately creative beings.

The best practice of my workshops is that we . . . honor all participants, invite all to participate at their own level, and make the participation dynamic, active, novel, and engaging.

My favorite model or metaphor for a workshop is . . . improvisation and/or the dramatic arc.

My role as teaching artist is . . . mentor, teacher, model, entertainer, storyteller, agent provocateur, collaborator, and learner.

My students' role is . . . to enter the work with openness and good intentions.

My approach, attitude, or philosophy is . . . we all learn and grow when we engage actively and meaningfully when we play with each other and our chosen content.

The strategy I use to bring all this together is . . . a combination of patience, listening, and instinct.

—BARRY STEWART MANN (Actor, Storyteller, Educator/Atlanta, GA)

The social contract of my workshops is that we see ourselves as . . . collaborators and co-learners.

The best practice of my workshops is that we . . . create an environment of trust and mutual respect and allow for multiple perspectives to be voiced and understood.

My favorite model or metaphor for a workshop is. . . community-building, risk-taking, collaboration, and co-creation of artistic work.

My role as teaching artist is . . . as a facilitator of creative experiences and inclusion.

My students' role is . . . to share their knowledge, experience, and strengths while taking risks creatively.

My approach, attitude, or philosophy is . . . that when we can create an atmosphere of mutual respect and trust, then meaningful learning and dialogue happens.

The strategy I use to bring all this together is . . . by focusing on community-building, honoring and building on participant experience and strengths, and facilitating respectful dialogue.

—HEATHER BRYCE (Dance/Vermont and NYC)

The social contract of my workshops is that we see ourselves as . . . human beings and therefore people who must enter the historical process critically; human beings, in a social lattice of official and sanctioned factories of various economic, political, and military purposes, who therefore learn and create in order to humanize ourselves and others.

The best practice of my workshops is that we . . . become our own teachers. Education is the art of convincing someone to be their own teacher; to enter a dialogical process of embracing and transforming reality.

My favorite model or metaphor for a workshop is . . . the classic Freirean learning circle.

My role as teaching artist is . . . to have one whole human experience; for my existence to not be bullied into living in internal compartments of psyche in order to conform to a power structure.

My students' role is . . . to open their mind to the potentials of liberation.

My approach, attitude, or philosophy is . . . history is the graveyard of empires.

The strategy I use to bring all this together is . . . patience and exertion. Exertion, but no narrative control. Consciousness. But consciousness in a living process.

—TONGO EISEN-MARTIN (Poetry/San Francisco, CA)

The social contract of our workshops is that we see ourselves as . . . creative instigators, a community of persistent supporters.

The best practice of our workshops is that we . . . build trust over time as a strategy to combat our vulnerable teenagers' hesitation to take creative risks.

My favorite model or metaphor for a workshop is . . . safe spaces where different perspectives are celebrated.

Our role is . . . motivator, questioner, prodder, access provider, community builder, preparer, connector.

Our students' role is . . . to ask questions, be curious, learn to effectively communicate, think independently, thrive in collaboration, and say yes to opportunities that expand their networks and communities.

Our approach, attitude, or philosophy is . . . to question and encourage inquiry, to create fertile ground to tease out new ways of thinking and creating, to deliver relevant and authentic programs, to encourage a sense of wonder, to create a culture where failure is viewed as learning.

The strategy we use to bring all this together is . . . long-term engagement, delivered by a team that includes a teaching artist, staff, classroom teacher, and a local cultural institution.

—CYNTHIA CAMPOY BROPHY
(Executive Director, artworxLA)

The social contract of my workshops is that we see ourselves as . . . creating action around shared story.

The best practice of my workshops is that we . . . co-construct meaning together.

My favorite model or metaphor for a workshop is . . . Come as you are. Leave as you are.

My role as teaching artist is . . . to never make any assumptions about what someone knows; to value all lived experience and prior knowledge as an opportunity to make our world bigger.

My students' role is . . . to never make any assumptions about what someone knows; to value all lived experience and prior knowledge as an opportunity to make our world bigger.

My approach, attitude, or philosophy is . . . What separates us keeps us fragile.

The strategy I use to bring all this together is . . . student-centered, student-led learning environments.

—DEREK FENNER (Poetry/Hayward, CA)

The social contract of my workshops is that we see ourselves as . . . co-learners, evolving, creative souls working together, focused on specific aspects of the creative process through art-making in order to bathe and delight in the satisfaction of co-creation.

The best practice of my workshops is that we . . . take the big words and lofty goals and carefully design developmentally appropriate plans in developmentally appropriate language that challenge students from Pre-K through the most senior of citizens, without presuming previous knowledge, so that all may succeed beyond their own expectations and the expectations of those around them.

My favorite model or metaphor for a workshop is . . . Toothpaste Tube Creativity: setting up meticulously crafted restrictions so that what comes out at the end can be spread all over creation

My role as a teaching artist is . . . constantly to aspire to excellence as an artist; to use that artistry to facilitate creativity in others; to plan with my colleagues with an open mind and heart; to give every class 100 percent of what's in me; to meet my students WHEREVER they are.

My students' role is . . . to give me a chance, as much as is possible within the reality of their present circumstances, and to participate as fully as possible—*whatever that looks like.*

My approach, attitude, or philosophy is . . . that every person has a birthright in the arts; that the arts help us understand and connect to each other as human beings, across cultural, language, experiential, and personal barriers.

The strategy I use to bring all this together is . . . to try to find out as much as I can about every situation in order to employ the right mix of artistry, knowledge, experience, humor, flair, collaboration, and planning, and planning, and planning.

—CAROL PONDER (Theater, Music, and Dance/Nashville, TN)

The social contract of my workshops is that we see ourselves as . . . global citizens. Contributors to society. Innovators. Leaders.

The best practice of my workshops is that we . . . collaborate. Have fun. Ask questions. Create.

My favorite model or metaphor for a workshop is . . . organized chaos.

My role as teaching artist is . . . facilitator of conversations.

My students' role is . . . leaders.

My approach, attitude, or philosophy is . . . within structure lies creativity.

The strategy I use to bring all this together is . . . culturally responsive pedagogy. If I respond to the culture of the participants, we can all work together toward a vision. If an educator doesn't respond to the cultures of the participants, then why teach?

—JAMES MILES (Theater, Executive Director, Arts Corps/Seattle, WA)

The social contract of my workshops is that we see ourselves as . . . makers working elbow to elbow. We are collaborators who know that collaboration itself is an art form that we can get better at with practice.

The best practice of my workshops is that we . . . consider how we all perceive and use space differently, depending on our cultural backgrounds, before we design anything together.

My favorite model or metaphor for a workshop is . . . infusion, like a tea bag. Introducing a TA into a school community, like dipping in a tea bag, changes the color and flavor of the water.

My role as teaching artist is . . . to co-coach students through the creative process (the Design Thinking Process) alongside educator partners and to chip away at outmoded, clichéd perceptions of who artists are in the community. And, oh yeah, hopefully get some art built that is fresh, not a re-hash of anything anyone has seen before.

My students' role is . . . to surprise me with their ideas, but more importantly, to surprise themselves with ideas that they contribute to the mix.

My approach, attitude, or philosophy is . . . working as a TA is a way of making art for social justice. Collaborating with lots of very different kinds of people to make art that belongs to no one and helps communities better understand themselves is the work I put myself out there to do, because this is where the revolution will begin.

The strategy I use to bring all this together is . . . to be a "utility player" in my partner schools. This means that, though I may be invited in to a school because of what I am best known for (and for me, that's community-based public art and environmental sculpture), once involved in that place, if I'm really paying attention to what is going on around me, I'll find multiple ways to be of use.

—JEFF MATHER (Visual Arts/Atlanta, GA)

The social contract of my workshops is that we see ourselves as . . . equally human. I present a space where connection and simple presence are the entry points, where we respect ourselves and each other.

The best practice of my workshops is that we . . . collaborate. Humbleness and presence matter, as do trustworthiness and stability, and a willingness to connect and be vulnerable, and to lead.

My favorite model or metaphor for a workshop is . . . weaving, stitching, building.

My role as teaching artist is . . . guide, mentor, instigator.

My students' role is . . . to show up as exactly who they are.

My approach, attitude, or philosophy is . . . that students can all begin by sticking one toe in the water. But this is the calculatedly off-hand approach, an entry point for the suspicious middle school student. I am also prepared for the deep dive that inevitably follows.

The strategy I use to bring all this together is . . . to enter the room prepared to weave our multiple visions together, modeling the weaving that my participants or students can also do.

—JEAN JOHNSTONE (Theater/San Francisco, CA;
also Executive Director, Teaching Artists Guild)

The social contract of my workshops is that we see ourselves as . . . works-in-progress and all at different points along the journey to being the practitioners, artists, humans we want to be.

The best practice of my workshops is that we . . . are open to new information and perspectives and that we listen to listen and build.

My favorite model or metaphor for a workshop is . . . a session to workshop new ideas, and also a cypher where learning and creating are communal, iterative, and fun.

My role as teaching artist is . . . to share my experience and expertise in a way that *facilitates* pathways to understanding and mastery. This only works if I also check power dynamics so that knowledge is moving in multiple directions, allowing everyone to grow along with, and because of, one another. I uphold the history and power of the art form as a powerful aesthetic and pedagogical tool.

My students' role is . . . to be open to learning with and from me, as well as each other.

My approach, attitude, or philosophy is . . . rooted in equity and inclusion and also about respecting and celebrating the cultural capital of the art form.

The strategy I use to bring all this together is . . . passion mixed with enthusiasm and curiosity.

—AYSHA UPCHURCH (Dance/Boston, MA)

The social contract of my workshops is that we see ourselves as . . . unfaltering inspiration for one another.

The best practice of my workshops is that we . . . scaffold instruction, allowing students to build applicable skills and understanding throughout a class, and over the course of a residency.

My favorite model or metaphor for a workshop is . . . ignite the spark.

My role as a teaching artist is . . . to create an environment in which learning and personal growth can be cultivated in and through the arts.

My students' role is . . . to be aware, to explore, to take risks, to rethink, to create, to collaborate, and to engage in the fun of making art.

My approach, attitude, or philosophy is . . . keep it fresh. While tried and true lesson plans have their place, I allow myself to be spontaneous, take risks, and try new things everyday.

The strategy I use to bring this all together is . . . to nurture myself as an artist, to recognize the responsibility of my role as a teacher, and to appreciate a career that allows me to share my passion and cultivate creativity.

—MAGGIE COSTIGAN (Dance/Maui, HI)

The social contract of my workshops is that we see ourselves as . . . equally responsible and active participants in shaping the classroom culture, my students as well as myself. If one child can not find their place in the circle, we must all adjust to make space.

The best practice of my workshops is that we . . . begin every class with individual check-ins and ends with check-outs. The check-in allows us to see each other as individuals with emotional and physical history. The check-out helps us internally process and reflect on the learning and to validate our shared experience of the work.

My role as teaching artist is . . . to provide a safe space for both learning and healing through dance.

My students' role is . . . to show up and be present for themselves and for each other. We can only be vulnerable and take risks if we are all in it together.

My approach, attitude, or philosophy is . . . . to meet my students where they are, allow time for everyone to find their own way into the class, and then to spark their curiosity and ask them to reach further and dive deeper than they knew was possible.

The strategy I use to bring all this together is . . . trusting in the power of dance as we come together to learn and heal, transcend our personal narratives, and realize our human potential.

—JENNIFER OLIVER (Dance/San Diego, CA)

A COMPENDIUM OF VIEWS (ORGANIZED BY PROMPT)

The social contract of my workshops is that we see ourselves as. . .

- co-creators of the learning, as innately creative beings. BSM/theater
- collaborators and co-learners. HB/dance
- human beings and therefore people who must enter the historical process critically. Human beings, in a social lattice of official and sanctioned factories of various economic, political, and military purposes, who therefore learn and create in order to humanize ourselves and others. TEM/poetry
- creative instigators, a community of persistent supporters. CCB/visual art
- unfaltering inspiration for one another. MC/dance
- creating action around shared story. DF/poetry
- co-learners, evolving, creative souls working together, focused on specific aspects of the creative process through art-making in order to bathe and delight in the satisfaction of co-creation. CP/theater

- global citizens. Contributors to society. Innovators. Leaders. JM/theater
- makers working elbow to elbow. We are collaborators who know that collaboration itself is an art form that we can get better at with practice. JM/visual art
- equally human. I present a space where connection and simple presence are the entry points, where we respect ourselves and each other. JJ/theater
- works-in-progress and all at different points along the journey to being the practitioners, artists, humans we want to be. AU/dance
- equally responsible and active participants in shaping the classroom culture, my students as well as myself. If one child can not find their place in the circle, we must all adjust to make space. JO/dance

The best practice of my workshops is that we . . .

- honor all participants, invite all to participate at their own level, and make the participation dynamic, active, novel, and engaging. BSM/theater
- create an environment of trust and mutual respect and allow for multiple perspectives to be voiced and understood. HB/dance
- become our own teachers. Education is the art of convincing someone to be their own teacher; to enter a dialogical process of embracing and transforming reality. TEM/poetry
- build trust over time as a strategy to combat our vulnerable teenagers' hesitation to take creative risks. CCB/visual art
- co-construct meaning together. DF/poetry
- take the big words and lofty goals and carefully design developmentally appropriate plans in developmentally appropriate language that challenge students from Pre-K through the most senior of citizens, without presuming previous knowledge, so that all may succeed beyond their own expectations—and the expectations of those around them. CP/theater
- scaffold instruction, allowing students to build applicable skills and understanding throughout a class, and over the course of a residency. MC/dance
- collaborate. Have Fun. Ask Questions. Create. JM/theater
- consider how we all perceive and use space differently, depending on our cultural backgrounds, before we design anything together. JM/visual art
- collaborate. Humbleness and presence matter, as do trustworthiness and stability, and a willingness to connect and be vulnerable, and to lead. JJ/theater

- are open to new information and perspectives and that we listen to listen and build. AU/dance
- begin every class with individual check-ins and end with check-outs. The check-in allows us to see each other as individuals with emotional and physical history. The check-out helps us internally process and reflect on the learning and to validate our shared experience of the work. JO/dance

My favorite model or metaphor for a workshop is . . .

- improvisation and/or the dramatic arc. BSM/theater
- community-building, risk-taking, collaboration, and co-creation of artistic work. HB/dance
- the classic Freirean learning circle. TEM/poetry
- safe spaces where different perspectives are celebrated. CCB/visual art
- Come as you are. Leave as you are. DF/poetry
- Toothpaste Tube Creativity: setting up meticulously crafted restrictions so that what comes out at the end can be spread all over creation. CP/theater
- organized chaos. JM/theater
- ignite the spark. MC/dance
- infusion, like a tea bag. Introducing a TA into a school community, like dipping in a tea bag, changes the color and flavor of the water. JM/visual art
- weaving, stitching, building. JJ/theater
- a session to workshop new ideas, and also a cypher where learning and creating are communal, iterative, and fun. AU/dance

My role as teaching artist is . . .

- mentor, teacher, model, entertainer, storyteller, agent provocateur, collaborator, and learner. BSM/theater
- a facilitator of creative experiences and inclusion. HB/dance
- to have one whole human experience. For my existence to not be bullied into living in internal compartments of psyche in order to conform to a power structure. TEM/poetry
- motivator, questioner, prodder, access provider, community builder, preparer, connector. CCB/visual art
- to never make any assumptions about what someone knows; to value all lived experience and prior knowledge as an opportunity to make our world bigger. DF/poetry
- to aspire to excellence as an artist; to use that artistry to facilitate creativity in others; to plan with my colleagues with an open mind

and heart; to give every class 100 percent of what's in me; to meet my students WHEREVER they are. CP/theater

- facilitator of conversations. JM/theater
- to create an environment in which learning and personal growth can be cultivated in and through the arts. MC/dance
- to co-coach students through the creative process (the Design Thinking Process) alongside educator partners and to chip away at outmoded, clichéd, perceptions of who artists are in the community. And, oh yeah, hopefully get some art built that is fresh, not a re-hash of anything anyone has seen before. JM/visual art
- guide, mentor, instigator. JJ/theater
- to share my experience and expertise in a way that *facilitates* pathways to understanding and mastery. This only works if I also check power dynamics so that knowledge is moving in multiple directions, allowing everyone to grow along with, and because of, one another. I uphold the history and power of the art form as a powerful aesthetic and pedagogical tool. AU/dance
- to provide a safe space for both learning and healing through dance. JO/dance

My students' role is . . .

- to enter the work with openness and good intentions. BSM/theater
- to share their knowledge, experience, and strengths while taking risks creatively. HB/dance
- to open their mind to the potentials of liberation. TEM/poetry
- to ask questions, be curious, learn to effectively communicate, think independently, thrive in collaboration, and say yes to opportunities that expand their networks and communities. CCB/visual art
- to never make any assumptions about what someone knows; to value all lived experience and prior knowledge as an opportunity to make our world bigger. DF/poetry
- to give me a chance, as much as is possible within the reality of their present circumstances, and to participate as fully as possible— *whatever that looks like.* CP/theater
- leaders. JM/theater
- to surprise me with their ideas, but more importantly, to surprise themselves with ideas that they contribute to the mix. JM/visual art
- to be aware, to explore, to take risks, to rethink, to create, to collaborate, and to engage in the fun of making art. MS/dance
- to show up exactly as who they are. JJ/theater
- to be open to learning with and from me, as well as each other. AU/dance

◻ to show up and be present for themselves and for each other. We can only be vulnerable and take risks if we are all in it together. JO/dance

My approach, attitude, or philosophy is . . .

◻ we all learn and grow when we engage actively and meaningfully when we play with each other and our chosen content. BSM/
◻ that when we can create an atmosphere of mutual respect and trust then meaningful learning and dialogue happens. HB/dance
◻ history is the graveyard of empires. TEM/poetry
◻ to question and encourage inquiry, to create fertile ground to tease out new ways of thinking and creating, to deliver relevant and authentic programs, to encourage a sense of wonder, to create a culture where failure is viewed as learning. CCB/visual art
◻ what separates us keeps us fragile. DF/poetry
◻ that every person has a birthright in the arts; that the arts help us understand and connect to each other as human beings, across cultural, language, experiential, and personal barriers. CP/theater
◻ within structure lies creativity. JM/theater
◻ working as a TA is a way of making art for social justice. Collaborating with lots of very different kinds of people to make art that belongs to no one and helps communities better understand themselves is the work I put myself out there to do, because this is where the revolution will begin. JM/visual art
◻ keep it fresh. While tried and true lesson plans have their place, I allow myself to be spontaneous, take risks, and try new things everyday. MC/dance
◻ that students can all begin by sticking one toe in the water. But this is the calculatedly off-hand approach, an entry point for the suspicious middle school student. I am also prepared for the deep dive that inevitably follows. JJ/theater
◻ rooted in equity and inclusion and also about respecting and celebrating the cultural capital of the art form. AU/dance
◻ to meet my students where they are, allow time for everyone to find their own way into the class, and then to spark their curiosity and ask them to reach further and dive deeper then they knew was possible. JO/dance

The strategy I use to bring all this together is . . .

◻ a combination of patience, listening, and instinct. BSM/theater

¤ to focus on community-building, honoring and building on participant experience and strengths, and facilitating respectful dialogue. HB/dance

¤ patience and exertion. Exertion, but no narrative control. Consciousness. But consciousness in a living process. TEM/poetry

¤ long-term engagement, delivered by a team that includes a teaching artist, staff, classroom teacher, and a local cultural institution. CCB/visual art

¤ student-centered, student-led learning environments. DF/poetry

¤ to try to find out as much as I can about every situation in order to employ the right mix of artistry, knowledge, experience, humor, flair, collaboration, and planning, and planning, and planning. CP/theater

¤ culturally responsive pedagogy. If I respond to the culture of the participants, we can all work together toward a vision. If an educator doesn't respond to the cultures of the participants, then why teach? JM/theater

¤ to be a "utility player" in my partner schools. This means that, though I may be invited in to a school because of what I am best known for (and for me, that's community-based public art and environmental sculpture), once involved in that place, if I'm really paying attention to what is going on around me, I'll find multiple ways to be of use. JM/visual art

¤ to enter the room prepared to weave our multiple visions together, modeling the weaving that my participants or students can also do. JJ/theater

¤ to nurture myself as an artist, to recognize the responsibility of my role as a teacher, and to appreciate a career that allows me to share my passion and cultivate creativity. MC/dance

¤ passion mixed with enthusiasm and curiosity. AU/dance

¤ trusting in the power of dance as we come together to learn and heal, transcend our personal narratives, and realize our human potential. JO/dance

Contributing Writers Key

BSM	Barry Stewart Mann (Theater/Atlanta, GA)
HB	Heather Bryce (Dance/Vermont and NYC)
TEM	Tongo Eisen-Martin (Poetry/San Francisco, CA)
CCB	Cynthia Campoy Brophy (Visual Art/Executive Director, artworxLA, CA)

DF   Derek Fenner (Poetry/Oakland, CA)
CP   Carol Ponder (Theater, Music, and Dance/Nashville, TN)
JM   James Miles (Theater, Executive Director of Arts Corps/
            Seattle, WA)
JM   Jeff Mather (Visual Arts/Atlanta, GA)
JJ   Jean Johnstone (Theater, Director of Teaching Artists
            Guild/San Francisco, CA)
AU   Aysha Upchurch (Dance/Boston, MA)
JO   Jennifer Oliver (Dance/San Diego, CA)
MC   Maggie Costigan (Dance/Maui, HA)

Design

to plan and make decisions (about something that is being built
or created)

to plan for a specific use or purpose

to create, fashion, or construct according to plan

to conceive and plan out in the mind

to have as a purpose; intend

to devise for a specific function or end

a method worked out in advance for achieving some objective

something that one hopes or intends to accomplish

the way in which the elements of a work of art are arranged

All the Right Questions

Etched into the glass of your office door: *Jessica Jamerson, Civil Engineer.* The phone rings, you answer.

"Hello, this is Jessica."

"Hey, Jess, it's Wilson from Town Planning. I've got a job, and I think you're the right person for it. Interested?"

"Hi, Wilson. Thanks for thinking of me. *What* do you need built?"

"A bridge."

"*Who* is going to use it?"

"Pedestrians. Oh, and some bikes."

"*Where* do you need it?"

"Between the two halves of Honey Creek Park, smack in the middle."

"What's your *timeline*?"

"Design in six weeks, ribbon cutting in eighteen months."

"*Why* does the park need a bridge?"

"We want to increase use of the park and connectivity between the shops on either side."

"Any *support* from your office on this project?"

"We'll provide a style sheet from the park designer, do all the subcontracting, and you get a nice big fee."

And after a meeting to gather more details, you begin your design for the Honey Creek Park Bridge.

The banner at the top of the main page of your artist/teaching artist website reads: *Jessica Jamerson, Choreographer/Teaching Artist*. Wilson from Educational Outreach text messages you: *Unit of Study at Harriet Tubman JHS—you up for it?* Your Design process has already started: you know a little about the *Who* (junior high), and something about the *When* (a whole unit, not just a one-off workshop). But like Jessica the civil engineer, Jessica the dance TA also needs the full *What, Who, When, Where, Why,* and *How* before she can accept the work:

What type of workshop?
    Preparation (and the associated work of art)
    Studio (and the associated media or materials)
    Arts integration (and the associated curriculum)

Who are the participants?
How many, what ages, grades, or skill levels are included?

When?
    Number of sessions
    Length of each session
    Unit start and end dates
    Fixed-schedule performances, showings, workshop sessions

Where?
    Rooms available—size and type
    Desks/furniture—fixed or moveable
    Smart Board
    Visual arts—sink, storage, drying racks, materials
    Music—percussion or other instruments; sonic isolation
    Dance—sprung floor, floor mats, barre, mirrors

Why/How is the workshop supported?
    Curriculum provided or teaching-artist-designed
    Contextual materials provided
    Recordings or images provided
    Materials budget
    Fee

If Jessica doesn't find the situation agreeable, as defined by the basic five Ws, she can negotiate the variables or turn down the work. But if the work fits her schedule and other criteria, she begins her Design in earnest. (For a more detailed list, of see the "Workshop Space, Time, and Resources Checklist" on page 219.)

THE ESSENTIAL PRACTICES OF TEACHING ARTIST CRAFT

Every Design is an expression of the designer's View as well as their *craft*, their knowledge of how to use various approaches and techniques to achieve an end. Bridge-builder Jessica already knows about spans, beams, cantilevers, suspension systems, and the wonderful world of trusses (it really is wonderful). As a certified civil engineer, she is required to have mastered these aspects of her craft. She also has to know how to Respond to the variables that come up during the construction process, when her Design is implemented in real time. Your teaching artist craft is your knowledge of how to use various approaches and techniques to achieve an end in a workshop. In this chapter, I'll present these essential practices used by all teaching artists *working in all art forms and workshop types*:

> *establishing safe space*—how we build trust and supportive communities of learners
>
> *accessing prior knowledge*—how we work with and build on what our students already know
>
> *using open questions*—how to formulate and make the most of open and closed questions
>
> *constructing analogies*—approaching unfamiliar works of art or processes via more familiar analogous processes
>
> *modeling*—how demonstrating a process can also serve to invite and facilitate student work
>
> *exploiting multiple modalities*—how students' different learning styles affect the way we design activities
>
> *placing contextual information*—the role of context in creative work and the study of works of art*reflecting*—different techniques for and approaches to reflection
>
> *define/analyze/interpret*—examples of reflective prompt types and alternate models of reflection

ACTIVITY = INVITE/WORK/SHOW

All activities are structured using some variation on a three-part sequence of Invite–Work–Show. We can all recognize these three consecutive steps in our

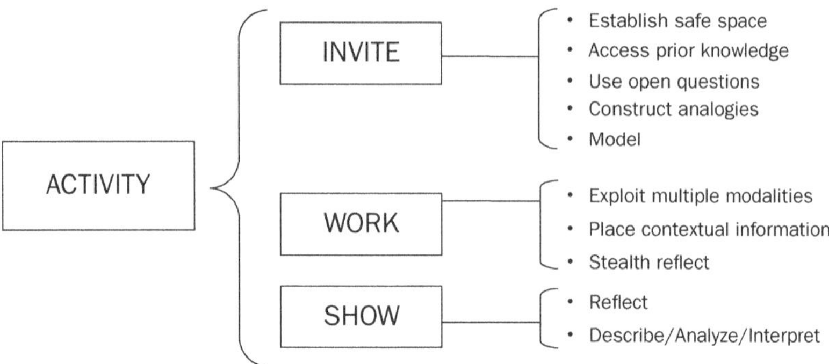

FIGURE 3.1 Essential Practices within an Invite Work Show sequence

work: a teaching artist invites, students respond with some kind of work that is shown or made visible. In this chapter, we'll examine the Essential Practices according to the place they most commonly appear in the *Invite–Work–Show* sequence (Figure 3.1).

Placing the Essential Practices in this framework is not meant to indicate priority (*establishing safe space* is most important) or sequence (*modeling* must always come before *constructing analogies*). And the organizational scheme I'm suggesting is not set in stone: you will certainly be able to find Essential Practices that are placed under Work on this list (*stealth reflection, placing contextual information, exploiting multiple modalities*) being used during Invite or Show out in the working world. Mini- or micro-instances of most of the Essential Practices occur in every workshop that you teach; they don't have a single home in our work. But there are some logical tendencies (for example, *accessing prior knowledge* most often appears in the Invite stage of an activity) that make this imperfect order useful.

DESIGN: TIGHT OR LOOSE?

What works best, a tight Design, or a loose Design? Aren't looser Designs more open to being responsive to students' needs? This chapter makes a case for deliberate workshop Design. The essential practices are presented as such so that they can be used in targeted ways. If this approach to Design sounds too tight for your teaching style, please remember your View-inspired intention to create a joyful, productive workshop space. I'm suggesting that a tight Design clarifies those intentions, making them specific enough to act on. This clarity allows us to be loose and responsive once we are in the workshop, as we Respond. A Design might be too tight in its planned use of time or materials (you end up disappointed because you didn't allow enough time or stuff), or if it *requires* certain kinds of student work to be successful (you end up disappointed because students did not hit your pre-selected marks). But from a Design point of view, specificity is going to pay off every time.

Can a Design be too loose? That has to remain an open question. Even what appears to be a free exploration centers on a finite set of materials. Even very loose-seeming Designs are not completely open. Perhaps showing up for a workshop with no Design at all—no objectives, no ideas, no idea what your students might find interesting or engaging—might be considered too loose. In that case, the first thing that would happen is probably a discussion along the lines of *Why are we gathered here? What are we interested in and what do we want to do?* A Design would be born, as the workshop that appeared too loose rectifies itself, designs itself on the spot. With the right group of students, this nondesigned Design might be the perfect approach.

You may not have to design your own curriculum, or design it on your own. In some cases, teaching artists are given support materials to help with the Design process. If you are in the Chicago area, and taking part in the Hive Chicago HOMAGO program (Hang Out, Mess Around, Geek Out), you'll have a twenty-page philosophy and practice guide to get you started. Many museums and performing arts presenters will have institutional philosophies or practices they ask you to master (MoMA's Visual Thinking Strategies). You might be asked to use a general Design process template, such as Design Thinking for Educators, or something more specific, such as Lincoln Center Education's combination of a philosophy-driven aesthetic education approach and a lesson planning page. But unless you are handed a curriculum and asked to follow it, you'll be creating your own workshop Design.

THREE WORKSHOP TYPES: PREPARATION, STUDIO, AND ARTS INTEGRATION

The Invite–Work–Show activities you Design all take place within the context of a workshop. In the working world, you'll encounter variations on three contrasting Arts-in-Education workshop types: Studio, Preparation, and Arts Integration. To be sure, many programs mix aspects from each of these three, but they also exist is fairly pure forms. For the moment I'm going to separate them from one another as cleanly as I can. Preparation workshops prepare students for an encounter with a work of art. Studio workshops are programs where students create works of art. Arts Integration workshops use a Preparation or Studio approach in service of some other curriculum area, usually English or social studies, sometimes math or science. Without getting too specific about actual activities, this outline shows what might happen in a typical six-session version of each type of workshop (Figure 3.2). The

Workshop Type Comparison			
	Preparation	**Studio**	**Arts Integration**
focus	work of art: dance / Thunderbird Dancers	studio practice: visual art / clay sculpture	subject area: social studies / dance
goal	study, experience, and connect with the work of art	create clay sculpture	use the Thunderbird Dancers performance to enhance Native American studies
Activities			
Session 1	students learn and perform traditional Native American songs and dances from the concert; analyze stories, photos, and artifacts from contemporary native culture; create new work that opens up their experience of the work of art.	establish studio procedures and familiarity with clay via small (quick) projects; analyze and catalogue traditional ornaments and marks on Hopi, Zuni, and Thunderbird Dancer costumes	build traditional Native American movement vocabulary; research tribe-specific mask and costume designs
Session 2			
Session 3		attend Thunderbird Dancers performance	choose myths to adapt; create story outlines
Session 4		TA model, then students work on large project	combine story, design, and movement in an original dance
Session 5	attend Thunderbird Dancers perfor-mance		attend Thunderbird Dancers performance
Session 6	reflect on our work and the work of art	complete and reflect on large project	Use elements from the Thunderbird Dancers performance to rework students' original dance

FIGURE 3.2 Workshop Type Comparison

Thunderbird Native American Dancers make an appearance as a work of art in all three of the workshops.

The three workshop types have similarities in many of their mechanics. There is generative and creative work in a Preparation workshop. All three include a sense of exploration, and include students developing some specific art-making skills. But Studio workshops will focus more on developing skills and work toward mastering a medium, technique, or set of materials. Preparation workshops emphasize experiential and exploratory work that connects to a specific work of art, and are much less concerned with developing skills. Arts Integration workshops have a subject-specific academic curriculum at their core; they reference and return to that subject area in the same way a Preparation workshop references and returns to a work of art. Preparation workshops are sponsored by institutions (art museums, performing arts presenters, education outreach branches of any cultural institution such as theater companies, poetry centers, YMCAs) who are interested in having students engage more deeply with the works of art they are showing, hosting, or producing. Studio and Arts Integration programs may or may not be associated with a presenting institution.

Preparation and Studio workshops also differ in the ways they engage with or use works of art. In Studio workshops (focused on the students' generative process and the artwork created), works of art from outside the workshop might be introduced as reference points along the way, or as fuel to feed the fire of the creative process. In Preparation workshops, a work of art that exists outside the workshop forms the center of an inquiry into the nature of that work, with the work of art as a single, constant point of reference. The inquiry may explore processes, or materials, or context, but ideally it will always be conscious of and serve students' direct engagement with this outside-the-workshop work of art.

For readers wondering why Social Justice Arts Education and Creative Youth Development are not included as workshop types, please "Four View, Design and Respond Based Programs," page 181 and "Materials For Professional Teaching Artists," pages 299–304 for sections devoted to that topic. There I make a case for seeing these programs as Arts Integration workshops that support a social justice curriculum.

The work of teaching artists in a higher education may appear to fall outside of the Preparation and Studio workshop continuum. But college lectures and read-and-discuss seminars can contain elements of both Preparation and Studio workshops. To the extent that undergraduate lectures and seminars taught by teaching artists revolve around works of art, they might be seen as Preparation workshops; creative writing classes are in essence studios or writing ateliers. So the Essential Practices (as well as the View–Design–Respond framework) should be useful to teaching artists working in higher education.

Later in the book, after Chapter 4, "Respond," and Chapter 5, "Four View, Design, and Respond Based Programs," Chapter 6, "Designing a Curriculum," walks you through the curriculum-writing half of the Design process. There, "Daniel's Guide to the Serendipitous Path of Designing a Unit of Study" details and supports arts-curriculum-specific writing steps with worksheets and other organizing tools.

Let's re-cap this introduction to Design. A Design consists of activities. Each activity is structured in a sequence we're calling *Invite–Work–Show*. In this chapter on Design, the Essential Practices of teaching artist craft (establishing safe space, accessing prior knowledge, using open questions) are presented one by one in separate sections, ordered according to where they most often appear in the Invite–Work–Show sequence.

CASE STUDY: INCLUDING EVERY ESSENTIAL PRACTICE

An activity sequence called "Night Thoughts" makes a good case for trying to include all of the Essential Practices in a given lesson. If you ask me for my *most successful* or *favorite lesson ever*, I'd choose this multi-stage preparation activity. In this case I'm measuring success by how many students were strongly engaged, how consistently they stayed involved through the lesson, how affected they were by the work, and how strongly the workshop work connected with the work of art. With "Night Thoughts," I was surprised by my students' investment in every part of these activities, pleased by their silent, focused attention to the video performance, and gob-smacked by the way most classes spontaneously applauded this slow, spacious, and quiet four-minute work.

In this activity, students are invited to make connections between nighttime feelings, images, poetry, and music. The lesson begins by eliciting students' experiences of and feelings about the night (using open questions, accessing prior knowledge). Students are invited to create poems using night images and feelings (verbal, visual, and intrapersonal modalities). The poems are performed with music in an improvisatory way, with a light touch (establish safe space), and interesting or resonant aesthetic choices are praised (stealth reflect). All the work up to this point is meant to set up our connection of the aesthetics of an ancient poem by Li Bo with those of a contemporary musical work by Wu Man that the poem inspired (construct analogies). We encounter Li Bo's ancient poem in Chinese as well as English characters (place contextual information), analyze the poem's imagery, and connect it with our own experience (reflect, access prior knowledge). Only then do we watch Wu Man's video performance of the musical work for solo pipa "Night Thoughts." Usually I played the video twice, and recited the Li Bo poem over the music during the second viewing. From 92Y's 2017–2018 Musical Introduction Series (Figures 3.3, 3.4, 3.5, 3.6).[1,2]

You may already be incorporating the Essential Practices into your work. To find out, use this checklist to recall and think through a few activities of your own (Figure 3.7).

ACTIVITY	STEPS & GUIDING QUESTIONS	SUPPORT

NIGHT THOUGHTS (20 min)
Part I: Our Night Thoughts
	• Create some short poems about night thoughts on chart paper.
	  o *What kind of music would go well with these poems?*
	• Read poems aloud with TA-improvised musical accompaniment, or with the *Night Thoughts* CD track.
		In this activity, students make connections between night-time feelings, images, poetry and music.
		
		Use "night words" to paint a picture in the listeners mind:
		• <u>Qualities</u>: dark, quiet, still, black, sleepy, slow, warm, lonely, happy, dreamy
		• <u>Objects</u>: bed, pillow, blanket, sheets, candle, moon, stars
		
		「靜夜思」
		床前明月光
		疑是地上霜
		舉頭望明月
		低頭思故鄉
		    —Li Bo (701–762)
		
		In front of my bed, there is a bright moonlight.
		It appears to be frost on the ground.
		I lift my head and gaze at the August Moon,
		I lower my head and think of my hometown.

Part II: Wu Man's Night Thoughts	• Introduce and read Li Bo's poem aloud. • Connect Li Bo's use of "hometown" with the idea of traveling the Silk Road. • Watch video: *Night Thoughts*. o *How does the pipa paint a picture of night thoughts?* 	Two contrasting videos of Wu Man performing *Night Thoughts* are on the CD. The second one is shot in close-up.

FIGURE 3.3 Night Thoughts Activity (page 1)

ACTIVITY	STEPS & GUIDING QUESTIONS	SUPPORT
MY CHINESE CHARACTER POEM (20 min)	<u>Prepare:</u> • Turn to My Music Journal pg. 26-27, My Chinese Character Poem. • Explore the poem and the characters. • Practice drawing characters with an imaginary brush. • Draw characters on a practice page <u>Create:</u> • Model creating a short poem using two characters and a few English words. • Create a poem on the My Music Journal page. • Share and celebrate work.	For K-1, a single line would make a poem. Older students may want to write longer pieces with more characters. Classroom teachers may want to take on this activity for their own. The word for poem in Chinese is Shi, which includes 言, the word for speech, and 寺 which is the word for temple; therefore, a poem is a "temple of speech." While exploring the characters, ask students to find the character for Moon in the Chinese version of the Li Bo poem.  Moon In this activity, students develop listening skills for pipa songs with no lyrics. You may want to define *vocal music* vs. *instrumental music*. Students may need you to model the listening, noticing, and enjoying process. Point out details that genuinely appeal to you, both objective (phrases, gesture, techniques) and subjective (feelings, images). Encourage students to begin with *I noticed... and I enjoyed...*

WHITE SNOW IN A SUNNY SPRING (10 min)	• *Wu Man's songs don't have any lyrics.*
	• *When Wu Man plays a song, what can we notice and enjoy, instead of the words?*
	• Cue up a video, and explain this process:
	  o <u>Viewing 1</u>: Watch the first minute, and silently find some things to notice and enjoy.
	  o <u>Viewing 2</u>: Watch the first minute again, stopping and starting to point out things that you noticed and enjoyed.
	• Watch, notice and enjoy.
		The CD includes three contrasting videos of *White Snow* and two of *Night Thoughts* that you might compare:
		White Snow...Video A (a slow, clear version)
		White Snow...Video B (a faster version)
		White Snow...Video C (a close-up version)

FIGURE 3.4 Night Thoughts Activity (page 2)

My Chinese Poem

「靜夜思」
床前明月光
疑是地上霜
舉頭望明月
低頭思故鄉

<u>Night Thoughts</u>
by Li Bo
In front of my bed, there is a bright moonlight.
It appears to be frost on the ground.
I lift my head and gaze at the August Moon,
I lower my head and think of my hometown.

<u>My Poem:</u>

Title: ____

By: ____

FIGURE 3.5 My Chinese Character Poem Activity (page 1)

FIGURE 3.6 My Chinese Character Poem Activity (page 2)

Essential Practices Checklist Check here if the activity includes…	
establishing safe space	
accessing prior knowledge	
using open questions	
using analogies or analogous processes	
modeling	
exploiting multiple modalities	
placing contextual information	
stealth reflecting	
reflection (describe, analyze, interpret)	

FIGURE 3.7 Essential Practices Checklist

INVITE

When we *Invite*, we assume the role of host in the community of learners. *Host* and *invitation* have resonances that *workshop leader* or *facilitator* may not, but inviting participants into an activity is clearly an act of leadership. Every activity necessarily begins with an invitation, since the Work of *Making & Doing* isn't going to begin without it. When an activity is recurring, familiar or ritualized, the Invite step may be understood (*we know we begin every session this way, so it doesn't need to be explained*). To Invite, the teaching artist sets up some Making & Doing in one of three ways—a query, an instruction, or by modeling (Figure 3.8).

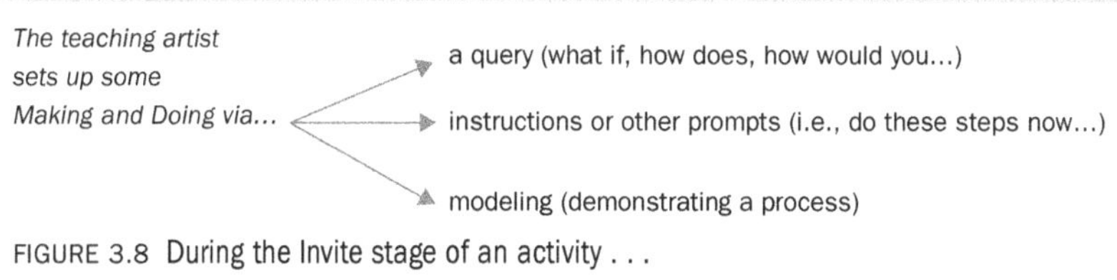

FIGURE 3.8 During the Invite stage of an activity . . .

A *query entices (What if we had to walk through this series of objects to get from point A to point B . . .? How does your family celebrate . . .? Which of these drums . . .?). Instructions or other request-style prompts begin a series of activity steps (Let's arrange ourselves in order of height . . . Everyone come with me and stand behind this line . . .). Modeling demonstrates something crucial about the activity process in which you are about to engage (wordlessly humming a melody or clapping a rhythm that will form the basis of the upcoming activity; using contact points on a partner's body to maintain balance; arranging and rearranging elements of a sculpture).*

The fact that students have been invited rather than required to attend is important to them, as is the tone of the offer, because both indicate what kind of relationship they are entering into. An invitation that's delivered with easy confidence and a light touch draws students in; invitations that express your natural curiosity and engagement appeal to students as co-learners (or even better, co-conspirators), whereas a sense of coercion or obligation tells them that they are subordinates (or even worse, ignorant subordinates). The good will and positive energy generated by an excellent invitation can add a forward momentum to the workshop that lasts beyond the activity itself, not unlike the way a Broadway show with a great opening number wins the audience's trust and willingness to suspend disbelief well into the first act. Let's take a close look at the Essential Practices related to the Invite stage: establish safe space, access prior knowledge, use open questions, construct analogies, and model.

ESTABLISH SAFE SPACE

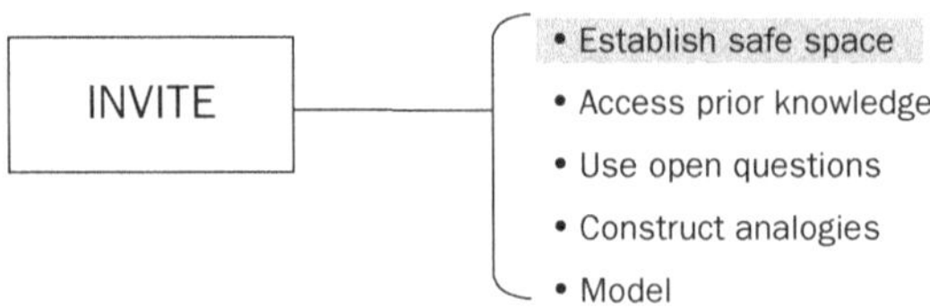

"Hello. My name is Daniel. Your teacher Ms. Hirsch and I have been meeting and talking about how we all might have some fun getting ready to see drummer Herlin Reily's Jazz Octet performance at the Civic Auditorium next week. Everything we do together is meant to help us all enjoy the concert. To start, we need some more space: please push all the desks to either side of the room, then meet me at that end." *Scrape crash thump* go the desks; the classroom space opens up. Students stand in a self-conscious clump. I offer one student the end of a roll of blue painter's tape. Together we make lines across the floor, one in front of the students, another near the far end of the room. Some kids are smiling, a few are looking skeptical, and all are wondering: *What is going on?*

"The Improv Zone" is an activity that can be used to explore any music that involves improvisation, particularly jazz song performances where a composed song both bookends and underlies the improvised solo sections. By the end of the first two sections of "The Improv Zone," outlined below, students have developed empathy for the performers who improvise, and are also set up to notice the shift of energy that happens when improvised sections begin. In the third section of the activity, students watch a jazz performance and discuss: *Can you tell when the musicians are improvising? What parts of the song are decided before the performance? Which parts are made up on the spot? What is special about the sound of improvising?*

I like to use "The Improv Zone" activity as the first lesson of a unit of study, my first interaction with the students (Figure 3.9). There is no established relationship between student and teaching artist at that time, so the activity is a jump-in-with-both-feet affair. The success of the activity is (as always) dependent on the students' engagement. Let's take a look at how this activity cultivates that engagement by establishing safe space, an environment in which students feel they are supported and can take intellectual and creative risks without fear of ridicule.

"The Improv Zone" depends on a strong analogy: a four-dimensional, physical realization of the formal structure of a jazz performance (*construct analogies* is an Essential Practice we'll look at in the next chapter). The invitations are easy to understand, and the instructions make it easy for anyone to do well: even the slightest shift into a freestyle walk will be a success.

THE IMPROV ZONE - Preparation Activity for Jazz Improvisation (40 Min.)		
Activity	**Steps**	**Support**

Walking plain and freestyle (20 min)	• Tape off the floor, a starting line and a finish line.
	
	• Model, then have students walk a plain, simple walk from start to finish, one at a time.
	
	• Model, then have students walk a freestyle walk from start to finish, one at a time.
	
	• Discuss:
	
	  o *How were the freestyle walks different from the plain walks?*
	
	  o *Did you pick up any ideas from your classmates?*
		Use the entire length of the room.

Walking in the improv zone (20 min)	• Define improvisation.
	
	• Tape off the floor into three zones:
	
	    Plain / Freestyle (improvised) / Plain
	
	• Model, then have students walk across each zone: plain, *freestyle (improvised),* plain
	
	• Repeat the same sequence, without "pre-deciding" the improvised section
	
	• Discuss:
	
	  o *What did it feel like when you crossed the line into the improv zone?*
	
	  o *How were your planned freestyle walks different from the unplanned ones?*
		At first most of the improvised walks may be pre-planned. Invite students not to plan, but to decide how to move on the spot, when they cross the line into the improv zone.

FIGURE 3.9 The Improv Zone activity

The activity starts with prior knowledge (walking), is playful (the freestyle walks will elicit laughter), and honors student work via immediate discussion. All these qualities contribute to the creation of safe space. The clear structures and instructions give students the sense that the teaching artist has a purpose; they are in good hands. Everyone is asked to take an equal risk (see how you feel when you are walking across a room with twenty-four of your friends and colleagues looking at you), so no one is singled out. The activity requires trust, the student's sense that they can take a risk and not be made game of, hurt, or harmed. A verbal declaration of the teaching artist's own trustworthiness probably won't create the trust that is needed, but direct experience might. As they participate, students come to learn that they will not be humiliated, a truth that gains in certainty with each step in the activity.

Twenty-five students require about ten seconds each to traverse a 25-foot classroom once. That's about five minutes to give everyone a chance to cross, multiplied by the two different kinds of walks in the "Plain and Freestyle" steps of the lesson plan. That makes ten minutes, plus five minutes for instructions, modeling, and answering questions. Fifteen minutes to walk across the floor? Is it worth it? Won't the students talk while they do it? Not if you clearly make not talking part of the fun. Won't they giggle and laugh? Hopefully, yes: the walks are amusing, and laughter is a wonderful, disarming, equalizing factor in the classroom. Everyone can walk across a room, and they know it. By taking the first fifteen minutes to straightforwardly do it, we honor the simplicity of the gesture. The teaching artist's willingness to allow the activity to unhurriedly unfold bespeaks confidence, and implies clarity of purpose. Everyone is allowed time to succeed. Also, everyone is equally exposed. Once exposed, if students safely accomplish their task or goal, their level of trust bumps up a notch, along with their willingness to risk more in the next step. Without the trust, risk-taking and learning will take place at a much lower level of intensity, if at all.

In the "Improv Zone" activity, exposure to risk, clarity of intent, and a patient use of time all work together to create safe space. Not the current hot topic "Safe Space" that Katherine Ho addresses in her excellent *Harvard Political Review* article "Tackling the Term: What Is a Safe Space?" where she notes that "today, it's particularly difficult to have productive conversations about safe spaces due to the term's multiplicity of definitions." The safe space I'm referring to is a "different (but also beneficial) type of safe space" Ho calls an academic safe space, which stresses "the end goal of encouraging individuals to speak. In this type of space, people are still made to feel uncomfortable, yet it's *safe* to take intellectual risks and explore any line of thought. Here, "safety" protects your right to make others uncomfortable with ideas and rational arguments. . . . In this setting, free speech is the end goal. This type of safety is commonly emphasized in in classrooms and discussion groups, where open dialogue is particularly valuable."

In his book *You've Gotta Connect*, veteran high school history teacher James Sturtevant uses a practical approach to creating safe space as he designs, asking himself a series of variations on the question "Does any student in my class spend any time being afraid?" I wish I could say that I can get through his checklist with only the desirable responses. With your own classroom and workshop experience in mind, see if you can do so.

> *Do undercurrents of threat flow around the classroom?*
> *Are any students subtly bullied?*
> *Are there any messages that some students are smarter than others?*
> *Are any students humiliated?*
> *Do I poke fun at students?*
> *Are any students ignored (by me or other students)?*
> *Is there any name-calling?*
> *Do I respond to any students with disregard or irritation?*

Is the seating arrangement safe for everyone?
Do I show that I believe in each individual as a student?
Do all students know they can ask for help?
Do I allow words or acts of disrespect to students?
Do I follow procedures that are set out?
Do I treat all students with equal regard?
Do I apply rules and consequences the same to all students?
Would any students doubt that I am their advocate?
Do students leave class confused about the concepts I taught?
Do any students get the message that they are failures?[3]

Sturtevant re-designs his classroom every year by finding new ways to make his safe space even safer, using this list as a rubric to measure success. If we are willing to apply a similarly rigorous lens to our teaching artistry, the effort will pay off in our planning, as well as in our manner. Of course our students perceptively track both what we say as well as the feeling behind what we say. As the Germans remind us with their truism "Der ton macht die musik," *the tone makes the music.* Every classroom is a container for experience; our care in establishing safe space is one of the ways we shape and maintain the container. For more about the idea of seeing the workshop as a container for teaching and learning, see "The Container" page 142.

Cultural Relevance in Juvenile Justice

I was teaching in a Los Angeles County probation camp for boys ages 12 to 18. After about three weeks, they trusted me and trusted that I would be returning to work with them. Each time I arrived with a cart of paints and brushes, the boys would come running across the field to greet me and help carry the supplies. One group of fifteen students created a large mural on an exterior wall of a building in the camp. Our classroom was only equipped with old American history textbooks, so we used those to cull images for the design. The boys were surprisingly interested in images they found of Mount Rushmore, and worked to create their own version. Instead of Roosevelt, Lincoln, Jefferson, and Washington, their Mt. Rushmore included Dr. Martin Luther King Jr., Cesar Chavez, Malcolm X, and Rosa Parks. In true hip-hop style, they *sampled* an iconic American image and made it their own. Teaching artists can make all of the arts relevant to today's young people. First, we can connect our students' lives with art-making using culturally responsive curriculum. We can make sure they can see themselves represented in the artists and instructors who teach them, and strive for multicultural teams of instructors—this way students not only can see their cultures represented, but can also see diverse groups of instructors working together toward a common goal. My takeaway: *Students in juvenile justice correctional facilities, probation camps, and juvenile halls are hungry to learn about the arts and to participate in art-making activities. Reach them on their own level first, then teach the arts.*— Glenna Avila, teaching artist and Wallis Annenberg Artistic Director, CalArts Community Arts Partnership (CAP), California Institute of the Arts

---

ACCESS PRIOR KNOWLEDGE

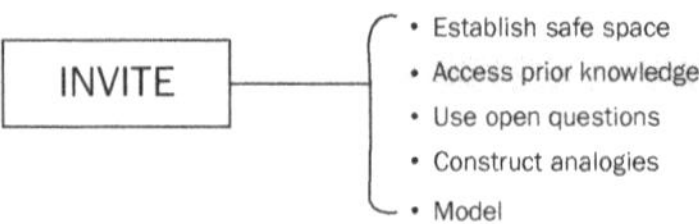

You've become curious about aesthetic education—*What is it, really*? You sign up for a workshop entitled *Introduction to Aesthetic Education*. Facilitator Eric Booth begins the workshop by asking you to take out paper and pen for some journaling. He puts you at ease and establishes some safe space by explaining that your journaling will remain private—you won't be asked to reveal or discuss what you write down. He invites you to take three or four minutes to respond to these prompts:

> *Step 1) I will name a general state of emotion, something everyone feels at some time or other. Would you come up with a title for what you might call that state when it happens to you, and write it down? I will name the general state, and you come up with a specific title that captures your experience. The general emotion is when you are "down in the dumps"; when you are feeling really low.*
>
> *Step 2) Please jot down two things you might notice yourself doing in your everyday life that would be indicators or evidence that you are down in the dumps.*
>
> *Step 3) Imagine you are in that low state of mind, and imagine two thoughts that might shoot through your head about other people when you are that low. Please write down those two things you might actually think about others when you are as low as you get. It's OK to write in code.*
>
> *Step 4) Please jot down something real that happens in your life that could or does lift you right out of that low place.*

Once all pens are still, Eric the Teaching Artist asks you to put aside your notebook. Then he steps to one side, takes a breath, and subtly transforms into Eric the Actor presenting a work of art, his performance of Shakespeare's "Sonnet 29":

> *When, in disgrace with fortune and men's eyes,*
> *I all alone beweep my outcast state,*
> *And trouble deaf heaven with my bootless cries,*
> *And look upon myself and curse my fate . . .*
> *Wishing me like to one more rich in hope,*
> *Featured like him, like him with friends possess'd,*
> *Desiring this man's art and that man's scope,*
> *With what I most enjoy contented least;*

Yet in these thoughts myself almost despising,
Haply I think on thee, and then my state,
Like to the lark at break of day arising
From sullen earth, sings hymns at heaven's gate;
For thy sweet love remember'd such wealth brings
That then I scorn to change my state with kings.

Eric the Actor obviously knows what he is about, gives a good performance, and applause naturally follows. You have just encountered a work of art: a live performance of Shakespeare's "Sonnet 29." Then Eric the Teaching Artist reappears and invites you reflect and discuss: *What was happening inside you during the sonnet?* And: *How did your journaling affect your experience with the sonnet?*

Booth's connection of our private journaling with the work of art is elegant, clear, and efficient. The activity works well, as long as students make some degree of a personal investment in the journaling. In this activity, the connection between the students' lives and the work of art is made explicit by inviting and honoring each individual's *prior knowledge*. In the case of this sonnet, the connection involves the work's *content*. Eric's questions led us to imagine a sequence of despair, stasis, and release that we could see mirrored in the sonnet. We make a connection with the work as we read it, and a connection with Shakespeare if our empathy is evoked.

The connection might alternately have been based on the work's *characteristics* (sonnet form, private note to a valued friend or lover), or *context* (poetic forms, subjects, and word choice in Shakespeare's time). Not all prior knowledge connections are created equal, nor are they equally attractive or engaging. But every work of art has some content or quality or context that opens the possibility of connecting with your students' prior knowledge. Some connections will be obvious, others will require some digging to discover. Those that intuitively seem more fun to you are probably good ones.

All of your students, even quite young ones, come to you as fully formed human beings, each with a unique worldview. Each individual has a wealth of life experience that informs their insight and self-expression. Your students know a lot and willingly bring a lot to the table. There are significant pre-existing overlaps between your students' experiences, memories, and ideas and the content, characteristics, and context a given work of art (in a Preparation workshop) or art-making process (in a Studio workshop). *As you design activities and units of study, how can you make the best use of what your students already know?*

In Socratic seminars (aka Socratic circles), all new knowledge is connected to prior knowledge. In this still commonly used form of discussion, students examine texts through questions and answers, based on the premise that all thinking comes from asking questions, and that asking one question should lead to asking further questions. Can you remember a teacher who began classes with a provocative question? Or Socratically answered your questions with a question, led you out? These teachers, by instinct or design, were helping you make a bridge between what you already knew and what you might not yet have known.

Piaget, Vygotsky, and Dewey all prominently address the role of prior knowledge. Vygotsky suggests that teachers scaffold student learning, building on prior knowledge. Piaget and Dewey both recognize the natural place of confusion in the learning process as prior knowledge is challenged by a new experience. In Piaget's theory, children, like adults, combine what he calls *prior schemata* with experience; when the *known* meets the *unknown* (when prior knowledge meets with new experience), a dis-equilibrium results. As this internal imbalance eventually rights itself, learning takes place. "Similarly, in Dewey's account of learning, what he calls *problematic experience* comes to the fore," as explained by University of Massachusetts at Dartmouth professor Jeremy Roschelle in his article "Learning in Interactive Environments: Prior Knowledge and New Experience."

> *By (problematic), Dewey means that we feel confused, uncertain, incoherent, unable to act. We are unable to coordinate prior knowledge and prior habit to cope with the exigencies of the moment. In the situation of problematic experience, we can engage a different mode of life from use and enjoying, which Dewey calls Inquiry, the reflective transformation of perception, thought, and action, re-unifies experience into a more satisfactory whole.*[4]

Classroom teachers, particularly those in middle schools and high schools, often design lessons to access a kind of prior knowledge that they call *background knowledge*, with the understanding that "Learning is controlled as much by experiences students bring to the learning situation as it is by the way the information is presented. . . . By starting with what students already know, teachers can be more precise in their teaching. They do not have to make guesses about areas of confusion or gaps in understanding. . . . Attending to background knowledge is like getting inside students' minds, which is a great place for middle level teachers to be."[5] Recent neuroscience research suggest that prior or background knowledge supports new learning in a way that is hard-wired in the brain, and that human being must necessarily "integrate new incoming information from the surroundings in relation to our pre-existing knowledge about the world . . . Information that doesn't make it into a pre-existing network of thoughts, ideas, [and] experiences is less likely to be retained over time."[6]

Rochelle places prior knowledge at the front end of what is in effect his View, one that also de-emphasizes the "specialized knowledge" of the facilitator and also stresses the role of social learning. He synthesizes Dewey, Piaget, and Vygotsky as he addresses designers of interactive experiences (the emphasis is his own):

> First, designers should seek to *refine prior knowledge,* and not attempt to replace learners' understanding with their own. Second, designers must *anticipate a long-term learning process,* of which the short-term experience will form an incremental part. Third, designers must remember that *learning depends on social interaction*; conversations shape the form and content of the concepts that learners construct. Only part of specialized knowledge can exist explicitly as information; the rest must come from engagement in the practice of discourse of the community.

Visual arts teaching artist Barbara Ellman taught to Matisse's painting *The Red Studio* at one of Lincoln Center Education's summer sessions, week-long workshops geared toward training classroom teachers in the basics of aesthetic education. The activity shown below took place just before our MoMA museum visit to see the painting (Figures 3.10 and 3.11). Notice the ways Barbara uses prior knowledge in her simple and effective preparation for an encounter with the work of art.

Matisse, THE RED STUDIO Activity (50 min)		
activity	**steps**	**support**
DRAW YOUR WORK PLACE (30 min.)	• Draw your workspace or studio, emphasizing the 3 or 4 most important objects or areas there. • Post drawings • *What visual strategies did each artist use to emphasize objects and areas?*	Materials: colored pencils, crayons, markers, and paper. Draw with enough definition that we can tell it is the place you work. Before you start, develop a strategy for emphasizing the 3 or 4 most important objects or areas in your studio; use or modify that strategy as you go. Draw 15 min., discuss 15 min.
THE RED STUDIO (20 min.)	• View slide: *The Red Studio* (Matisse) • *What do you notice?* • *What visual strategies were used to emphasize objects and areas?* • *How did your own art-making affect your engagement with the Matisse?*	

FIGURE 3.10 The *Red Studio* Activity

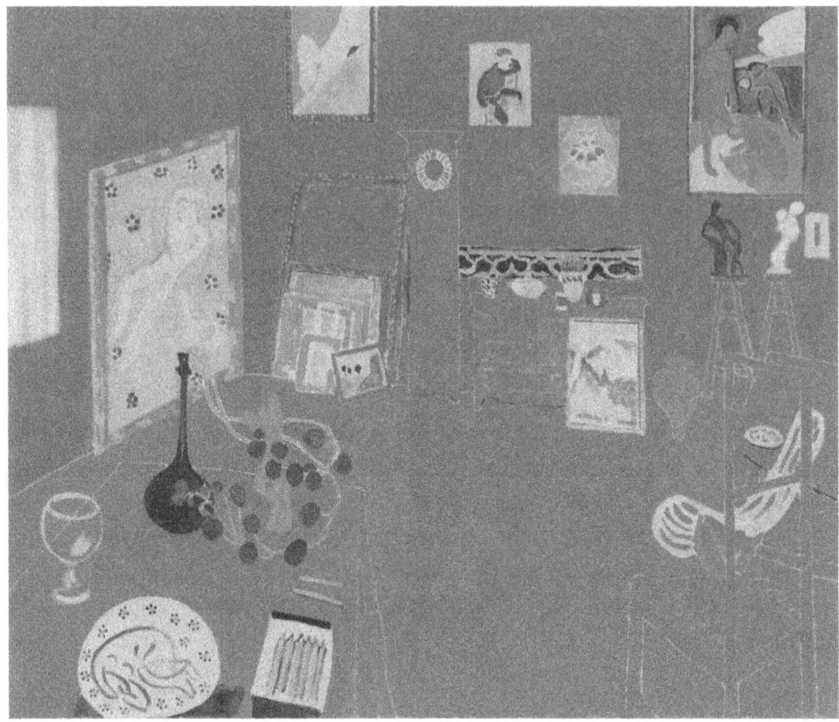

FIGURE 3.11 Matisse, Henri (1869–1954), The Red Studio (1911), © 2019 Succession H. Matisse / Artists Rights Society (ARS), New York

Digital Image © The Museum of Modern Art, Licensed by SCALA / Art Resource, NY

In the *Red Studio* activity, the students' art-making choices (practical, material, aesthetic) mirror or parallel those the artist made when creating this portrait of his workspace. We're not trying to be Matisse, or to visually mimic him. But we are placing ourselves in the position, similar to that of Matisse, of visual problem-solver. Embracing the original artist's role with this degree of directness is a dependably eye-opening experience that draws on students' prior knowledge. In order to emphasize or shape certain objects or areas, students draw on an intimate understanding of their creative or at-work space, how the physical arrangement of the space relates to what is important to them and what they want to accomplish there. The activity begins by inviting this prior knowledge, then asks the students to, Matisse-like, translate their personal priorities into a representation on paper. There is no way to respond to the invitation incorrectly, so students can't fail at the task. The more effort they put into the imagining, translating, and representing, the more rewarding their contact with Matisse's *Red Studio*—which remains hidden until after the drawing and discussion—will be.

Steven Sondheim's "Another Hundred People" from the Broadway show *Company* recently appeared as a song in a curriculum I was writing:

Another hundred people just got off of the train
and came up through the ground,
while another hundred people just got off of the bus
and are looking around
at another hundred people who got off of the plane
and are looking at us, who got off of the train
and the plane and the bus maybe yesterday.

It's a city of strangers, some come to work, some to play.
A city of strangers, some come to stare, some to stay.
And every day, the ones who stay
can find each other in the crowded streets and the guarded parks,
by the rusty fountains and the dusty trees with the battered barks,
and they walk together past the postered walls with the crude remarks.
And they meet at parties through the friends of friends who they
     never know.
"Do I pick you up or do I meet you there or shall we let it go?"
"Did you get my message? 'Cause I looked in vain."
"Can we see each other Tuesday if it doesn't rain?"
"Look, I'll call you in the morning or my service will explain."
And another hundred people just got off of the train.[7]

It's a sophisticated and lonely song. The curriculum was for urban children between the ages of six and ten who have prior knowledge and experience of elevators and public transportation. In a preparation activity that is meant to take place before students read the lyric or hear the song, I set up the work of art by drawing on students' prior knowledge, as well as their empathy:

Part One: Imagine and Connect (10 minutes)
   How many people live . . .
      in your building?
      on your street?
      on your block?
      in your neighborhood?
      in all of New York City?
   How many people fit . . .
      into an elevator?
      on a city bus?
      into a subway car?
   Are all these people sharing streets and buses and subways strangers, or are they friends and neighbors? Does living close to so many people make you feel less lonely, or more lonely? Have you ever been in a crowded, busy park or playground filled with people, but still felt lonely?

These are open questions, invitations similar in quality to those asked in the Sonnet and *Red Studio* activities. In the next step of this activity (still before they've heard the song), students make aesthetic choices (the rhythmic setting of the text, which includes the tempo of the accompaniment as well as the speed, density, and rhythm of the spoken text) that parallel choices Sondheim made when he composed the song:

Part Two: Explore the Lyric (20 minutes)
    Introduce "Another Hundred People"
    Read the lyric aloud
    Discuss:
        What kinds of pictures does this lyric paint in your mind?
        What is the person who sings this song noticing?
        What is the person who sings this song feeling?
        What would be a good beat for this song?
    Tap or clap your invented beats.
    Perform the first part of the lyric as a rap while you play your beat.

USE OPEN QUESTIONS

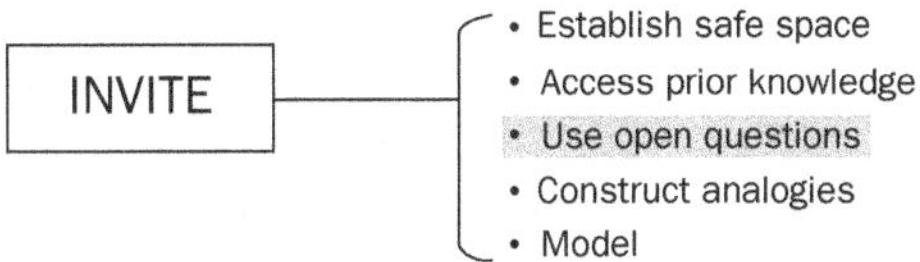

A matching game: draw a line from the question to the most accurate description of its type. You may not use up all the types; you may use some types more than once.

In a courtroom, trial attorneys examine witnesses via crafted sequences of

QUESTION	QUESTION TYPE
What can I get for you folks today?	desperate
Would you please pass the hot pepper flakes?	burning
Do we have to go to the shore again this summer?	loaded
Are you going to keep doing that all day and night?	rhetorical
Have you stopped beating your dog?	polite
What if we attached all the balloons to the lawn chair?	practical

questions. Their questions elicit specific bits of information in a pre-planned, controlled order. They are careful to ask only those questions to which they already know the answer. The goal of the sequence of attorney questions and witness responses is to shape a compelling argument in the listening judge and jury's mind. Neither the specific questions nor the general argument are meant to have a sense of open-endedness. They are designed to eliminate the need for further questions, not invite them. They also thwart any sense of exchange: the witness being examined or cross-examined doesn't have a chance to question back.

In a classroom, questions lead happily unpredictable lives. They might be repeated, rephrased, abandoned, noted, temporarily shelved, or twisted back on themselves, dissected, or even answered. In a *container* (see page 141) that *honors every response* (see page 149), questions are designed to be open-ended, to invite and inspire further questions and deeper or broader inquiry. In a classroom there are few if any limits on who might pose a question at any time. The questioner might quickly become the one being questioned. And the social contract agrees with these conditions: since we have gathered in a community to learn and grow, inquiry in its many forms is at the heart of what we are about. With all this fluidity in mind, *what is the role of questions in a teaching artist's work?*

Students' questions reveal some aspect of their understanding. The More Experienced person (the teaching artist) to whom a question is addressed can sometimes *deduce* what the Less Experienced questioner (the student) does not know, aka what they need to know or *believe* they need to know in that moment. Many of these deductions are straightforward: *When's lunch?* might mean *I'm hungry*, or *I'm confused*, or *I'm so confused that I'm bored*. Some questions posed by students invite some untangling. The student who wants to know *How many chords are in this melody?* might be noticing that the tune of a work (the notes) implies a specific harmony or range of harmonic possibilities (the chords), a pretty sophisticated observation. Or they may have a problematic understanding of what the terms *melody* and *chord* might mean and how the two relate, or they are interested in generating an accompaniment instead of playing the melody, or they can't imagine such a melody even having chords. Perhaps it is most accurate to say that students' questions *indicate* some aspect of their thinking.

When teaching artists question students, we are either confirming or instigating. *Confirming questions* are practical, even mechanical. They stabilize, reassure, focus, or redirect. When confirming, we need to know that a specific idea is understood so that we can move forward with confidence. Our students' accurate responses confirm that the work has a sound basis upon which to proceed:

> *Does everyone understand the instructions?*
> *How many instruments will be in your quintet?*
> *What three pencil shading techniques might we explore in this drawing?*

Confirming questions are often a gateway to more substantive instigating question. Here a confirming question (about a play that includes overlapping dialogue) sets up the instigating question that immediately follows it:

> *In this scene, does the interlocutor have to wait for the other person to finish speaking before they begin? Why would the playwright want this?*

Instigating questions have probing or even destabilizing qualities. These more open questions are a teaching artist's bread and butter, a constructivist-inspired version of what are commonly called Socratic questions. Socratic questions invite student engagement by asking them to clarify their thinking (*Why do you say that? Could you explain further?*), or challenging their assumptions (*Is this always the case? Why do you think that this assumption holds here?*), or asking them to provide evidence (*Could you point out where that is happening for us? Is there any reason to doubt this evidence?*), explore viewpoints (*What is the counter-argument for? Does anyone see this another way?*), imagine consequences (*But if . . . happened, what else would result? How does . . . affect . . .?*), or question the question (*Why do you think that I asked that question? Which of your questions turned out to be the most useful?*).

But a traditionally defined Socratic dialogue emphasizes objectivity, and doesn't include the aesthetic and emotional components of our full engagement with works of art. For those purposes, what are commonly called *open questions* are more useful. Functionally they might implicitly confirm, but mainly they instigate. Open questions encourage curiosity (*What's happening in this picture?*), model systematic thinking (*How would you design the set of this play if you wanted to . . .*), and dig beneath the surface of ideas while inviting and valuing subjective experience (*What subtitle would help the audience understand this piece?*). Open questions assume that students have ideas, and that those ideas matter. When training teaching artists, Eric Booth calls out and discourages *closed questions* (those with a single correct answer). In *The Music Teaching Artists' Bible*, Booth champions open questions as the antidote to un-artistic, control-oriented classrooms:

> *Good questions are not only open questions (don't have a single correct answer), they also grab people with inherent interest, invite the discovery of personal relevance, and launch an interesting answering journey. The quality of your questions, those that are clever, subtle, elegant in some way, will make a major difference in the quality of the answering by the students . . .*[8]

As we've noted, a teaching artist is constantly inviting. Open questions invite a variety of responses and create an atmosphere of adventure and acceptance. A lively spirit of inquiry can be a dependable aspect of our workshops if we're in the habit of creating high-quality open questions. One way to test the quality of your open questions is to measure how well they awaken your own internal motivation to answer. (And at the very least you have to be able to answer your own question, always worth a trial run). Which of these questions are more compelling, A or B?

A) *When did Beethoven compose this piano sonata?*
B) *What do you think Beethoven might have been feeling when he wrote this music?*

A) *What colors is the artist using?*
B) *How is the artist using color?*

A) *Who is the soloist?*
B) *What sets the soloist apart from the other dancers?*

A) *Is this music fast or slow?*
B) *How is this music moving?*

A) *Can you hear the oboe playing the melody here?*
B) *Which sounds seem important here?*

The closed questions have fixed answers, are pretty easy to formulate, and reinforce a sense of right and wrong. The more open questions (B in the A/B pairs) should be more fun. The closed questions also imply a teaching artist's or teacher's expertise; using them reinforces the expert's authority and status. When open questions are the norm, the teaching artist's authority stems from some combination of enthusiasm, humor, genuine expertise, and fearlessness in being willing to ask questions without hard and fast or predictable answers. For example the question *Is this a solo?* is closed (you will be right or wrong when you answer), while *How can our ears tell the difference between one instrument playing, and more than one?* opens up the students' subjective experience, honors their prior knowledge, and may yield new listening tools that the class can share.

If Moses had been a teaching artist, he might have put it something like this:

The Eight Commandments of Open Questions

I)   Thou shalt not require yes and no answers

II)   Thou shalt not employ questions that contain built-in assumptions or didacticism

III)   Thou shalt generally avoid asking "when" and "what" and "who"

IV)   Thou shalt invite greater participation by asking "why" and "how"

V)   Thou shalt avoid the extremes of too specific or too vague

VI)   Thou shalt avoid the extremes of too easy or too hard

VII)   Thou shalt take thy time constructing quality questions

VIII)   Thou shalt correct thyself and rephrase thine own poorly worded questions as needed, on the spot, for the benefit of all thy brethren

In their defense, confirming (or closed) questions can be energizing when they allow younger students to demonstrate and celebrate their own expertise, as in *How do you hold a cello?* And clear-cut *yes* or *no* answers to closed questions are important at transition points, as in *Before we start our drawings, who can explain the difference between the violin and the viola*?

There is really only a single open question, and all other open questions are variations on the theme of that one: *What do you notice?* After that, ny questions we ask are Socratic-circle-style follow-up. That same single open question is at the heart of the Visual Thinking Strategies approach used at MoMA and in many museums across the country. VTS-trained teachers and teaching artists open discussions with: *What's going on in this picture?*

The question is easy to love. "What's going on . . ." might refer to mark-making, color, artist's intent, iconography, or depiction—in other words, anything and everything, but with a sense of energy and relationship. "What's going on . . ." avoids the relative flatness of "What do you see?" and has more spice than "What do you notice?" VTS facilitators follow up "What's going on . . ." with two questions and three support techniques. The two follow-up questions aim to clarify detail and meaning in the speaker's ideas:

Follow-Up Questions
What do you see that makes you say that?
What more can we find?

The three support techniques help the rest of the community of learners follow and connect with the speaker:

Support
 a) paraphrase student comments, neutrally
 b) point at the area being discussed
 c) link and frame student comments

These questions and follow-up techniques are all notable for the way they encourage *continued* openness. They are honest invitations, which will be followed by further invitations to suspend judgment and keep looking at the work of art in its myriad possibilities. We might compress and translate the VTS process this way for use in any art form:

What's going on in this poem/dance/scene/music?
What do you see/hear that makes you say that?
What more can we find?

In Visual Thinking Strategies, students are invited to look carefully at works of art and talk about what they observe. They are also invited to back up their ideas with evidence (many classroom teachers require supporting observations with evidence as part of *responsible talk*), and listen to and consider the views of others as they discuss possible interpretations. As soon as they are familiar with these VTS methods, the students themselves can facilitate the discussions. The beneficial effects of working this way can be far-reaching. The Center for Creative Community's description of VTS is as good an argument for Arts-in-Education, and the power and potential of open questions, as one might hope to read:

VTS provides a way to jumpstart a process of learning to think deeply, applicable in most subjects from poetry to math, science, and social studies. Art is the essential first discussion topic because it enables students to use existing visual and cognitive skills to develop confidence and experience, learning to use what they already know to figure out what they don't; they are then prepared to explore other complex subject matter alone and with peers.[9]

CASE STUDY: WHERE CLOSED QUESTIONS MASQUERADE AS OPEN

For this unit of study, the work of art was a concert of traditional Chinese folk tunes arranged by the Shanghai String Quartet. During my activity Design process, I saw a connection between the aesthetics of traditional Chinese Sumi-e ink painting, such as *Miu Mountain Morning* (Figure 3.12), and the musical sources for the tunes and arrangements the quartet was playing (solo songs for the ehru, the Chinese two-string violin, Figure 3.13).

FIGURE 3.12 *Miu Mountain Morning* (Sumi-e ink painting)

FIGURE 3.13 Ehru (Chinese two-string violin)

To my mind, the simplicity of the lines, a connection to nature, and use of open (empty, negative) space were important in both the ink painting and the ehru music. Specifically, it seemed to me that the empty or negative space in the painting was like the silence spaces in the music, the clear ink marks were like the clearly articulated notes, the emphasis on foreground like the emphasis on melody, the lack of background like the absence of accompaniment, and the biomorphic shapes like the free rhythm and fluid tempo. These shared characteristics led me to design this activity (Figure 3.14).

Preparation Workshop Activity: Shanghai String Quartet	
Activity	**Steps**

COMPARE EHRU SOLO & SUMI-E PAINTING (15 min.)	• Discuss *Miu Mountain Morning* painting
	• Introduce the ehru
	• Play CD: Solo ehru demo
	• Discuss:
	  How is the ehru solo like a Sumi-e painting?
	  What is there, and what is not?
	  What do silence and empty/negative space have in common?

FIGURE 3.14 Shanghai String Quartet Activity

In this activity, I am asking what may appear to be open questions. But without a lot more preparation, I am probably the only person in the room capable of answering them, so from the outset the questions are poorly conceived. The questions are also so abstract that they are not likely to be of interest to young students, which makes them developmentally inappropriate questions. The questions are meant to sound open, but the truth is that I already had the preferred, that is, correct answers in hand: *the empty or negative space in the painting is like the silence spaces in the music; the clear ink marks are like the clear notes; the emphasis on foreground emphasis is like the emphasis on melody; the lack of background is like the absence of accompaniment; the biomorphic shapes are like the free rhythm and fluid tempo.* Here is a fine example of a teaching artist/designer who is enamored of his own insight and aesthetic pleasure at the expense of his student's experience. I'm inspired, but selfish. I'd like my students to have my insight, rather than their own. Please avoid this kind of thinking: double check your open questions and make sure they really are open.

No Wrong Answers—Really?

Teachers and teaching artists of all stripes sometimes tell students "There are no wrong answers." This is meant to express the educator's openness to students' varied responses. But the statement can be confusing. Students are accustomed to being asked for the one right answer. They know from experience that right answers have a vital place in learning—so why would a correct answer suddenly *not* be important? When we are (legitimately or not) fishing for a single right answer, our students know it. In that case, "no wrong answers" might feel like a trick, provoke anxiety, and shut down creativity. And students know for sure that kicking your neighbor is a wrong answer, complete nonparticipation is a wrong answer, intentionally derailing the workshop is a wrong answer. What we really mean by "There are no wrong answers" is that there are multiple right answers—as many right answers as people in the room, and as many different right answers as each of them can think of. Teaching artists know that every individual's response to a question, work of art, or artistic process will be different. Each response is valid (and potentially useful) as long as it is authentically tied to the question, work of art, or artistic process under scrutiny, no matter how "left field" it may (at first) seem to be. My takeaway: *instead of using the shorthand statement* There are no wrong answers . . ., *I go a little deeper:* There are lots of right answers to this question. I want to know what you think, how you react to this question or challenge. When I'm fishing for a single right answer, I'll let you know.—Carol Ponder, theater, music, and dance TA, Nashville, TN

CONSTRUCT ANALOGIES

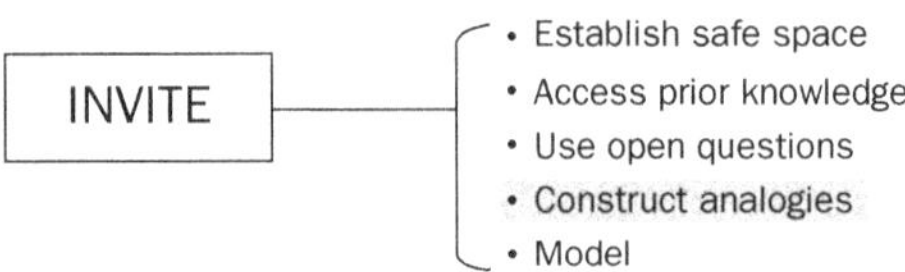

Analogies work with our prior knowledge to open up a new area of experience, using the known to illuminate the unknown. In writing, *analogy* is often confused with its close cousins *metaphor, simile,* and *allegory*. All four emphasize similarities and parallels between different things, but analogies are used to help explain complex ideas by likening them to something familiar.

As Adam Cohen tells us, "The power of an analogy is that it can persuade people to transfer the feeling of certainty they have about one subject to another subject about which they may not have formed an opinion." Thus, "when Karl Marx wanted to arouse the workers of the world, he compared the proletariat's condition to slavery and, in 'The Communist Manifesto,' urged them to throw off their figurative chains."[10] In teaching and learning, we can access our students' prior knowledge, rather than approaching a work of art or art-making process head on, and use analogy as an entrée into meaning, process, or structure.

An *a cappella* vocal work with eighteen independently sung parts by Renaissance composer Thomas Tallis is structurally a lot like a frog pond with eighteen different frogs croaking away in different combinations: first this one,

Cup is to coffee as bowl is to

    a) dish.

    b) soup.

    c) spoon.

    d) food.

Window is to pane as book is to

    a) novel.

    b) glass.

    c) cover.

    d) page.

Secretly is to openly as silently is to

    a) scarcely.

    b) impolitely.

    c) noisily.

    d) quietly.

Artist is to painting as senator is to

    a) attorney.

    b) law.

    c) politician.

    d) constituents.

Play is to actor as concert is to

    a) symphony.

    b) musician.

    c) piano.

    d) percussion.

Careful is to cautious as boastful is to

    a) arrogant.

    b) humble.

    c) joyful.

    d) suspicious.

Reptile is to lizard as flower is to

    a) petal.

    b) stem.

    c) daisy.

    d) alligator.

Marathon is to race as hibernation is to

    a) winter.

    b) bear.

    c) dream.

    d) sleep.

then those three, then five at once and five more that echo them back again. The frogs differ in size, shape, and to a certain extent the tone color of their individual croaks, but their croaks (the pitch, volume, and tone color of their croaks) all fall within given limits of male and female frog vocal mechanisms. This frog pond analogy can be a starting point for activities that would help participants experience and notice the contrapuntal, multi-timbral qualities of a Thomas Tallis piece, qualities that can be said to be the essential springs that drive and organize Tallis' music. Building a workshop around the frog pond analogy allows students to begin with a place and phenomenon that they are familiar with or can easily imagine, then *translate it* from a four-dimensional, comfortably narrative froggy world into the more or less abstract and invisible world of music. Such a translation is possible (and fun) because the initial image is familiar and a little goofy, and because the analogy itself is resonant and maps accurately onto the music itself, the work of art under study. For students not trained as musicians, gaining this kind of insight into a complex music structure would be difficult without an analogy lighting the way.

A successful analogy might also be less narrative, but still familiar and direct in its visual and physical qualities. Felix Mendelssohn's Octet for Strings is a classical chamber work, scored for four violins, two violas, and two celli. Imagine you want to explore the ways the eight instruments speak back and forth to one another in constantly shifting configurations, the contrapuntal interplay that drives the piece. Imagine too that you want your students to work in multiple modalities, with an emphasis on the visual and kinesthetic; you want them to have the experience of composing for and playing in an octet before they encounter the Mendelsohn's Octet. Enter the analogous ensemble (Figure 3.15): an octet of eight home-made shakers.

Within each of the octets, the instruments all hail from the same family (string family, percussion family). Bigger shakers are mechanically heavier and move slower by nature, and their deeper tones play specific roles in the musical structure, much the way slower-moving celli are differentiated from the higher, lighter, and more nimble violins. Because the size and relative tone of the percussion instruments corresponds with that of the string instruments, the analogy is strong. Since it is easier for students to compose and perform music using a shaker octet than for a string octet, the opportunities to Make & Do open up in a nice way (see page 231, "Technique, Theory, and Developmental Appropriateness").

When Mendelssohn wrote his string octet, he made practical, material, and aesthetic choices about the instruments at his disposal. In any given moment or phrase, he had to ask himself: *How many instruments should I use? How many layers of sound is too many? Which sounds go together best? What*

FIGURE 3.15 A string octet and a home-made shaker octet

is the most satisfying thing I can make happen right now? When students compose music for their shaker octets, they'll ask themselves the same questions. Because the music is layered, a sandwich analogy is one fun way to start the composing process. . . .

It's late at night. You're hungry. You open the fridge and start taking out stuff to make a sandwich (Figure 3.16). You have a lot of options. How do you start? What layer comes first? Then what? If you have meat, do you stick with one kind, or mix them together? Why? If you have mayo, is it good to have mustard too? How many layers or ingredients is too many? How do you know when the balance of ingredients is just right? Which flavors go together best? Which do you avoid? What is the most satisfying bite you can make happen?

At this point we've imagined a midnight snack. But we are also now predisposed to think along certain lines when creating a multi-layered thing. Our sandwich-building process mirrors Mendelssohn's octet-building. And we've identified the prime mover in the process, the basis of all aesthetic choices: *pleasing ourselves.* That is an empowerment we want to maintain all through the composing process. As layered-thing-builders, we are also tuned in to Mendelssohn's first three questions regarding *What/Which* and *How Many* layers or ingredients. The sandwich analogy warm-up takes just a few minutes, draws on prior knowledge, and establishes a safe and light-hearted work space. It leads into composing for the shaker octet when the teaching artist offers a transition: *Like a good and tasty sandwich, tasty music has layers too . . . How do you start? What layer comes first? Then what?*

FIGURE 3.16 A familiar item with multiple layers

Analogies like the frog pond and shaker octet act as lenses though which we see a work of art in a new light or in greater detail. A student who creates and performs music for a frog pond sees themselves as something of an expert in frog pond music, and rightly so. With a little prompting, new masters of frog pond or shaker octet counterpoint can see into Tallis or Mendelssohn, comparing and connecting their own practical, material, and aesthetic choice-making with that of composers. The sense of recognition that comes with this connection, the understanding of how much the student creators have in common with authors of the work of art, evokes a feeling of engagement and ownership within the student. *Engagement* because there is delight in discovering the similarities between the work of art and the analogous process. *Ownership* because the students' own ideas and choices were the first creative step.

Successful analogies are user-friendly, familiar to the students, based in their prior knowledge. Successful analogies are also apt, truly reflective of the qualities and characteristics of the work of art they reference. An accurate analogy opens up the possibility for understanding in some *modality* that runs *parallel* to that of the work of art. For example: noticing and working with the qualities of movement involved in a baseball pitching machine or a hot-air popcorn popper *might* enable a student to perceive or describe the way Trisha Brown uses space and rhythm at the beginning of a dance piece, if the students are familiar with the machine or the popper, and if the analogy is true to Brown's work in a big way, and not merely as a momentary detail. You might use analogies as a passing reference to illustrate a concept, or the inspiration for a short activity, or as the basis for an entire unit of study. Analogies may appear according to your Design, written by you, or be spontaneously offered by students during activities. In all cases, they can be challenging to formulate well.

An inaccurate analogy can only confuse and slow the process it is meant to serve. For example the interactivity of a string quartet, the ways that players alternately take turns, lead and follow, call and respond, or share musical materials brings up any number of possibilities for analogy. Let's evaluate the accuracy of five different analogies for the ways those four string quartet musicians interact. You won't have to be a musician to do this.

> *Analogy #1—A string quartet is like a family of four with a mother, father, and two children.*

This seems like a good match: the violins are smaller, have higher voices, and could be seen as the "children," with a lower-voiced viola mom and a bigger, deep-voiced cello dad. Everyone knows about family structures, so this analogy has a firm basis in prior knowledge. Children generally move faster than adults, just as violins generally move faster than the heavier celli. But does a cello actually sound like a dad? What does it objectively mean, to "sound like a dad," and how many students will share that opinion? And in terms of a cello's musical materials in any given piece, the notes and rhythms played may not be dad-like at all, even if the general sound of the instrument is considered to be so. To get the family to "line up" with the instruments, this analogy requires the teaching artist to be prescriptive, so the invitation to explore the idea will indicate a right answer, rather than being genuinely open. In the end the "like a family" simile makes too subjective assumptions, and has too many weaknesses to make it worth setting up or exploring. Analogy Grade: C+

Analogy #2—A string quartet is like the four wheels of a car.

This one sounds good: the car really does need all four mutually dependent wheels to roll . . . or does it? Also a car never hops up and rolls on one wheel (like a violin solo), and only does so rarely on two wheels (like a viola and cello duet), and the wheels never take turns (as quartets so often do). And car wheels always roll at the same rate, whereas the instruments in quartets often "move" at different speeds. Finally the wheels and tires on a car are all basically the same, interchangeable— not so the violin, viola, and cello. So this is a poor, misleading analogy. Analogy Grade: D−

Analogy #3—A string quartet playing music is like four people carrying a balloon.

Everyone can invent ways of getting a balloon across a room (carry a tune) without having it touch the floor (without having the music stop), so this analogy is friendly and light-hearted. Four balloon-carriers can take turns, all do the same thing, all do different things, selectively lay out, or have three support the efforts of one, the way a string quartet shares or supports a melody. So this analogy accurately reflects the range of relationships that composers employ with four-voice ensembles, emphasizing the types of string quartet interactivity. But it misses the boat by a) referring to "music," which is too broad a term, and b) not including the contrasting qualities of the instruments in the analogy. Analogy Grade: B−

Analogy #4—A string quartet playing music is like four people carrying a balloon, where each person has a limited range of motion in an important body part.

Strings are differentiated largely by their ranges, and the differences are fairly easy to see and hear. They could also be said to be differentiated by tone color, but that is a pretty subtle aspect of sound to teach to. Adding this detail of *limited range* to the previous analogy makes it more precise. Analogy Grade: B+

> *Analogy #5—The opening passage of Mark O'Conner's String Quartet No. 2, first movement, is like four people (where each person has a limited range of motion in an important body part) carrying a balloon at the same time in the same way—all of them are doing the same rhythm at the same time.*

Adding the detail of a specific passage from the work of art (*Mark O'Conner's String Quartet No. 2*) brings this one up another notch. String quartets change texture often, sometimes every measure or even every couple of beats. In this analogy, the texture we are referring to goes on for many measures, so naming the passage helps us avoid the pitfall of trying to hear what is happening in an excerpt that is too short to be substantive, representational, or aesthetically satisfying. We are teaching more directly to a work of art, and not to a general idea of how textures work in string quartets. The opening passage of the work is probably a theme that gets developed as the movement progresses, so the passage contains an important idea, not just a passing detail. The designer makes it easy for students to connect the analogy (already familiar, fun, and apt) with the source music that inspired it. Analogy Grade: A

Some cultural sensitivity is called for when constructing analogies. I was teaching to a performance of traditional Irish *sean-nós* singing, intricately ornamented a cappella vocal solos in Gaelic. I was moved by this haunting music, and the vocal ornaments (improvised) and their relationship to the underlying melody (fixed, known) fascinated me. As a prior-knowledge entry point to the work of art, I drew a large Christmas-tree-style pine tree . . . and invited students to ornament the tree with various paper decorations (Figure 3.17). We experimented with different kinds of ornaments, placements, groupings, densities. We analyzed our work: *How many ornaments is too many? What is the relationship between the shape and structure of the tree and that of the ornaments? If we had a differently-shaped tree, would we want differently-shaped ornaments?*

As soon as we became experts in 3D ornamentation we encountered a highly ornamented *sean-nós* melodies. Through repeated listenings, we discussed: *What is happening in this music? What is the relationship between the tune of the song and the ornaments? Are there too many ornaments, not enough, or just about the right amount?* And somewhere is the activity sequence we try to sing, draw, and physicalize (draw in the air, re-create as a whole body gesture) the individual ornaments. Finally, with *If we were listening to a different song, would these ornaments still work, or would we want different ornaments? Why?*, we open up to other works of art in the *sean-nós* genre (in fact to any works of art that include vocal ornamentation, from Beyoncé to Indian ragas) and contextual questions of lyric content, styles, and traditions.

FIGURE 3.17 A Christmas-tree-style pine tree

But my original choice of a Christmas tree was, as you may have guessed, an issue. An experienced educator, a teacher of teachers at Columbia University, no less, attended a professional development where I presented this activity as an example of teaching artist practice. She informed me, not unkindly, that not everyone in a classroom setting is necessarily knowledgeable about nor comfortable with Christmas trees as an object of focus for an activity. I was put off by the idea of making students and teachers uncomfortable, and stopped using the activity. I tried using jewelry as a replacement for the tree, where the underlying form was the human body and the ornament was jewelry. Students lay on large pieces of paper; we traced outlines of our bodies, then added ornaments. Sometimes the underlying individual was so obscured by ornament that they could hardly be seen. *How much jewelry is too much, too little, just right?* The jewelry analogy worked just as well as the tree, without the cultural baggage.

MODEL

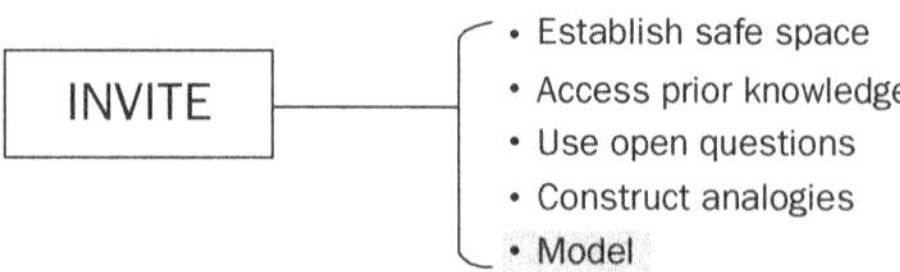

It's 8:15 a.m. at the Spuyten Duyvil School in Riverdale, and Ms. Keheyas' gifted and talented first-graders are already warmed up and ready to make something. The classroom is appointed with a Smart Board (a 4′ x 5′ touch-sensitive screen attached to a computer, projector, speakers, and document camera). I've photocopied and handed out pages with pictures of three musicians that my students already know by name and instrument, and empty musical staves for an activity called "Squiggle Scores."

The basic instructions: *imagine the sound you want each instrument to make, and draw lines or shapes that represent that sound.* In a concert scheduled for the following week, live musicians will interpret and play the marks the students make on these pages in much the same way they interpret any musical score. The activity feels like play, since it involves crayons and markers, and has *squiggle* in its name. The students are precocious, so I won't be surprised if they do some deep and creative scoring. I have taught some version of this activity twenty or thirty times, so I am confident that it will engage students and produce good results. On this particular morning, we practice drawing sounds in the air to make the connection between sound and gesture explicit, then begin creating our hard-copy Squiggle Scores.

But the scores I see taking shape don't look like much. The marks lack a sense of clarity and purpose. The students are almost all making long wavy lines, and then they are all suddenly finished. There are few if any interesting textures on their score pages—mostly just wandering lines. *What is wrong with these children this morning?* is (unfortunately) the first question I asked myself. *Why is their work so mediocre?* The marks they were making showed me that they had not followed or perhaps not understood my instructions. But the instructions had been clear; I'd taught this lesson many times, so I had the activity prompts pretty well honed.

"Ms. Keheyas . . . I'm not happy with these scores. I don't think the children are making much of a connection between their drawn marks and sounds in general, let alone sounds they want the instruments to make. What are we . . .", notice I am still avoiding taking full responsibility, "doing wrong?" Ms. Keheyas is polite but also direct. "It might be good if you modeled it for them on the Smart Board." Ah—hm, yes. Ms. Keheyas is right. Modeling is what I had done every other time I taught this activity, and what I had failed to do that morning. I had become complacent with my preparation and assumed I knew how to present this familiar lesson. As a result, the work suffered on every level: it was less engaging, less interesting, less fun to do, and the resulting scores, from a usually outstanding group, were pretty awful.

Ms. Keheyas and I both knew how much fun the Squiggle Scores *could* be. We started over. We made sure we had enough new paper score templates to do it all again and literally went back to the drawing board. The students needed to make a kinesthetic connection between the marks and the sounds, so my re-modeling addressed this. A blank score appeared on the Smart Board (a replica of the paper score template students work with). I modeled mark-and-sound-making, and we all sang the short, long, high, and low notes, sometimes drawing them in the air as we do, mimicking the motion of drawing them on paper. Two or three different students came up and made new marks, and we sang those too (see page 234 for some examples of student-drawn Squiggle Scores). For children who were ready to work in more detail, we modeled how instruments can copy one another, or lay out and rest. The students' excitement built as their understanding of the possibilities grew. In the sliver of remaining class time that the re-modeling process allowed, they completed (or almost completed) scores that were much more creative and thoughtful than those from the first poorly-modeled round.

(Note: The precipitating action that led to my poor modeling was not a Design problem, but my not having adhered to an existing design. Based on trial and error, I had already learned that it took at least twenty-five minutes to do the modeling well, more than half the allotted forty-minute class time. Once the Squiggle Score process had been modeled and students felt confident and empowered, the drawing of the score could happen in a quick, intense ten minutes. This balance of preparation time versus process time looks lopsided on paper, but for this activity it is the right balance. With the right modeling, that is, enough time exploring the physical mechanics and aesthetic possibilities of the Squiggle Score process, students succeed (Figure 3.18). But some part of my mind had always resisted that balance of preparation versus creative process; part of me, ignoring past experience, simply wanted the modeling to take less time. I took a road-tested, dependable activity and tweaked it just enough to make it developmentally inappropriate. Ideally we would schedule two sessions to get the most out of the activity, the first to model and create a draft or experimental score, the second to look at each other's scores to sing and appreciate the possibilities before creating a final version.)

Most teaching artists find themselves modeling a lot. In any subject or art form, the master teachers I have observed are all proficient modelers, succinct and effective. Students see practical, material, and aesthetic choices being made during the modeling, the same kinds of choices they will be asked

FIGURE 3.18 The author with a projected Squiggle Score, 2013

to make. The pleasure of creating something becomes apparent and often awakens students' intrinsic motivation, as in "I want to make one too." This is a human response, not limited to an age group. Modeling a process gives students a chance to observe and reflect, examine any artifacts produced, and ask questions. The questions students ask will tell you exactly what you left out of your model, so that you can put it in the next time around.

The richness and messiness that might become apparent during the act of modeling an art-making process are encouraging; students experience the fact that there is room within the work process for subtlety, grossness, boldness, shyness, ridiculousness, confusion, wrong turns, corrections, and, ultimately, a meaningful product or shared experience. Modeling confirms that students are safe to laugh, have fun, experiment, and that their work will be honored, so it bolsters students' sense of community and safe space. If you draw or sing or move easily, model in visual, aural, and kinesthetic modalities: your ease will help put your students at ease. If you are weak in any particular area (I'm a clumsy dancer), don't let that stop you from working in that modality: your willingness to be imperfect (dance a clumsy slip jig, a hopeless hornpipe) *also* helps put your students at ease. Modeling can also open up your relationship with classroom teachers, who can often provide pinch-hit modeling, once they know what the goal is, or can, as Ms. Keheyas did, help identify when their students need more modeling.

Good modeling doesn't imply rigidity or direct imitation in the creative work that follows. Students can choose how closely they want to imitate the modeled process. Some may mimic or directly copy what you do during modeling and keep it as their own work, and copying may be a genuine and therefore positive choice. Students who copy your modeling may need more or perhaps clearer modeling, and they may be providing it for themselves by repeating the teaching artists' model. See their staying so close to home as an indicator that they need more process time or support before venturing beyond reproducing the model.

Hand Out Tools and Get Out of the Way

At a gathering of teaching artists interested in cross-training in each others' disciplines, I was asked "How do you manage to get such large-scale sculptures built so quickly at the schools you visit?" Off the cuff, I replied, "My job is to hand out tools and then get out of the way." That might have sounded as if I wasn't concerned about the safety of students using power tools. But since I take great care when it comes to safety, I just let the remark hang in the air. Teaching artist colleagues who overheard me still quip, "I loved it when you said that about handing out tools and getting out of the way, Jeff!" Maybe the comment resonated with the other teaching artists because having a short time to work with a school group can be frustrating for any of us. Especially if too much of our time is taken up with talking about what we might want to create together, rather than jumping right in to make art. My goal, as much as possible, is *Engagement Before Information* (a concise reminder I learned from Eric Booth). Talking is highly valued in schools. I try to counter-balance all that talking by offering other ways for teachers and students to communicate and learn. My takeaway: *Teachers may tend to over-explain things, but as a teaching artist, I can choose to "under-explain" things. Often this swings open the door to greater engagement and student ownership of the creative process.*—Jeff Mather, visual arts, Atlanta GA

Discovering Neutral

As a dancer, my body is my instrument, my tool for making art. As a teaching artist, I nurture the relationship that my students have with their own instrument. At the beginning of each residency, I ask students to *please find an empty space and show me neutral position.* In a class of twenty students, perhaps one or two will accomplish this seemingly simple task, but that is all I need. I call attention to a student who has succeeded: *This is an excellent example of neutral. What do you notice about the way she is standing?* A student responds: *Her arms are by her side.* Four more students achieve neutral. *Look, here's another great example of neutral, his arms are by his side. What else do you notice?* Another student: *He's not touching anything.* Five more students find their neutral. *Look, her arms are by her side and she has empty space around her whole body; she is definitely in neutral. What else do you notice?* A chain reaction begins to happen. *Her legs are together.* Eight more students find their neutral. *Another great example—arms by his side, not touching anything, legs together; this is neutral. What else do you notice?* Another student: *He isn't moving.* By observing and describing their peers, students guide themselves and achieve neutral. With this heightened sense of awareness and control of their instrument, they're now ready to embark on their journey into movement. My takeaway: *Mindful, self-directed learners develop when I invite active discovery and model noticing.*—Maggie Costigan, dance, Maui, HA

WORK

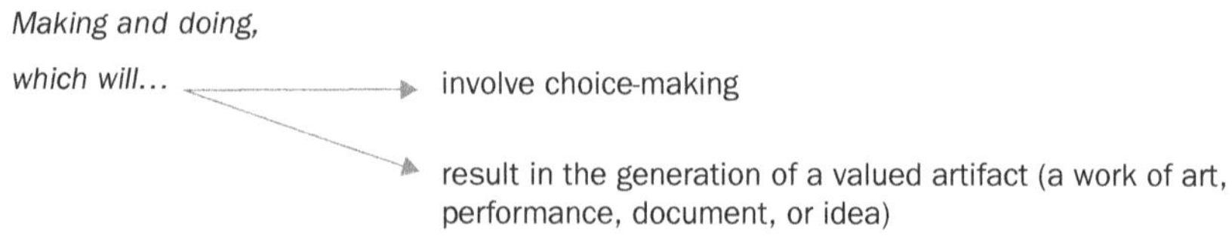

FIGURE 3.19 During the Work stage of an activity . . .

Work is moving, drawing, singing, stepping, navigating, deciding between, marking, separating, replacing, substituting, responding, improvising, drumming, jumping, verbalizing—all the fun stuff that our students actively *make* and *do*. This Making & Doing involves *choice-making*, making that results in the generation of a valued *artifact*: a work of art, performance, document or idea (Figure 3.19). "Choice-making" is a way of describing an art-making process. As they work, students make practical choices (*What will work? Will this work?*), material choices (*Do I want this, or this?*), and aesthetic choices (*Do I like it this way, or this way?*). The common quality that animates all of these practical, material, and aesthetic choices is the students' genuine desire to *please themselves*. Pleasing the teaching artist or "getting it right" are lesser goals, from an engagement and learning point of view. Pleasing one's self is intrinsically rewarding and intrinsically motivating, so the experience of choice-making has value *even before that experience yields any artifacts*.

EXPLOIT MULTIPLE MODALITIES

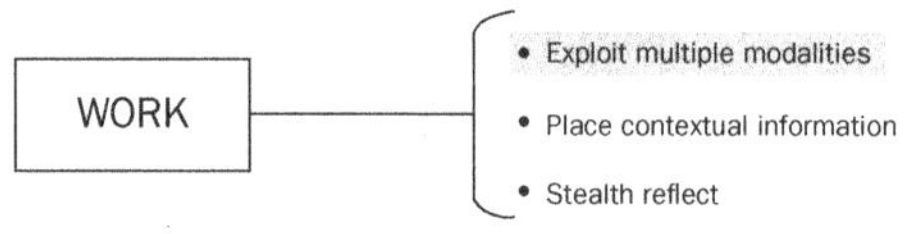

On a primal level, our brains are tickled by what film composers refer to as "Mickey Mouse scoring," where a visible action or movement is tightly accompanied by a sound: Mickey falls down, a drum goes BOOM. Infants find the coordination of sight and sound delightful. Five minutes watching *America's Funniest Home Videos* will show that in this regard we never really grow up: when the startled cat jumps into the air, the post-production sound designers add a "boing." Choreographers play with our adult sense of how sight and sound work together. In films, a one-to-one correspondence between action and sound might seem like kid stuff or broad comedy. But skillfully used, soaring music with soaring images might evoke your own inner soaring.

Composer Steven Malinowski's "Music Animation Machine" links qualities of sound with parallel qualities of shape and color. Music and image are synchronized in real time; short duration sounds appear as short-length shapes (reading from left to right), longer sounds as longer shapes; high-pitched sounds (high notes) appear higher up on the screen, lower pitch sounds (lower notes) are closer to the bottom of the screen. As the music plays, the notes we hear at any given moment turn white; otherwise notes appear in various colors, organized by layers of rhythm or by instrument groups. By setting up these relationships, Malinowski makes the invisible *visible*. I'm going to use the way Malinowski translates sound (aka an aural modality) into shape, color, and motion (aka visual and kinesthetic modalities) to help make a case for exploiting multiple modalities in every lesson we teach.

See if you can find the shapes representing the famous "dit-dit-dit-daaaah" or "short-short-short-long" from the opening bars of Beethoven's Symphony No. 5 on this Music Animation Machine screen shot (Figure 3.20), even without the real-time sound and animation:

If you found it, congratulations. When the image is in motion and linked to sound, as you can experience on Malinowski's website, the connection is impossible to miss, and delightful to witness. You don't have to possess a strong auditory intelligence or have any musical training to succeed because you can *see* the structure of the pitches and rhythms, and they *linger* in your visual world. Of course the moment-to-moment sounds soon end and are replaced with new ones, but their visual representation lingers within the frame,

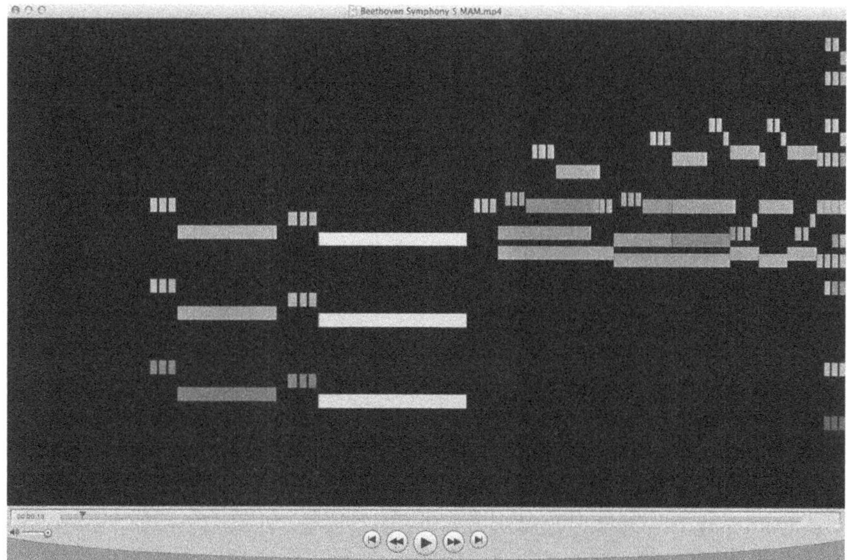

FIGURE 3.20 Screen shot from Steven Malinowski's *Music Animation Machine* version of Beethoven's Symphony No. 5, Mvt 1

allowing you to track them for longer than you might if they remained as invisible, ephemeral waves in the air. If you know what a *pattern* is, Beethoven's pattern *short short short long*, which is the engine that drives the entire seven-minute movement, is there for anyone to observe. I use this graphic Music Animation Machine version of this piece as an introduction to the importance of pattern and sequence in music with young children as well as groups of adults in studio workshops for composers creating new work. We mine the Beethoven for composing techniques.

Using animated Beethoven videos to inform students' composing is an example of *multiple modalities*. I'd like my students to *discover* the inner workings of Beethoven's motifs and orchestration without having to be conservatory-trained. Once they are able to *see* Beethoven, they experience invisible sound as a visible phenomenon in real time. The musical structures Beethoven uses are present as a kind of graphic map that anyone can observe, describe, and analyze. In a short time students can become Beethoven pattern experts at a simple but quite genuine level. Their understanding of patterns and sequences takes a developmental step. Any composing or listening they do in the future will be informed by their knowledge of Beethoven's pattern-making.

"Multiple modalities" is my practical application of one of the most influential ideas in education theory in the last thirty years, Howard Gardner's theory of Multiple Intelligences. Here is the current and most simple form of the multiple intelligences list:

Howard Gardner's Multiple Intelligences

Visual-Spatial
Bodily-Kinesthetic
Musical
Interpersonal
Intrapersonal
Linguistic
Logical-Mathematical

According to Gardner, "We are all able to know the world through language, logical-mathematical analysis, spatial representation, musical thinking, the use of the body to solve problems or to make things, an understanding of other individuals, and an understanding of ourselves. Where individuals differ is in the strength of these intelligences—the so-called profile of intelligences—and in the ways in which such intelligences are invoked and combined to carry out different tasks, solve diverse problems, and progress in various domains."[11] He inveighs against the educational status quo, explaining that the existence of these different, fluctuating, and differently applied profiles of intelligence "challenge an educational system that assumes that everyone can learn the same materials in the same way and that a uniform, universal measure suffices to test student learning. Indeed, as currently constituted, our educational system is heavily biased toward linguistic modes of instruction and assessment and, to a somewhat lesser degree, toward logical-quantitative modes as well."

Gardner's *Frames of Mind* (1983) and *Multiple Intelligences* (1993, revised 2006) substantiate his observation that students learn in ways that are identifiably distinctive. Without being prescriptive, he urges educators to use their knowledge of Multiple Intelligences to alter the way they approach teaching and assessment: *The broad spectrum of students—and perhaps the society as a whole—would be better served if disciplines could be presented in a number of ways and learning could be assessed through a variety of means.*

Whenever Gardner came up in teaching artist conversations at Lincoln Center Institute's TA Collaborative Lab in the mid-1990s, we discussed the overall validity of his observations and argued about his theory's usefulness for us in the field. For me, the idea that "students . . .would be better served if disciplines could be presented in a number of ways" was especially resonant. And I was particularly concerned with the "broad spectrum of students" he talked about—I wanted to reach more of my students more of the time. All the teaching artists at Lincoln Center Institute did. Could Gardner's Multiple Intelligences point of view help this happen?

I assessed the validity of Gardner's assertions by observing the mechanics of teaching and learning. As I watched my colleagues at work, it became clear that the best of them were masters of *multiple modalities*. This, in effect, is the theory applied as practice: *multiple* intelligences are addressed via *multiple* modalities within a lesson. I began making sure my lessons included multiple avenues of engagement that were meant to appeal to different students on different days. It seemed a completely practical thing to do, since it was apparent that not every approach engaged every student every time. To make multiple avenues of engagement possible in every lesson, I had to translate musical ideas and structures into more or less parallel languages and analogous forms in the different areas Gardner identified.

Here is my current Gardner-inspired list of the most useful (fun, engaging, effective) of these modalities for students of any age:

Modalities Checklist

Kinesthetic	(to sing, play, dance, move, work in four dimensions)
Visual	(to decode, draw, design, chart, graph, reproduce, enhance)
Narrative	(using original or pre-existing stories)
Authorial	(to write, improvise, generate)
Reflective	(to wonder, imagine, question, posit, hypothesize)
Aural	(to listen)

Interpersonal   (regarding self and others, empathy)
Intrapersonal   (regarding personal relevance, ethics)

The list is provisional, not definitive. Once you've generated an activity or direction, evaluate your Design: *How many modalities have I included in the unit of study? Am I too dependent on a single modality? Have I missed an opportunity to reach more students with a more effective modality?*

In practice, the first five on the list (Kinesthetic, Visual, Narrative, Authorial, Reflective) are usually combined or hybridized; some Visual or Kinesthetic work is involved whenever students work in any modality, and Reflection is ubiquitous. And art forms may lend themselves more directly to certain modalities. For example when teaching to works of art that are text-driven (plays, any narrative work in dance or theater, figurative work in visual art, music with lyrics) Interpersonal (between two people) and Intrapersonal (within one's self) modalities are often the most vitally connected to the work of art. As a music teaching artist, I found that connecting with the work of art often meant leaning heavily on students' listening abilities, the Aural modality. But students seemed to be able to stay with Visual and Kinesthetic work for longer than they could actively listen. Their ability to notice detail in what they saw and did was much more developed then their ability to describe what they heard. The Aural modality was, for whatever reason, generally weak. If I were to ignore this tendency during music workshops, I would be depending on what might be my students' weakest modality or intelligence. I'd be making it *more* difficult for the majority of my students to feel confident and be active. Instead I approach musical ideas via the Visual, Kinesthetic, and Narrative, "Narrative" being my take on the stories that comprise the Intrapersonal and Interpersonal modalities.

This multiple modality approach has proven robust and become essential for all of my teaching; I consider the other non-aural modalities as a varied means to reach an aural-musical end. Examples of these adaptations are sprinkled throughout this book. The counterpoint-as-frog-pond analogy (page 85) creates an almost theatrical analogue (potentially Visual, Kinesthetic, and Narrative all at once). The Squiggle Scores (page 238) and Music Animation Machine version of Beethoven's Fifth Symphony (page 97) are exuberantly Visual. The blue tape on the floor of the Improv Zone (page 66) is musical form made manifest on the floor (Spatial) and in our bodies (Kinesthetic).

One of the rewards of a multiple modality approach is the playfulness it engenders, both for you as you design and teach, and for your students, who you'll find are always ready to do something fun. In being willing to open up and experiment with alternate modalities, we're opening the classroom community's sense of the possible, with a light touch. A little silliness (imitate a frog pond?) can bring a lot of positive energy to a classroom, and help our serious planned endeavors avoid being heavy or too teaching-artist-directed.

Being able to change modalities as needed is like having a roadside emergency kit for when lessons, for whatever reason, break down. Even well-designed lessons fall apart, without our being to ascertain the cause, as any sympathetic, experienced classroom teacher or teaching artist can tell you. If an idea or concept isn't coming clear for students during a lesson in master teacher's math, English Language Arts (ELA), and other K–12 classrooms, many are able change gears by switching modalities, on the spot. Doing so seems to be part of a standard classroom teacher skill set, something I try to emulate. Switching modalities is the teaching equivalent of approaching a topic from another angle during a debate or argument; if one approach is not working, try another—while staying on topic.

Barbara Solomon and Richard Felder at North Carolina State University make a good case for multiple modalities being essential to the development of a well-rounded, capable person. They urge educators to "strive for a balance of instructional methods (as opposed to trying to teach each student exclusively according to his or her preferences.) If the balance is achieved, all students will be taught partly in a manner they prefer, which leads to an increased comfort level and willingness to learn, and partly in a less preferred manner, which provides practice and feedback in ways of thinking and solving problems which they may not initially be comfortable with but which they will have to use to be fully effective professionals."[12]

Their Index of Learning Styles provides an interesting counterpoint to Gardner's Multiple Intelligences. The index began as a paper that described the learning styles of engineering students, then evolved into a more general tool. I like the way it re-orients me to pay attention to the (sometimes momentary, sometimes inscrutable) needs of the learners in my charge. It also evokes my empathy: I know how I feel when asked to work outside of my preferred type.

Types of Learners

Active
Reflective
Sensing
Intuitive
Visual
Verbal
Sequential
Global

The Visual and Verbal types refer to modalities, but the rest of Solomon and Felder's types draw our attention to the teaching and learning dynamic. Notice the pairs that emerge (Active vs. Reflective; Sequential vs. Global), and the way the list corresponds with the author's assertion that all of us benefit from developing our abilities to take on any of these types as needed.

During Design, keep tabs on how often the modality of your activities varies within individual lessons and across whole units of study. Strike a balance between modalities. Use the Multiple Modalities Checklist at the end of this section as a provisional rubric for evaluating your Design. Re-define the modalities listed according to what you find most meaningful (Figure 3.21). During Respond, as you interact in the classroom, you'll need to track the

A Multiple Modalities Checklist

1) How many modalities have I included in the unit of study?

☐   Kinesthetic   (to sing, play, dance, move, work in four dimensions)

☐   Visual   (to decode, draw, design, chart, graph, reproduce, enhance)

☐   Aural   (to listen)

☐   Narrative   (original or pre-existing stories)

☐   Authorial   (to write, improvise, generate)

☐   Reflective   (to wonder, imagine, question, posit, hypothesize)

☐   Interpersonal   (regarding self and others, empathy)

☐   Intrapersonal   (regarding personal relevance, ethics)

2) How many types of learners am I addressing?

☐   Active

☐   Reflective

☐   Sensing

☐   Intuitive

☐   Visual

☐   Verbal

☐   Sequential

☐   Global

☐   _________________

☐   _________________

3) Am I too dependent on a single modality?

4) Have I missed an opportunity to reach more students with a more effective modality?

FIGURE 3.21 A Multiple Modalities Checklist

efficacy of any chosen modality, and switch to an alternate approach whenever your planned modality isn't working. Many teaching artists already do this instinctually. Take your insight further. Experiment with the modality translation process, apply what you learn to your subsequent Designs, and eventually you'll earn your MMM degree: Master of Multiple Modalities.

CASE STUDY: TRADITIONAL IRISH MUSIC VIA MULTIPLE MODALITIES

Students were preparing for a performance by Lúnasa, contemporary masters of the Irish musical tradition. The song types Lúnasa plays are referred to by their underlying rhythms: jig, slip jig, reel, march, waltz, schottische. All of these rhythms are connected with the Irish dance tradition. Most of the concert the students would see was to be jigs, slip jigs, and reels, so we chose to focus on the concert's most sing-able examples of each type (Jig: "The Irish Washerwoman"; Slip-jig: "The Minor Bee"; Reel: "The Miller of Drohan"). We knew our young students (and their classroom teachers) generally preferred activities in Kinesthetic, Visual, and Aural modalities. With all these factors in mind, we designed a unit of study where students would dance, move, count, sing, and play their way to becoming self-confident experts in the rhythms of Irish jigs, slip jigs, and reels. The kinesthetic modality was especially emphasized. This was not a dance unit of study; these were all preparation activities for a live musical concert, taught by music teaching artists for a Music in the Schools program. But we danced or moved almost everything we explored; musical ideas became whole-body experiences.

The Lúnasa activities took advantage of two Design approaches: multiple modalities, and scaffolding. In construction, a scaffold is a temporary structure that is put up to support a building process, and removed when no longer needed. When teachers scaffold instruction, they typically break up a learning experience or skill into discrete parts, and then give students the assistance they need to learn each part. Scaffolding theory was first introduced in the late 1950s by cognitive psychologist Jerome Bruner, inspired in part by Vygotsky's zone of proximal development. Instructional scaffolding, content scaffolding (starting with familiar, highly interesting, or easy content), task, and material scaffolding are all variations on this theme. Teachers who scaffold lessons strategically support students' creative processes, then remove the support as soon as it is no longer needed. Backward Mapping (aka Backward Design, popularized in Wiggins and McTighe's influential book *Understanding by Design*) is an excellent way to reverse-engineer a scaffold. To use a Backward Mapping approach, teaching artists who wanted students to reach a creative goal or skill would start by thoroughly defining the goal then working backward: *In order to do this, we first have to be able to do this . . .*, and so on, all the way back to students' current knowledge or skill level.

Traditional Irish Music via Scaffolded Multiple Modalities		
Scaffold step	Activity summary	New or added element
1 Jig Windshield Wipers I	move to a jig beat	We imitated a windshield wiper rhythm to establish a jig's basic one-two duple meter (kinesthetic + visual) while music played. 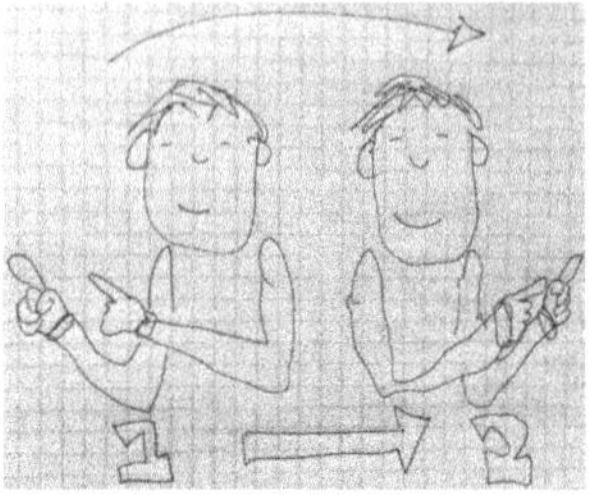
2 Jig Windshield Wipers II	move to a subdivided jig beat	We subdivided the basic two-beat windshield wiper pulse, and counted out the **ONE**-*two-three* **FOUR**-*five-six* accent pattern in the underlying rhythm (ONE and FOUR are stronger, louder) while we continued our windshield-wipering (kinesthetic + verbal). 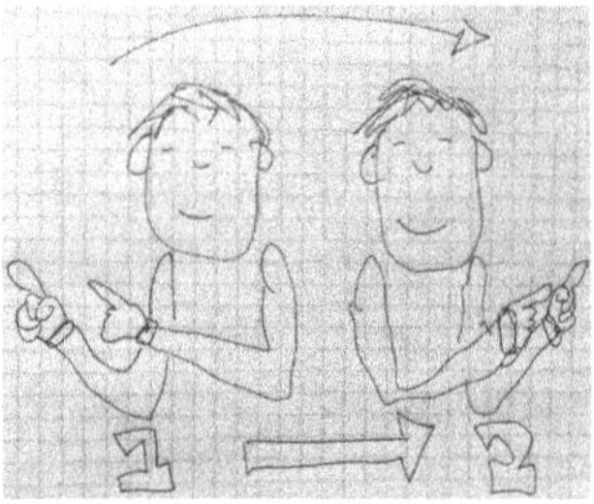
3 Add Chanting	count a jig beat	We added poetic-mnemonic modality to the windshield wipers, chanting *jiggety-jig, jiggety-jig:* 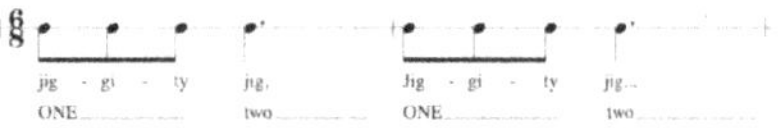

FIGURE 3.22 Traditional Irish Music via Scaffolded Multiple Modalities

The Lúnasa activities were scaffolded to build from the most basic ideas (*move to the two-beat pattern you hear in this song*) up to students being able to hear a unknown song, identify and explain its rhythmic feel, and dance the appropriate traditional step to the beat (Figure 3.22). Each workshop session restarted the scaffold sequence from the very beginning, with the "Jig Windshield Wipers." Students who had not mastered any particular step had multiple opportunities to do so, and those who had mastered any step enjoyed

4	Add Slip Jigs	move to and count a slip jig beat	Into the musical mix comes the Slip Jig (*jiggety-jiggety-jig,* i.e., three accented beats, a windshield wiper with an extra wipe, aka 9/8), which has to be separated from its by now familiar close cousin the Jig (*jiggety-jig,* i.e., two accented beats, aka 6/8). While music plays, we move, count, and chant to either Jigs or Slip Jigs, depending on how we identify them, and where we feel the accent patterns falling.

5	Sing Jigs and Slip Jigs	connect melody, beat, moving, and counting	Into the musical mix comes our singing the actual melodies of the songs that we've been hearing and moving to. We freely mix moving, counting, chanting, and singing the tune. Teaching artists are provided with audio and video the Lúnasa songs (played by the band's uilleann piper Cillian Vallely) at slow, medium, and performance speed to make it easier to learn the intricate melodies. Jig: The Irish Washerwoman Slip Jig: A Minor Bee

6	Jig Jam Jump (version 1)	assess knowledge gained so far	A game. Music plays: only jigs or slip jigs, unannounced. Students have to feel and hear the rhythmic pattern, and jump on the downbeat (demonstrating their differentiation of 6/8 jig and 9/8 slip jig). Familiar and unfamiliar songs are used. This also acts as a mid-unit assessment of our learning: do we know what we need to know .

FIGURE 3.22 Continued

showing off their knowledge. Activities that needed ten minutes to set up and run the first time might only last two or three minutes when revisited.

After exploring so vigorously in all those modalities, students should be able to recognize, feel connected with, and respond positively to any jigs, slip jigs, or reels that come their way for many years to come. All these movement-driven activities took place as music played; all the movements connected directly with the music's particular pulse, meter, subdivided rhythms, accent

7	Dance Sing Jigs and Slip Jigs	add traditional dance steps	We use online videos to learn the basic steps for jigs and slip jigs. Each has its own verbal mnemonic (step, hop, kick).  Traditional ways of "doing it correctly" (arms straight at your sides, eyes forward) are encouraged. We freely mix moving, counting, chanting, singing and dancing the songs.
8	All About Reels	move to and count a reel beat	Into the musical mix comes the Reel *(this is how a reel goes,* i.e. four accented beats, aka 4/4), and its dance step. 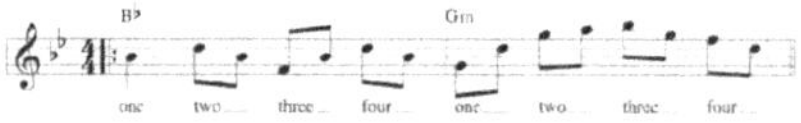 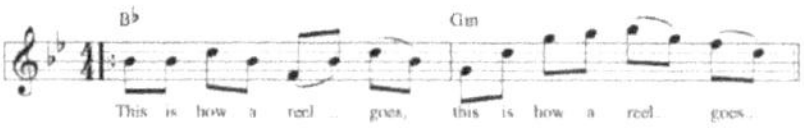 While music plays, we move, count, chant and sing to reels, using one of Lúnasa's slower reels, "The Miller of Drohan."
9	New York City Reel	re-imagine traditional dance steps	We dance to a Reel using familiar hip-hop moves, then blend Irish and American dances to make a New York City Reel. All the contemporary urban dances the students know are counted in fours, so the three, six and nine-count jigs and slip jigs might have been problematic for this activity.
10	Reel Variations	celebrate & imitate dance virtuosi	We play a video from Ireland's County Sligo that features a succession of children dancing virtuosic variations on reels. The invitation: try to imitate everything you see on the screen. We try to match the dancers move for move in real time.
11	Jig Jam Jump (version 2)	assess and celebrate knowledge gained	The game again: a musical contest to see who could most quickly and accurately match their movements, counting, singing, and dancing with a unpredictable mix of recorded jigs, slip-jigs, and reels. This also acts as an assessment of our learning.

FIGURE 3.22 Continued

patterns, melodies, and syncopations. It would be challenging for anyone to explain the nature of the defining musical principles of traditional Irish music in words, let alone in technical or musical terms. But these students knew the essentials in their bodies and could show you: *this* is a jig, *this* is a slip jig, *this* is how you count and feel them, *this* is how they work. *This is how a reel goes . . .*

PLACE CONTEXTUAL INFORMATION

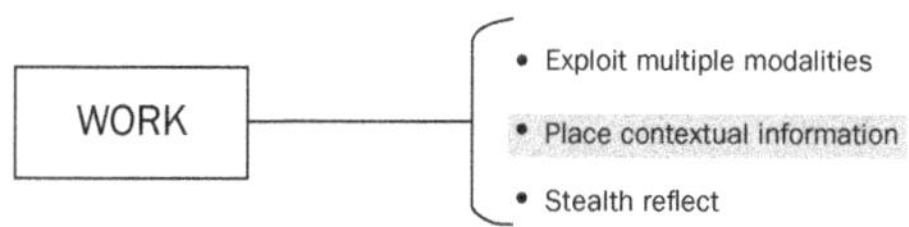

You're at your favorite art museum, entering an exhibition of work that's new to you: the paintings of Cy Twombly. At the entrance to the exhibition, do you read the two-paragraph orientation blurb painted on the wall beside the entryway, or walk directly in? Soon you enter a room where a massive scribbly drawing occupies a large portion of wall (Figure 3.23). A small card next to the work gives the artist's name, the title, year of completion, and materials used in making of the work. Just to the side of that card is a larger card that describes some of the history surrounding the work and the artist's stated or possible intent. What do you do first, read the card, or the longer description, or look at the art? Look at the art briefly then read the description? Bounce back and forth between art, card, and description?

In this exhibition, curators provide the work of art, chosen from many possible works and placed just so within the exhibition. They also offer support for your encounter with that work in the form of contextual information that surrounds or informs the work; in effect, they are offering to be your guide. Of course you are free to choose how you will attend to the work. You decide what to look at, how long to look at it, from what distance or angle you wish to view it. You may also find the contextual information on the cards that accompany the work of interest: the *where, when,* and *how* of the work, what the artist might have been exploring or interested in, and other social, political, or philosophical connections to the work. Ideally, this information sparks your insight or interest and encourages you to look longer and go deeper.

We *should* feel free to choose how we bestow our attention and respond to the work, but less confident or less experienced museum-goers don't always feel these freedoms. They may instead feel anxiety or embarrassment when encountering an unfamiliar work of art, and wonder what they are *supposed to* feel or do. The contextual information they encounter can be mistaken as an

FIGURE 3.23 Cy Twombly
Untitled, (Munich/Rome), 1972
Oil paint, wax crayon, lead pencil on canvas
78 3/4 × 102 3/8 inches
The Eli and Edythe L. Broad Collection
c/o The Broad Art Foundation
Photo credit: Douglas M. Parker Studio, LA

indicator of work's true meaning, the expert's authority writ large, to be valued more than their own thoughts and experience. When this happens, less experienced museum-goers (and music, dance, and theater audience members) may retreat: *Someone else who knows more than they do has already decided what this work of art means.* Since the expert has spoken, they feel less need to engage with the work. Imagine an actor prefacing a performance by telling you what she finds meaningful about the play, the connections she feels with the text, how the biography of the playwright may have influenced the work. After that kind of set-up, wouldn't you be primed to look for evidence that confirmed or denied the actor's point of view? Once that dynamic is in place, how much room is there for you to draw your own inferences and conclusions about the work? I would guess that our well-intentioned actor did not deepen your sense of engagement with the work, but instead led you away from the satisfaction of making your own meaning.

As a preparation workshop teaching artist guiding your student's approach to a work of art, you take on the role of co-curator as you choose contextual information and decide when and how you'll present it. Given the possibility of turning our students on or turning them off, *what is the best way to use contextual information in our teaching?* Let's start by defining what kinds of materials we are referring to. Here is a checklist that will help you brainstorm possible contextual information for a unit of study (Figure 3.24), categorized as text, image, or sound and video.

The most valuable piece of context is any information that makes your students feel more able, more curious, more engaged. Remember that your

Contextual Materials Search Checklist

<u>Text</u>
- ☐ quotes from the artist
  - ○ personal letters, notes, journals
  - ○ public statements, publications, manifesti
- ☐ biography and chronology
- ☐ quotes from critics, contemporaries, biographers
- ☐ texts that inspired the artist
- ☐ contemporary history and culture
- ☐ anecdotes (substantiated)

<u>Images</u>
- ☐ of the artist
  - ○ at work
  - ○ at leisure
  - ○ as a child
- ☐ of the artist's work
  - ○ finished
  - ○ in process
  - ○ in situ
- ☐ of other related works of art
- ☐ of materials related to the work
  - ○ tools or instruments
  - ○ costume, set, and other designs
  - ○ references the artist used

<u>Audio or Video Recordings</u>
- ☐ of the artist's life or process
- ☐ of the artist's other work

FIGURE 3.24 Contextual Materials Search Checklist

overall goal is to open up students' experience of the work of art, not to fill their minds with facts and figures. There is no hard and fast rule as to which types of contextual information are consistently effective. But there is a small constellation of ideas to consider as you choose what to share with your students: qualities of objectivity and openness within the materials, your own inner sense of the materials' resonance, your timing (when you present the materials), tone (your voice and manner as your present), and the density of the materials themselves. Let's examine each of these in turn.

1) Objectivity

Your contextual information should be reliable and as objective as possible. But finding well-written text that isn't subjective is challenging, especially in the jazz and classical music worlds, where opinion and anecdote are too often presented as scholarship. Scholarly or critical texts are a likely starting point for sources of contextual information. Does the writing describe and analyze the work in a way that is supported by evidence? You may end up paraphrasing or rewriting text to get the objectivity you are looking for. If the writer does interpret or judge, are the writer's opinions presented as opinions, or as fact? If interpretations and judgments are offered by one writer, can you find contrasting opinions from other writers for your students to read, or use the writer's opinion as a jumping-off point as your students create counter-arguments according to their own experience?

2) Openness

Some pieces of contextual information feel more open than others, in that they seem to invite us in. They free up our willingness to explore what the work of art might mean or become to us because they are less indicative of a single pre-determined meaning. Does this Cy Twombly photograph and quote feel open in that inviting way (Figure 3.25)?

> *When I work, I work very fast, but preparing to work can take any length of time . . . I sit for two or three hours and then in fifteen minutes I can do a painting, but that's part of it. You have to get ready and decide to jump up and do it; you build yourself up psychologically, and so painting has no time for brush. Brush is boring; you give it and all of a sudden it's dry, you have to go. Before you cut the thought, you know?*—Cy Twombly

The photograph of Mr. Twombly might feel open or closed, depending on who is decoding it, but I'd guess students might read it as representing who Twombly is, and feel that they have enough information: *an older man, sort of grandfatherly and nice—now I know him, and I don't need any more infor-mation.* If that is the case, their interest has been dampened instead of stoked. (As an antidote to that kind of turning off, if the photo seemed important, it might be worth talking about unconscious ageism, or the potential difference

FIGURE 3.25 Cy in front of Bacchus painting after finished

© Fondazione Nicola Del Roscio. Courtesy Archives Nicola Del Roscio. Photo Nicola Del Roscio.

between the way be people appear and the reality of what is happening in their minds and hearts.)

The quote leads back to the work of art. Twombly's language is a bit mysterious, which can serve to lure us into the artist's world. To guide reflection, ask:

What is he really saying?
If we look at his other work, does this quote bear out?
What about his preference for pencil over brush?

Why do we ourselves prefer certain tools?
Does he always think long and work fast?
What does it feel like to do so?

If I were leading the workshop, I might asks students for their own stories of *think long then work fast* and offer up my own story: being a college junior with a weekly Thursday morning music composition lesson, at which I was expected to show my week's work. For six days in a row, Friday through Wednesday, I would make time to walk, think, and dream of the music I was composing, playing it again and again in my mind for at least an hour a day, often more. Then on Thursday morning I would get out of bed at 6:00 a.m., plug in the coffee maker and sit and drink coffee (which went cold in the cup and had to be repeatedly run back through the coffee maker to heat it up) and furiously score my ideas onto music paper. At 10:30 I'd fly my bike downhill all the way to my caffeine-enhanced 11:00 a.m. lesson. I would guess the Twombly quote and my own story would help students make a more immediate and personal connection with the artist, and include both in my Cy Twombly museum visit unit of study design.

In *The Music Teaching Artists Bible*, Eric Booth stresses engagement before information. "Before" meaning "is more important than," as well as "preceding in the sequence of events":

> *Not everyone agrees with me about this, but I place engaging learners, getting them to participate actively in your work, as a higher priority than the actual information you deliver. This prioritization respects students as people, reminding us that they have to be involved participants in the work you present rather than merely acquiescent recipients of your information. After they are engaged, your information will have a far greater impact and relevance, will be desired, retained and used.*

Booth also takes the point further, reframing any use of contextual information as part of a more fundamental choice on the teaching artist's part:

> *It can be argued that the key question TAs ask themselves in every challenge is: "How can I best engage this particular individual or group, for this particular learning goal, in this specific situation?" Once that entry point is discovered, and pursued as the priority, the pertinent and valuable information begins to become clear.*[13]

3) Resonance

As you research and weigh materials, some will of course appeal to you more than others. It's not a connection one can predict. Particular photographs, journal entries, stories, and quotes simply speak to us. When the information has a strong positive effect on how you yourself engage with the work of art, and you share it with that sense of wonder, chances are the information will open up the work for your students, too. You may say to them, "I don't even know why I like knowing this, but . . .," or "I love the way this information changes how I see the work of art." Either way, you'll be modeling and encouraging a natural, easy habit of connecting context, personal engagement, and the work under study. This is different from having the performer speak about a work. The actor who explained the meanings of the play does so as an expert, not a co-learner; she isn't responsible for the community in the way a teaching artist is. So feel free to model engagement with materials that are personally resonant for you.

4) Timing, Tone, and Density

Imagine that you are a music teaching artist leading a preparation workshop for a concert of Antonio Vivaldi's *Four Seasons.*

Vivaldi became a priest (with red hair, called "The Red Priest") and ran a famous all-girl orchestra at an orphanage where the girls had to remain hidden behind a screen as they played. The orchestra was exceptionally good, and some of the girls he taught there in early 1700s Venice (no streets—canals) at the Ospedale della Pietà developed into ace (virtuoso) violin, viola, and cello players. He's a colorful figure from a colorful time and place who wrote colorful music (Figures 3.26 and 3.27). Your instinct is that a combination of life story, anecdote, and music-specific connection will help make the composer more human and accessible in your students' eyes.

As you decide how to use this information, consider the effect of your *timing* (when you present the information), your *tone* (your voice and manner as your present), and the *density* of the information (too simple, too esoteric, or just right?), which in a way also includes the strength of the connection between the information and the work of art itself (how possible is it to "hear" the context in the music?).

The best *timing* for introducing aspects of Vivaldi's working life might be early in the unit of study. In this example, the biographical information engages students' imaginations and leads directly back to the work of art: *With an orchestra of virtuosic, hard-working string players at your disposal six days a week, what kind of music would you have written?* If this question is posed before students hear any of Vivaldi's music, they imagine the music before they encounter it, an approach I am borrowing from Rudolf Steiner's method of teaching science, where students form a mental picture of a phenomenon before experiencing or observing it in the world. Imagining before experiencing becomes a useful lens during the actual encounter: *this* is what I imagined beforehand, but *this* is what it really is. The *tone* of the Vivaldi information is colorful and anecdotal, appealing to social relationships, Inter- and Intrapersonal intelligences, as well as our Visual and Narrative imaginations. In terms of

FIGURE 3.26 Antonio Vivaldi (image courtesy of the International Museum and Library of Music of Bologna)

density, the information is brief, and memorable, and you can in fact hear the "virtuoso" aspect of the contextual story in the virtuosic playing.

After students imagine and then listen to Vivaldi's music (timing: midway), you might introduce this quote from *New Yorker* music critic Alex Ross' blog/book *The Rest Is Noise*. Ross teases us with two interesting metaphors (tone and density: colorful) instead of a dry explanation: *"Most movements of Vivaldi concertos go on no longer than a fifties pop hit, but they are packed with information, invention, and emotion; each work is a game of twists and turns, an arrangement of artful shocks."*[14] But if you do quote an expert such as Mr. Ross, avoid presenting the quote as the citation of an expert's truth. Instead use it to focus our attention on the qualities he mentions, a prompt to do further and more intensive listening: *What is Alex saying? Is he correct? Let's listen to some Vivaldi and see if we can see what he means . . .*

With Vivaldi (or any other composer or artists of any stripe), you might also invite students' empathy and imagination, again in the service of rendering the artist more human and familiar, by asking them to recall or even *invent* contextual information (Figure 3.28). At the end of one unit of study (timing: late) at a public school in East Harlem, students and teachers volunteered to don

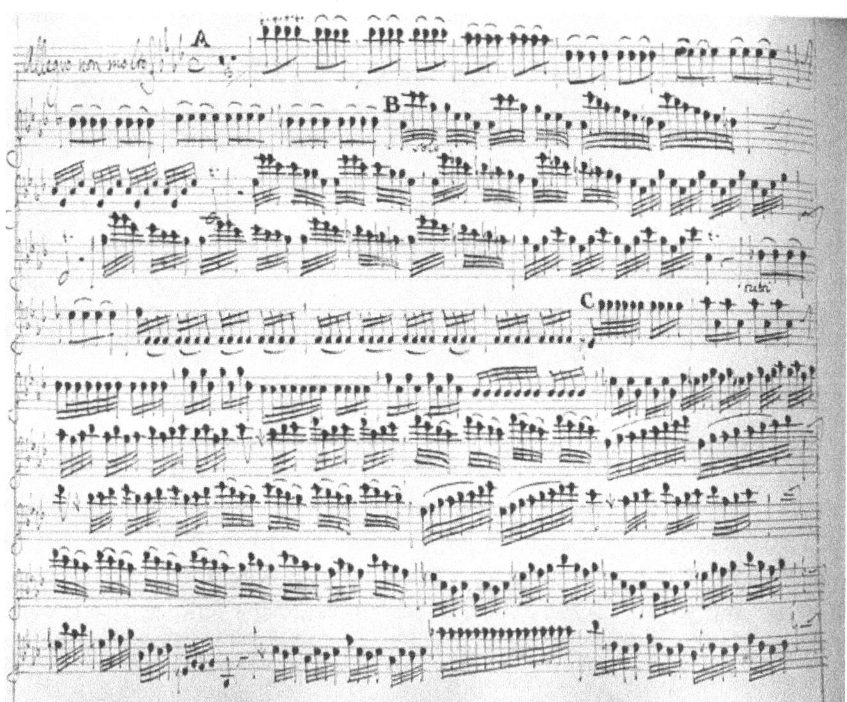

FIGURE 3.27 Antonio Vivaldi manuscript, Concerto No. 4 in F minor, Op. 8, RV 297, "L'inverno" (Winter) (image courtesy of the Beinecke Library, Yale)

a Vivaldi mask, complete with wig, quill, and sheet music (tone: playful); the class invented interview questions which the individual who was role-playing Vivaldi was obliged to answer, whether or not they actually knew the answer (density: according to each student's ability to recall or invent).

> *What is that in your hand, Mr. Vivaldi?*
> *How much music have you written?*
> *What is your favorite instrument?*
> *Is that your real hair?*
> *Why do you put nature in your music?*
> *Do you like hip-hop?*
> *Is* The Four Seasons *your best piece?*
> *What is the hardest thing about composing?*

When your contextual materials are recorded audio or video, edit them to serve your teaching goals. Consider your students' experience of the material's density and duration. Dances, operas, concerts, and plays move through time and continuously evolve as we watch or listen (in contrast to the projected JPGs that visual arts teaching artists show to students, which sit still and do not change over time). During even a very few seconds of viewing, a student

FIGURE 3.28 Students interviewing Antonio Vivaldi

can observe a lot of detail: actions, events, the qualities of those actions and events, and various sonic, physical, and narrative relationships that arise and dissolve. If your teaching goal is to have students freely notice and discuss what they see and hear, then experiment with showing different lengths of excerpt, and see which yield the best responses during reflection. If you are interested in having students notice some particular details in the work, you can gently nudge the conversation toward those details. When you have such specifics in mind, shorter and simpler excerpts work as enabling constraints, in that they focus students' noticing by providing fewer divergent paths to go down. If you want students to be able to recognize the sound of an oboe, don't play an MP3 of an oboe with piano accompaniment and expect them to differentiate the two. Instead, find an actual solo oboe passage that meets any style or other content criteria you might have.

Also consider your student's experience of the material's quality. Use the highest definition media you can find. Your slides or facsimiles of artwork, videos, photocopies, and sound recordings are already a few steps removed from the energy of the actual work of art. Keep the student's experience of the work at as high a level of quality as you can manage. Higher-definition video and audio (HD video, WAV audio files) and better-quality projectors and speakers can reproduce levels of contrast, range, and intensity that lower-definition formats (lower video resolutions, MP3s) cannot.

Contextual information is an essential part of every teaching artist's toolkit—but is it essential for every unit of study? If your View is *a community of learners / making & doing / in an atelier setting*, then making and doing trumps delivering contextual facts and figures, and you'll want to interrogate each piece of context: *How will this information enhance our Making & Doing?* Or, to turn the question around, in the spirit of Hippocrates: *Am I sure this information will do no harm?*

Imagine you are a fledgling playwright, choreographer, or songwriter and your teaching artist hands you a "How To . . ." worksheet, with the intention of being helpful. A "Playwriting Step-by-Step" worksheet handed out at the beginning of a process may well dampen a dramatist's ardor, if it is understood to say *you don't know how to do this process* or *you are doing it wrong* or *you are not capable of inventing your own process.* The same worksheet, presented after a scene exists in its first draft, that is, in process, becomes a more welcome, less threatening way for the student/artist to self-evaluate a process that they've already initiated. In presenting the worksheet later, the teaching artist may be seen to say *you are already off to a good start—here is a tool that may help you get to the next level, and if this does not work, other tools are at your disposal.* The contextual information about playwriting processes is a reflective tool that students might *choose* to use, as opposed to a boilerplate that indicates what they probably should be doing. Similarly, contextual information intended to fuel discussions may work best after the community encounters the work of art or art-making process. For example, with Cy Twombly, I'd save the quote for after the students encounter the work of art, because in this case I believe there is something important to be gained from a viewing unmitigated by anything but the students' direct experience of having made parallel work; before they read a quote about *think long and work fast,* I'd like them to try thinking long and working fast.

STEALTH REFLECT

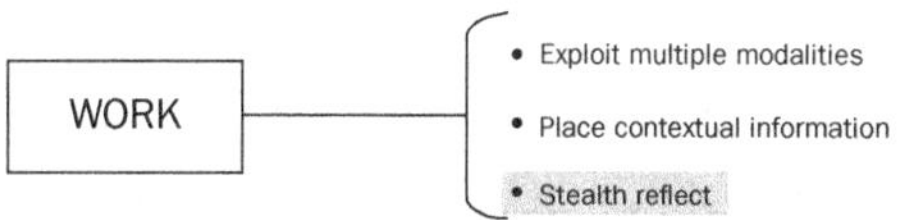

The scene: twenty-five second graders equipped with egg-shaped shakers or glockenspiels and wooden mallets, spread out around a room, facing a lone guitarist. They are about to begin the ritual that opens each session with their teaching artist, a semi-guided improvisation. The shaker players stand next to their partners, knowing they are invited to *move to the groove* once the music begins. The glock players sit, reviewing the location of the suggested "good notes" they are going to improvise and experiment with. Everybody is jiggling, malleting, and bantering until they hear "Mallets up," when the room gets quiet and suddenly *poised*—something fun is about to happen.

If your View recognizes the importance of reflection, you'll build reflective practices into your Design. One way to reflect is to set aside time to do so within the structure of a given session, perhaps the kind of guided reflection discussed in the section "Describe/Analyze/Interpret" (page 131). In the "Hello, Composers Daily Warm-Up" (Figure 3.29), we Stealth Reflect, a form of spontaneous but targeted praise of student work. *Stealth* because it feels more like fun than a "sit and talk" reflection; students may not even be aware they are reflecting. There is an unpredictable energy in Stealth Reflection that sets it apart from other more formal reflective practices.

To begin Stealth Reflecting, keep your radar up for moments of particular quality or interest during an activity. As soon as you discover one, bring the community's attention to the action or choice (practical, material, or aesthetic) of interest. If a large group improvisation is happening, and a student invents a juicy musical pattern, you can press the pause button on everyone's playing and highlight that student's work, then question the observers to make sure they noticed what took place and can articulate what they noticed. This spontaneous reflection stays close to the process at hand. Ask the originator to demonstrate the idea, give it a space in which it can be clearly seen and heard. You might ask other students what they notice, or ask them to reproduce the idea themselves, or ask the originator to explain their choices or their thinking.

Stealth Reflection Steps

1) all students are making and doing
2) TA notices a student's noteworthy choice
3) TA pauses the activity
4) a student demonstrates their choice
5) all students reflect on the nature of the choice

Stealth Reflection's oblique approach can be useful when you want to establish a particular principle or technique. Instead of modeling the idea, you can wait for a clear example of any idea that aligns with your instructional

Studio Workshop Activity: *Hello, Composers* Daily Warm-Up		
activity	**steps**	**support**
IMPROVISE & EXPERIMENT (5-15 min.)	• TA: *the good notes are a, c, and e* • students warm up on glockenspiels (find *a, c, e*) • TA begins a rhythm on guitar, using chords suited to the "good" notes • students improvise *en masse* along with guitar • TA brings attention to interesting choices made by improvisers • Repeat the sequence w/new "good" notes and rhythms.	Let each guitar accompaniment rhythm firmly establish before counting students in. Once you notice an interesting musical choice, Stealth Reflect.

FIGURE 3.29 Hello Composers Daily Warm-Up

goals to arise within your students' work, and bring the spontaneously arising thing to everyone's attention. I have never led a workshop where noteworthy or useful material did not arise out of the students' creative work, no matter what the prevailing skill level.

The Stealth Reflection used in the *Hello, Composers* program is outlined in the activity plan that begins this section. In *Hello, Composers*, named for our ritual greeting, grade school students self-identify as composers on a mission to create a concert of original music for professional musicians to play. Each workshop session begins with students improvising on glockenspiels while I play two or three guitar chords with a repeated, often syncopated strum, something with some musical heft. This activity feeds the creative fire in the room because there is enough structure in the activity and in the musical accompaniment to guarantee success and enough openness to allow for genuine aesthetic choice-making. While we are cultivating the composerly habit of choosing notes we love, we are also accurately working with an instrument to reproduce the sounds we want, in order, in rhythm, and in relationship to another sound.

While I am strumming, I am scanning the room to make sure students are locking in with the main pulse, the basic heartbeat of the music that makes us tap our foot. If students are not locking in, it isn't a bad sign; most often it means their mind is taken up with note-choosing and the sound of the notes, so much so that they aren't really taking in the sonic information around them (the clear, steady pulse embedded in the guitar strum). Or sometimes they are trying to execute a fancy move of some kind, and again their consciousness of the pulse is bumped to the side by their need to focus on the fancy move. Sometimes I'll coach a little, but most often I will just remind them to try to hear what I am doing and what they are doing at the same time and make sure they are going together, so that we are playing together and not separately.

At the same time I am making eye contact and smiling at students who seem uncertain or who are just having a good time. I reinforce our musical connection with body language, dance moves, eyebrow raises, nods, and a few encouraging words. If I can, I call out to them by name with some genuine praise (name tags are a big help here). But the eye contact and smiles do most of the work. My smile is not forced; I am genuinely pleased to see everyone whacking away at the labeled metal bars on the glocks, thinking or murmuring the note names as they go, making musical choices involving rhythm, pattern, range. Unless a student is having a very bad day indeed, she eventually smiles back, and even if she does not, we're still taking steps toward connectedness.

I am also on the lookout for some spark, a student doing something above average in terms of interest, boldness, or some other ineffable quality that I am attracted to as a fellow artist. Usually it is some confident or clear musical pattern that connects with what I am doing in a delightful way, an energy that I appreciate. Once I notice an individual who stands out in this way, I stop strumming, and the students all stop playing and look up. I invite the chosen student to continue with me, explaining that there is something she has done that I like and want everyone to hear. Together, the student and I perform or demonstrate her idea. As we play it a few times, other students attend without my prompting any *specific* reflection—but in that moment they are all already reflecting: *Daniel is doing this for a reason . . . what is special or interesting about this?*

Deciding what to praise is a creative act. The teaching artist is called on to be aware of what is happening aesthetically, creatively, and collaboratively in the classroom, and decide in any given moment which students are making choices that all students would benefit from knowing about. Of course all students are equally valued, but not all of their contributions are equally musical, interesting, or valuable as exemplars and potential teaching tools. By allowing musical ideas to rise out of the students' work and selectively praising the ideas that will be the most immediately useful, the teaching artist avoids having to teach or lecture. More importantly, students come to see themselves as the very capable composers that they are, since they are recognized as a primary source of musical ideas.

For example, professional composers value and use empty space—silence or rests—in much the same way a painter values negative space, or a dancer values stillness. Empty space is a basic and important tool in composing. But the idea of working with silence doesn't have to be formally presented to student composers, since it eventually arises in the course of their improvising. When a student generates a pattern that includes a lot of empty space during the improvisatory play-alongs that begin most sessions, I take advantage of the moment. *"Mallets up." Everyone stops playing and looks at the teaching artist. "Mallets and shakers in the baskets" In they go, and the room quiets. "Dante is doing something really interesting, and I'd like everyone to hear it. Dante, would you please play a duet with me? Just you and I playing the same thing you were playing just now?" Dante nods, and performs his pattern with all the empty space while the teaching artist repeats the original accompaniment, then stops. "Awesome, thank you. What was Dante doing?"*

The closed question *What is Dante doing?* serves better than an open question here. Dante has independently invented what, for our community, is a new technique, an approach that is vital for creating interesting patterns (and even more important for making layers of patterns): the bold use of empty space. As a community of learners, we need to notice it, articulate it, and add it to our composer's toolbox. After this discovery, whenever a student puts silence to good use, I will intone "I love empty space" to bolster and encourage the idea, this new tool for composing that came from Dante, an individual in the community, and not from me.

After a featured student's musical idea is clear, I sometimes make sure the class experiences it in a parallel modality. We might mimic the featured pattern vocally or physically, translate it into sung syllables, or reproduce it on our own instruments so that every student makes aural as well as kinesthetic connections with the idea. Once we have some kinesthetic knowledge of the featured idea, I might prompt reflection. "What is Maya doing? Isn't that cool? Why is it so cool?" It helps to keep the remarks brief, the tone celebratory, respectful, and interested. Some days we might simply enjoy the featured pattern for what it is, fist bump the creator, and move on. But usually I'll take a moment to define what it was I found delightful, why I felt it was worth stopping to notice this individual artist's work, and make sure the creator and his classmates hear some gentle, specific praise. Whatever the teaching artist praises is in effect highlighted in the students' mind: *This is important.*

Pointing out and praising work this way enhances your students' sense of safe space. Even though your praise is directed toward an individual, other students respond positively to hearing it because it reinforces their sense that creativity will be protected and rewarded within the community. The more often they see this happen, the more confident they'll feel, and the easier it will be for them to take creative risks. Some students may feel envious of those who receive praise, but they will also be aware that while exemplary work may be praised, no one is in danger of being derided or disrespected for creating work that is less than exemplary.

Stealth Reflection interactions feel good. Since the idea that drew all the attention and praise came from them, the *less experienced learners* (as per Vygotski), instead of from the teaching artist or the classroom teacher, the *more experienced learners*, everyone gets a little burst of confidence. *The teacher even interrupted what everyone was doing so the idea could be shared— it must be important.* A classroom-wide jolt of collegiality occurs when work is praised this way. You confirm for your students that in your eyes they too are artists, fully capable of understanding art-making choices and techniques. In that moment the social hierarchies of the classroom are set aside; you and your students are speaking artist to artist. Interestingly, it is often the usually quiet or struggling students who end up shining. In those moments, Stealth Reflection becomes an invaluable tool for folding them into the community, praising students who are too seldom praised.

SHOW

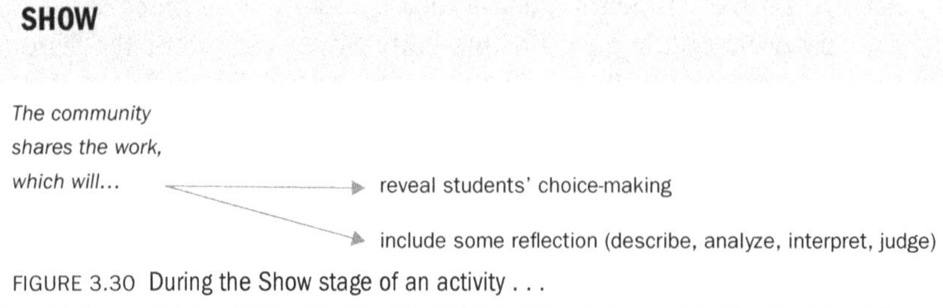

FIGURE 3.30 During the Show stage of an activity . . .

To *Show* our work is to share it with the classroom community by per-forming, posting, or displaying. By sharing their work, individuals or small groups publicly acknowledge it as their own. In those moments of showing, the practical, material, and aesthetic *choices* we've made are on display, so the classroom community can *reflect* on our Making & Doing process (Figure 3.30). By attending to the Work that is being shared (its qualities, and the story of its creation), students demonstrate their re-spect and regard for one another. Students value Showing for the sense of accomplishment and recognition it brings. Risk-taking is rewarded with positive attention. The community affirms the value of the individuals' choice-making process: *you made choices, and we the community confirm that your choices mattered.*

Showing and reflecting can be used to open up the internal workings of the creators. Because an artifact (a collage on paper, a recorded beat, a dance on video) is more easily observable than an ephemeral performance, students can use it to help them recall the sequence of choices made when they were creating or performing. We can point at an image or a sculpture to question what it is, and how and why it came to be; we can stop and start a video or piece of music to isolate events and structures. Let's look at the Essential Practices related to the Show stage, which I'm calling Reflect, and Describe/Analyze/Interpret.

REFLECT

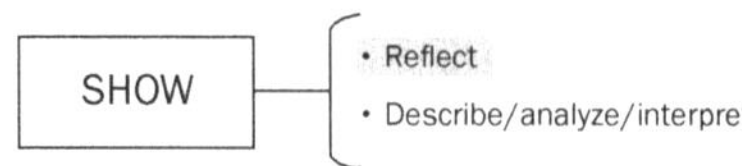

Seventeen incarcerated men sit in a circle in a down-at-heels cinder block schoolroom. The floor is cracked, and thick bars cover the windows. The men are mostly wearing green, but a few sport regulation-approved white polo shirts or thick red sweatshirts. The black and blue I have on are reserved for officers and civilians. Two Bose computer speakers sit atop a stack of milk crates alongside a portable CD player. Together we are listening to a recording of a musical concert the men performed for other prisoners two weeks earlier, a mix of original songs and covers. The live concert and our post-concert listening comprise the Show phase of a long arc of Invite, Work, and Show.

The men listen to each song attentively, respectfully, but not silently. They can't seem to help it: they call out to one another, shouting praise or delight at almost every well-sung or well-played passage, "That's right," "Go Flaco," or "Watch out, now." Songwriters and performers alternately grin or hold their heads in their hands, taking deep breaths while they listen to their work. For many of the men this is the first time they have heard a recording of their own voice or guitar. They tap their feet, sway, bop around in their chairs, or mime music-making. As each recorded song ends, I invite them to reflect: *Tell the creators—what's hot?* They let each other know what moved them in the songwriting and performances. Their comments embody generosity, empathy, attentiveness, and sensitivity. They are polite yet direct. They are obviously enjoying this extended moment of normalcy and human dignity, rare in that place of punishment. How the rest of their days play out in this maximum security facility as they serve their long sentences for violent offenses is hidden from me. But in this room, for this time, they are excellent, noble friends to each other. Just the kind of guys you'd be happy to have move in next door or give guitar lessons to your child.

Twenty-seven second graders sit at standard-issue desks at PS130 in Queens, New York. Near the end of a unit of study that focused on the layers of sound in jazz drumming, I've allowed five minutes for them to reflect on our experience together. I explain that we are going to use a "Question-on-Question" technique. The rules: anyone can ask any question they want to ask about the work of art or our workshop, but no one will answer any of the questions. We will each probably *think* of our own answer as soon as we hear a question, but we all agree not to *say* that answer out loud. *"When you have a question to add, raise your hand, and I will nod to you to indicate that it is your turn to speak, otherwise we get too many overlapping questions that we can't hear."* I gently suggest that sometimes another person's question will make us think of a new question, and that if one of these connected questions floats up in our minds, we should raise a hand and say *that* question out loud. Once the rules are confirmed, I check the clock on the wall, and say "Five minutes of Only Questions starting . . . now."

And nothing happens. Students look at each other a little nervously. The classroom teacher and I look at each other, but she knows that *wait time* is crucial; we can be patient. Ten seconds can feel like a long time to wait. Twenty seconds pass. Thirty seconds. Forty. Then a hand goes up, and another, and another:

> *How many drums does he have?*
> *How does he know which drums to hit?*
> *Why are all the drums different?*
> *Are the drums different?*

Five minutes of questions flows smoothly, and the teacher and I are pleased with the quality of the questions. Our eyes meet again. We both shrug and nod and decide to let it go on another five minutes, out of curiosity as to whether or not the students can sustain the process. They seem to be hearing each other's ideas, making some linkages from question to question. At around the ten-minute mark, something new starts to kick in. Up to that point, I have been "responding" to questions with a nod and a smile, or sometimes a raised eyebrow as if to say "Hmm, that's a good one." Students are picking up on this as modeling and start to really enjoy each others' questions. Some questions are greeted with little murmurs of approval or laughter. The energy in the room is shifting. Hands aren't coming up any faster, really, and there is still wait time, but the questions are getting freer, more random, and at the same time more connected, a positive quality teachers sometimes call *divergent*. Some students realize that we are well beyond the planned five minutes. We pass fifteen minutes, and the questions keep coming like popcorn slowly popping, a kernel here, a kernel there, a sudden flurry of five kernels. Every time I think we are at an end, and consider closing out the process, I make myself wait just a few more seconds . . . and up goes another hand. We pass twenty minutes, and the teacher and I grin at each other. Students are responding to each other's questions with smiles and exclamations of "Oh," delighted either by the actual question, or by the fact that we are *still asking questions*, as if we were on the verge of winning an Olympic question-asking event. I egg them on a bit, dropping my jaw in semi-mock surprise, beaming at their success and achievement. After thirty minutes, the class period is about to end, and we have to stop. The students applaud. We are all a little dazed, and happy, looking at each other: *something marvelous just happened, didn't it*?

In the Question-on-Question activity, each person in the room constructs meaning internally, as they A) pose questions or B) consider the questions they hear being posed. New connections and possibilities are revealed with each question, some mundane, some brilliant. Students' sense of self-worth and community are bolstered because the work is transparently community-dependent. We all own the discussion. The teaching artist is not controlling the quality of the discussion: it simply arises. There is room for laughter, seriousness, ill-formed and well-formed inquiry, divergence, and mutual support within the ongoing questioning.

The Sing Sing and PS130 stories illustrate some of the methods and potentials of *reflection* in teaching artist practice. Why do so many educators stress the importance of reflection? John Dewey's 1934 treatise on aesthetics is titled *Art as Experience.* He is often quoted with what is actually a paraphrase: *We do not learn from experience . . .we learn from reflecting on experience.* Let's combine Dewey's book title with the popular paraphrase: *We do not learn from making art . . . we learn from reflecting on the experience of making art.*

Opportunities for reflection come up in the Work and Show phases of each Activity's *Invite–Work–Show* sequence. During Work, students naturally reflect; one might even say that reflection *comprises* any art-making process, since anyone Making & Doing engages in an internal dialogue with the work they are creating: *How does that look? Do I like that color? Should I add another mark? Repeat, or move on? Ignore that stimulus, that possibility, or pick up on it?* This kind of spontaneous reflection is built in to any art-making process. Teaching artists might also prompt students to reflect on the art-making experience during the Work phase using *Stealth Reflection* (see page 117). During the Show phase, we commonly invite students to describe, analyze, and interpret their experiences as makers and observers. Reflection might be formal, built into a Design strategically, as a necessary step in a process, or serendipitous, guided by your inner sense of when to stop and invite your students to take a longer, deeper look at a work of art or their process. In the remainder of this chapter, we'll define reflection and look over some contrasting models of the mechanics of reflecting. In the next chapter we'll take a more specific look at how the Describe, Analyze, Interpret, Judge sequence plays out in teaching artist work.

Professional educators, psychologists, and cognitive theorists have been defining reflection (in educational contexts) for a century or so. The materials I've included here are mere headings, but the work of these six educator/writers are a good place to begin if you are interested in a deeper exploration of this topic. Here again is John Dewey, defining reflection:

Active, persistent, and careful consideration of any belief or supposed form of knowledge in the light of the grounds that support it, and further conclusions to which it leads. . . . [I]t includes a conscious and voluntary effort to establish belief upon a firm basis of evidence and rationality."[15]

Notice Dewey's opening modifiers. If your consideration is not active, persistent, and careful, it doesn't qualify as reflection. Reflection is work, requiring effort. Dr. Jennifer Moon, author of *Reflection in Learning and Professional Development: Theory and Practice* (2000) and staff development officer at the

University of Exeter, offers a definition of reflection that also stresses the effort involved, but also adds an emotional component:

> *Reflection is a form of mental processing—like a form of thinking—that we use to fulfill a purpose or to achieve some anticipated outcome. It is applied to relatively complicated or unstructured ideas for which there is not an obvious solution and is largely based on the further processing of knowledge and understanding and possibly emotions that we already possess.*[16]

Moon also asks us include in our definition of reflection a broader constellation of activities, including metacognition (considering the process of our own learning), inquiry, critical review, and resolving uncertainties. As we engage in these activities, we are self-developing, and "empowering or emancipating ourselves as learners." Her "Characteristics of Reflective Learners" also connects reflecting with what educators and activists might call a growth mindset:

Characteristics of Reflective Learners

Self-aware and self-critical.
Honest about themselves.
Responsive to criticism and feedback.
Objective in weighing up evidence.
Open/prepared to try different approaches to learning.
Curious.
Motivated to improve.
More able to learn independently.

Professor Graham Gibb's Model for Reflection, from his book *Learning By Doing*,[17] comes complete with graphic arrows, and makes the general sense of purpose and directionality found in Dewey and Moon more explicit (Figure 3.31). Gibb's invites us to see reflection as cyclical. His model reminds me of the way Joseph Campbell describes the archetypal "Hero's Journey," which begins with an event or disruption that must be noticed, and ends with the hero bringing new information back to his community.

Professor and Apple Distinguished Educator Peter Pappas's blog posts on the Taxonomy of Lower to Higher Order Reflection began in 2010. Here Pappas describes a ladder of increasingly sophisticated types of reflection: *remembering, understanding, applying, analyzing, valuing, creating.* But Pappas goes further than a simple list of types of reflection (Figure 3.32). His taxonomy[18] is more of a hierarchy, not unlike Professor Abraham Maslow's 1943 Hierarchy of Needs which moves from foundational to higher level needs (basic, then psychological, then self-fulfillment needs—see page 168, where the higher levels are only achieved after the lower levels are in place.

Professor David Kolb, a psychologist and educational theorist and the professor of organizational behavior at the Weatherhead School of Management

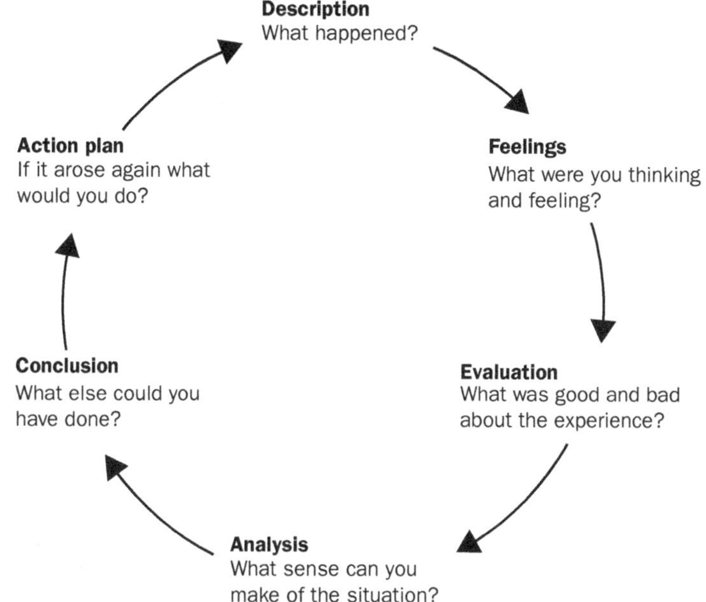

FIGURE 3.31 Graham Gibb's Model for Reflection

FIGURE 3.32 Peter Pappas's Taxonomy of Lower to Higher Order Reflection

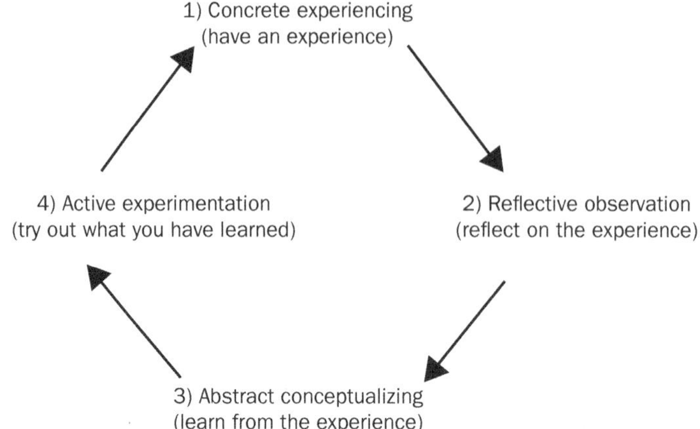

FIGURE 3.33 David Kolb's Learning Cycle

at Case Western Reserve, defines learning as "the process whereby knowledge is created through the transformation of experience.",[19] His Learning Cycle is based on his belief that deep learning (learning for real comprehension) comes from a sequence of *experience, reflection, conceptualization, and experimentation,* as explained by Saul McLeod in his article for *Simply Psychology,* "(1) having a concrete experience followed by (2) observation of and reflection on that experience which leads to (3) the formation of abstract concepts (analysis) and generalizations (conclusions) which are then (4) used to test hypotheses in future situations, resulting in new experiences."[20] The sequence of experiences in Kolb's cycle (Figure 3.33) is not unlike that of a teaching artist's View–Design–Respond cycle (diagrammed on page 33). In both cycles, the reflective practitioner experiments and applies whatever they learn, solidifying or altering their previously held View, and beginning the cycle anew. Kolb's sequence substantiates the Dewey paraphrase about the necessity of reflection: a learning cycle isn't going to take place without that second step, "reflective observation."

In her education blog *Stable Transitions,* Karen Barnstable turns the jewel of reflection in four contrasting directions, Four Dimensions of Reflection, so that we might better appreciate the facets of the practice. As with Gibbs, Pappas, and Kolb, Barnstable's conception of reflection contains a sense of sequential movement: *Thinking Back, Thinking Forward, Thinking Inward,* and *Thinking Outward.*[21]

Karen Barnstable's Four Dimensions of Reflection

I. Thinking Back
   What was the original purpose of this project/experience?
   What was my motive for completion of this project/experience?

What were the critical factors helping or hindering completion of this project?

What specific skills/knowledge/attributes were necessary for completion of this project?

What did I actually learn from this project/experience?

When did the most learning occur? How do I know this?

II. Thinking Forward

If I had chosen to do "x" or not to do "x," what might have happened?

How significant are the outcomes of either direction?

If I had the chance to do this again, what changes would I make?

How might this project or experience shape the goals that I set for my future?

How might what I have learned affect my future learning decisions?

III. Thinking Inward

Why was this project or experience meaningful to me?

What are my personal beliefs regarding this learning experience?

Do I agree or disagree with the way I learned this? Why or why not?

What differences has the learning made in my intellectual, personal, or ethical development?

What were the highest and lowest emotional moments in my learning experience?

IV. Thinking Outward

How am I looking at this topic?

Can I identify another point of view?

How might a person from another culture or religion look at this?

Which of these viewpoints makes the most sense?

Is my current concept about a topic causing problems for others?

Does the problem or question in my mind have historical, ethical, scientific, political, or economic considerations?

When Reflection Trumps Making & Doing

I was leading a visual arts workshop for arts-in-healthcare providers, experienced practitioners who work with elders, individuals with dementia or memory loss, and people suffering from a debilitating chronic illness or mental illness. My Inkblot Workshop (making, drawing into, games for interpreting) had been a hit with this group before. The conference setting meant that participants had already been talking and listening for days, so I was hesitant to alter my usual hands-on focus to reflect. But this particular time I set aside twenty of my ninety minutes for the attendees to talk about how they might use the Inkblot Workshop with their populations. Their ideas were wide-ranging: some wanted to use the workshop as a team-building activity for staff, some wanted to do it one-on-one with bed-bound patients. One woman worked with mentally ill patients and wanted to make sure people knew that using abstract inkblot images might make some mentally ill art-makers unstable, and had ideas of what to do if that happened. We talked about how to make the materials safe for people who might be at risk for getting sick from germs on shared art materials. We brainstormed the idea of making a giant inkblot that many people could work on together. It was a fantastic discussion. And the drawn-into inkblots that the participants did next were subtle and interesting. They were on fire about taking the Inkblot Workshop back to their worlds, and drew into their inkblots all through their lunch break. They felt empowered beyond their instant-expert status as inkblot artists, and became inkblot ambassadors. Our profession-targeted reflection had changed everything. My takeaway: *More reflection and less hands-on work might be what brings it all home for participants. Offer them time and space to connect and reflect.*—Margaret Peot, author and visual artist, New York, NY

DESCRIBE/ANALYZE/INTERPRET

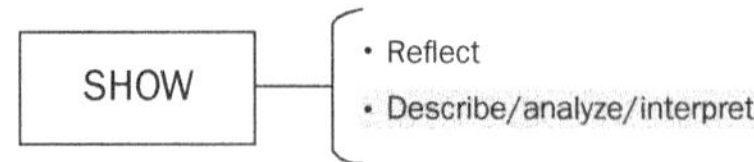

Any time we guide a discussion or reflection, we're asking students to go beyond a cursory glance at or brief encounter with a work of art: we are asking them to attend to the work as well as to their own experience in a sustained way. As Maxine Greene suggests in her *Variations on a Blue Guitar*, when we take the time to reflect, we lend our lives to the work of art so that we might be able to find and make meaning in the transaction: *We understand aesthetic education to be an intentional undertaking designed to nurture appreciative, reflective, cultural, participatory engagements with works of art by enabling learners to notice what there is to be noticed, and to lend works of art their lives in such a way that they can achieve them as variously meaningful.*[22]

"Variously meaningful" is a wide open door: we meet the work of art and make our own meaning, unfettered and on-going. To make meaning, we take time to "notice what there is to be noticed" and give voice to those ideas. Many experienced audience members and museum-goers have internalized the process. Students new to encountering works of art may benefit from a somewhat formal, ordered approach; teaching artists who want to encourage reflection can support these students by asking them to *Describe, Analyze,* and *Interpret.*

Arts educator, theorist, and critic Edmund Burke Feldman first presented Describe–Analyze–Interpret in *Practical Art Criticism* (1994). The sequence (with or without a fourth *Evaluate* or *Judge* phase, omitted for the moment) is taught in criticism courses and widely used by teaching artists. The elegant idea that reflection takes place in three discrete steps becomes messier when we observe actual reflections. It is almost impossible not to let some analysis creep into our descriptions, or interpretation into our analysis. Even Feldman himself wasn't immune: in his first book, *Varieties of Visual Experience* (1967), he begins with a careful analysis of Picasso's *Les Demoiselles d'Avignon*, but soon conflates his own description with interpretation. Any messiness in workaday application notwithstanding, Feldman's Describe–Analyze–Interpret remains a useful framework for reflection.

Let's apply Feldman's sequence to teaching artist work. In *Describe–Analyze–Interpret for Teaching Artists* (Figure 3.34), each column begins with two typical invitations to either *Describe, Analyze,* or *Interpret,* followed by examples of the types of responses, words, and phrases that students might use within each reflective mode.

When it works well, the three step sequence creates an arc of experience, beginning with a cooler objectivity and culminating in a warmer, wholly subjective engagement with the work. If we don't take the time to Describe, we probably won't have the raw materials needed to Analyze the work, and will need to backtrack a bit in order to do so. Once we've objectively observed elements of and relationships in the work of art, we're able to ascribe subjective meanings to the work. In this way, the Describe, Analyze, and Interpret sequence can lead to deeper engagement.

Let's track different types of observations students might offer up as they Describe, Analyze, and Interpret. Each of the three charts that follow begin with basic *Describe, Analyze, or Interpret* prompts. The prompts on the Describe chart below are *What do you notice? What has the artist done?* Words and phrases that students might use to answer those prompts (i.e., student observations that stay in a describing mode, not analyzing or interpreting) are listed under visual art, dance, music, and theater headings (the four right-hand columns) (Figure 3.35). What students specifically notice as they Describe tends to fall under one of the fourteen possible aspects of a work of art (for example: size, scale, primary art form) listed on the left-hand side of the chart.

First we *Describe: What do I see?* Here we try to remain objective, and delay subjective comment. Describe honors the work itself, and also guides us to value our own direct experience, as if to say: *What you notice is at the heart of this transaction—please linger here.* Most of us will jump to analyzing or interpreting based on a brief encounter with the work of art. But works yield more meaning and significance when we take time and simply attend. Holding *Analyze* or *Interpret* in abeyance means suspending judgment. Ask students to put statements of *I felt . . ., I thought . . ., I wondered . . ., I liked . . .* to one side so that they can abide, observe, and soak in what *is.* Describing slows us down and creates a sense of open space where we can explore the work of art and find out what it has to say to us. Taking time to describe what we notice has the effect of stretching out the initial noticing period. In that time we notice the thing-ness of the work of art. When we don't take time to *Describe,* we *lend ourselves* less to, and receive less from, our interaction with the work of art. If we previously skipped or skimped on attending to the work of art, describing it makes sure we invest at least a little time to do so.

Describe–Analyze–Interpret for Teaching Artists

Describe			Analyze	Interpret
What do you notice? *What has the artist done?*			*How are the elements you noticed used?* *What relationships exist between elements?*	*What was the artist's intention?* *What does the work mean to you?*
art form	technique	location	There is a lot of ___.	The artist is saying…
size	composition	surface	There is more ___ than ___.	The artist is wants us to feel / see / know…
scale	elements	similarity	All of the _______ always _____.	I believe…
shape	subject matter	closeness]	This part is _____, but this part…	I think…
texture	line	contrast	Sometimes it ____, but then it _____.	I imagine…
color	light	sequence	The sections go back and forth between…	I feel…
palette	shape	direction	The middle is really different sections where…	I interpret…
artist	color	rhythm	The ending was set up in the middle, when…	
title	temperature	symmetry	Each of the ____ is brought out by ____.	
medium	quantity	balance	The _____ relate to each other like a _____.	
tools	space	completeness		

FIGURE 3.34 Describe–Analyze–Interpret invitations and responses

Describe				
What do you notice? What has the artist done?				

Aspect of the observed work of art	Examples of descriptive observations			
	VISUAL ART	DANCE	MUSIC	THEATER
primary art form(s)	*sculpture*	*ballet*	*string quartet*	*play*
size and scale	*huge*	*trio*	*multi-movement*	*one-act*
shape	*spidery*	*spread-out arms*	*slow fast slow presto*	*series of arguments*
texture	*bumpy*	*jittery*	*ornamented*	*thick*
color and palette	*earth tone*	*plastic-like jewel tones*	*bright*	*dark*
artist	*sculptor's name*	*choreographer's name*	*composer's name*	*playwright's name*
title	*title of sculpture*	*title of ballet*	*title of quartet*	*title of play*
medium or tools	*earth and stone*	*three dancers and water hoses*	*two violins, viola, cello*	*five actors in a car*
technique	*piling, tamping*	*jump, spin, slide*	*different in each section*	*dialogue, direct address*
composition	*site-specific*	*theme and variations*	*motif-driven*	*1-hour unit of time*
identification of elements	*central hump, projecting curved arms*	*water used as lubrication between dancers and plastic floor*	*low drones, skittering high notes, tapping, plucking*	*family relations, deadline clock*
relationships between elements (these might also appear in Analyze)	*hump as hub for arms, variations in tamped and raw earth*	*constant back and forth between high-level movement and low-level sliding*	*instruments take turns, trade and echo melodies*	*two characters flip their points of view*
subject matter	*not clear without interpreting*	*kids in summer*	*not clear without interpreting*	*teen pregnancy*
original location/date	*Utah 1975*	*Jacob's Pillow 2006*	*Vienna 1821*	*New York 1964*

Other more art-form-specific Describe aspects include line, light, shape, color, temperature, quantity, space, location, surface, similarity, closeness, contrast, sequence, direction, rhythm, symmetry, balance, completeness, closure.

FIGURE 3.35 Describe examples organized by art form

Using details from our responses to the Describe prompts *What do you notice?* and *What has the artist done?*, we are ready to Analyze: to make connections, notice structures, qualities, points of emphasis, and relationships while maintaining objectivity (Figure 3.36).

The same structures and qualities noticed during Describe and objectively observed during Analyze are referred to more subjectively when we *Interpret* (Figure 3.37).

When describing and analyzing we should ask our students to provide evidence, to be able to point out to others the basis of what they are noticing. And sharing descriptions and analysis is useful for everyone present: we learn what is there to be noticed from each other. But interpretations are not subject to the same rigors of proof as description or analysis. During Interpret, we feel, we think, we imagine without having to provide evidence or justification. Most of us can't dependably articulate why we've interpreted something in a particular way. Sharing our interpretations may or may not deepen our own engagement with a work of art, or have any effect on the engagement of other observers and audience members. Some interpretations stay within the world of the work of art, others go far afield. On the positive side, shared interpretations ask us to entertain divergent ideas and opinions, and can be persuasive when they

Analyze
How are the elements you noticed used?
What relationships exist between elements?

principles of the work of art	examples of analytical observations
contrast	There is a lot of ___.
repetition	There is more ___ than ___.
unity	All of the _______ always ______.
movement	This part is ______, but this part…
balance	Sometimes it _____, but then it ______.
organization	The sections go back and forth between…
structure	The middle is really different sections where…
planning	The ending was set up in the middle, when…
points of emphasis	Each of the _____ is brought out by _____.
subjects or characters	The ______ relate to each other like a ______.

Analysis via more art-form-specific questioning might include: *Where is this happening? Who lives here? What did they do? Why did they do it? Are the represented events real or potentially real? Was this place seen, remembered, or invented? Where are we in relation to what we see? What happened before we arrived? What will happen afterward?* With some works of art, these questions might prompt interpretation, rather than analysis.

FIGURE 3.36 Analyze examples

<table>
<tr><td colspan="2" align="center">Interpret

What was the artist's intention?

What does the work mean to you?</td></tr>
<tr><td align="center">aspects of the work of art

subject to interpretation</td><td align="center">examples of interpretive observations</td></tr>
<tr><td>Meaning, mood, intention, effect on viewer, i.e., any subjective observation, not necessarily supported by any evidence.</td><td>The artist is saying…

The artist is wants us to feel/see/know…

I believe…

I think…

I imagine…

I feel…

I interpret…</td></tr>
<tr><td colspan="2">Prompts to interpret might include: Is there a larger concept or idea that sums up all the separate pieces? What is the feeling you get when looking at this work? How does it relate to your art knowledge, particularly with art history and artistic styles? How does it relate to your knowledge of life? How does it relate to your art experiences? What does the artist want to say? What strategies and techniques is the artist using to convey that message? How effective are those strategies and techniques? What would have to change to give the piece more or less impact? Who are the people in these paintings? Why did the artist choose to paint them?</td></tr>
</table>

FIGURE 3.37 Interpret examples

correspond with qualities we can observe in the work of art. These well-made interpretations "invite us to see for ourselves and to continue on our own," as author Terry Barrett suggests in his Principles of Interpretation:

1) Artworks have "aboutness" and demand interpretation.
2) Interpretations are persuasive arguments.
3) Some interpretations are better than others.
4) Good interpretations of art tell more about the artwork than they tell about the critic.
5) There can be different, competing, and contradictory interpretations of the same artwork.
6) Interpretations are not so much absolutely right, but more or less reasonable, convincing, enlightening, and informative.
7) Interpretations can be judged by coherence, correspondence, and inclusiveness.
8) All art is in part about the world in which it emerged.
9) All art is in part about other art.
10) No single interpretation is exhaustive of the meaning of an artwork.

11) The meanings of an artwork may be different from its significance to the viewer. Interpretation is ultimately a communal endeavor, and the community is ultimately self-corrective.

12) Good interpretations invite us to see for ourselves and to continue on our own.[23]

As your students describe, analyze, and interpret, what they notice may not be as directly connected with the work of art or process at hand as you would like. Help them by modeling the kind of reflection you want them to contribute. Notice some of the qualities, structures, or relationships you want them to be noticing. Think aloud; reveal your personal process of noticing. Because you are an artist-expert with an unusual way of looking at the world that they value and an evident expertise that they respect, students will be interested in at least following along the reflective paths you lay out. Students are already familiar with mirroring their classroom teachers' reflective techniques. Some classroom teachers use a Columbia University Teachers College language arts program called Readers and Writers Workshop, which includes a type of modeling called a *think-aloud*, in which the teacher stops and reflects aloud at various points as she reads a text to students, in effect an artist-expert revealing how she processes a text. Teaching artists can apply the same approach to our texts and works of art. With this kind of think-aloud modeling, students come to know that describing, analyzing, and interpreting is a vital and everyday aspect of being an artist, and a way for them to embrace the artistic attitude of mind.

The Kennedy Center's ArtsEdge program outlines *Describe–Analyze–Interpret* with teachers and teaching artists in mind using specific prompts, and adds a decisively subjective *judgment* step:

Description

Describe the work without using value words such as "beautiful" or "ugly":
What is the written description on the label or in the program about the work?
What is the title and who is (are) the artist(s)?
When and where was the work created?
Describe the elements of the work (i.e., line, movement, light, space).
Describe the technical qualities of the work (i.e., tools, materials, instruments).
Describe the subject matter. What is it all about? Are there recognizable images?

Analysis

Describe how the work is organized as a complete composition:
How is the work constructed or planned (i.e., acts, movements, lines)?
Identify some of the similarities throughout the work (i.e., repetition of lines, two songs in each act).
Identify some of the points of emphasis in the work (i.e., specific scene, figure, movement).

If the work has subjects or characters, what are the relationships between or among them?

Interpretation

Describe how the work makes you think or feel.

Describe the expressive qualities you find in the work. What expressive language would you use to describe the qualities (i.e., tragic, ugly, funny)?

Does the work remind you of other things you have experienced (i.e., analogy or metaphor)?

How does the work relate to other ideas or events in the world and/or in your other studies?

Judgment or Evaluation

Present your opinion of the work's success or failure:

What qualities of the work make you feel it is a success or failure?

Compare it with similar works that you think are good or bad.

What criteria can you list to help others judge this work?

How original is the work? Why do you feel this work is original or not original?[24]

The Kennedy Center and other institutions often provide professional development workshops to help their teaching artists build reflection into their planning and teaching. With or without institutional support, you'll find yourself developing your own individual approach. Reflection feeds the fire of student engagement. The words *recall, remember, revisit, re-evaluate*, and *re-imagine*, all those "re-" prefixed terms we associate with *reflection*, invite us to *return* to the immediate past. Returning allows students to become aware of the practical, material, and aesthetic choices they made during Making & Doing. They become more process-aware, and aware of their roles as creators, observers, and participants. When students respond to each other's reflections, they reinforce with workshop's sense of community.

What is your view on the role of reflection? What kinds of reflections and reflective strategies are a natural extension of your own character, interests, and humor? During Design, strategize how you will make reflection an integral part of your workshops and build these elements into your plan (Figure 3.38).

Designing Reflection Checklist

☐ where to invite students to describe, analyze, or interpret

☐ how to word reflective prompts

☐ how to allow for informal moments of reflection

☐ when to leave space to follow up on ideas that might arise during reflection

FIGURE 3.38

CASE STUDY: INVITE–WORK–SHOW

Let's track the *Invite–Work–Show* sequences in a modest fifteen-minute activity, titled "Families of Instruments." The three column form (activity, steps, support) is my own design, and has proven useful for 92Y's Musical Introduction Series teaching artists and classroom teachers, who share a written curriculum (Figure 3.39).

The chart below (Figure 3.40) breaks the "Families of Instruments" activity into its component Invite–Work–Show steps, and lists the Design Practices and Respond Principles that make an appearance.

What I like most about the "Families of Instruments" activity is that—without any telling or lecturing—students can become conversant with the orchestral instruments' appearances (color, shape, size), the materials used in their construction (wooden or metal tubes, reeds, double reeds, wooden boxes, strings, horse hair, metal or gut strings), observable mechanisms and structures (slides, valves, bells, f-holes, finger holes, mouthpieces, bridges, bows, keys, pads, separable sections, mutes), and how the instruments produce sound (via breath, buzzing lips, fingers, bowing, striking, shaking, scraping). This familiarization doesn't happen automatically; the teaching artist does a lot of following up to draw students out. What keeps the whole

Families of Instruments—Preparation Activity For Orchestral Concert		
activity	**steps**	**support**
Families *of* *Instruments* (15 min)	• *What do we know about families?* • *What do we know about orchestras?* • Hand out Orchestra Game bags • Model mis-organizing the instruments into families (TA) • Organize instrument pictures into families (students) • *What are the instrument families? What makes them so?* • Hand out Orchestra Layout Chart • *What does this picture tell you?* • *What is the best / loudest / highest / loneliest / fiercest instrument of the orchestra?*	The Orchestra Game Bag is a clear plastic bag with a lot of small color images of individual orchestra instruments, unlabeled and unsorted, one bag for each team or pair. TA models mis-organizing: describe and sort, make goofy mistakes, invite students to correct you. As pairs or teams organizing instruments: *be prepared to explain WHY it is a family.*

FIGURE 3.39 Families of Instruments Activity

Families of Instruments—Preparation Activity For Orchestral Concert (15 minutes)		
Activity Step	**Invite Work Show**	**Design Practice Or Respond Principle**
What do we know about families? What do we know about orchestras?	Invite via a query	use open questions, access prior knowledge, honor every response, all of which establish safe space
Hand out Orchestra Game Bags	Invite via a material prompt	predict and remove impediments (by avoiding any need for participants to be able to read: all pictures, no words or names unless the participants choose to write them); track developmental appropriateness (by welcoming and honoring more experienced student's prior knowledge)
Model mis-organizing the instruments into families (TA)	Invite via modeling	modeling (describing instrument qualities); establish safe space (with a lighthearted tone)
Participants organize instrument pictures into families.	Work via making choices and creating an artifact: a classification system	construct analogies, access prior knowledge, and reflect
What are the instrument families? What makes them so?	Show via revealing their choice-making process	reflect; use open questions; honor every response; follow-up; exploit multiple modalities by working visually (pictures and charts), interpersonally (work in pairs), logically (when we support our reasoning), kinesthetically (when we mime instruments being held and played), and aurally (when we mimic the sounds of instruments)
Hand out Orchestra Layout Chart	Invite via a material prompt	place contextual information
What does this picture tell you? What is the best (loudest, highest, loneliest, fiercest) instrument of the orchestra?	Invite via a query; Work and Show at the same time	exploit multiple modalities by working visually (pictures and charts), interpersonally (work in pairs), logically (when we support our reasoning), kinesthetically (when we mime instruments being held and played), and aurally (when we mimic the sounds of instruments)

FIGURE 3.40 Families of Instruments Activity broken down into Essential Practices

process from being a boring version of "show me what you know, and get it right or else" is that the discussion is genuinely open. Even though the characteristics of the instruments are concrete and not open to interpretation, there are no predetermined correct answers to the sorting questions, only sharp or less sharp observations, clear or less clear support of one's assertions. And better still: everyone in the room knows that they are not being *told* what the answers are, but are contributing to a live, active inquiry as they work.

Did you roll your eyes when you saw the words *handout, chart,* and *sort* in the activity plan? I too am wary of these devices, which can stifle inquiry or create a false sense of engagement. But this isn't one of those lessons, according to the students who have done the work. In mixed-age groups at family homeless shelters in the Bronx, I watched older children gently and considerately helped younger ones through the process. They all seemed to love the small pictures, the puzzle-solving atmosphere, the sorting as well as the arguing. At the end of the workshop, they wanted to keep their pictures and charts. I think that was in part because the pictures were evidence of something they had in a sense both invented and discovered, valuable knowledge that, by the end of the activity, belonged to them.

4

Respond

to say or write something as an answer to a question or request

to do something as a reaction to something that has happened

to have a good or desired reaction to something

to make an answer

to react

the activity or inhibition of previous activity of an organism (or any of its parts) resulting from stimulation

the output of a transducer or detecting device resulting from a given input

The Container

A champagne flute's stem allows the drinker to hold the glass without affecting the temperature of the drink. The tall, narrow shape helps retain champagne's signature carbonation by reducing the surface area at the opening of the bowl. The clear glass or crystal allows us to easily see the color, effervescence, and amount of champagne in the flute. The flute is a *container* designed with both the properties of champagne as well as the champagne drinker's experience in mind. We appreciate, use, and prefer containers that are well-matched with the qualities of that which they contain: sieves make terrible containers for soup, while bowls or cups are known as excellent containers for soup. A good container is functional, allowing us to have and hold something we value within something else.

Teaching artists serve their students and workshop participants by designing *containers* for teaching and learning. These environments or spaces are an expression of what we as educators and artists believe is important (our View). When we do a good job establishing them, our containers make the relationships, structures, and processes we want to make possible. Our container Designs strengthen those factors that improve the quality of students'

FIGURE 4.1

Photo courtesy of Libbey Glassware

experience within the enclosure, and mitigate those qualities that might potentially degrade that experience. Often our physical workshop spaces are borrowed from classroom teachers; often we are guests in a pre-existing community; often there are factors and conditions outside of our control that affect our students. But for as long as we are there, the responsibility for the container is effectively ours. Teaching artists respond to anything and everything that takes place there: planned events and unpredictable circumstances, bursts of energy, certainties and mysteries. I believe our success during the Respond phase of our work is largely determined by how well we create and maintain a good *container* for teaching and learning.

Good containers provide boundaries and support. A few years ago I participated in a traditional Buddhist four-week silent meditation retreat called a *dathun*. In a converted farmhouse and barn on a snowy mountainside in Vermont, twenty retreatants lived a more or less monastic life, supported by the retreat center's small staff. A *dathun* is designed to maximize reflection and self-transformation. The tradition stipulates strictly observed periods of sitting meditation, study, service (cleaning the center or helping in the kitchen), mindful silent *oryoki* meals (Figure 4.2), walking meditation, a few rest breaks, and sleep.

FIGURE 4.2 An *oryoki* meal in progress

The support staff made it possible for the retreatants to take part in the retreat without distractions or material worries by providing what they called a *container* for the experience. Mostly *dathun* veterans, they did whatever was needed to create an appropriate environment for meditation, providing an overall sense of what they called an *uplifted presence*, including food, shelter, practice support from experienced meditation instructors, security services, and staff available to address any conflict or health issues that arose in the community.

There was nothing casual about the *dathun* staff's approach to creating and maintaining the container. At daily meetings they reviewed every conceivable aspect of the retreat experience, from the practical (*Is there enough bread and butter at the tea break table?*) to the aesthetic (*clean floors, good light?*), from the community discipline-related (*Are folks rolling up and stowing their sleeping mats no later than 6:45 a.m.?*) to the personal (*individual meetings with qualified meditation instructors*). Being responsible for these details is a form of Buddhist practice, in this case one of service, called the *dorje kasung*, which as Barry Boyce explains in the *Shambhala Sun* magazine,

> *[Dorje kasung] roughly translated means those who protect the teachings and help make them accessible. The kasung could help the teacher create a good container in which the teachings can be heard and experienced. A meditation hall that is clean and quiet and well lit and ventilated provides an excellent container for mindfulness practice and to hear teachings. Likewise, if someone sits at the gate in an upright posture looking out as a reminder to students to enter attentively—and make a transition from the speed of daily life—they'll be inspired to hear the teachings, take them to heart, and wake up.*[1]

Teaching artists are the *dorje kasung* of their workshops, defining and maintain their classroom containers in similar ways. As defined by Trungpa Rinpoche, who brought *dathun* practice to the West in the 1970s, a container holds something safe—a substance, activity, or state of mind. It simultaneously constitutes a boundary and offers structure, organizing the ground of a situation while allowing the content to manifest in various ways, as the walls of a house delineate the boundary between public and private, but also provide a secure living environment and making certain freedoms possible. The boundary isn't meant solely to keep undesirable things out, but also to regulate the energy flow between the inside and the outside.

TEACHING ARTIST AS WARM CHALLENGER

Master Teacher James Sturtevant's *You've Gotta Connect* (2014) makes the value of personally connecting with students clear as he tells stories of his own experiments with establishing a classroom community—his container for teaching and learning. In evaluating his own practice, Sturtevant measures the student engagement that did, or sometimes did not, result from his efforts to connect. The practice of *acceptance* is high on his list—making sure that he is willing to accept who and where his students are, each day, without needing to change them. Verbal and nonverbal communications, enjoyment, advocacy, and safety all play a role. Sturtevant cites educational researcher Judith Kleinfeld's phrase *warm demander* (a nurturing yet firm friend who holds you to high standards) as a model that many successful full-time classroom teachers embody. Sturtevant prefers *warm challenger* as being more appropriate, less aggressive or controlling. In my own informal ongoing survey of successful teaching artists, I have found warm demanders (aka challengers, guides, coaches) facilitating the most vital and successful workshops. Their warmth is explicit, spoken aloud, as well as implied or embodied, simply part of who the teaching artist is as a human being, à la Booth's "80 percent of teaching artistry is who you are." With these experienced teaching artists, high expectations or demands were both explicit and implicit; even in the midst of play, there was an overall sense of the earnestness or even seriousness of students' endeavors.

Sturtevant and other warm demanders/challengers like him form containers that are highly functional, with clear rules and a sense of shared responsibility. They often create these communities within the first few days of any given year. Teachers who are unable to shape their communities during those first few days can end up stuck with whatever they did develop for the rest of the year; once a classroom's dynamic is established, it can be tough to change. As you enter different classroom communities, take on a researcher's role and ask yourself: *How does this container function?* In high-functioning containers, participants want to be there, to be active members of the community. They want to do well and want others to do well, because those attitudes are intrinsically rewarding. Participating in and contributing to the classroom community feels wholesome and right. When actions that do not fit within this ethos seem strange or absurd (*Why would anyone want to do that, or act that way?*), classroom management issues are fewer. A strong classroom community makes it easier to notice and help students who are distressed or struggling for non-school-related reasons. If you admire a teacher's community-building style and substance, the classroom container they have created, take that individual to lunch and ask *How do you do it?* Every teacher will have a different set of answers—but most of them will be warm demanders, with strong Views and excellent Respond skills.

TEACHING ARTIST AS FACILITATOR

From a constructivist perspective, a teaching artist forming a container might be seen as the facilitator of a *community of learners*. Russian psychologist and constructivist Lev Vygotsky (1896–1934) believed that all human learning takes place in a social context, between people. In his View, we *construct* our understanding of life experiences through interaction with others in a *community of learners*, a gathering of *more experienced* and *less experienced* individuals working side by side where learning takes place. In constructivist classrooms, as summarized by Ozgur Ozer in "Constructivism in Piaget and Vygotsky,"

> *Unlike the conventional lecturer, the teacher is a facilitator and a guide who plans, organizes, guides, and provides directions to the learner, who is accountable for his own learning. The teacher supports the learner by means of suggestions that arise out of ordinary activities, by challenges that inspire creativity, and with projects that allow for independent thinking and new ways of learning information. Students work in groups to approach problems and challenges in real world situations; this in turn leads to the creation of practical solutions and a diverse variety of student products. . . . A Vygotskian classroom emphasizes creating one's own concepts and making knowledge one's property. . . . In a Vygotskian classroom, dynamic support and considerate guidance are provided according to the learner's needs, but no will or force is dictated.[2]*

Vygotsky's assertions are thrilling and empowering because of their broad implications for teaching artist practice. If you embrace *community of learners* as a unifying metaphor (as I do in my View), you'll naturally strive to make your containers (i.e., your Design and Respond phases) correspond with what turn out to be Vygotskian ideals:

The teacher is a facilitator and a guide.
The learner is accountable for his own learning.
The teacher supports the learner by means of challenges and projects.
Students create a diverse variety of products.
Cognitive strategies of questioning, predicting, summarizing, and clarifying.
Dynamic support and guidance is provided according to the learner's needs.

If you view yourself as a facilitator and a guide, you won't lecture much, since you will be busy imagining, setting up, maintaining, and tweaking optimal learning situations for your group. If you believe that the learner is accountable for his own learning, you design supportive, open opportunities for imaginative play. Those first two beliefs already include your supporting the learner by means of challenges and projects. Since you are not lecturing, your more Socratic approach will necessarily include the cognitive strategies of questioning, predicting, summarizing, and clarifying as skillful means to an end. Since you are a responsive leader, you'll improvise dynamic support and guidance according to the learner's needs. That students would create a diverse variety of products is implicit in your open invitation to create.

A constructivist-inspired facilitator or guide might sometimes be a demonstrator. For a few action-packed days every September, hundreds of artist-blacksmiths gather in a little-used corner of the Dayton International Airport for the QuadState Round Up, an event hosted by Southern Ohio Forge and Anvil, an affiliate of ABANA, the Artist Blacksmith Association of America. These men and women come to the Round Up because they are interested in *iron*: how to grade it, heat it, shape, form, manipulate, control, and work it. They gather to swap or sell tools, raw stock, plans, stories, ideas, and expertise. There is something decidedly egalitarian about this *community of learners*. Craft and skill are honored. Nationally recognized smiths present free workshops on everything from beginner-level forge welding to expert-level Damascus steel blade-making.

FIGURE 4.3 Artist-blacksmith Brian Russell; photo: Nigel Kaines

The demonstrators are in effect teaching artists of forge-based Making & Doing, *modeling* forging processes from start to finish, often *thinking aloud* as they go, by doing the real work in real time. A QuadState demonstration falls somewhere between a workshop (there is some participation) and a show (there is an interested audience), and the demonstrators themselves might be called teachers, lecturers, or facilitators depending on how they are communicating with the gathered community at any given moment. The format really works for this community. Attendees come away from QuadState buzzing with new ideas and creative energy.

As you demonstrate Making & Doing, or any time you model, do you see yourself as teaching, or facilitating? Is the difference important? In the April 2015 *Journal of Social Sciences, Literature and Languages'* article "Review of Constructivism and Social Constructivism," Roya Jafari Amineh and Hanieh Davatgari cite a cross-section of articles that make a case for good constructivist teaching as *facilitating*:

> According to the social constructivist approach, instructors have to adapt to the role of facilitators and not teachers (Bauersfeld, 1995) . . . Whereas a teacher gives a didactic lecture that covers the subject matter, a facilitator helps the learner to get to his or her own understanding of the content. In the former scenario the learner plays a passive role and in the latter scenario the learner plays an active role in the learning process. The emphasis thus turns away from the instructor and the content, and toward the learner (Gamoran, Secada, & Marrett, 2000). This dramatic change of role implies that a facilitator needs to display a totally different set of skills than that of a teacher (Brownstein 2001) . . . A teacher tells, a facilitator asks; a teacher lectures from the front, a facilitator supports from the back; a teacher gives answers according to a set curriculum, a facilitator provides guidelines and creates the environment for the learner to arrive at his or her own conclusions; a teacher mostly gives a monologue, a facilitator is in continuous dialogue with the learners (Rhodes and Bellamy, 1999).[3]

These writers' assertions bring up questions about modeling that are useful for us, as Inviter-Warm Demander-Demonstrator-Facilitators called teaching artists, to ask ourselves: *Where, when, and how are my students passive or active? Where, when, and how am I teaching (telling), as opposed to inviting? Have I created an environment where my students are able to make meaning and arrive at their own conclusions? To what extent am I in a continuous dialogue with my students?*

In this opening section of the Respond chapter, we've looked at our workshops as containers for teaching and learning, with their own boundaries and dynamics. The Respond phase of our work takes place within these Designed spaces, where we support, challenge, and guide to facilitate student learning.

The remainder of the chapter explores approaches to responding, practical support for teaching artists working in all art forms and workshop types:

Respond Principles of Teaching Artist Craft

The Container—seeing the workshop space as a container for teaching and learning

Honor Every Response—how to work with the range of positive and negative responses that students offer

The Art of the Follow-Up—response strategies that can help us draw out students' ideas and insights

Thriving and Struggling—how arts education students thrive, and the many ways they can struggle, with a look at classroom management and the effects of social toxicity.

I Cannot

I asked my middle school students to create a piece of art in a medium of their choice, beginning with a concept sheet explaining their idea for the piece. Lisa's only reply was, "I cannot draw, paint, or do anything artistic." She was steadfast in her belief that she was no visual artist. I showed her some examples of artists who do not render pieces that are perfectly photo real, including Jean-Michel Basquiat. We talked about his simplistic style, and that an artist does not have to create works like da Vinci or a famous photographer in order to be an artist. We also talked about how art is a representation of self. I asked Lisa questions about what her interests were and what she liked doing in her spare time. Lisa was an avid swimmer, as well as an accomplished violinist. These self-reflections gave her the courage to sit down and create—to her own astonishment and joy—a fabulous watercolor painting of herself swimming through a sea of musical notes that floated up from an image of her violin. To this day, Lisa's piece is one of the best works that a student has ever done in one of my classes. My takeaway: *"I can't" means "I don't feel safe," or "I don't know how to begin."*—Greg Thornton, visual arts, Seattle, WA

Honor Every Response

A teaching artist stands in an East Harlem grade-school hallway, pacing back and forth in front of a bulletin board. From a distance, you hear him muttering, discreetly talking to himself. In two minutes, he's scheduled to begin teaching the twenty-eight third graders in the next room. His pacing continues. If you move closer, you might hear that his muttering is a repeated phrase: *honor every response, honor every response.* The teaching artist is me, and the scene recurs in some form before just about every workshop I teach.

Mantra: a phrase meant to alter some aspect of one's consciousness or awareness via repetition. As a teaching artist, I embrace *honor every response* as a mantra in the hope that the words will soak into my consciousness deeply enough that I become permanently predisposed to do so. If I remind myself of the principle often enough, I may be able to maintain the practice of honoring every response all the way though the next workshop session, every minute, without fail. If and when that happens, I am a better teaching artist because I am a fearless and intrepid Responder, and an enthusiastic, unfettered Engager with whatever arises within the container. No response will put me off; every response is welcome. After twenty-five years of teaching artist work, I still say it, I am still working on it, and it is still a good reminder.

How do you prime yourself to do your best work in the classroom? What thought is on your mind the moment you walk in?

The Respond phase of View, Design, and Respond consists mainly of two related practices: creating and maintaining a good container for teaching and learning, and drawing out our students' ideas using open questions and skillful follow-ups. Within the container, teaching artists are constantly inviting. Activities all begin with invitations (as in Invite–Work–Show, see page 56). And every question you pose during a workshop is also an invitation to students: *come notice, come wonder, come engage.* Each teaching artist invitation receives a student response, which teaching artists do, or in various ways do not, honor.

The ongoing sequence of teaching artist invitations and student responses is not unlike a partner-dancing situation. On the dance floor as in a classroom, a social contract is implicit: we are about to enter into a mutual give and take. In dancing, we arrive at a dance floor, and music begins to play; in a classroom or workshop space, we meet and an activity begins. A dancer invites their partner to dance; teaching artists begin activities with an invitation— modeling, prompting, posing a question. An invited partner accepts the invitation to dance, stands up and joins the inviter; a student responds to a teaching artist's invitation. Once the invitation is accepted in either realm, all partners have in effect made a promise to do the best partnering they can, to look out for one another, to be considerate.

The main difference in the two scenarios is status. Dancing partners are more or less equals on the dance floor. Teaching artists and students have very different sets of responsibilities in the classroom, which render them different and unequal. The teaching artist is responsible for designing and guiding the students' exploration and learning. So once a student joins the classroom dance of invitation and response, it is initially up to the teaching artist to be a responsive and sensitive partner, to know what it means to be such a partner under any and all conditions that may arise—to honor every response.

Each interested, supportive response you give will make the responding student, *as well as all the other students observing the interaction*, more interested in engaging with you. When the classroom community witnesses the teaching artist's care and precision with an invitation-accepting partner, they can imagine that their own trust in the teaching artist would be well-placed, their own risk-taking similarly rewarded, or at least protected. If, however, having accepted your invitation your student partner finds herself being ignored, or having her toes stepped on . . . imagine her frustration and confusion. When partners are observed being treated in this way, new volunteer partners will grow fewer and more reluctant. In a workshop, this reluctance can range from a subtle cooling of engagement to a painfully obvious checking out. This would be bad enough with a single student, but the whole class is affected by what they observe happening between the teaching artist and the invitation-accepting student. Responses to your invitations will also decrease if the invitational questions you pose are problematic (too specific, too vague, too easy, too hard), any of which indicate that you may be unreliable, or unpredictable, or inexperienced. Would you enjoy dancing with an unreliable or unpredictable or inexperienced dance partner? However: each question is a new invitation, and even if you get off on the wrong foot, each response a student gives is another chance to draw them into the work. Even a problematic question/response/follow-up sequence can turn on a dime and become a fabulous dance, if we have the tools to make it so.

Mastering the dance of inviting, responding, following up, and drawing out students' responses makes it possible for us to stay present with the moment-to-moment dynamics of each classroom and sustain a living exchange of experience and ideas. If, instead of honoring every response, we allow ourselves to fish for the answers we *really* want, or if we are disappointed in or disapproving of student's responses, they will know it immediately, and that knowledge will shape how they relate to us. Better to create a classroom community where students feel free to let fly with ideas and questions. Our honoring every response creates a safe space in which to do so, when students feel rewarded for accepting our invitations.

When we successfully establish this atmosphere of exchange, our dancing partners may grow bold enough to take the lead. When a student asks you a question, make the most of the opportunity. What your students *know* and *don't know* is inherent in their questions. This glimpse is full of potential. It is a measure of your students' trust in and comfort with you that they are willing to expose their own "not knowing." Their questioning is a creative act, a foray into what educational philosopher Maxine Greene refers to as "imagining the possible." Giving voice to that imagination puts the speaker in a vulnerable position. Questioning—yours or your students'—involves a temporary suspension of judgment, a willingness to remain undecided and curious, which is valuable in a world where forceful, decisive opinions often rule.

Your clarity of purpose (*honor every response, honor every response . . .*) matters. As you evaluate your own teaching, take yourself back to the workshop/dance floor, and ask yourself: *How consistently am I creating a safe space for dancing? What can I do to increase my ability to work with whatever moves my partners make? Do my actions match my intention to honor every response?*

Students on Strike

I was working at a school for students with language and learning challenges, basically as an adjunct who came in twice a week to teach a high school drama class. The students were engaged, but very lively. We had started a unit on oral interpretation with poetry. One day the students remained out in the courtyard instead of coming in for class. When I stepped out to invite them in, one of the more outspoken girls told me they weren't coming—they didn't like the poetry unit, so they were on strike. I told them to stop playing around, but they resisted. (Of course, the courtyard was just below the headmaster's office window; I imagined my days at that school were numbered). I explained that in strike situations, the workers always had demands for the management, and that they should come in to give me their demands. Unsure at first, they ultimately came inside. I gave them time to confer and give specific demands. When they did, I told them I could grant some but not all, so we should, as many do in such situations, submit to arbitration. We agreed to invite the high school principal in to mediate. Then I added in one more element, which the students embraced: each of us would play someone else during arbitration. The next day the principal came, and we began, with a student playing me (insensitive, unyielding), me playing a student (defiant, inattentive), and the rest of the students playing each other (with love and exaggeration). Through the improvisation, we came to a mutual understanding about how the class could move forward, and we had an absolute blast. It was wonderfully healing. The class resumed, stronger than before—and I kept the gig. My takeaway: *don't ignore what is really happening inside (or outside) the room: Respond.*—Barry Stewart Mann, actor, storyteller, educator, Atlanta, GA

The Art of the Follow-Up

There are these four ways of answering questions . . . There are questions that should be answered categorically (straightforwardly yes, no, this, that). There are questions that should be answered with an analytical (qualified) answer (defining or redefining the terms). There are questions that should be answered with a counter-question. There are questions that should be put aside.

—BUDDHA, in the Pañha Sutta

Spend an afternoon being a spy. Next time you are in a position to surreptitiously witness a conversation, perhaps in a Starbucks or on a bus, track the exchanges you hear there. Examine the flow of invitations, responses, counter-invitations, lures, dead ends, restarts, the rise and fall of each interlocutor's interest, and the overall sense of momentum. A teaching artist might be particularly interested in those conversations where one individual draws out another: interviews, press conferences, interrogations, verbal tests, classrooms, and workshops. As you spy, note which exchanges and strategies result in interlocutors opening up and giving voice to their ideas and opinions, and which make them pause or retreat. Often the interviewer's skill is evident not so much in their initial questions as in their follow-ups.

When teaching artists *follow up*, that is, respond to their students' observations and responses, it's as if they're a partner in a game of "keep the balloon in the air." The right tap back to the student, and the game continues: the student can keep responding. The wrong tap sends the balloon to the ground. When teaching artists follow up skillfully, inquiry comes to life and stays lively, students feel affirmed, and playfulness and improvisation rule: the balloon stays in the air.

How do teaching artists master the art of the follow-up? There's no official list of correct follow-ups to memorize. But in this section we'll consider the language and dynamics of eight common follow-ups that embody empathy and support our container:

waiting
drawing out
feeding the fire
knowing right from wrong
next times, mental post-it notes, and hold that thought
fielding the non-response response
resisting the expert (you)
redirecting the expert

FOLLOW-UP #1—WAITING

When you plunk a stone into a pond, you expect immediate ripples on the surface of the water. Plunk a question into the middle of a classroom and the immediate response will almost always be quiet, an apparent stillness. The stillness you observe after you pose a question can feel like a small eternity. Nearly every student response to a teaching artist's question begins with this silence. However it is anything but still. You are expectant, curious, ready for whatever response you might get, while wondering what that response might be. Your students are processing what you've just said, and processing takes time. Imagine the steps involved in responding. Each student first mentally replays the question. If they understand the terms and ideas involved, they formulate one or more responses, judging which response they prefer to give voice to. If they are eager, they'll have a hand up before they have quite figured out what they want to say, or may blurt out what they are thinking even as it forms. If they don't feel they understand the terms and ideas, students may rework the question, recasting it until it makes sense. Then they can formulate a response that they feel good about, or get discouraged and close down. Your students also may be trying to determine which answer you might prefer, and editing their response accordingly; pleasing the teacher is a strong motivator for some. Other students want their answer to be funny or clever. (That sometimes funny but mostly annoying kid who always has to twist every answer into something funny? That was me from kindergarten through high school. I have a high tolerance for this kind of kid now. I remember that for my part there was no malice in it, just a certain need for attention, a habitual questioning of authority, and a mind that was spinning a bit in search of intellectual gears to mesh with, needing to engage, as gears do). In all these cases, students are hard at work, and any physical stillness is the calm exterior of a busy interior.

Classroom teachers refer to the period of students' silence after a teacher's prompt as *wait time*. The truth is that in posing a question you have put yourself in a position where you must wait—all you can do, for a moment, is wait. Lecturers don't have to be concerned with this. If they pose a question, it is because they are about to answer it, or it was rhetorical in the first place. In that setting you, a member of the audience, aren't invited into a direct exchange. Your imagination is welcome, but not your participation. Lecturers don't have to create or maintain a container for inquiry or creativity, so their View is profoundly different from that of a teaching artist—in many ways diametrically opposed. When a teaching artist or classroom teacher poses a question (in particular an open question, one without a single correct answer—see "Use Open Questions" on page 77), they invite participation, something that can't or should not be forced . . . and so we wait.

You may hope you won't have to wait too long. Wouldn't a long wait time be a bad sign, an indication that you hadn't posed a good question, or for some reason you were not understood? Long wait times may make you feel like you have made some mistake, and that valuable time is passing while the class sits frozen. But even when it feels too long, wait time is worth the wait. You may or may not have posed a fabulous question. But in waiting you demonstrate your willingness to relinquish control over the interaction, to enter the process thoughtfully, as if to say: *Let's start here. If this makes sense, great. If not, I trust that you will let me know, and together we will figure out how to proceed. But I will not simply stick to a script. I am here to interact, and I am willing to wait for your response so that we can do so.* Without your willingness to wait, your invitation may have a hollow ring, as in *yes, I am inviting you to dance, but if you do not dance a certain way, with a certain rhythm* (within a certain amount of time) *and with certain moves* (actual content in your answer), *then your dance will not be welcome.* A particularly long wait time can signal your determination to have students be responsible for their own learning.

Some answers come quickly. All classes have a few shining stars that are ready to answer; if they are consistently successful, they become identified as leaders. Not only do they respond readily to prompts, but they often come to be seen by the classroom community, teachers included, as dependable answerers: *If you need a good answer to a question, ask one of these kids.* During wait time, less engaged students and students who are struggling to formulate a response may have learned to use wait time to hang back and wait for one of the more verbal students to respond. When we let this happen, we're not maintaining our container as well as we might. Students that have interesting, original things to say may be holding back, in which case we miss out on some of the divergent thinking that is happening right in front of us. And when students' answers all fall within predictable borders, we risk losing the community's sense of adventure.

The *I'll let someone else answer* dynamic develops even in high-functioning classes led by master teachers, but the teachers usually work against it, adding wait time, and calling directly on less verbal students when they don't volunteer (add "name tags for all students" to your list of planning session requests—you will not be sorry). A few classroom teachers don't even use raise-your-hand volunteering: everyone is on notice that they may be asked to give a response at any moment (sometimes supported by the use of equity sticks: an open jar of popsicle sticks, each inscribed with a student's name; teachers pull sticks from the jar at random when choosing students to ensure an equal chance of participation; there may be a second jar to hold the sticks of students who have already had a turn). If I find the class leaning on the more verbal students, I might thank the students who have been so active and ask them to keep thinking but stop volunteering for a while so that other students might feel an open space in which they can respond.

FOLLOW-UP #2—DRAWING OUT

Given appropriate wait time and some initial response from a student (we'll look at students' non-responses in Follow-Up #6), the most basic and general follow-up is to *draw out* a student's thinking. The root of the English word *educate* is the Greek *educare*, "to draw out." A teaching artist's drawing out their student's thinking involves empathy. We've all been students, and have been in the potentially vulnerable position of the less experienced individual. As lovers of learning, we have a natural sympathy for our students as they work to express ideas. We know that works of art touch our hearts and minds in ways that can be difficult to put into words. When students' attempts to cast what they notice into language fall short of being fully formed observations, gently draw them out. Hold a space for them in which they can make meaning. When they are moved, connect with what they are feeling. Students need to know that they are heard, even if they are not immediately understood. They are watching you not so much as a mirror, to reflect back to them the content of what they are saying, but to be reassured that they are on the right track, that there is substance in what they are saying, and that what they say matters to you. Our first job is to listen, to accept what is being offered as completely and graciously as we can. (And if you are not initially pleased with a student's response, in spite of your commitment to *honor every response*, some graciousness may need to be applied.)

Drawing out begins as we acknowledge our student's response verbally, or with a nod. Then we invite them to go deeper, be clearer, say more, with some version of *Can you tell me more about that?* Your curiosity about a student's response has to be genuine, or the students will immediately smell a rat. Keep eye contact with the student. Remember that your tone and facial expressions carry weight. You don't need to repeat what students say, especially if you want to encourage a classroom culture where speaking clearly and listening to other students as they speak is the norm. You don't need to praise an observation, unless you are genuinely moved to do so (and praising too broadly or too often sets a low bar, transforming you from a *warm demander* into a *warm puffball*). There is nothing negative about a teaching artist being interested and respectful regarding the student, while somewhat non-committal regarding the student's observation. Take time to consider what was offered, process it; doing so can be a model for students learning to evaluate ideas. This slight distance is not based on coolness, but on the recognition that a student's response has its own energy in the moment, and doesn't require enhancement. Your students' contributions can be valued for what they are. A discussion that gets its momentum from a teaching artist cheerleading every response will grow tiresome for everyone, first because it requires the teaching artist to pump everything up, which is exhausting, and second because the unspoken implication of doing so is that student's responses are not adequate all by themselves.

It may seem paradoxical, but we can honor responses for what they are *and* ask for more at the same time. Modified versions of our drawing-out invitation, with the *Hmm* indicating *I am still processing what you just said*, include:

> *Hmm, I think I know what you mean. Can you tell me more about that?*
> *I am so interested that you would say it that way . . . can you please tell me more?*
> *Wow, I never thought of that . . . can you please say more about that?*
> *Hmm, I think I know what you mean, but I need you to tell me a little more. What do you mean by . . .*

Drawing out gives the responding student time to think and articulate, more space in which to wonder. In our culture of snap judgments and stalwart opinions, this is a rare space to occupy. To the extent that a student's responses reflect the larger group's understanding and abilities, those responses can be used as an assessment tool: *This is what my students know or do not know at this moment.* With that in-the-moment information, you can modify your use of language, your choice of modality, or the sequence or duration of activity steps to stay in sync with students' immediate learning needs.

Moving a discussion forward may require a step backward, a *reconnection.* The word *connect* comes from a Latin root meaning *to bind.* The prefix *re-* comes into English via Latin and the Old French for *back to the original place, again.* To revive forward motion in an activity or discussion, we *reconnect* by making students aware of their own original experience and unexamined knowledge, *binding* it with their present awareness, a drawing-out in reverse. This is something we do naturally in the course of everyday conversation: if an exchange between friends falters on either side, we assume that something has been missed, and take a step back to find it. In a workshop or classroom, we similarly notice when something has been missed, because the community conversation falters. Teaching artists can help students pause and locate the missing link using one or two of these guided reflections:

Reconnect Follow-Ups

> *What did we do earlier that might help with this?*
> *What did we do earlier that connects with this?*
> *Where have you seen something like this before?*
> *Can you think of anything else that . . .*
> > *works like this?*
> > *looks or sounds like this?*
> > *reminds you of this?*
> *When in your life have you experienced something similar to this?*
> *What were we doing just before I asked you this question?*
> *Why do you think we have been (previous activity)?*
> *What is our goal?*

If you are in a healthy co-teaching situation, follow-ups may be a fruitful place to collaborate. Many classroom teachers are good at drawing out students' ideas. During planning sessions, or casually at the beginning or ending of class, invite your partner teacher to be an active part of discussions, and express your interest in making the most of their follow-up skills. Follow-up collaboration between classroom teachers and teaching artists during your workshop also makes it possible to connect student work in other classroom subjects and curriculum with the art-centered work.

FOLLOW-UP #3: FEEDING THE FIRE

When passion and interest start to manifest in your students' responses, follow up by feeding the fire. Share their enthusiasm. Jump aboard their train of thought, and invite the entire class along:

> *All right! Now you're getting hot. Can you keep going with that idea?*
> *I love that idea . . . what else could we do / could it be?*
>> *where else would that go?*
>> *then what would happen?*
>> *and then we could . . . (teaching artist models continuing the idea)*

One of the ways genuine engagement makes itself visible is laughter. A spontaneous outburst of laughter during a lesson is the result of attentiveness, and we want to notice and value our students' attention. Laughter tells us that we've touched upon a truth. It doesn't matter if the laughter is contained or free, silly, based in nervousness or fear, or born of delight—it is still a connected, gut response, and worthy of our appreciation. Enjoy the laughter along with your students, then follow up and feed the fire by asking them to meta-cognate, to think about their thinking:

> *We all just laughed. Why did we laugh?*

Your willingness to investigate laughter's visceral source will probably be rewarded. At the very least the classroom community will know that in welcoming laughter the container welcomes spontaneous expression. Your embracing and reflecting on serendipitous laughter may help your students make a connection with the work of art that might never have arisen according to a plan. Laughter puts you at ease, too. In her *Guardian Weekly* article "Learning with Laughter," Rose Senior notes that "Teachers can often pinpoint a particular moment when (their) class laughed spontaneously for the first time—often at quite a trivial event. When this happens the teacher relaxes, feels more confident—and is inspired to teach more imaginatively and enthusiastically."[4]

FOLLOW-UP #4: KNOWING RIGHT FROM WRONG

Students will say *it goes up* when something goes down. They'll refer to a saxophone during a solo piano piece. They'll say *high* but mean loud, or *quick* when they mean short. They will inevitably be technically inaccurate in their use of a term, or be factually inaccurate, or misuse arts-specific vocabulary. These responses can open up into teachable moments. The time it takes to follow up on this potential falls somewhere on a continuum between a quick fix and a deeper dive.

When you are pressed for time, opt for the quick fix: *Sorry, but we need to finish this before 10:30, so I'm going to* tell *you . . .* Every teaching artist does this once in a while, intervening in a learning process that wouldn't need intervention if given adequate time (although if you had an extremely rigorous constructivist approach, you might care less about time and the activity progressing or concluding, and more about your students' constructing meaning with less intervention from you, and allow their discovery and understanding to proceed at its own pace. Imagine Socrates saying "No, you've got it all wrong. I'm going to give you the correct response, so we can all go home.")

Sometime you may need a quick fix to be sure that everyone understands a key point before you can go on with an activity. This necessity puts wrongness in a different category altogether: the student's wrong-seeming response isn't wrong—it is a reflection of the teaching artists' not having yet clearly communicated an important idea. In intervening, the error you are correcting is your own, and you can say it that way:

> *Oh, I see . . . Sorry I didn't make this clear before: what we all have to understand is . . .*

Or when a term being *misunderstood* has the potential to wreak havoc with the learning process:

> *The thing that you are observing is correct—good job! But it's going to be important that we use a word for it that we all understand. We all have to agree on the word and what it means, or the whole class and I may end up confused. Sculptors (or dancers, or film-makers) call this . . .*

In this way, everyone gets some inside information, and becomes an initiate into discipline-specific art-speak. You won't need to walk on eggshells; your everyday social sensitivity is a good guide for how to redirect students. And as always your own comfort level (in this case with stepping in and clarifying meaning) sets the tone for students as they respond emotionally to being corrected.

When you have time, opt for the deeper dive. Treat wrong-seeming or inaccurate-seeming responses as invitations to further conversation and more careful attending, a somewhat awkward tap that calls on you to tap back and keep the balloon in the air. Unsupported thinking (a different kind of *wrong*) can also be approached in the same way. When your students make an observation but cannot support it with evidence, that's a teachable moment. Help them be more observant and articulate by drawing out their reasoning. If your students misuse a term, you have a chance to check in with the entire group's understanding of the term. Every wrong, fuzzy, or unsupported response opens up a path by which the teaching artist and student can approach a clearer or deeper understanding.

While correcting a student's use of language can have a cooling effect on discussion, declaring any honestly proffered response *wrong* puts a damper on everyone's willingness to risk speaking up. The whole class receives the message that there will be *right* answers and *wrong* ones in your container. The evidence of their senses tells them that if they'd prefer not be embarrassed, they should perhaps stay still and quiet unless they are certain they have the right answer. Instead of correcting your students, draw them out. Say *Yes*, or at least *OK*, to a student's answer, and then work from there, using all the follow-up techniques in your toolkit.

Finally, two response-correcting temptations to avoid. When teaching artists despair of getting the answer they want and start answering their own questions, students get the message that they don't need to respond, or take the risk of responding, because the expert teaching artist already knows the right answers and will fill in for them. When we ignore what one student offers and ask for other opinions in the hopes of getting a *better* answer, that is, an answer we'd prefer to work with, we pass up a teachable moment. I've given in to these temptations when I was tired or discouraged, and never felt good about the results. A positive-spirited quick fix or a confident deeper dive is always a better option.

FOLLOW-UP #5: NEXT TIMES, MENTAL STICKY NOTES, AND HOLD THAT THOUGHT

In the middle of workshop activities, students will come up with fabulous ideas. They'll unexpectedly ask a beautiful question, one that is worthy of its own inquiry and exploration. They'll extend what you are working on in an interesting, unexpected direction, saying *I know! Why don't we . . .* When the activity they suggest or the question they pose is in line with your inquiry, you have the option of folding it into what you are doing, or even embracing it as a new direction. But when an idea is a certain number of degrees away from the direction you are already committed to going, it falls outside of your Design. Resonance and depth notwithstanding, you may need to gently defer:

> *That is a fantastic idea/question. We could do an entire workshop on that idea/question all by itself, and that would be a lot of fun. But for today, I want us to stick with the direction we're already going. I hope we can explore your idea/question another time.*

When your intuition tells you that the activity at hand will soon answer or modify or otherwise affect the insightful student's idea, ask them to flag the idea with a mental sticky note. Doing so honors their idea and makes them responsible for their own process as they track their insight through the activity:

> *That is such a great question/idea that it makes me want to stop everything we are doing and try to figure it out. But instead, here is a mental sticky note: I'm going to ask that you remember your idea/question, keep it in mind, and at the end of the work we're doing please bring it back again, and we'll see if we have any new thoughts then.*

Sometimes an individual jumps two steps ahead of you with an appropriate, inquiry-centered insight, question, or idea. It's a sign that you are reaching them. They are not only motivated to go forward, but are already teaching themselves. Share their excitement, and praise their insight. If you sense that most of the students are ready to jump ahead, get some confirmation of that readiness and jump. But if the perspicacious one is alone in being out ahead of the crowd, bring them back to the activity at hand:

> *Fabulous—but hold that thought. You're about two steps ahead of me and I want to get all of us caught up. Please ask that question/say that idea again in about ten minutes. I might forget, but I want you to remind me.*

FOLLOW-UP #6: FIELDING THE NON-RESPONSE RESPONSE

You've just posed a wonderful open question, but for some reason your students seem to have nothing to say. The same three students who always raise their hands just raised their hands, but no one else is moving. You've allowed adequate wait time, you've restated the prompt, but the situation seems frozen. This non-response is still a response, and your students are communicating with you even in that moment, saying *This is where we are*. When this happens, what can a teaching artist do to get back into the flow? Classroom teachers use Turn and Talks to jump-start conversation by making a semi-private space where everyone can speak and be heard, and Read-Alouds give students clear models for responding. I've adapted these classroom teacher techniques (which might be structured into lessons for many different reasons) for teaching artists to use as follow-ups to non-response responses.

Turn and Talk

If students are reluctant to speak owing to some shyness or social pressure not to stand out, *Turn and Talks* are an easy way to open up classroom conversations. In a Turn and Talk, for a short time everyone in the community speaks, is heard, or both. It works in many different situations; as a warm-up, as a focusing activity during a journaling process, as a step before whole-class discussion to raise the quality of what is offered there, or as a closing reflection activity. I use it most often to up the energy level in the room and loosen everyone up when students have been sitting or quiet too long. Once you have a juicy open question, pose it as a Turn and Talk prompt:

Tell the person sitting next to you: Why do you think . . .

Encourage one or two minutes of person-to-person conversation: everyone talks. Some start more slowly, others jump in. Some students will not talk at all. You may want to quietly, personally draw them out, or not. Since it is meant to be a moment for students' free choice and free expression, unshaped by the teacher or teaching artist, I prefer to leave it alone. Students who don't talk will eavesdrop on other students' conversations. As soon as the discussion's overall volume starts to fade, or conversations digress, call students back to focus. Ask them to share what they heard or thought.

Some classroom teachers prefer a variation of Turn and Talk called Think-Pair-Share, which begins with a moment of silent reflection (Think), followed by a Turn and Talk (Pair), and ending with a whole group discussion highlighting what was shared by the pairs (Share).

Think-Aloud

When students aren't able to articulate what they notice, they may not understand or feel confident about how to respond. They'd like to respond, but are impeded by not having a model as to how to do so. In the Teachers College Readers' and Writers' Workshop Interactive Read-Alouds, classroom teachers read the text of a book, while students listen but usually do not follow along with the text visually. As she reads, the teacher models good reading habits, judiciously interrupting the flow of the text by giving voice to what are usually internal, personal reading-process comments:

I wonder if . . .
That reminds me of . . .
I predict . . .
I don't really understand . . .

Using this technique, the teacher can introduce texts that include more challenging concepts and language than students can read independently. Interactive reading aloud stimulates imagination and emotion, enriches vocabularies, and shows students how to question, visualize, and make predictions while they read. Teaching artists can adapt this classroom tool for artistic uses by thinking of the work of art as the text, and interactively

Think-Aloud Examples in Four Art Forms				
	Dance	Theater	Visual Art	Music
I love the...	... pattern of shapes that all the arms make.	... way the actor breathes during this section.	... way this appears to be real but at the same time is obviously not real.	... sound of that instrument that is going... (imitate instrument).
This is a great...	... gesture, makes me want to try it (perform the gesture).	... line, makes me want to quote it (perform the line).	... use of mass, makes me want to see if I could get a rock to do that (perform the gesture).	... rhythm, makes me want to move (move to the rhythm).
I wonder...	...if the choreographer is inspired by...	... how they co-ordinate the two sides of the stage when they...	... which of the layers was created first.	... how the composer decided on thirty-three variations.
I notice...	... a lot of eye contact.	... a lack of eye contact.	...the way the subject seems to be avoiding eye contact.	... the times the musicians look up and make eye contact.
This _______ reminds me of...	This twisting reminds me of a wisteria vine, the way the...	This suitcase joke reminds me of clowns at the circus, the way the...	This pile of backpacks reminds me of refugee children, the way the...	This quiet section reminds me of flowing water, the way the...

FIGURE 4.4 Think-Aloud Examples in Four Art Forms

"reading" it while students observe (Figure 4.4). I call it a Think-Aloud because you are not performing the text, as in the Read-Alouds. The main idea is to model good art-engagement habits in ways that students can imitate and eventually make their own. To Think Aloud, present a work of art (on prerecorded media) and model the noticing process, stopping and starting the recording as needed.

To help bring the practices you are modeling home, ask students to reflect on your Think-Aloud: *What kinds of things did I notice?* Help them notice details of your process. When they seem clear on the model, turn the process over to them with a new or related work of art. Many students and teachers are habitually passive listeners. Combat that passivity by stopping, starting, and repeating recorded materials. Focus on short examples, and praise attentiveness. And if your Think-Alouds include questions you personally have about the work of art (*I have no idea . . ., I really don't understand . . .*), you become a co-learner in your students' eyes.

When All Else Fails

What if your excerpts are well-prepared, Turn and Talks and Think-Alouds attempted, and you are still having a hard time engaging students in observation and discussion? You may have landed in (or taken part in creating) a classroom culture that doesn't allow for unfettered noticing. The boundaries you have established for acceptable behavior and expression may not leave room for open questions. Even in a safe container, *What do you notice?* might evoke some concerns unintended by the teaching artist in a student's mind: *I think I notice . . . Am I right? What happens if I am wrong? Is this what the teaching artist wants me to notice? What if I use the wrong word?*

When you aren't sure what to do next, simply start over. Do some transparent partnering with the classroom teacher, explaining your concerns about your own effectiveness and eliciting her help: *Ms. Walsh, I'd like to hear more from students about this work, to know what they are thinking and noticing—but I am not getting very many responses. What should we do differently?*

You can also tell your students that you mean for them to have fun and experiment with noticing, and that you will support what they say and help them articulate it if they aren't sure how. And finally if that doesn't work, give up the reins and ask a student to lead the discussion, or give up the need for an open discussion that day and use the day to help students develop the habit of articulating their responses: ask each individual to write their responses on paper (super-safe, even if they grumble about having to write) before possibly sharing them with each other privately, Turn and Talk style.

FOLLOW-UP #7: RESISTING THE EXPERT (YOU)

At some point in your follow-ups, it is going to seem compelling and expedient to launch into a brief but erudite lecture that will make all things clear for your students, inspiring them and cheering them on to greater heights of artistry and achievement. When this temptation arises, remember the emphasis that your View places on Making & Doing, and that you are facilitating a community of learners, not an undergraduate lecture hall. Ask yourself, *As a learner, do I prefer being provided a model and time and space to actively explore an idea, or absorbing a set of spoken facts for use at some later time?* Remember the kind of inquiry-driven engagement you are trying to cultivate, and your faith that Making & Doing are more effective than telling. Instead of telling, help your students to be curious by being openly curious yourself.

The San Francisco–based, poetry-inspired Youth Speaks program has a Creative Youth Development approach that emphasizes student empowerment and control over their own learning. Their published methodology decries the effects of traditional expert-centric leadership which renders students, at best, passive recipients of an education: *Traditional classroom settings embody a narrative-like character where little decision-making relies on the concerns and perspectives of students in the class. Even in a "democratic" class setting, youth may not always feel comfortable exercising their right to speak up or be heard, especially when giving voice to thoughts, ideas, or beliefs that are unpopular. This may leave students feeling alienated and/or discouraged from participating in class.*[5]

Or, to play devil's advocate: in a world of limited time and resources, which ideas are best laid out in down-and-dirty lecture fashion, in order to allow more time for modeling and inquiry? If you are sure that a brief talk will move the inquiry forward, it may be just the thing. Experiment. The only way you'll know when to put on (or shun) the professor's hat is by trying it on every so often and watching the results.

FOLLOW-UP #8: REDIRECTING THE EXPERT

Many workshops include an unofficial resident expert, someone who has genuine knowledge of your subject or materials. They'll raise their hand every time, often give accurate, even insightful answers, and use arts-specific vocabulary with some degree of precision. Leaning on these experts to answer your questions may be tempting. It is especially tempting to resort to these shining stars when discussion is flagging and you feel discouraged, or when observers are present (especially funders) and you want the class to appear in its best light. If the resident expert answers too many questions, the other students may naturally begin to defer to them, relaxing into a passive mode where the teaching artist and the expert student will do all the work and have all the fun while they, self-demoted, sit by and watch.

How can you balance your desire to honor your expert's prior knowledge with your desire to include the entire class on an equal footing? Remembering your intention to *honor every response*, employ some genuine collegial sympathy between the expert student and yourself. If the expert is burning to answer every question, try:

> *Fantine, you've been great about answering questions and I love your enthusiasm, but I also want to hear from some other students, so hand down for a little while, please.*

Fantine will either lay out for a while, or she'll lay out completely and need to be specifically invited back into the action. Being clear with her is worth the effort; a teaching artist's careful handling of a student's feeling helps put all the students at ease: *Here is someone who is respectful and gentle, someone I can trust.* Alternatively, push *pause*:

Fantine, I love it that you are so accomplished at the piano, and that you have so much to share. But for right now I'm going to push the pause button and ask you to please think all your answers, but don't say them out loud.

You might want to engage with the expert's observations directly. Chances are that the expert student will use an arts-specific term. Whether the usage is correct or incorrect, the arrival of an unknown word becomes a teachable moment. Music plays, then . . .

TA: What do you notice about this music?
EXPERT STUDENT: Those notes are all staccato.
OTHER STUDENTS: Huh?

As a teaching artist, you know that *staccato* is Italian for a type of notated articulation that in performance shortens a written note value. Add a *staccato* mark (it looks like a small dot directly above the note head) to a note that is one beat long, and the attentive performer will play a note that is somewhat shorter than one full beat; the sonic effect is that the *staccato* note is detached from the next note (the opposite of *legato*, or connected). When this technical term is used by your expert student, you might choose to take everyone directly back to the music, to listen again and try to identify and describe, together, the quality that the expert student is naming. Or you can detour into the word itself (its Italian origin, what the musically notated mark looks like, what it is meant to denote), then go back to the music with new, more informed ears. Including both approaches and making the most of the teachable moment might look something like this:

EXPERT STUDENT: Those notes are all staccato.
TA: Hmm . . . what do you mean by *staccato*?
EXPERT STUDENT: An articulation that makes a note sound short. *(more or less correct)*
TA: Right—staccato is an Italian word that means short. *(for correct)*

- **or** -

EXPERT STUDENT: It's a kind of a loud note. *(incorrect)*
TA: It might be loud, but staccato is an Italian word that means short. *(for incorrect)*

Once the term is defined, make it experiential by demonstrating detached sounds:

TA: Now – I – am – do – ing – sta – cat – to – sounds. Do it with me please, and lets make our hands follow our voice.

ALL *(using choppy, detached gestures)*:
Now – I – am – do – ing – sta – cca – to – sounds.
TA: Staccato is the *opposite* of legato, and Italian word that means connected.

(speaking or singing in a smooth, connected manner)

Nowwwww Iiiiiiiiiiii ammmmmm dooooooo innnnnng leeeeee gaaaaaa toooooo.

Do it with me please, and lets make our hands follow our voice.

ALL *(doing smooth gestures)*:

Nowwwww Iiiiiiii ammmmmm dooooo innnnnng leeeee gaaaa tooooo.
(An optional digression: *In fact, the* marks *that musicians put on the music-paper pages look just like your gestures: little short dots for staccato, and long smooth lines for legato*—which the teaching artist draws and demonstrates.)

TA: So *staccato* and *legato* are two Italian words that musicians sometimes use to describe short disconnected notes or smooth connected notes. Who can show me the difference between staccato and legato? Who can go back and forth between legato and staccato notes? Now lets go back to the music and see where we can hear any *staccato* or *legato* sounds.

That degree of attention may have an appropriate, gently cooling effect on the student expert, who might think *if all my answers are going to receive this kind of scrutiny, I'd better be sure of what I'm saying*. For an expert who is bold, your attention acts as a higher bar, a call for their best work. In the eyes of the students observing the interaction, the expert is held to a higher standard, which levels the playing field. The presence of the expert raises the bar for the teaching artist, too, calling for greater sensitivity to the diversity of the prior knowledge in the room.

Thriving and Struggling

After the junior high school students tumbled out, Ms. Baxter unexpectedly stayed behind and faced me. We'd never spoken before, but I could tell she had something to say, and was hesitant to begin. The room was quiet, at rest between two workshops. Ms. Baxter had observed the session that had just ended, which had been an almost complete failure. Only three out of twenty-five students had been prepared to rap their rhyming couplets on camera to document many weeks of work. At one point, more curious than anything else, I had told them "I feel responsible that you are not ready to do this today. Please tell me: what could I have done differently so that you would have been prepared?" But they had not had an answer, at least not one they wanted to tell me in that moment. The classroom teacher (not Ms. Baxter—she had been observing) did have some answers, and I already had some ideas of my own, but I was more interested in how the kids would analyze their process, which at that point looked like a *failed* process. And here was Ms. Baxter, who said, "You didn't do anything wrong. It's a lovely program. These activities are fun. But the things you are asking these children to do . . . it's not that they *won't* do them. They *can't* do them." Yes, she said, she believed all children should have access to the arts. But she did not think that all of them were ready to *make art*, and she wanted me to know that it was absolutely not my fault when they could not. I thanked Ms. Baxter, and told her I was glad to have her advice. But I'm still working on what went wrong in that residency. And I know the responsibility is mine.

Our students don't always participate. They can't always absorb and embrace the experiences we offer in the container. They avoid eye contact, respond slowly or not at all, hang back from activities and conversations. As the Designers and keepers of the container, responsible for everything that happens there, how should we respond when our students aren't doing as well as they might? Throughout *A Teaching Artists' Companion*, we've looked at our practice from a teaching artist's perspective. Let's now examine the continuum of students' experience from their perspective. *What do our students experience when they thrive? What are they going through when they struggle?*

In the song "What Keeps Mankind Alive?" from *The Threepenny Opera*, composer Bertolt Brecht and librettist Kurt Weill tell us that basic human needs necessarily take precedence over anything philosophical: *Food is the first thing—morals follow on.* Similarly, psychologist Abraham Maslow's Hierarchy of Needs (Figure 4.5) outlines his theory that psychological health (self-actualization, self-fulfillment) is predicated on basic human needs being fulfilled. You may remember this chart from the psychology course you took in high school or undergrad.

In Maslow's schematic, *physiological* needs are foundational, and necessarily come first: air, food, water, shelter, sleep. *Safety needs* are next, an individual's sense that the environment is physically and psychologically

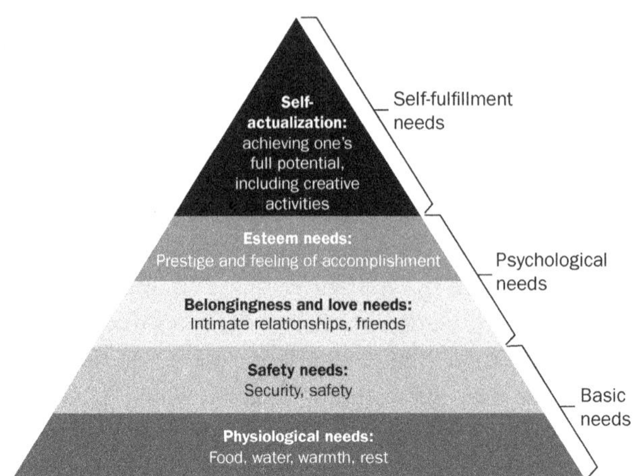

FIGURE 4.5 Maslow's Hierarchy of Needs

secure. Satisfying these basic needs makes *Belongingness and Love, Esteem,* and *Self-actualization* possible. Maslow's theory is sometimes criticized for lacking scientific grounding, and you may differ with his labeling or ordering of the upper three-fifths of the hierarchy, but his basic observation makes good common sense; few of us are at our best when we are cold, tired, hungry, or afraid.

Who might be responsible for a student's needs being met at each of Maslow's five levels in a teaching and learning situation? Teaching artists depend on the students themselves, their families, and our institutional partners (schools and arts presenters) to make sure students' basic needs are met: food, shelter, and rest, Maslow's Level One. Schools, we assume, provide students with a safe, clean, well-lit, ventilated space, kept at reasonable temperature, Level Two. If family and school community conditions are healthy, students are already experiencing belongingness, love, and esteem, Levels Three and Four. And whether or not those needs are met, there is every reason to continue providing for them within our workshops; who ever suffers from too much belongingness, love, and esteem? Self-fulfilling *creative activities* appear at the apex of the pyramid, Level Five. Most of a teaching artist's work would appear to come under that definition, making our main area of responsibility *creative activities,* with a good measure of *belongingness, love, and esteem.* Some of our work also addresses Level Two's *safety;* learners need a safe container in order to take creative risks. A fair distribution of materials (enough for all participants), and equal opportunities for everyone to create and respond appeal to participants' sense of fairness—a good place to start. We also establish a safe container more subtly, with our choice of words, tone, and eye contact, and more subtly still as students relate with our energy, honesty, openness and the personal connection we offer. Our responsibilities range almost all the way up and down the Hierarchy of Needs. But we don't do any of it alone. Those Level Five *creative activities* that are our main focus are only possible when they are supported by the entire community (students, their families, schools, arts presenters) working in consort to meet student's more basic needs. It really does take a village.

Nourishment

We were a collective of young and inexperienced teaching artists, presenting a series of after-school creative workshops on Fridays. The students' energy was all over the place, their attention scattered, and the program wasn't going well. We tried making our end-of-the-week presentations more energetic and engaging, but nothing worked. Then we went on a retreat day for students and teaching artists. The retreat center provided frequent healthy snacks to keep everyone, kids and adults, sustained through a long day. Aha! Everyone benefitted from first having a snack, a cup of water or juice, and a chance to socialize before entering into a focused creative space. We realized our after-school workshops needed to be preceded by a half hour snack and informal social time, a chance for kids to breathe and for energy to gather. It worked. Now we make sure to offer healthy snacks so the kids are not doing a lot of sugar but are getting some real sustenance, a practice that has become part of the culture of Community MusicWorks. Most students talk about food as a central part of their CMW experience. When we have family performance activities, student retreats, or our weekly "All Play Day," there's always food that helps to center us and prepare us for an engaged learning experience. Students feel our respect and care for them, and then offer it back once the program begins. My takeaway: *Learners are not in a learning mindset until their whole being is prepared to be.*—Sebastian Ruth, founder and artistic director, Community MusicWorks, Providence RI.

WHAT THRIVING LOOKS LIKE

You already have an informed opinion as to what students' *thriving* in your workshops looks like. Make a quick list of the *verbs* of thriving: *I know students are doing well when I see them . . .* See how your verb list stacks up against these three influential perspectives in list form (Figure 4.6), the Project Zero Studio Thinking Framework, Kallick and Costa's Habits of Mind, and the Lincoln Center Education Learning Framework.

The particular benefits associated with arts education started to attract serious examination in 1967, when philosopher Nelson Goodman founded Project Zero at the Harvard Graduate School of Education (at a time when "zero," aka nothing, had yet been firmly established in their field of research). In their Studio Thinking Framework[6], Project Zero investigators used the following verb-headings to organize their observations of students at work in Arts-in-Education settings. Teaching artists might use this as a checklist for "what students' thriving looks like":

Studio Thinking Framework (aka Eight Studio Habits of Mind)

Develop Craft—Learning to use and care for tools and materials; learning artistic conventions (e.g., perspective, color mixing).

Engage and Persist—Learning to embrace problems of relevance within the art world and/or of personal importance, to develop focus and other mental states conducive to working and persevering at art tasks.

Envision—Learning to picture mentally what cannot be directly observed and imagine possible next steps in making a piece.

Express—Learning to create works that convey an idea, a feeling, or a personal meaning.

Observe—Learning to attend to visual contexts more closely than ordinary "looking" requires, and thereby to see things that otherwise might not be seen.

Reflect, Question, and Explain—Learning to think and talk with others about an aspect of one's work or working process.

Stretch and Explore—Learning to reach beyond one's capacities, to explore playfully without a preconceived plan, and to embrace the opportunity to learn from mistakes and accidents.

Understand the Art World—Learning about art history and current practice; learning to interact as an artist with other artists and within the broader society.

In a related project, the Institute for Habits of Mind founders Arthur Costa and Bena Kallick asked themselves *What behaviors are indicative of the efficient, effective problem solver? Just what do human beings do when they behave intelligently?* They identified a set of sixteen problem-solving skills necessary for human beings "to effectively operate in society and promote strategic reasoning, insightfulness, perseverance, creativity, and craftsmanship." The authors do not make an explicit connection with arts education, and their work isn't documented with the academic rigor that Project Zero work is. But the headings in Costa and Kallick's 2002 *Habits of Mind*[7] (full explanations are available on the Habits of Mind Institute website) read like an alternate version of the Project Zero list, with the addition of resonant modifiers: *empathy, precision, wonderment, awe* (Figure 4.6).

Most recently, Lincoln Center Education has articulated the benefits of teaching-artist-led programs under the banner of "Think Like an Artist." The teaching branch of the Lincoln Center consortium of arts presenters, LCE promotes students' "Developing Skills of Imagination, Creativity, and Innovation," more specifically broken out into their *Capacities for Imaginative Learning*, recently renamed as their *Learning Framework*. This inspiring set of possibilities makes an excellent entrée into LCE's approach to aesthetic education. You might use this framework when explaining the potentials of arts-based learning to a parent association, or a classroom teacher professional development. I use them to remind myself of our broadest goals.

Lincoln Center Education's Learning Framework

Noticing Deeply—to identify and articulate layers of detail in a work of art or other object of study through continuous interaction with it over time.

Embodying—to experience a work of art or other object of study through your senses, as well as emotionally, and also to physically represent that experience.

Questioning—to ask questions throughout your explorations that further your own learning; to ask the question, "What if?"

Making Connections—to connect what you notice and the patterns you see to your prior knowledge and experiences, to others' knowledge and experiences, and to text and multimedia resources.

Identifying Patterns—to find relationships among the details that you notice, group them, and recognize patterns.

Exhibiting Empathy—to respect the diverse perspectives of others in the community; to understand the experiences of others emotionally, as well as intellectually.

Living with Ambiguity—to understand that issues have more than one interpretation, that not all problems have immediate or clear-cut solutions, and to be patient while a resolution becomes clear.

Creating Meaning—to create your own interpretations based on the previous capacities, see these in the light of others in the community, create a synthesis, and express it in your own voice.

Taking Action—to try out new ideas, behaviors, or situations in ways that are neither too easy nor too dangerous or difficult, based on the synthesis of what you have learned in your explorations.

Reflecting/Assessing—to look back on your learning, continually assess what you have learned, assess/identify what challenges remain, and assess/identify what further learning needs to happen. This occurs not only at the end of a learning experience, but is part of what happens throughout that experience. It is also not the end of your learning; it is part of beginning to learn something else.[8]

These three lists share a number of ideas and terms, for example Project Zero's *Observe*, Costa and Kallick's *Gathering Data Through All Sense*, and LCE's *Notice Deeply*. But Project Zero and Costa and Kallick are defining students' experience (Engage and Persist; Persisting; Question and Explain; Questioning and Posing Problems), while Lincoln Center Education speaks from an Arts-in-Education point of view. Lincoln Center also distills the verbs of our work (Embody, Pose, Identify . . .) as they are enacted by teaching artist and students together, as in *Together, we notice deeply; together we make connections.*

Studio Thinking Framework (Harvard Project Zero)	Habits of Mind (Kallick and Costa)	Learning Framework (Lincoln Center Education)
Develop Craft Engage & Persist Envision Express Observe Reflect Stretch & Explore Understand Art World	Persisting Managing Impulsivity Listening to Others with Understanding and Empathy Thinking Flexibly Thinking About Our Thinking Striving for Accuracy and Precision Questioning and Posing Problems Applying Past Knowledge to New Situations Thinking and Communicating with Clarity and Precision Gathering Data Through All Senses Creating, Imagining, and Innovating Responding with Wonderment and Awe Taking Responsible Risks Finding Humor Thinking Interdependently Learning Continuously	Notice Deeply Embody Pose Questions Identify Patterns Make Connections Empathize Live with Ambiguity Create Meaning Take Action Reflect/Assess

FIGURE 4.6 Evidence of thriving (three published perspectives); Lincoln Center Education's Learning Framework provided courtesy of Lincoln Center for the Performing Arts, Inc. Copyright 2017

Except that sometimes we don't work well together, and students don't notice, or empathize, or make connections, or even engage with workshop activities. They might very much want to engage, but in some moments, instead of thriving, students struggle.

THE NATURE OF STRUGGLING

In the workaday teaching artist world, we're asked to serve students whose basic needs for health, safety, belonging, and esteem remain unfulfilled (see Maslow's Hierarchy, page 168). We need to be able to differentiate between and respond appropriately to different types of struggling, from simple classroom management issues (transitions, equity, physical environment) to special needs and trauma-related behaviors. Let's begin in this section with the simpler problems—how we define disruptions, and what we do about them—and work our way toward the effects of trauma and social toxicity on students. In a later section, "Special Needs and Special Education," we'll add a working definition of disability to our View, and some essential strategies for working with students with disabilities to our Design and Respond toolkits.

"Classroom management" refers to the ways classroom teachers a) set up and maintain safe space in their classrooms as they move students through various invitations, tasks, and transitions, and b) how they work with the confusion and diversions that arise as they do. For teachers, classroom management is an accepted part of their professional craft, with its own developmentally appropriate techniques. Teachers share tips, study, and attend professional development to improve their classroom management skills. Management is considered essential and positive in schools, much as it is in the corporate world, where management can be as sensitive and artistic as the person who is managing, helping teams and individuals do their best work.

The number one most requested professional development training requested by teaching artists is classroom management. But for many teaching artists, the word "management" has some unsavory resonances, as though students were worker bees or employees, entities to be controlled. It may be difficult to reconcile a top-down/management frame of reference with our creative and community-centered work. In their "14 Ideas About Classroom Management" (from *Teaching Artist Handbook*, Vol. 1), Jaffe, Barniskis, and Cox even suggest that teaching artists . . . "Consider never using the term 'classroom management.' . . . Ninety percent of a good learning and teaching environment has to do with curriculum . . . that if you have something real to teach, some clarity about what it is and how to teach it, and some genuine enthusiasm about it, students will almost always respond and engage with the work. If any of these things are lacking, engaging students will inevitably be difficult."[9] At the same time, what might be labeled behavior issues will come up in every teaching artist's practice, so it makes sense for us to learn how to work with disruptions in our containers. Of course we cannot *control* what happens in the container. But it falls to us to Respond in a manner that serves the integrity of the community, every moment, every time. That includes having clear boundaries, and when needed quite firm, inflexible boundaries. There should be certain things that are not permitted because they threaten the nature of the container. This honors and protects all participants.

As you manage your classroom/container, you might find yourself resorting to old models of management that you might have learned in school (how your sixth grade math teacher kept order), or trying to work it all out in the heat of the moment (not all of us are gifted in this way, and with emotionally disturbed students it is not even appropriate to do so). Instead, prepare for the moment by interrogating your View of disruption and control.

1) *What is your definition of "disruption"?* Is it noise? Rustling about? Talking and whispering? Whatever it is, make sure that what seems disruptive is not simply an expression of the natural energy of your container. Noise might be the result of impassioned work; whispered conversations may result from students' inability to control their excitement as to what is developing in the moment, or the work they are about to do. Are students not paying attention? Students are always paying attention to something . . . but perhaps not to what you want them to in a given moment. Often students are so determined to complete a task well that they have difficulty stopping work and attending to anything else. The noise and movement you pick up on your radar during an activity or transition may be excess energy left over from the last thing you did. If the disruption is this kind of natural byproduct of process, you might be able to enjoy it as such, and let it ride. In some cases, talking or even outright strife may be indicating a teachable moment, something you want to draw attention to and work with: if one set of collaborators is having difficulty negotiating the nature of their partnership, odds are that others are too. Taking the time to help them define their problem and making the negotiation public may benefit everyone in the room. Squeaky wheels get the grease for a reason: they need it, or they wouldn't squeak.

2) *How pronounced or prolonged does a disruption need to be before you address it? Do you address it privately, or more publicly?* Most disruptions are short-lived, and simply fade out. But you don't have to wait for them to do so. If a behavior seems out of place, eye contact or a raised eyebrow can gently say "Hi, I see you, and I know you see me seeing you—is everything OK?" In the right tone, more publicly clarifying instructions can communicate a similar concern without seeming punitive, as in "Please remember that we're making shapes wordlessly, deciding what to do without talking." In all cases, the right tone is an aspect of the community you have already established, as well as an expression of who you are. You don't have to construct an alternate voice and persona to be a teaching artist. Instead, be your genuine self, and cultivate a community where every act (even a classroom-management-style behavioral tweak) is understood to be a supportive, nurturing act. Do your best to maintain a panoramic awareness, taking in *everything*. Your constant attentiveness has a profound effect on the way your guidance will be received. And the genuineness of your Response to what you notice can't be faked. Students can and will on some level perceive your clarity of purpose as well as the quality of the connection between your intention (your View and Design) and your actions in the classroom (how

you Respond), so when you are able to notice and Respond in a consistently clear and supportive manner, your container knows it, and hums with a wholesome sense of security.

3) *Are your own instructions contributing to the disruption, or have you yourself caused the problem, and if so, can you reverse course and provide a remedy?* This question is meant to shift your frame of reference away from the idea of *disruption* per se and toward clarifying your role as the Designer and keeper of the container. Are students struggling, and is that struggle a disruption? If their struggles are part of an unfamiliar process (students making practical, material, and aesthetic choices), help students embrace the experience, give them room to work, and some warm support. If disruptive struggles are the result of a Design problem (not enough time allotted to accomplish a task; too many choices; unclear modeling) or a problematic View (*I believe that all students benefit from using a strict classical technique*), then it's back to the drawing board, perhaps even in the moment. In all those cases, what might have been seen as a disruption is really a call to attention that you can welcome and act on.

Struggle and a certain amount of confusion and uncertainty is inevitable in any creative workshop. Here I'm talking about the challenges involved in any artist's Making & Doing. Teaching artists bring their (hopefully) calm acceptance of these predictable problems with them into the classroom. We can reassure our struggling students that their travails are a normal, healthy part of the art-making process. Normal, healthy, and more: Paul Tough documents the necessity of certain adversities in child development in *How Children Succeed: Grit, Curiosity, and the Hidden Power of Character*, where he compellingly claims that "What matters most in a child's development . . . is not how much information we can stuff into her brain in the first few years. What matters, instead, is whether we are able to help her develop a very different set of qualities, a list that includes persistence, self-control, curiosity, conscientiousness, grit, and self-confidence."[10]

You may hear a strong echo of the Project Zero, Costa and Kallick, and Lincoln Center Education lists of the student experiences associated with Arts-in-Education in Tough's assertion. Wendell Barry reminds us of the value of struggling with impediments in his poem "The Real Work":

> *It may be that when we no longer know what to do*
> *we have come to our real work,*
> *and that when we no longer know which way to go*
> *we have come to our real journey.*
> *The mind that is not baffled is not employed.*
> *The impeded stream is the one that sings.*[11]

But sometimes the impediments are overwhelming, and make engagement or even a positive response to an invitation difficult. When our students' struggles are rooted in trauma, grit alone isn't an antidote. The Substance Abuse and Mental Health Services Association (SAMHSA) explains trauma as the result of "an event, series of events, or set of circumstances that is experienced by an individual as physically or emotionally harmful or life threatening and that has lasting adverse effects on the individual's functioning and mental, physical, social, emotional, or spiritual well-being." In their book "Life After Trauma—A Workbook for Healing," Dena Rosenbloom, Mary Beth Williams, and Barbara E. Watkins identify "five basic needs often disrupted by trauma," an alternate take on Maslow's Hierarchy (page 168) that more intimately brings us to a traumatized person's point of view (Figure 4.7).

In this schematic, *Safety* for yourself and others is foundational, "the feeling that you/your loved ones are reasonably protected from harm inflicted by yourself, by others, or by the environment." *Trust* in yourself and others comes next, "the ability to rely on your own judgment and on the support of others," followed by *Control* (of yourself and others: the feeling that you are charge of your own actions and can impact others), *Intimacy* (with yourself and others: The ability to know and accept your own feelings and thoughts, and to be known and accepted by others) and at the apex *Esteem* (for yourself and others: The ability to value what you feel, think, and believe, and to value the same in others.)[12]

Students whose lives are disrupted by trauma may be experiencing emotions of fear, insecurity, loss, anxiety, stress, or hopelessness. James Garbarino, author of *Raising Children in a Socially Toxic Environment*, identifies these negative states as a *social toxicity* that arises from social inequality:

> *Social toxicity refers to the extent to which the social environment in which families develop and operate is poisonous, in the sense that it contains serious threats to the development of identity, competence, moral reasoning, trust, hope, and the other features of personality and ideology that make for*

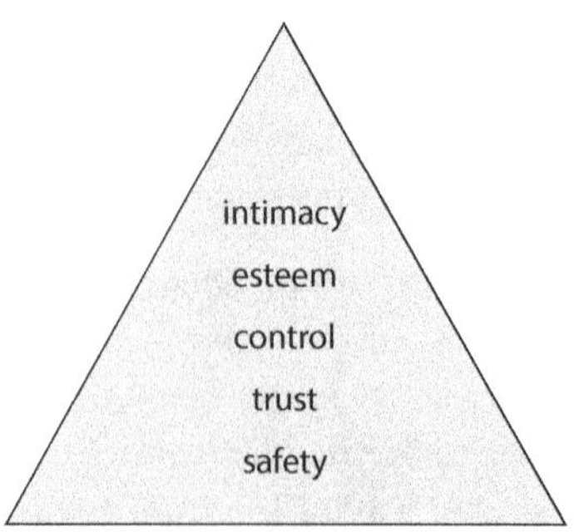

FIGURE 4.7 Rosenbloom, Williams and Watson's five basic needs often disrupted by trauma

success in school, family, work, and the community. Like physical toxicity, it can be fatal—in the forms of suicide, homicide, drug-related, and other life style-related preventable deaths. But mostly it results in diminished "humanity" in the lives of children and youth by virtue of leading them to live in a state of degradation, whether they know it or not.[13]

Author and activist Shawn Ginwright urges educators to combat social toxicity by "creating spaces that relentlessly foster hope" so that all participants can "imagine a different future." Hopelessness expresses itself in violent behavior, fatalism, and depression. Ginwright calls us to detoxify toxic environments with hope, which takes root as courageous educators develop loving personally and politically empowering relationships with students. He explains that we the educators have to be whole and healthy to begin with if we are to accomplish this; our ability to heal ourselves and be happy directly effects our ability to help our students heal and be healthy. See his book *Hope and Healing in Urban Education* for more on "how social change can be enacted from within to restore a sense of hope to besieged communities and counteract the effects of poverty, violence, and hopelessness."[14]

If you identify your teaching artistry with working for social justice, then your work is already directly addressing some of the roots of social toxicity. While you give of yourself in this pursuit, recognize that there are practical limits to what you can address in the classroom. When you have the sense that a child is struggling in a manner that is beyond your expertise or your ability to immediately address, ask for help. Teachers and facility staff know the students' and participants situations and needs. Let them know what you are seeing, and what concerns you. Their insight into students' daily difficulties and the presence of (or lack of) positive support systems can be your source for insight into individual students' needs. There are limits to what they can share with you, rules that govern confidentiality (for example only certified teachers can be privy to family matters, diagnoses, and evaluations, including a student's IEP, Individualized Education Program). But the information that can be shared, and the mutually supportive relationships you cultivate with the teachers, staff, and caregivers who share it with you, is essential if you are to respond to your students' special needs in an effective way.

A Personal Invitation

A diverse class of ninth graders at an urban school was developing scenes based on oral histories as part of a project to create a play about neighborhoods in the city. This class was focused on a neighborhood several miles down the road, but worlds away—an upscale area known for theaters, bookstores, and a vibrant LGBT community. Regina was an African-American girl who was all attitude. After several days of her refusing to join in warm-ups or pick up a pencil to write, and many dismissive utterances, I asked her to join me in the hall. She likely expected a dressing down. Instead, I told her, "You understand this stuff. Drama is about people getting what they want from each other. From the first day of this project, you've been pressing all our buttons. You're making my job hard. I can make sure you get a low grade, and send you to the office and all that. But you could be a leader here." She smiled in spite of herself. "You understand how people's minds and feelings work. This is easy for you. You might as well put a little work in and get credit for it. Think about it." Then I sent her back in. She didn't become an obvious leader, but from then on she joined in warm-ups, contributed to discussions, and stopped disrupting. My takeaway: *meet each student where she is.*—Barry Stewart Mann, actor, storyteller, educator, Atlanta, GA

Culturally Responsive

Early on in my career, as a white male working in the juvenile justice system, I came to understand that my mere presence (representing two oppressor patterns immediately, white and male) might cause more harm than good. If I wasn't willing to be reflective of this contradiction, I had no business in these settings. I chose to walk in that contradiction and remain steadfast in acknowledging and overcoming where I messed up. This kind of choice is at the core of what it means to be culturally and linguistically responsive. Being responsive does not mean checking things off a to-do list in your classroom. It is really about the stance you take; a perspective shift. It's not just about unpacking bias and privilege; it's about moving from empathy models to solidarity. Empathy just makes someone feel better about themselves, where solidarity is the action of effecting change in the world. This kind of transformation takes time, but the that fact that it takes time does not deny its urgency. Every single time we gather in learning environments we are creating a new culture. We should make sure that no one has to give up any of their past, present, or future cultures to take part in these new cultures we are co-creating. My takeaway: *We are always smarter together. What separates us keeps us fragile.*—Derek Fenner, poetry, Hayward, CA

5

Four View, Design, and Respond Based Arts-in-Education Programs

What exactly is a *curriculum*?

You'll find that the terms used to describe the components and structures of teaching artist-led projects have yet to be standardized. Arts in Education programs are differentiated by their unique titles. But within the programs, program managers and artist-educators seem to use any number of words interchangeably. A teaching artist–led project within a school-based program is commonly called a *unit of study* (for Preparation workshops) or *residency* (for Studio workshops). Then again, residencies can be organized into units of study, and a teaching artist facilitating a unit of study may be said to be in residency. Our field's use of the terms *inquiry, big idea, overarching theme, aim, learning arc, essential questions, scaffold, blueprint,* and *learning outcomes* makes them seem almost equivalent. *Modality, frame,* and *window* all have multiple possible meanings in our work. The most common terms that are used by artists and institutions to describe and define the way teaching artist work is organized are listed here, along with their most commonly used meanings:

activity	a classroom interaction involving making, doing, or reflecting
exercise	an activity
workshop	a session
session	a workshop
class	a workshop or session
lesson	a workshop, session, or class, or a plan for one
unit of study	a series of workshops

residency	a series of workshops
workshop	a series of workshops
program	a series of workshops
plan	the specific steps involved in any of the above
design	the specific steps involved in any of the above
pedagogy	the specific steps involved in any of the above
curriculum	the specific steps involved in any of the above

Three of these terms have more standardized meanings. The common understanding is that *activity, lesson,* and *curriculum* refer to progressively longer periods of time. More experienced educators also understand them as hierarchical, implying a set of dependent or nested relationships:

activity	Invite–Work–Show; the basic unit of a Design (5–30 min. each)
lesson	a series of activities (30–60 min. each)
curriculum	a series of lessons (3–10 sessions)

For classroom teachers, the term *unit of study* means a multi-step exploration of a specific topic that takes place over weeks or months. Each classroom session is planned, organized as a series of individual activities. Each session supports a clearly stated goal, and the individual goals all support an overarching theme, inquiry, or result. Organizing schoolwork into units of study is a big-picture approach that helps teachers to be clear about their View (*What do I believe is important?*) and their Design (*What are the steps I need to do to accomplish my goal?*). That clarity guides their choices as they Respond: at any given moment, teachers have an informed idea about whether to press ahead, or loop back and rework an essential idea, because at any given moment they know where they are along an intended learning arc. For each subject area they teach, classroom teachers follow a written curriculum (purchased, borrowed, provided by the school, or created from scratch) that lays out units of study.

Teaching artist–led workshops are usually sponsored by institutions: schools, arts presenters, or both in collaboration. We're either provided with some kind of lesson or activity plans or asked to create our own. In our *View–Design–Respond* framework, the Design process is complete when the plan (the institution-provided or teaching artist–created Design) takes written, shareable form as a curriculum.

The Discovery Series: Music curriculum published by the 92nd Street Y's Center for Arts Learning and Leadership (formerly the 92Y Center for

Education Outreach's Musical Introduction Series) is typical in its organization. Activities, lessons, and units of study are treated as nested units of time. This year-long curriculum contains four three-week units of study, corresponding with the four concerts that students attend during the school year. Each of these units of study is divided into five forty-minute lessons that straddle the performance, before and after. Each lesson divided into three or more individual activities. Working back out from micro to macro, each activity has a stated purpose that supports the overall goal of the curriculum (Figure 5.1). In this program, classroom teachers and teaching artists are free to choose those activities that they are most interested in doing.

This chapter presents four contrasting workshop models, two for children and two for adults. The first two models are Studio workshops (where students create works of art). In the *Hello, Composers* program, first and second graders compose music to be played in concert by professional musicians. In the Sing Sing Correctional Facility Music Workshop, incarcerated men in a maximum security facility also compose music to be played in concert by professional musicians. The next two models are for Preparation workshops (preparing students for an encounter with a work of art). *Walking in Beauty* prepares grade school children for a concert featuring Native American musicians and dancers. The *Fatherhood Family Concert Workshop* prepares fathers to share family concert experiences with their children.

All four models show how similarly the aspects of View, Design, and Respond discussed earlier in the book play out with students with widely varied ages and backgrounds. I'll make explicit connections between each program and the Design practices and Respond principles presented earlier in the book. Dance, theatre, and visual arts teaching artists who have a basic familiarity with those chapters should find the models easy to translate and apply to their specific disciplines. The first of the four programs described, *Hello, Composers*, is described in particular detail. *Hello, Composers* is the most thoroughly developed and consistently successful program I currently teach; it's my hope that the an intimate look at the moment-to-moment mechanics of that work will be useful for all readers.

Each of the programs described in this chapter have been or are currently being used in New York City, facilitated either by the author, or by other teaching artists, or both, so all have been field-tested, and in some cases revised many times according to which practices were the most consistently successful for the largest percentage of participants. Each program in this chapter is presented in anecdotal form, along with an outline. Some specific activity descriptions and lesson plans will also be included. All of them embody the same View I stated back in the first part of the book: *a community of learners / making & doing / in an atelier setting.*

The Music of the Silk Road

92nd Street Y Educational Outreach: Musical Introduction Series 2017–2018 Curriculum

Units of Study (2–3 weeks each)	Classroom Lessons (45 min. each)	Individual Activities (15 min. each)		
Unit 1	classroom teacher	"Silk Road" video	Silk Road book	My Camel Caravan
	teaching artist	"This Season" video	"Meet Wu Man" video	Chinese poem / music
	teaching artist	My New music for pipa	Dancing "Ambush"	Music without words
	92Y LIVE PERFORMANCE	(during the interactive performance, the artist features the works we studied)		
	both	Co-taught. Reflect, revisit, re-do, connect, and complete unfinished explorations.		
Unit 2	classroom teacher	"Meet Zulal" video	Silk Road Role Play	Silk Road Bargaining
	teaching artist	"This Season" video	Storyboard Five Goats	Story / song #1: Mountain Sweetheart
	teaching artist	Story / song #2: At The Moks Market	Singing In Three Parts	Compare instruments (NYC, China, Armenia)
	92Y LIVE PER-FORMANCE	(during the interactive performance, the artist features the works we studied)		
	both	Co-taught. Reflect, revisit, re-do, connect, and complete unfinished explorations.		

Jiva Dance / India

Gaida / Syria

Unit 3 	classroom teacher	"Meet Jiva" video	Silk road mysteries	My Camel Caravan
	teaching artist	"This Season" video	Bharatnatyum Facial expressions & make-up	Compare instruments (NYC, China, Armenia, India)
	teaching artist	My Mridangam Drum	Bharatnatyum hand mudras	Krishna Stories
	92Y LIVE PERFORMANCE	(during the interactive performance, the artist features the works we studied)		
	both	Co-taught. Reflect, revisit, re-do, connect, and complete unfinished explorations.		
Unit 4 	classroom teacher	"Meet Gaida" video	Silk Road Role Play	Silk Road Bargaining
	teaching artist	"This Season" video	Darbouka Rhythms	Compare instruments (NYC, China, Armenia, India, Syria)
	teaching artist	Syrian Wedding Song	Syrian Wedding Dance	Social Justice Song (Arabic)
	92Y LIVE PER-FORMANCE	(during the interactive performance, the artist features the works we studied)		
	both	Co-taught. Reflect on revisit, the entire year.		

FIGURE 5.1 92Y Music of the Silk Road curriculm overview

Caravan illustration by Nilesh Mistry, from Cherry Gilchrist's *Stories from the Silk Road* (Barefoot Books 1999)

There are no Creative Youth Development (CYD) or Arts Integration workshops modeled in this chapter. CYD workshops use Studio approaches in service of social or personal transformation, so many aspects of the Studio models in this chapter will be applicable in that context. Arts Integration workshops use Preparation or Studio approaches in service of some other curriculum area (usually English or social studies, sometimes math or science), so many aspects of those Preparation and Studio models will be applicable in Arts Integration situations. Each Arts Integration workshop grows out of a particular combination of needs (academic, developmental, programmatic) that are largely defined by the school, not by the teaching artist. A school might need a theater-based anti-bullying program, or an ELL program (English Language Learners, formerly ESL, English as a Second Language) that uses choral singing, or a mural or dance theater work that comes out of the student's study of their state history. In these workshops, the school-defined academic goal comes first; the art-making is there to (at best) serve and support that learning, or (at worst) enliven something that might otherwise be dreary. Heads up, teaching artists: some Arts Integration workshops sideline art-making and engagement with works of art while paying lip-service to the presence of the arts.

Workshops for teachers and administrators, including planning sessions, end-of-unit reviews, and other professional development are also a common element of teaching artist work. Models and other support for these types of workshops are presented in Chapter 7, "Working with Teachers and Administrators." For readers who want to go deeper into the program designs outlined in this chapter, please see websites of the sponsoring institutions.

Curriculum Model #1: *Hello, Composers*

FIGURE 5.2 *Hello, Composers* Workshop at PS54, Bronx. Photo by the author, 2018

Program Type:	art-making Studio/Preparation workshop hybrid
Students:	public school first and second graders
Location:	New York City
Sponsoring Institution:	The Little Orchestra Society

Hello, Composers is one of the Little Orchestra Society's grade school education programs in the New York City area. Every session begins with a ritual greeting, which takes place just outside of the work space, before we sit down at our instruments. Students and I make eye contact, and the first thing I say is "Hello, composers." In the early sessions, I also ask them all to look around, make eye contact with students near them, and greet each other with the same phrase to encourage them to see themselves and each other as composers. At the end of the session, the last thing I say is "Goodbye, composers."

The program is a hybrid of a Preparation workshop and an art-making residency. Two teaching artists divide the work. The first visits each class before and after each concert doing preparation work. Students attend four lovingly produced orchestra concerts, all with dance, animation, puppetry, or other story elements structured in. At the same time, a second teaching artist runs a ten-session residency where students compose original music that is performed at an interactive, intimate event we call a *celebration*. The outline I'm presenting here focuses on the art-making residency.

The phrase "Hello, Composers" neatly expresses my *View*. Addressing students collectively, I identify them as a creative *community of learners*. With each "Hello, Composers," we re-affirm our identity as makers of new music, and declare the primacy of *Making & Doing* in our community. The room we meet in contains our tools, and is seen as a particular kind of space, where the community of learners will Make and Do: an *atelier setting*. In this *container*, we act and interact differently from the way we do in other rooms in the school. Here everyone will succeed, and anything we need to learn can come out of our process as we make music together. *Hello, Composers* activities are scaffolded with increasing openness in mind: Improvising, Name Songs, Book Text Melodies, Squiggle Scores, and Celebrations.

IMPROVISE

A ritual warm-up and skill-builder. The teaching artist plays an accompaniment-style rhythm on guitar, and students invent melodies that go along with what the guitar is playing. Students play glockenspiels and shakers, switching and taking turns. The guitar rhythms are different every week. Students learn to find specific notes on the glock (A, B, C . . .), and get better at inventing interesting rhythms. This is something of a devil-may-care jam band, and the energy is infectious.

NAME SONGS

FIGURE 5.3 Book Text Song, student work for *Dancing Pants* (handwritten)

FIGURE 5.4 Book Text Song, student work for *Dancing Pants* (notated)

Student learn the mantra *Say It and Clap It and Put It on the Glock*, which means to say your name with a beat, clap your name with the same beat, then find notes that you like on the glockenspiel that follow the same beat. Students are encouraged to be bold and inventive with their rhythms. Each name becomes the basis for a short melody. Once several names are captured on Noteflight (online notation and playback), we begin experimenting with layers—playing more than one name at the same time.

BOOK TEXT MELODIES

Students collect titles, phrases, or character names from books that they like, then we *Say It, Clap It, Write It, and Put It on the Glock*. It is a lot like making a

Name Song, only the book text phrases are longer and more complicated, and often funny, too (Figures 5.3 and 5.4). Sometimes our sentences are all from different books, and putting them all together makes a crazy new story.

SQUIGGLE SCORES

Composers make marks and squiggles on music staff paper to show the musicians just what they'd like them to do: high and low notes, long and short notes, and patterns of notes, going up or down. A project page provides a blank staff for each musician. Students notate with crayons and markers. For more about Squiggle Scores, see "Model" on page 91, and "Predict and Remove Impediments" on page 232.

CELEBRATION

Students hear their music played by professional musicians in an intimate, informal, lab-like setting. Composers sit very close to the players, instead of in a traditional performer-audience relationship. Students experiment with new patterns and layer combinations of instruments, almost like a musical Lego session with live musicians.

We use the online application Noteflight, a kind of web-based tape recorder for music notation. The application's main working window is projected on a Smart Board during every class. Noteflight makes it easy to notate, play back, and save students' music. The application has a magical immediacy. A student sings or plays a melody for the teaching artist, who acts as a scribe and inputs the pitches and rhythms (in standard notation). As she does, the student's idea appears as visible and audible notes, and the computer can play it accurately for everyone to hear. Composers sing along with their new songs, and experiment with changing the instrument sounds, rearranging the notes, or making the computer play the songs faster or slower. Whenever students' melodies are played by the computer, or by the teaching artist, or sung by the class, or looked up online at home, each composer enjoys a sense of accomplishment. The telling smiles and satisfied looks that come over each composer's face when they first see and hear their work realized are a beautiful thing.

In the *Hello, Composers* Design, we limit materials, vocabulary, and the range of creative choices offered to students. These limitations act as *enabling constraints* that focus and intensify our art-making process, not unlike the way the libretto compresses a story into fewer scenes and words in order to focus and intensify an opera's dramatic effect. In both cases, the creator wants to maximize an effect within a limited time frame. Dance, visual arts, theater, and other teaching artists: *When does a narrower focus merely limit a student's choice, and when does it empower them to be more creative and expressive?* Let's look at *Hello, Composers'* use of limited tools (one main instrument), vocabulary (four terms), organization and transition prompts (four), means of documenting and sharing work, and creative choices.

The first enabling constraint in our atelier involves the range of materials we make available to our twenty-six composers: glockenspiels, wooden mallets, a basketful of egg-shaped shakers, and a computer connected to a large-screen Smart Board. Glocks and shakers are easy to play, so we sidestep any need to master instrumental technique or technical skill beyond being able to choose pitches and execute rhythms (the glock keys are labeled according to pitch name (A, B, C . . .). The "limited instrument" constraint is enabling because there is very little struggle with playing technique, and we get to genuine music-making on day one.

We work with a vocabulary of only four terms: *composer, improvise, pattern, layer*. These words hover above our Smart Board work area, printed large and ready to remind us how to describe what we're about. Here the enabling constraint allows us to go narrow and deep, rather than wide and shallow. We don't need a more comprehensive or ambitious set of terms to do the work. And in nine sessions, we can only master a limited number of ideas. While we depend on prior knowledge for common terms such as *instrument* or *experiment*, and while any terms students bring up are welcome, I generally avoid using musical terms other than *composer, improvise, pattern, layer* and the instrument names.

Workflow and classroom management are made simpler by our use of a few recurring phrases, all of which have special meaning within our community:

> *Say It / Clap It / Write It / Put It on the Glock (our main composing process)*
> *Love Your Notes (take time to experiment and please yourself)*
> *Mallets Up (everyone stops playing and looks at the TA)*
> *Mallets and Shakers Switch (partners change instruments)*

Our *Hello, Composers* musical decision-making involves improvising (fast, impermanent, free, and exploratory) and composing/notating (slower, more deliberate, and, in our workshop, somewhat permanent). These two practices mirror the creative processes of professional composers. Many teaching artist–led workshops make a similar link between professional and student practice, with good reason. In many of the best Preparation workshops, students are presented with a set of options and choices that are similar to, parallel, or directly reproduce the practical, material, and aesthetic choices made by the artist during the creation of the work of art under study (see "Technique, Theory, and Developmental Appropriateness," page 233).

The *Hello, Composers* program Design strategically *removes* a number of practical, material, and aesthetic choices by making several key decisions for the student composers before the workshop begins. The student's instruments, aka their means of determining pitch (glock or voice), are predetermined. So are their means of notation: composers use the letter names of notes, but are not asked to notate rhythm. Everyone dictates their letter-notated ideas to a transcription-skilled teaching artist armed with a computer notation program. Each composing process modeled by the teaching artist gives students a way to

FIGURE 5.5 *Hello, Composers* Name Song (notated excerpt)

confidently begin within limits that serve to bypass potential impediments (see "Predict and Remove Impediments," page 232). For example in the Name Song (Figure 5.5), students set their own name to music by inventing a rhythm (*Say it and clap it . . .*) and choosing a pitch for each syllable (*. . . and put it on the glock*):

The number of notes needed is limited by the number of syllables in a student's name. This enabling constraint opens up other kinds of flexibility. Students are not discouraged from creating melismas (more than one pitch for a given syllable, although only one in fifty students will think of doing this) or repeating syllables within their names (which is modeled and encouraged as a good way to create a cool beat, very popular with kids who have short names, or rhythmic gifts). The rhythm, meter, and pitch choices are up for grabs. Any student's name might be set any number of ways. The process of choosing rhythms and pitches is enveloped by one global requirement: *Love your notes. Don't just settle for any old notes. Keep working until you've got something that really pleases you.*

All of these predetermined limitations make it easier for students to be successful and productive as quickly as possible within the allotted time. If student composers are not struggling with notation, vocabulary, or instrumental technique, they are freer to invent and experiment. It sounds paradoxical, but the teaching artist encourages students' free expression by inviting them to work within enabling constraints.

Wouldn't starting from scratch and allowing the students to invent all their own methods and notational systems enable creativity better than all the limitations Hello, Composers *imposes?* Yes, given enough time and support. Students could happily invent their own developmentally appropriate methods as well as workarounds for the notation and instrumental proficiency issues. In the 2014–2016 school years in the Spuyten Dyvil neighborhood of the Bronx, self-selecting classroom teachers and I experimented with a more constructivist atelier. My main concern going in was the first and second graders' ability to collaborate and self-structure. I remembered what David McGreevy, an inspired classroom teacher who ran a public grade school art program during the 1990s, had told me about an experiment he once tried. Instead of his usual careful, structured approach to in-class work, David set out large lumps of clay, then invited the second grade class to work with it any way they wanted to for thirty-five minutes. The girls and boys instantly retreated into separate corners of the classroom. The girls formed small partnerships, discussed what they might make, and collaborated as they made it. The boys gathered into a single group and spent the entire period howling with laughter as they fashioned a variety of clay turds. If we similarly handed over control of the creative process to the students in the Bronx, would the group end up with music they were pleased with (and that the professional players at the final celebration could perform) within the eight-session time frame, or would the result be the musical equivalent of the clay-wielding boys' sculptural output?

Four teachers committed to trying an un-Designed process with me. Our first procedural question was about modeling: should we stack the deck by demonstrating possible uses of the instruments and computer, or wait for students to ask for certain tools and capabilities? Should we model listening and responding to musical ideas, or wait for students to structure all of their own work? In the end, we split the difference. Classes began with guided improvisations, where good listening and responding was praised. For several weeks we followed that warm-up with a completely open invitation: *Now what do you want to do?* Students invented various activities and groupings. They were happy enough, but to my eyes and ears listless. The quality of collaboration was low. Many students appeared not to know how to listen to each other, to attend or respond in the way we were modeling in the warm-up at the beginning of every session. Students didn't seem to be becoming more capable, and there were no lasting artifacts from their work. Was this a cue for the teaching artist and classroom teacher to intervene? I was tempted to do so.

Then around session number four, two of the four classes said that they wanted to remember what we played from week to week, and students began notating their ideas with pencil and paper. Once they tried to do this, they realized that they could notate pitches (A, B, C . . .), but not rhythms, at least not in a way that could be retained from session to session. Not being able to notate rhythm was a big impediment. In response, I offered help, and unveiled the Noteflight music notation application. Students were excited to hear their music played by the computer, and gratified to see their names on the screen, acknowledging their work. We all learned to sing each other's notated patterns. Once the students saw that single lines of music could be notated and played back, it dawned on them that more than one line of music could play at the same time. Layers of music could be stacked up, perhaps unlimited layers. Getting to this insight, and creating new music with this understanding, is an essential goal of the program. It was reached in the "Un-Designed" classes almost as well as it was in the Designed classes.

Even so, achieving our Un-Design involved a lot of Design. There was a constant flow of *sotto voce* conversation during class, and after-class emails between the self-selecting constructivist teachers and myself. *How do you think it's going? Should I mention this idea, or wait? Is it OK if they just flounder around for twenty minutes? If they are playing duets but not listening to each other, do we intervene?* In the end, the constructivist-friendly classroom teachers and I agreed to go back to the teaching artist–led model: easier on us, and just as effective and meaningful for the students.

In the *Respond* phase of *Hello, Composers*, the teaching artist supports and praises specificity and musicality. The support mostly takes the form of being the students' musical amanuensis. Support also is expressed in every bit of eye contact, every smile, every *I like that!* and *Nice pattern, Julia.* These little moments of recognition do a great deal to shape the feeling in the room and each student's sense of their own potential. These exchanges have to be honest, if they are to resonate: the student has to have made a practical, material, or aesthetic choice that was specific and had some musicality that the teaching artist subjectively appreciated. Genuine praise can't be faked. But praising interesting work is an easy habit to get in to, especially since the quiet smiles you see in return (especially those from students who are otherwise seen as struggling) are lovely.

In the introduction to this book, I said that the music activities I'd present would be translatable into other art forms. *Hello, Composers* is a good place to start. I've presented it in detail to make your translating easier. If you'd like to translate part of the *Hello, Composers* approach for your art form, here is a worksheet (Figure 5.6) that walks you through many aspects of the program Design.

Worksheet: Translating Hello, Composers for Your Art Form

Hello, Composers (music) Activity, practice, or approach	Your workshop / art form Translated activity, practice, or approach
Limit vocabulary and materials (to go deeper with just a few concepts)	Limit vocabulary and materials
Use software to record ongoing student work (to support reflection and rehearsal)	Use this software or tech gear to record ongoing student work
Improvise (to establish safe space, encourage playfulness, practice making basic musical choices)	Experiment with…
Play-Alongs (to cultivate playfulness, listening; practice making basic musical choices)	Add to an existing or TA-generated work; collaborate
Name Songs (a name-driven composition process to create and develop many different very short pieces)	Use a model or template to create a short new work
Book Text Melodies (a text-driven composition process to create and develop more complex pieces)	Use skills learned in the previous activity, create a longer, more complex work
Squiggle Scores (invent a notation system, connected to working vocabulary)	Invent a notation or instruction system that can be interpreted by other artists
Attend performance (connect choices made by featured artists with those we make in the workshop; see ourselves as fellow artists)	Attend a theater, concert, performance or museum visit
Celebration (perform and share work; see the same work played by professions; alter work on the spot)	Display, perform, share work

FIGURE 5.6 Translating *Hello, Composers* Worksheet

Curriculum Model #2: *Sing Sing Correctional Facility Music Workshop*

FIGURE 5.7 Sing Sing Composition Residency (2017)

Photo by Stephanie Berger (Carnegie Hall)

Program Type:	Art-making studio preparation workshop hybrid
Students:	Incarcerated men, 22 to 60 years of age
Location:	Sing Sing (maximum security), Ossining, NY
Sponsoring Institution:	Musical Connections at Carnegie Hall

The *Sing Sing Correctional Facility Music Workshop* is part of Carnegie Hall/Weill Music Institute's Musical Connections program. As of this writing, the program is entering its ninth year. I designed and led the first four years of the program, which continues and evolves based on my original idea for an impediment-removing hybrid of a concert preparation workshop and an art-making residency. The men play guitars, bass, piano, trumpet, and violin, instruments they own and are allowed to have in their cells. They meet with Carnegie Hall artists in the prison's school building once every two weeks to develop several types of music projects at the same time. The men prepare for the four concerts that visiting artists will present by learning some of the visiting artists' music, later joining them on stage for selected pieces. The talent Carnegie brings in to perform includes New York's best Latin jazz bands, opera stars, classical string and woodwind quintets, and Indian, Eastern European, and Haitian music masters. The men in the workshop also compose new music for the visiting ensembles to play, with each ensemble's specific talents and instruments in mind, music that is premiered at concerts for as many as 350 incarcerated men. To support the creative work and the men's longer-term development, the teaching artist facilitates the composing and arranging as well as an ongoing study of music theory, technique, notation, and improvisation, creating support materials as needed (for example, a one-page *How to Write for String Quartet)*. The teaching artist's specific, genuine praise provides a model for all participants: *These are the musical qualities that matter; this is the way artists notice and speak about them.* The most accomplished men teach guitar lessons and general music classes to other incarcerated men.

The program participants become known and admired throughout the facility as players and composers. They come to self-identify as artists, and find sustenance in their artistic processes, products, and relationships. The Sing Sing container emphasizes a sense of community, which includes a shared responsibility for the well-being of the group. We take time to reflect on our work, collectively commiserate with each other's creative struggles, and celebrate breakthroughs and achievements. When we are at our best, we look out for one another in a manner similar to that found in high-functioning families and places of work or worship.

The men find themselves in the middle of a true inquiry into their own potential as musicians and composers. No one in the workshop knows what will happen next, what will be improvised, invented, or said. The teaching artist leading the workshop also commits to an unknowable course, not knowing what the men will bring to the table or what support they will need on any given day. Creating community and feeding the fire will require—*what?* A workshop leader takes their best guess, and adjusts day by day as the work progresses. The teaching artist predicts and removes impediments, designing and maintaining the container, and creating invitations, but doesn't attempt to control or limit the work. The whole community understands how open-ended the inquiry is, a quality that energizes every exchange. As the men's music making becomes more accomplished, the potential length and depth of their musical study reveals itself to be endless.

The Sing Sing workshop *View* is identical to that of the *Hello, Composers* work with first and second graders: *a community of learners / making & doing / in an atelier setting.* There are striking similarities in the way that View plays out in the two workshops' Designs. Both use ritual openings (at Sing Sing, it is eye contact, handshakes, and "How are you?") and encourage the participants to see themselves and each other as artists. In both workshops, a *community of learners* is *Making & Doing*: improvising, composing, and notating original music. Stealth Reflection (praising qualities of attention, responsiveness, and musical specificity at every opportunity, see page 117) plays an important role in both programs. The grade school students depend on digital gear and software to notate and hear their work. The incarcerated men use a digital projector rig to show everyone's written work on the wall for all to see during discussions. In both places, each individual's work is recognized and celebrated by the larger surrounding community.

The similarities end with the *atelier setting*. In the *Hello, Composers* grade school setting, the classroom in which we work is not very different from the other classrooms where students meet and work. At Sing Sing, our atelier needs to be a world apart from the rest of the facility if it is to be functional. It is telling that one of the first questions the men asked was "What are the rules of how to compose music?" It may have been that the freedom to operate without guidelines had become unfamiliar, or that abiding by rules meant safety to them. But the men's question helped me understand just what we were up against if we were going to be creative and expressive in such a place.

A maximum security correctional facility is, of course, a container designed to punish. It is a discouraging and often dangerous world of spoken and unspoken rules. To keep the population and staff as safe as possible, every facet of daily life is strictly regulated. Every movement is controlled, every aspect of activity (who, what, where, when, how) evaluated by the administration then approved or forbidden. Even the smallest infraction of the rules can result in being locked out of a job or educational program, or all programs, for a year. Conformity is mandatory, originality is discouraged. From a social point of view, any kind of standing out or appearing different, special, or privileged might bring unwelcome attention. Throughout most of the facility, men serve out their sentences in literal, mental, and emotional boxes.

In order for a music-making atelier to function at Sing Sing, a particularly focused container would be needed, a box within the box, somehow separate from the rest of the prison, a place where originality could be celebrated, where men would (or at least could) feel safe enough to express ideas and opinions. No one enters into creative work without that sense of safety and freedom.

Fortunately, the men in the program have a strong desire to learn, grow, and self-transform, and already appreciate the need for a safe space in which to create. Most of the negative conditions inside the facility that might threaten the stability of our container are counterbalanced by the mens' hunger for genuine work, to be treated as men and not prisoners, to experience beauty. Sing Sing is an institution noted for its historically progressive attitude toward rehabilitation, so our program is made to feel welcome within the walls, at least as welcome as possible for a maximum security facility. Within our workshop space in the school building, physically separated from the cell blocks and prison yards, procedures are not quite as restrictive as they are in the rest of the prison; a sense of possibility already exists as soon as we sit down together.

To address the men's feelings of isolation and powerlessness, each activity or interaction the teaching artists invites should reinforce the feeling of community (including a sense of responsibility for both self and others), and feed the creative fire that already exists within the men. With these goals in mind, our work includes:

IMPROVISING

Anything from duets to all-in ensembles. Some improvisations are free, others follow invented rules. Everyone who participates is equally on the spot. We also collectively analyze both the audience's experience of our improvisations and our internal experience as players: what we thought about, what we noticed, how we made choices.

JAM SONGS and PLAY-INS

We learn to read charts of increasing complexity by playing popular songs. At the same time, we learn to play works from each visiting artist's repertoire. For some pieces, we join the visiting artists onstage as part of their ensemble.

NEW WORK

The men present drafts of new work every week, played live as best we can, for group comments and critiques. Handwritten scores, sketches, and lyrics are digitally projected so that everyone in the room can see them.

STRUCTURED REFLECTION

For new work that is presented and post-performance feedback, we use my version of Liz Lerman's Critical Response Process. After the artist presents their new work without comment:

- the observers say what is "hot" about the work
- the artist asks questions of the observers (did you notice, like, feel . . .)
- the observers asks question of the artist (how did you, why did you . . .)
- the observers offer comments (if the artist wants to hear them)

OPEN DISCUSSION

It is important for the men to have unstructured time to speak about concerns and ideas, and to collectively problem-solve. Since the moment that the men are called back to their cells at the end of the day is somewhat unpredictable, we often have these discussions while waiting for the bell.

A young teaching artist-in-training recently asked me how she could pursue getting work in correctional and other social-justice-related settings. She wanted to serve underserved populations. But she had not yet done any professional teaching artist work. I suggested that she first do a few years of work in schools. Once she had some experience in that more supportive, predictable setting, and had developed her own style and substance, she'd be better able to serve elsewhere. I hope she followed up on her interest. Leading a program in a correctional facility, health care setting, homeless shelter, or other community-service setting may be the most challenging and satisfying work a teaching artist ever does. It may also be the most personally involving, the most apt to keep us up at night or weigh on our minds as we contemplate the real-life struggles of our students. But these non-school settings are generally less supportive, less predictable, and more demanding than schools. Out of consideration for those we wish to serve, it might be best to gather experience in schools and build a foundation for our teaching artist practice first, before we try to serve in more complex and challenging settings.

There is a small wealth of video documentation of the work at Sing Sing: a fourteen-minute documentary, a Google Arts & Culture Exhibit (Music at Sing Sing Correctional Facility) that includes concert footage of currently and formerly incarcerated men from the program, a CBS News report, video from a TEDx event at Sing Sing, and my own TED-style talk at the DiMenna Center. For links to these materials, visit www.DanielLevyMusic.com

Curriculum Model #3: *Walking in Beauty*

FIGURE 5.8 Valerie Dee Naranjo

Program Type:	Preparation workshop
Students:	public school first, second, and third graders
Location:	East Harlem, New York City
Sponsoring Institution:	The 92nd Street Y Center for Arts Learning and Leadership

The 92nd Street Y's Center for Arts Learning & Leadership *Discovery Series: Music* presents four concerts during a school year, ranging from string quartets to klezmer stars, Middle-Eastern folk singers, to Broadway and jazz masters, sometimes drawn from main stage concerts 92Y is already producing during their season. Each year there is a central theme (women in music, immigration and music, music of the Silk Road), and the work is almost always new to the young students, musically and culturally unfamiliar. Pre-concert Preparation workshops with teaching artists immerse students in the artists' songs and kid-friendly cultural and contextual information in multiple modalities. The teaching artists use a printed curriculum (which I author, and teach in the South Bronx), but the choice and sequence of activities is up to the classroom teacher and teaching artists.

Teaching artists are often asked to design and facilitate workshops that will prepare students for an encounter with a more or less unfamiliar work of art and its context. In these Preparation workshops, the Making & Doing are less focused on student-generated artifacts than they might be in a Studio art-making workshop. In the 92Y workshops, students sing, dance, draw maps or charts, make comparisons, and improvise rhythms in a way that makes it possible for students to connect the dots: workshop activities, work of art, and context.

The *View* here remains the same as in the other programs we've been looking at: *a community of learners / making & doing / in an atelier setting.* At the beginning of each class, and each concert, students sing and sign in American Sign Language, "We're reaching out to say hello . . . ." Each classroom session and concert concludes with my own Goodbye Song:

> *Now it's time to say, "Adios, amigos"*
> *Time to say goodbye*
> *We'll remember every song we sang*
> *Every low and every high*
> *And the next time we're together*
> *Making music side by side*
> *We'll be listening and laughing and learning*
> *Until it's time to say goodbye . . .*

When 92Y asked me to create a unit of study for the Thunderbird American Indian Dancers and Valerie Dee Naranjo, I had a head start on the *Design.* I had already seen the Thunderbirds perform twice, and Valerie and I had worked on a West African drumming unit of study for the Musicians for Harmony high school music program. They were all accomplished artists, experts at connecting with kids, and had extensive repertoire from which to draw. The dancers and Valerie hadn't shared a stage before, but they brought so much to the table that assembling a cohesive performance wasn't difficult. The Native American songs and dances we chose to include in the performance (the work of art under study), were authentic and rich, as well as accessible, easy to listen to, sing along with, dance with, and otherwise embrace. Valerie was in the midst of recording an album at the time, and kindly provided re-corded instrument demonstrations to use in the classroom, along with semi-deconstructed versions of almost all her songs (for example, just the main rattle part of a song instead of the two rattles, drum, and voice usually used in performance). Some performers are willing to create these kinds of special-ized educational materials, especially audio without video. It doesn't neces-sarily take long for them to do so, given the ubiquity of the hand-held digital recorders we commonly call smartphones. Valerie also provided a spoken re-cording of her personal story, so the students had a strong sense of who she

FIGURE 5.9 Thunderbird American Indian Dancers' 36th Annual Dance Concert and Pow-Wow at Theater for the New City, NYC, 2011. (L) Carlos Ponce/Eagle Feather (Mayan) and (R) Alan Brown—Shooting Star (Delaware/Dutch).

Photo by Lee Wexler/Images for Innovation.

was before they met her at the concert. Tailor-made instrumental recordings and personal messages from the artists to the students give our 92Y design a lovely specificity, allowing students and teaching artists to become intimate with the deconstructed works of art, and form something of a personal connection with the artists themselves.

With these kid-friendly materials at hand, the Design set out to clarify the Native American context. We wanted to organize the unit of study around a unifying idea that was robust (in terms of history and culture) but also age-appropriate, without having to write a social studies textbook. Valerie guided us to the Navajo concept of *Walking in Beauty*, or the Beauty Way, which became our cultural touchstone. We crafted this text to help teaching artists introduce the idea in the classroom:

> *When do you feel that everything is right with the world? That you are safe, happy, content, and connected with every part of your world? What was it like for you? Do you have a word for that way of being (feeling)? The Navajo*

> *people call it Walking in Beauty, or the Beauty Way. These words are difficult to translate, but they are connected with the idea of beauty, perfection, harmony, goodness, success, well-being, blessedness, and happiness.*
>
> *Walking in Beauty mainly means being in harmony with all things and all people, with all objects, all the animals, all the feelings, the plants, the weather, and all the events in your life. When you are at peace, knowing that all around you is well and that you are well with everything in your life, with nothing that pulls you in one direction or the other, you are ready to Walk in Beauty.*[1]

The introduction and discussion of *Walking in Beauty* ends with students learning to sing the Navajo song *I Walk In Beauty*, which is featured in the concert:

> *I walk in beauty, yes I do*
> *I dream of beauty, yes I do*
> *I beam with beauty, yes I do*
> *just for you and only you*
> *Hey-oh, hey-oh*

During the workshop sessions, teaching artists all *Respond* in their own ways, while following the sequence of activities in the written curriculum. Written, but not scripted, so teaching artists describe, model, paraphrase, comment, and interact according to their own lights. The only scripted aspect of the curriculum is the guiding questions, which are usually *open questions*, and certain critical transitions. Of all the challenges involved in creating a curriculum, the formulation of open questions may top the list (see "Use Open Questions," page 77). The 92Y Design relieves the teaching artist of this burden. The activities are laid out using a three-column "Activity, Steps, Support" format that makes them visually easy to follow (see "Three Column Template," page 225). The layout makes it easier for teaching artists to internalize parts of the lesson beforehand, then briefly refer to the lesson plan as needed during the classroom session. The curriculum also includes contextual information (audio recordings, photos, PowerPoints). An online Dropbox holds all the media examples, including videos of the artists that we edit to support specific activities in printed curriculum.

For a relatively small program (we serve some 7,500 students), the support for teaching and learning is remarkably robust. A combination reference and workbook called *My Music Journal* is provided for every child. The degree to which students become attached to these books surprises me: they love them, and want to take them home. At the end of the program when they do take them home, I ask the students to use the book to share everything they learned that year with their siblings and parents: *It's your turn to be the teacher.*

In 92Y student learning outcomes are stated in the form of three "Essential Questions." During our Design process, any activity that doesn't clearly connect with work of art and these questions doesn't make the cut. For Valerie and the Thunderbird Native American Dancers, these were:

Who are Native Americans?
What does it mean to "walk in beauty"?
What do songs and dances mean to Native Americans?

Near the end of the unit, after singing, drumming, and dancing Native American songs and looking at the ways we walk in beauty in our everyday lives, and after experiencing the work of art at the performance, students begin to be able to answer our main inquiry question, *What do songs and dances mean to Native Americans?* In that moment, the end becomes a beginning. Students finish the unit with the sense that the meaning of the work of art is still unfolding: *I know a few things about Native American songs and dances, and feel a connection . . . what else is out there in the world?*

To view the published curriculum for Walking in Beauty and other recent curricula from the Musical Introduction Series (renamed the Discovery Series: Music in 2018), visit 92Y's Center for Arts Learning & Leadership at www.92Y.org.

Curriculum Model #4: *Fatherhood Family Concert Workshop*

FIGURE 5.10

Photo courtesy of the CUNY Fatherhood Academy

Program Type:	Preparation workshop
Students:	fathers experiencing homelessness or at-risk fathers 16 to 45 years of age
Location:	support groups in New York City homeless shelters and CUNY's Fatherhood Academy
Sponsoring Institution:	Musical Connections at Carnegie Hall

This workshop is for fathers who have made a commitment to being better parents. They already attend weekly support groups (meetings facilitated by social workers or therapists) at their shelters or in programs like the City University of New York's Fatherhood Academy. In this add-on to those on-going meetings, the men are invited to come to free concerts with their children, without mothers or partners. The *just-Dad-and-me* approach is meant to strengthen parent-child bonding as fathers and children share a pleasurable experience with a work of art. In the short term, the shared experience creates a unique opportunity for communication and connectedness between parent and child. Longer-term, the ways parent and child successfully engage and interact can be repeated with other works of art and other unfamiliar life situations.

The *View* of *a community of learners / making & doing / in an atelier setting* permutated with this workshop. A single workshop session with the fathers and teaching artist sets up what will be in effect the men's own teaching-artist-like relationship with their children. Teaching artistry is modeled, and the men are invited to make that approach a part of their own parenting style. The *community of learners* is a community of dads, myself included, all of whom have a strong and natural interest in helping their children develop an ability to navigate unfamiliar situations and experiences in their lives. We all want our children to feel that the world is open to them. A concert featuring unfamiliar works of art being presented in an unfamiliar and perhaps imposing place, Carnegie Hall—established by Andrew Carnegie himself, like his libraries, with public benefit in mind—isn't a bad place to start. The *Making & Doing* in this workshop is the men's making and following through on a plan to do something positive for their relationship with their children. The creative spirit of *an atelier setting* is embodied in the open questions inherent in the effort: *What can we notice, say, and do to make the most of this concert experience?*

If the teaching artist spends an hour with the group and participates in their regular meeting before the official music workshop begins, personal connections form, some trust may be established, and a stronger container can take shape. Even just a few minutes of casual visiting and chatting would help establish trust and make it easier for the men to participate (see "Observe the Existing Community," page 242). The *Design* is for a simple sixty-minute pre-concert workshop, where the *Respond* work is to facilitate discussion:

Fatherhood Family Concert Workshop (60 min.)

1) music-making warm-up (15 min.)

goal: build community and enthusiasm, have some fun

activity: any rhythmic or other music making, directly connected with the music in the video excerpts of the work of art (but not announced as such)

2) TA presents the idea behind the program (5 min.)

what we are doing tonight and at the concert (in broad strokes)

the family concert experience as an extension of our role in helping our children connect and have a positive experience with the world

3) the work of art (15 min.)

watch video excerpts of the work of art in performance

discuss: *What did you think of that? What did you notice? Any physical or emotional responses? What did you picture or imagine as the music played? What are the ways we usually listen to music? What are the ways we respond to music?*

watch the same video again, with your child's experience in mind
discuss: *How will your child connect with this work of art?*

4)   planning family interaction (20 min.)
goal: planning our actions, understanding why they matter
activity: experiment with modeling and expressing . . .
enthusiasm (before the concert)
enjoyment (during the concert)
reflection and connection (after the concert)

5)   open discussion/end workshop (5 min.)

In the first three segments of the workshop, the fathers experience several modes of engagement with the work of art: making music, listening and responding, watching and reflecting. Then they reflect on their experiences of engagement, and imagine themselves in their children's shoes at the event: *How will your child connect with this work of art?* In the *planning family interaction* segment, we model for each other how to be co-learners with our children before, during, and after the concert experience, trusting (based on the evidence of media excerpts we just saw) that the encounter with the work of art can be joyful and resonant. The men imagine interacting with their children, and are encouraged to try out their ideas and phrasing on the group:

What might you say or do to express your enthusiasm . . .
   before the concert?
   during the concert?
   after the concert?

The men know their children are tuned in to them, and that the cues and indicators they display will be noticed. To help us be more aware of these opportunities to positively affect our children's experience, we isolate and consider *before, during,* and *after* separately. The fathers' enthusiasm *before* the event will set the tone for their children's' experience:

Let's go look at this artist's videos online to see what we might see . . .
I am looking forward to this concert . . .
I wonder if they will . . .

Their expressions of enjoyment *during* the event models engagement and appreciation as well as socially and culturally appropriate public behavior in a live concert setting:

eye contact with the child in significant moments

clapping with the beat
applause
conversation: Wow, did you hear that?
comments: She's a great sax player . . .

The men's interactive reflection and connection with their children *after* the concert brings additional substance to the experience, making it somewhat less ephemeral:

Which songs did you like best?
It touched my heart when . . .
I keep thinking about . . .

As they invite their children's' reflections, the fathers recognize and celebrate the importance of their child's point of view, ideas, and personal experience. They take on a teaching-artist-like role as they encourage, praise, and draw out their children's expression of their experiences. In the workshop, the teaching artist models this encouragement by drawing out the fathers' ideas and plans, and praising insight. By role-playing *before, during,* and *after* and rehearsing the things they might say to their children, the men not only imagine but also practice how their most generous selves might best express the love, affection, and responsibility they feel for their children.

Chapter 6

Designing a Curriculum

Daniel's Guide to the Serendipitous Path of Designing a Unit of Study

It is Monday morning. Your email inbox contains a note from the program manager of a local arts institution: *Dear Teaching Artist—I hope all is well with you. Are you available to teach a unit of study? This will be a Preparation workshop. Info on the focal work of art and a schedule are attached. If you accept the work, your workshop lesson plans are due by Friday noon, please. Sincerely, Your Favorite Program Manager.* You ask about the details (see "All the Right Questions," page 53), and accept the work. Lesson plans are due in five days, so you want to start designing your unit of study right away. Where do you begin?

"Daniel's Guide to the Serendipitous Path of Designing a Unit of Study" can help you shape your ideas and intuitions into focused, workable units of study. "Daniel's Guide" is both a road map and a rubric for creating preparation workshops. The road map helps you keep track of where you are in the process. The rubric aspect helps you assess your curriculum writing. You might also see the guide as a musical score that asks you to improvise, a supportive and suggestive structure that calls on you to invent at every turn. Or if you enjoy and take comfort from working your way through a list, treat "Daniel's Guide" as a To Do list. I use the Prepare, Sketch, and Outline and Revise steps differently for each Design, depending on what I discover about the work of art's qualities, artist, context, and the possibilities for teaching and learning that arise out of this information during my preparatory steps. Strangely enough, works that at the outset seem easy to teach to can turn out to be difficult to design for, and works that you found uninteresting before the design process may come to be respected or even loved, once you know them at the level of detail that a good Design requires. In any case: with "Daniel's Guide" in hand, please dive in, jump ahead, loop back, speed through some parts, and linger on others according to your sense of what you need next, knowing that in the end either you or your editor will have to complete all of the steps I've included.

FIGURE 6.1 The author's curriculum design sketch for a Metropolitan Opera Guild residency

Although the guide is set up to support a Preparation workshop (centered on a *work of art*), many steps can also support Studio or Arts Integration workshop planning. To read the guide with Studio workshop planning in mind, substitute the words *art-making process* for *work of art*. For Arts Integration planning, substitute the words *curricular goals* for *work of art*.

As you work through the guide, just about every aspect of your artist-educator self—your individual artistry and your understanding of technique and context, materials, methods, and pedagogy—will be called upon as you wend your way along the path. You'll *Prepare* by getting to know the work of art and workshop circumstances. Inspired by what you discover during your preparation, you'll imagine, *Sketch,* and focus the teaching and learning that might take place. This is the most creative and personal part of the Design process. Your View is embodied in this sketching step; no two teaching artists will invent the same activities and sequences. You'll refine your sketched Design as you *Outline and Revise* the unit of study. Here you make sure your ideas and aspirations for the work are clear, clearly communicable to others, and will function well within the given limitations of time, space, and other resources.

In this chapter, an Overview as well as the Prepare, Sketch, and Outline and Revise steps are each laid out on checklist-style worksheets. Each checklist refers to a separate support document. Here is the order in which these materials appear in this chapter:

Checklists
   Overview of All Steps (page 209)
   Prepare Steps (page 210)
   Sketch Steps (page 211)
   Outline and Revise Steps (page 212)
   Workshop Space, Time, and Resources (page 218)

Prepare Support Documents
   About the Study Prompts (page 213)
   Visual Art Study Prompts (page 214)
   Dance Study Prompts (page 215)
   Theater Study Prompts (page 216)
   Music Study Prompts (page 217)

Sketch Support Documents
   Brainstorming Guide (page 220)
   Focus Your Inquiry (page 222)

Outline and Revise Support Documents
   Three-Column Template (page 223)
   Single-Page Template (page 227)
   Design Self-Assessment (page 228)

Depending on your familiarity with the work of art and other factors, some of the detailed sub-steps in the support documents may take five minutes, others five hours to complete. If you embrace any single part of "Daniel's Guide," make it the Prepare sequence. The support pages for the Prepare step asks you to consider focal works of art from four different perspectives: Qualities and Characteristics, the Artist, Context, and Teaching and Learning. All the activities you'll Sketch and Outline and Revise grow out of this frame of reference, that is, your experience with and what you know about the work of art. We want our students to inquire into, engage with, connect with, open up to, explore, illuminate, and make meaning with the work of art being studied. The better we know the work of art, the better able we are to facilitate all these possibilities. As questions about content, priorities, and direction arise during your Design process, you'll find that the answers you need lie in the work of art itself.

OVERVIEW OF ALL STEPS CHECKLIST

Prepare

- [ ] become familiar with the work of art

- [ ] gather materials

- [ ] experience the work of art

- [ ] get to know the work of art

- [ ] study contextual materials

- [ ] become familiar with the time, space and resources available

- [ ] determine who, what, where, when; special needs and opportunities

- [ ] assess potentials via a diagnostic visit

Sketch

- [ ] imagine the teaching and learning

- [ ] choose an inquiry/theme

- [ ] sequence your inquiry/theme

- [ ] focus your inquiry/theme

Outline and Revise

- [ ] define your unit of study

- [ ] write out your unit using a template

- [ ] proofread and rewrite

PREPARE CHECKLIST

1 Become familiar with the work of art . . .

☐   gather materials (artists' recordings, video, websites, bios, a list of work(s) and artists involved

☐   experience the work of art
study the work of art (make notes of anything and everything you notice about the work of art; imagine the performance or museum visit).

support: *About the Study Prompts, page 214, Visual Art Study Prompts, page 215, Dance Study Prompts, page 216, Theater Study Prompts, page 217, Music Study Prompts, page 218*

2 Study contextual information (research the work of art's history and cultural origins)

3 Become familiar with the time, space, and resources available . . .

☐   determine who, what, where, when; special needs and opportunities

☐   assess potentials via a diagnostic site visit

support: *Workshop Space, Time, and Resources Checklist (page 219)*

SKETCH CHECKLIST

1 Imagine the teaching and learning

☐   envision the container you want to establish

☐   list the main artistic and aesthetic ideas that drive the
work of art

☐   list fun *Make and Do* activities that connect with those ideas
in that type of container

2 Choose a direction

☐   look over your *notes* and activity lists and see what themes
or inquiries emerge

☐   choose the best, juiciest, hottest, most fun single theme/
inquiry to develop

☐   state your specific chosen inquiry as a question

3 Sequence your activities

☐   place your activity ideas into an order that supports your
stated theme/inquiry

☐   look for opportunities to repeat or ritualize activities or
activity structures within that sequence

support: *Brainstorming Guide* (page 221)

4 Focus your activities

☐   With your first-draft, sequenced inquiry in hand, review
your use of multiple modalities, prior knowledge,
scaffolding, honest timings, etc.

support: *Focusing Your Inquiry* (page 223)

OUTLINE AND REVISE CHECKLIST

1 Define your unit of study by

☐ content: *students will learn about* . . .

☐ skills: *students will be able to* . . . (improvise, create, explore)

☐ essential questions to be explored: *What is . . . How can . . . What might . . . How does* . . .

☐ vocabulary

2 Write out your unit using a template

support: *Three-Column Template* (page 224), *Single Page Template* (page 229)

3 Proofread and rewrite

☐ review to make sure activity, steps, and guiding questions and support texts are all in the right places

☐ rework your text for simplicity, brevity, and clarity

support: *Design Self-Assessment* (page 230)

ABOUT THE STUDY PROMPTS

For all Preparation workshops, getting to know the work of art is the first order of business. But it is business mixed with the pleasure of being afforded the opportunity to dig deep into a work of art. The *Watch, Listen,* and *Study Prompts* are divided into four frames of reference (Qualities and Characteristics, the Artist, Context, and Teaching and Learning) to facilitate your becoming familiar with a work. Many of the prompts are identical for all four art forms. The better a teaching artist knows the work of art at the heart of their curriculum, the easier it will be for them to design activities and workshops that connect with and open up that work. Later in the Design process, if you become unsure as to how to proceed, you can come back to the work of art, do a little more steeping or delving, and let what you discover guide your choices. The answers and ideas you are looking for are embedded in the work itself, waiting there for you to find.

As you Prepare, allow the work of art to speak to you as both an artist and a Designer. You're looking for the main ideas and materials that drive or animate the work of art, *readily perceivable* aspects of the work you'll want to teach to. Most of the prompts are slanted toward helping you notice characteristics that might suggest activity ideas, especially in visual, kinesthetic, or narrative/verbal modalities. Even without the prompts, as you get to know a work of art some part of your mind is already tracking which characteristics, ideas, and materials suggest activities or interesting questions. You may not want to separate the processes of studying the work of art and spinning activities related to what you discover. Sometimes you'll intuit an activity before you've even defined the characteristic with which it connects. Other times the important characteristics will be obvious but coming up with a related activity will challenge you. Either way, it is natural and beneficial to stay loose with your process. Keep notes and outlines of your ideas as they pop up, and keeping digging into the work.

VISUAL ART STUDY PROMPTS

Qualities and Characteristics

Describe the elements of the work of art (line, color, form).

What is delightful about this work?

What makes this work unique, vital, bold?

How are materials used?

Featured materials or techniques?

What is the main idea at work?

Artist

What makes this artist unique, vital, bold?

Does the artist have a story we can connect with?

Are the artist's writings good/appropriate for study?

Context

The role of artistic genre, tradition, innovation?

Historical connections to people, places, events?

Cultural connections to writing, poetry, dance, costume, crafts, music, geography?

Music, dance, theatrical, or architectural connections?

Origin stories for the work of art, artist, or materials?

Teaching and Learning

What kinds of materials might need to be created to make a visual aspect clearer?

Which work-of-art-based materials or processes are classroom-friendly?

Are there characters, animals, or other narrative embedded in the work of art or its origin?

What alternate works of art might be fun to use for comparison?

In what ways is the work familiar or unfamiliar to students?

What aspects of the work, forms, or materials might the students easily connect with?

What aspects of the artist's life, approach, persona, or art-making might the students most easily connect with?

Related teacher-friendly books and websites that could serve as resources or destinations?

What about this work/artist would the classroom teacher love to explore?

DANCE STUDY PROMPTS

Qualities and Characteristics

Describe the elements of the work of art (line, form, rhythm, use of space).

What is delightful about this work?

What makes this work unique, vital, bold?

How is the human form used?

Featured materials or techniques?

What is the main idea at work?

Artist (authors and performers)

Does the work of art have a story we can connect with?

Context

The role of artistic genre, tradition, innovation?

Historical connections to people, places, events?

Cultural connections to writing, poetry, music, costume, crafts, geography?

Musical, theatrical, visual arts, or architectural connections?

Origin stories for the work of art, artist, or materials?

What makes this artist unique, vital, bold?

Are the artists' writings good/appropriate for study?

Teaching and Learning

What kinds of materials might need to be created to make the choreography clearer?

Which work-of-art-based movements or processes are classroom-friendly?

Are there characters, animals, or other narrative embedded in the work of art or its origin?

What alternate dance works might be fun to use for comparison?

In what ways is the work familiar or unfamiliar to students?

What aspects of the work, forms, or materials might the students most easily connect with?

What aspects of the artist's life, approach, persona, or art-making might the students easily connect with?

Related teacher-friendly books and websites that could serve as resources or destinations?

What about this work/artist would the classroom teacher love to explore?

THEATER STUDY PROMPTS

Qualities and Characteristics

Describe key themes, characters, action, settings, texts, and rhythms of the work of art.

What is delightful about this play or performance?

What makes this work unique, vital, bold?

How is improvisation used?

How are human performance potentials used (singing, acrobatics, stage fights)?

What is the main idea at work?

Artist (authors and performers)

Context

The role of theatrical genre, tradition, innovation?

Historical connections to people, places, events?

Cultural connections to writing, poetry, dance, costume, crafts, music, geography?

Design, visual art, or art-making connections?

Origin stories for the play or artists?

What makes this artist unique, vital, bold?

Teaching and Learning

What kinds of materials might be need to be created to make a theatrical aspect clearer to students?

Which work-of-art-based text appropriate for narrative, language or cultural study?

Dance or movement possibilities?

What materials are classroom-performance friendly?

Are there characters, animals, or other narrative embedded in the songs or their origins?

What alternate or related texts might be fun to include?

In what ways is the work familiar or unfamiliar to students?

What aspects of the production might students most easily connect with?

What aspects of the artist's life, approach, persona, or music-making might students most easily connect with?

Related teacher-friendly books and websites that could serve as resources or destinations?

What about this production/artist would classroom teacher love to explore?

MUSIC STUDY PROMPTS

Qualities and Characteristics

Describe and/or notate the work of art's important melodies, harmonies, bass lines, riffs, rhythms.
What is delightful about this music?
What makes this work of art unique, vital, bold?
Lyrics form and content?
How is improvisation used?
How are the instruments used? Featured instruments?
What is the main musical idea at work in this piece?
Artist (authors and performers)
Does the work of art have a story we can connect with?

Context

The role of musical genre, tradition, innovation?
Historical connections to people, places, events?
Cultural connections to writing, poetry, dance, costume, crafts, instruments, geography?
Visual art, dance, or art-making connections?
Origin stories for the song, artist, or instruments?
What makes this artist unique, vital, bold?

Teaching and Learning

What kinds of recordings might need to be created to make a musical aspect clearer?
Lyrics good/appropriate for rhyme, narrative, language, or cultural study?
Dance or movement possibilities suggested by the work?
What work-of-art-based materials are singing- or clapping-friendly?
Are there characters, animals, or other narrative embedded in the songs or their origins?
What alternate recordings might be fun to use for comparison?
In what ways is the work familiar or unfamiliar to students?
What aspects of the music, lyrics, or instruments might the students easily connect with?
What aspects of the artist's life, approach, persona, or music-making might the students most easily connect with?
Related teacher-friendly books and websites that could serve as resources or destinations?
What about this song/artist would the classroom teacher love to explore?

WORKSHOP SPACE, TIME, AND RESOURCES CHECKLIST

What

Type of workshop (preparation/studio/arts integration)

Work of art

Who and When

Co-coordinator's names/phone numbers/emails
Building location
Workshop dates or date range
Number of participants in each session
Number of sessions
Duration of each session
Actual daily schedule

Where

Sizes and types of room available

Moveable desks/furniture

Acoustics

Power

Lighting

Ventilation

Floor cleaned daily?

Wall tape allowed?

Amenities

Smart Board

other computer access

recording and playback devices (video/audio)

copy machine access

coat/bag storage

student work storage

materials storage

wall space or bulletin board

rolling cart for TA materials

Art-form-specific needs

Visual arts—sink, storage, drying racks, projector, materials

Music—percussion or other instruments; sonic isolation from other spaces

Dance—sprung floor, floor mats, barre, mirrors

How

Fees and payment schedule

Curriculum provided?

Contextual materials provided?

Recordings or images provided?

Assessment process required or provided?

Other Details

Differentiation—How many grade or skill levels are involved?

Special leadership required (is it a new program, or new facility?)

Documentation or work or performances required or provided?

Restrictions regarding posting work online?

Teaching artist professional development or certification required?

Structure for planning with co-teachers and collaborators?

Provide professional development with co-teachers and collaborators?

Provide demonstration or other workshops for funders, PTA, or parents and children?

Photo and video releases provided or completed?

Fingerprinting or special ID required?

BRAINSTORMING GUIDE

Here is an alternative to the "Daniel's Guide" sketching process, created by Lincoln Center for the Performing Arts' Education Department: Lincoln Center Education (LCE), their Brainstorming Guide for Designing an LCE Instructional Unit (Figure 6.2).[1] This document is actually a serious unit planning form masquerading as friendly Brainstorm boxes. Using it, you'll address (in any order) *The Work of Art, Questions, Contextual Information, Personal/ Curricular/Standards Connections*, and *Activity Ideas*. LCE emphasizes the centrality of the work of art, so any brainstorming is predicated on familiarity with the work to which you'll be teaching. Key ideas that arise from the brainstorming can be captured in the box at the lower right. These key ideas are first checked for alignment with LCE's Capacities for Imaginative Learning (see page 172 for more details), then winnowed down to a single Line of Inquiry, stated as a question, lower right, that specifically includes the title of the work of art and/or the artist. On another page, lesson plans can be created to support that Inquiry.

Lincoln Center Education
Helping young minds perform in a dynamic world

BRAINSTORMING GUIDE FOR DESIGNING AN LCE INSTRUCTIONAL UNIT

Focus Work of Art: _______________________

THE WORK OF ART	QUESTIONS	CONTEXTUAL INFORMATION
What do you notice in the work of art? What do you see? Hear?	What questions occur to you about the work of art? What are you curious about?	What surrounds this work socially, culturally, historically?
PERSONAL/CURRICULAR/ STANDARDS CONNECTIONS	**ACTIVITY IDEAS**	**KEY IDEAS**
What personal or curricular or Standards connections does this work of art evoke?	What experiential activities are you envisioning? Gather the ideas for future reference.	Reflect on all the responses documented during the brainstorming process, and identify the key ideas that stand out to you. These elements and concepts ARE the key ideas.
CAPACITIES FOR IMAGINATIVE THINKING		**LINE OF INQUIRY**
Identify what *Capacities* will be developed in students based on these key ideas.		Distill your list of key ideas and shape them into a Line of Inquiry. Craft a question that contains those key ideas, the title of the work of art and/or the artist.

FIGURE 6.2 Lincoln Center Education's "Brainstorming Guide for Designing an LCE Instructional Unit" (provided courtesy of Lincoln Center for the Performing Arts, Inc. Copyright © 2017)

FOCUS YOUR INQUIRY

With your first-draft activity sequence in hand . . .

☐ Review your activities to make sure you have included multiple modalities and emphasized the visual, kinesthetic, singing, moving, narrative, and generative work over telling or explaining (less talking, more doing).

☐ Review by backward mapping. Ask: *What do I want the students to experience at the museum visit or performance?* Work backward from that moment, step by step: *What do my students need to have experienced to make that step possible?)*

☐ Confirm and clarify the links between your classroom activities and the work of art. *What will happen in the museum visit or performance? What will the major connections between the classroom activities and the museum visit or performance be?*

☐ Review your honest timings for each activity, including transitions.

☐ Devise clever ways to make the work easier or more fun (photos, videos, charts, handouts, games, contests).

☐ If classroom teachers are involved, anticipate any difficulties they might have with the lessons, and rework them to be more accessible without sacrificing effectiveness or quality.

☐ Re-confirm that every activity directly supports your inquiry and clearly connects with the work of art.

THREE-COLUMN TEMPLATE

This template has been in use at the 92nd Street Y since 2007. We needed a standardized format that would present lesson steps in a manner that was easy for teaching artists to read while on their feet in class. The format has proven popular with the teaching artists and classroom teachers, ranging from newbies to masters, who use it to co-teach units of study. Here is a working example of the template in use (Figure 6.3) from the "Music of the Americas" unit on Cuban musician Pedrito Martinez:

This version outlines the intended use of each column in a typical music unit of study (Figure 6.4).

The *Activity* column lists an activity title that separates one invite-work-show activity sequence from another and provides an activity duration. Teaching artists look at this column during a lesson for reminder of what to do, how long to do it, and what comes next as they teach.

The *Steps* column describes a titled activity step by step, using bullet points followed by a simple verb (sing, play, complete, find, watch, create, introduce, try, try out, explore, read, imagine, model, make, curate, discuss, connect, stretch, take, turn to, revisit, act out, pretend, set up, provide, complete, move to, review, outline). For any given moment, teaching artists decide for themselves what in-class grouping is best (all, pairs, small groups, individuals). Important questions, prompts and transitions are also scripted here.

Scripting can be a dirty word regarding a lesson plan or any teaching situation, since it implies control of the process by someone other than the educator in the room. But in this case the scripting is selective, and acknowledges the importance of –and difficulty of formulating—the often crucial prompts upon which an activity or inquiry pivots (see "Use Open Questions" page 77). A poorly-worded question or prompt slows down our already time-limited process by being confusing, uninteresting, or off the track. A well-worded question or prompt invites divergent responses, and creates a sense of space, and encourages curiosity and trust: *Hmm, that is an interesting question . . . and I can tell that the facilitator is thoughtful and prepared.*

The *Support* column includes contextual and other reference materials that a teaching artist might need during the lesson: images, song lyrics, important names, dates, definitions, musical notation, lists, quotes, reasoning, goals or activity details that don't fit into the *Steps* column. The teaching artist would be familiar with all of the items in this column before teaching, but would not be expected to hold them all in mind. The information in Support might comprise the total contextual information needed for the activity, or there might be other additional pages available, but the idea is to put the references needed in easy reach. On the Pedrito Martinez sample page (Figure 6.4), materials mentioned in the "Steps" column (thumbnail versions of the student workbook pages, and a video screen shot) are shown in the Support column.

ACTIVITY	STEPS	SUPPORT
My Conga Patterns (5-15 min)	• Complete the Play the Conga activity • Stretch and warm up hands and wrists • Turn to MMJ Page 20: Play the Conga • Review the four strokes • Model creating and notating 8-beat (8-box) patterns • Make and share patterns	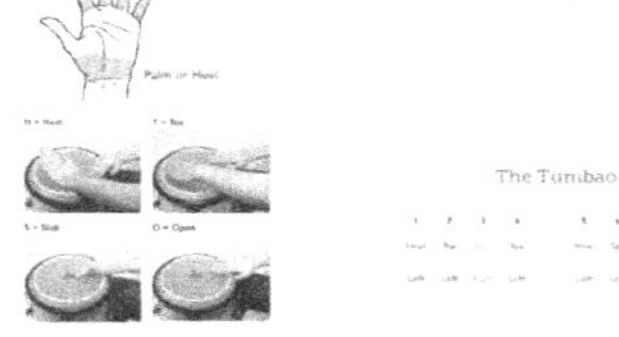
Play the Tumbao (10-15 min)	• Complete the Play the Conga activity • Stretch and warm up hands and wrists • Turn to MMJ Page 20: Play the Conga • Review the four strokes • Try out the tumbao pattern • Watch and play along with video: Tumbao • Take turns playing tumbao solos, duets, and ensembles	Son cubano is a genre of music and dance that originated in the highlands of eastern Cuba during the late 19th century, and is arguably the most important genre of Cuban popular music. The son montuno is a subgenre of son cubano. The basic son montuno conga pattern is called marcha, or tumbao.

FIGURE 6.3 Three-column template from 92Y's Musical Introduction Series

Activity	Steps	Support
Apt Title (duration)	• scripted prompt • verb / step a • verb / step b • verb / step c • scripted prompt	lyrics, names, dates, definitions, musical notation, lists, quotes, reasoning, goals or activity details

FIGURE 6.4 Three-column template column functions

The three columns address deeper levels of detail as you move from left to right through Activity, Steps, and Support. Before the lesson begins, the document functions as a straightforward curriculum guide, supporting teaching artists as they make themselves conversant with the activities, taking in the goals and guiding questions, and becoming familiar with the specific materials. During the actual lesson, each teaching artist works with the printed document in their own way. They might read the descriptive text, rather than memorize it (*Walking in Beauty mainly means being in harmony with all things*[2]), or they might glance at the text as a reminder and create their own version on the spot. Teaching artists are encouraged to use the scripted prompts as written. The timings and lesson steps are reminders that can be glanced at as needed. The spiral-bound book that contains the unit plans is designed to lay open flat on a desktop for easy reference.

During planning sessions, classroom teachers and teaching artists tailor the curriculum materials to their own needs. The Classroom Teacher and Teaching Artist Collaboration page (Figure 6.5) invites them to differentiate instruction and determine which student groupings, activity durations, and activity sequence will best serve their students.

The Classroom Teacher and
Teaching Artist Collaboration

92Y believes that classroom teacher and teaching artist partnerships are the best way to serve our students. As you meet in planning sessions and in the classroom with your students, please approach the work as co-teaching, and make the most of one another's expertise.

In planning sessions, you will review the Music of the Americas frame, the artists, and possible CT and TA activities. Choose those activities which are best suited for your students and interest you as educators. As you do, you'll find that the Guide activities and My Music Journal (MMJ) pages provide structure (lesson plans) and support (contextual information), but many decisions are left up to you. These should be addressed collaboratively during planning or in the moment with students:

Differentiating Instruction: *Which activities and modalities are best for our students? How should the activity plan be altered to make it as effective and appropriate as possible?*

Groupings: *What configuration(s) will work best—individual work, partners, small groups or splitting the class between CT and TA?*

Durations: *How long should we spend on this activity? How deep do we want to go? Is there another activity we want to make time for?*

Sequence: *What is the most effective orderofactivities for the whole Unit, and also on any given day?*

CT + TA co-teaching agreement: *How do we intend to work togetherin the classroom? How do we see our roles and our relationship? What will make our collaboration easier?*

FIGURE 6.5 The classroom teacher and teaching artist collaboration

Three-Column Template

Activity	Steps	Support

FIGURE 6.6

SINGLE PAGE TEMPLATE

You may prefer a simpler outline than the three-column form, especially if you will be the only person using the Design, and if you are comfortable with a less detailed approach. Lincoln Center Education's "Suggested Lesson Plan Format" (Figure 6.7) works along those lines:

Suggested Lesson Plan Format

Name:

Work of Art under study:

For grade(s):

Supplies:

Contextual Materials:

Specific Concerns of Students:

Line of Inquiry:

Consider

- How does each activity within this lesson relate to or explore the line of inquiry?

- Think of each activity as a layer building upon the previous layer to result in a deep exploration.

- What are some open-ended questions, related to your line of inquiry, that you will ask students to help guide their noticing and reflecting during the activity?

- At the end of the unit, what capacities do you think you might have elicited or that the students have gained?

ACTIVITY #1:

Estimated time for this activity:

Description of the activity:

Questions guiding the learning during the activity:

ACTIVITY #2:

Estimated time for this activity:

Description of the activity:

Questions guiding the learning during the activity:

FIGURE 6.7 Lincoln Center Education's "Suggested Lesson Plan Format"

DESIGN SELF-ASSESSMENT CHECKLIST

Activity Qualities

- ☐ Activities are fun.
- ☐ Activities all clearly connect to the work of art.
- ☐ Activities all support the stated inquiry.
- ☐ Activities build in a sequence.
- ☐ Activities minimize potential impediments of technique and skill.
- ☐ Activities are developmentally appropriate.
- ☐ Activities emphasize making, doing, choice-making.
- ☐ Activities emphasize visual, kinesthetic, and narrative modalities.
- ☐ Activities include some interpersonal and intrapersonal modalities.
- ☐ Activities avoid too much teaching artist talk-and-explain.
- ☐ Activities work with students' prior knowledge.
- ☐ Activities spark students' intrinsic motivation (they want to do them).
- ☐ Activities use contextual information in a inspiring way.
- ☐ Activities balance multiple modalities.
- ☐ Activities exploit technology well.
- ☐ Activity timings are honest and realistic.
- ☐ Activities include structured reflection.
- ☐ Activities allow space for spontaneous reflection.
- ☐ Activities differentiate instruction as needed.

Design Clarity and Completeness

- ☐ Invite–Work–Show activity plan steps are complete and clear.
- ☐ The reason(s) a student might be motivated to attend to each activity are clear.
- ☐ Make and Do prompts are clear/scripted.
- ☐ Reflection prompts are clear/scripted.
- ☐ Open questions are clear/scripted.
- ☐ Important analogies are clear.

Teaching Artist Strengths

In this unit, I have a clear sense of . . .

The most important personal qualities I bring to this unit are . . .

The most important artistic qualities I bring to this unit are . . .

In this unit, I look forward to enjoying . . .

I possess an unquestioning belief in [your answer], so my Design . . .

Connection to View

The social contract in this workshop is that we see ourselves as . . .
    such as when we . . .

The main best practice of this workshop is that we . . .
    such as when we . . .

The model or metaphor for this workshop is . . .
    such as when we . . .

In this workshop, my roles as teaching artist include . . .
    such as when we . . .

In this workshop, my students' roles include . . .
    such as when we . . .

In this workshop, my approach, attitude, or philosophy is . . .

In this workshop, the main strategy I use to bring all this together is . . .

Predict and Remove Impediments

The Saw Mill River Parkway traces a curving tree-lined route from my northern Manhattan apartment to Sing Sing Correctional Facility, a forty-five-minute drive away. Sing Sing is a maximum security facility, where some 70 percent of the prison population have been convicted of a violent crime, and most men there are serving long sentences. It is considered one of the more progressive state correctional facilities in the United States, with a well-attended school, GED, and college degree programs. I've made some eighty trips there to facilitate music workshops sponsored by Carnegie Hall. When I am alone, I use the drive up to review my workshop plans and clarify my intentions, and the trip back to review the successes and failures of the day. But often I'm ferrying a musician or Carnegie staff, and the shared commute turns into a mutually-assisted reflection session. The workday at Sing Sing is already quite long without adding previews and post-mortems, but the situation there is so fluid and complex that it is easy for everyone involved to get caught up in the challenge and excitement of figuring out how best to serve the incarcerated men who participate in our program.

On her way to observe one of the early workshops, educational researcher Dennie Wolf asked me, "How do you see your role in these workshops?" I started to say something like "the designer of activities," but then struck on a term I liked better: *a Predictor and Remover of Impediments*. That answer may have had something to do with the context of the question, given the challenges of working at a maximum security facility, but teaching artists who I've shared the idea with since then have found it useful in various settings. The act of designing any unit of study might be seen as *an informed mitigation of any circumstances that would impede learning*. Every aspect of a Design should ultimately serve to remove an impediment—anything that might hinder an individual's learning. This approach can have a bracing effect on our work. When *Predictor and Remover of Impediments* is included in our View, we recognize the directness of our responsibility for our charges' success. We express our willingness to change what we do to adapt to the circumstances of each workshop. This conscious adaptive attitude becomes essential to our Design. I now ask two basic questions at the beginning of a program Design process: *What are the potentials of my students in this situation? What can I do to remove impediments to my students realizing their potential?*

This section of the Designing A Curriculum chapter details three types of impediments that commonly come up as we Design, then explores the idea of observing and even joining existing communities before we begin teaching there. The section ends with looking at the ways our use of terminology can create or remove impediments.

TECHNIQUE, THEORY, AND DEVELOPMENTAL APPROPRIATENESS

Not all impediments in a teaching situation are predictable. But the most common impediments that arise will be in the areas of technique, theory, and developmental appropriateness. Anticipating obstacles to learning is something educators of all stripes already do to some extent, according to common sense. We don't hand just someone a saxophone and say, "Now improvise a solo," because we know that individuals need some *technique* in order to do so. We don't do Shenkarian analysis of melodic forms in a workshop with anyone except undergraduate music students because we know that the intensively *theoretical* approach involved will only be of genuine interest to experts and experts-to-be. And we shouldn't (though we sometimes do) get too abstract with second graders, because it isn't *developmentally appropriate* to do. Children are geared to connect with the narrative, physical, concrete aspects of a work of art; abstractions (for example, how harmonies are defined and labeled) are too ephemeral to be of interest, until a special effort is made to make them experiential or concrete.

By *technique* I mean the difficulties posed by the manual skills or physical realities involved in certain art-making processes: ballet *en pointe*, welding steel sculptures, playing most musical instruments. When teaching artists want to replicate Richard Serra's or Alexander Calder's monumental sculpture-making processes, they don't bring a welding rig into a ninth grade classroom. Many of us would love to do this, and there are some fine arguments to be made for doing so, but in most situations developing the skill of welding is too cumbersome in terms of time and materials. Instead, visual arts teaching artists create a workaround that allows students to do an exploration similar to that of the artist, with analogous materials or techniques. With a smaller-scale Calder mobile in mind, foam core, colored paper, wire, scissors, and pliers stand in for Calder's sculpted metal, sheet metal shears, pliers, files, and hammers:

In choosing foam core and paper, we hope to remove technique-related and technical impediments from our students' art-making process. We're still referencing Calder's processes and technique. The foam core, paper, wire, and string behave not unlike Calder's sheet metal, and allow us a chance to deal with weight, form, balance, color, and movement, and solve material and aesthetic problems similar to those he faced. Foam core won't be as tactilely satisfying to work as Calder's materials, and the objects we create won't have the sense of permanence or the paradoxical quality of a heavy thing appearing to be light as Calder's do. But if the substitution works, and our students dig in to the Making & Doing, then the compromise is worthwhile, as John Dewey observes in Art and Experience:

> . . . to perceive, a beholder must create his own experience. And his creation must include relations comparable to those which the original producer underwent. They are not the same in any literal sense. But with the

perceiver, as with the artist, there must be an ordering of the elements of the whole that is in form, although not in details, the same as the process of organization the creator of the work consciously experienced. Without an act of recreation, the object is not perceived as a work of art. The artist selected, simplified, clarified, abridged and condensed according to his interest. The beholder must go through these operations according to his point of view and interest.[3]

Impediments in the area of *theory* can develop when students over-value it. By theory, I mean those terms and systems that label, organize, or explain the inner workings of works of art in any art form, including schools of practice, historical movements, and art-history periods. Individual artists create and innovate according to what pleases them; theory comes along afterward and attempts to explain or describe aspects of what the creative person did. Because theory *follows* practice in the arts, it is inevitably of lesser importance. We should exercise discretion when we refer to theory, just as we do with any other contextual information (see "Place Contextual Information," page 107). When we do reference theory, we should connect it with practice, as directly and experientially as possible. Otherwise we run the risk of alienating and discouraging the student-practitioner, creating a situation where art-making is one thing and theory its heinous cousin.

Also, when we delve too deep into theory, our students can get the impression that we are saying, "This is what the experts say or do," or "This is how the truly accomplished practitioners speak about this," as though statements of theory were some kind of oracle. For students who hear the theoretical information this way, a sense of separateness from other practitioners can come up, a perceived separation into beginners and experts in the classroom community, unintended by the teaching artist. We don't have to completely avoid topics of theory or avoid using accurate, discipline-specific terminology, and more mature students have a higher tolerance for (or even an interest in) these areas. But theory will be most interesting to practitioners of an art when it is *immediately useful tool* for Making & Doing.

For many years I resisted listening to expert opinions on *developmental appropriateness*. During shared planning sessions, classroom teachers would tell me that a particular activity "was not right for their kids." I assumed they were underestimating their students' potentials. I knew in my heart that their students could do more than the teachers thought, and I was motivated to bring the student achievements I imagined into being. And every so often a teacher would in fact underestimate her students' ability to create. But the activities experienced teachers gently warned me against usually faltered or failed. As assiduous students of their own students' capabilities, classroom teachers have a deep knowledge of the sweet spot in their students' engagement, the place where teacherly ambitiousness and the students' natural proclivities at a given age meet. They ignore this kind of knowledge at their own peril, since doing so can render teaching a chore instead of a joy. I learned to listen more carefully to their advice. I became more observant of the dynamics classroom teachers described. I took outstanding teachers out to lunch to ask them how they knew what they knew. Most often direct experience, trial and error, had taught them what they were sure of—even as they continued experimenting with the kinds of activities they designed, pushing the envelope, broadening their experience base.

Let's track some impediments that might come up in a studio workshop activity for young composers. Imagine a group of second grade students with little or no formal musical training who will be attending a series of orchestral concerts. You want to explore "orchestral music" by composing, notating, and orchestrating short pieces of music. Composing and orchestrating on a professional level requires an understanding of counterpoint, instrument ranges, the comparative weights and colors of the sounds the instruments can make, not to mention composition, all the aspects of musical notation (pitch, meter, rhythm, harmony, melody, articulation, dynamics), and all the standard practices used by arrangers and music copyists. Given the technique and knowledge of music theory required to do so, asking second graders to create a musical score using standard notation would be far from developmentally appropriate.

But some strategic compromises could mitigate that impediment. Enter a simpler, more intuitive system of notation: the Squiggle Score.

Here the students don't invent their notation system from scratch, which would be fun, but would a) require a lot of time and b) be far-removed from the focus of the art-making, orchestral music. Instead, Squiggle Scores depend on a few straightforward graphic qualities: time flows left to right, high and low marks indicate high and low pitches, long and short marks (lines and dots) indicate long and short sounds (Figures 6.8–11). Since Squiggle Scores don't invite a lot of creativity in the notation, we have more workshop time to delve into each composer's intentional control of an orchestrated texture. This compromise makes everything that follows possible, the way replacing Calder's steel plates with foam core did. We also remove potential impediments by making the work brief. One page of Squiggle Score may only encompass a single texture, a few seconds long, so we avoid any issues of form. Instead of requiring the student's notation to be information-dense and hyper-accurate, students use their prior knowledge of *layers* to draw a four-layer Squiggle Score. During a performance, interpretation and dialogue shape the sound of the work as four trained musicians are coached by the young composers as to how to interpret the marks. Only then do the musicians choose a key or specific harmony (chord) to anchor the piece, and begin to play.

FIGURE 6.8 Squiggle Score composer at work

FIGURE 6.9 Olivia's Squiggle Score

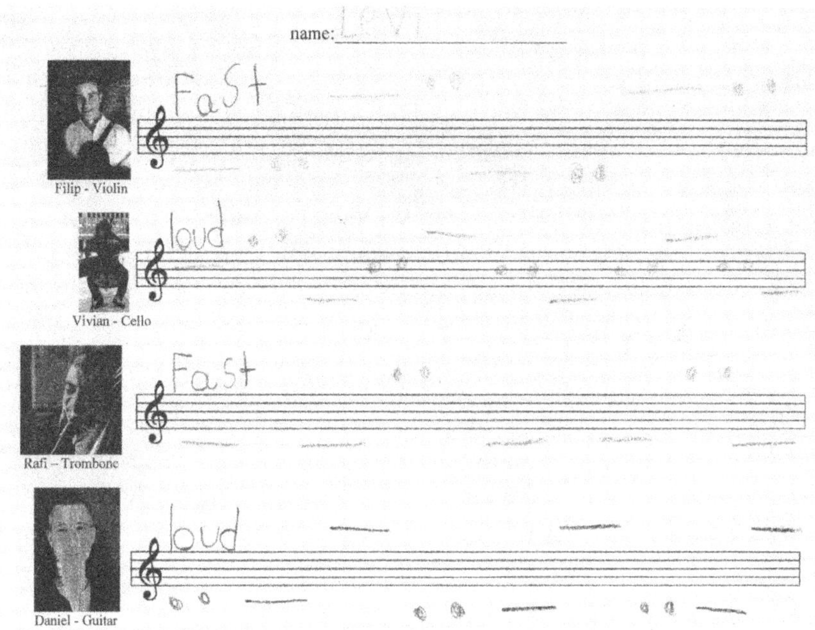

FIGURE 6.10 Levi's Squiggle Score

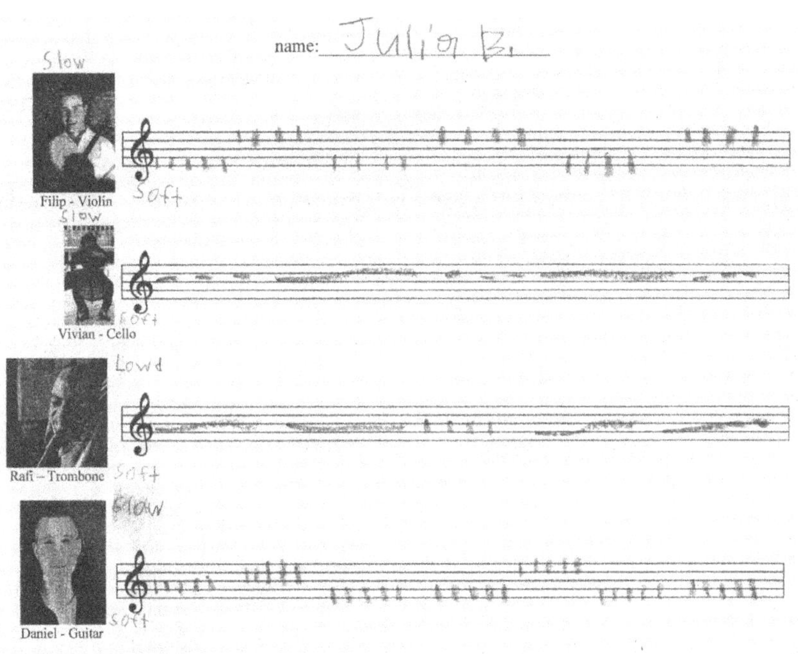

FIGURE 6.11 Julia's Squiggle Score

Non-music-readers, please stay with me for just a few more sentences—this won't be as arcane as it might threaten to be. Each left-to-right five-line staff on the Squiggle Score is reserved for an individual instrument (Filip/violin, Vivian/cello . . .). Each colored mark on a staff indicates certain qualities of sound: short and long marks indicate short or long notes, marks higher up or lower down on the staff indicate relatively higher or lower pitch for that staff's instrument. The width of the staff from left to right indicates a certain measurement of time that is fluid, determined only when the score is performed. Time passes at an identical rate on all staves, so vertical alignment of marks in different staves indicates simultaneity. The general idea is clear to students after a few minutes of modeling. The teaching artist helps students adjust the level of detail represented in their score according to their individual capabilities. Students who more easily connect the shapes with sounds will have more time to add detail or reconsider the choices they have made, and may add dynamics (*loud*) or other expressive markings (*quick like raindrops*).

CASE STUDY: DISASTER BY DESIGN

I'm watching twenty-two first graders squirming and rolling on the colorful carpeted floor of Ms. Lovano's classroom at PS130 in Queens. This display isn't part of a planned activity; they have simply had enough of me. The kids are showing a fair amount of self-restraint, being pretty polite, since they are stopping short of actually getting up and walking away. I'm humiliated. Ms. Lovano is watching me work myself into a mess. She seems intrigued. I know these students never behave this way when Ms. Lovano is in charge. What am I doing wrong?

This kind of scene plays out at various intensities many times in our work—perhaps you recognize the dynamic? It happens with children as well as adults, although the adults roll on the floor less often than the first graders do; adult tuning out is usually subtler. As a teaching artist in the moment, I desperately needed to diagnose and fix the problem. In the situation described above, I've obviously failed to spark intrinsic motivation. I'm looking for a tune-out trigger to un-trigger. Were we engaging with a high-quality work of art? Yes. Was it just before lunch, or was the room oxygen-deprived? No, that wasn't the problem. Had the students taken against me for some reason (I have seen it happen—an entire high school class going livid by degrees as they realized I was not simply going to tell them what a piece of music meant and why it was important, oy . . .), or was the teacher signaling by her behavior that I wasn't worth paying attention to, reading a newspaper while we worked? No, everyone was on board with the program, happy to be doing a music class, and the classroom teacher—bless her—was participating and looking on with a bemused smile.

Was I presenting an interesting idea? Yes, potentially: the sounds of the different vocal ranges in a chorus. Was I presenting the idea in an interesting manner? This might have been the first question in my diagnostic. No, the manner of presentation was not interesting, and my original vision of delivering a scintillating discourse on the topic to a reverently hushed and admiring class was dead in the water. I had somehow rendered my topic utterly boring. But I could not in the moment figure out why.

"Ms. Lovano, this is not working. What am I doing wrong?"

This kind of exchange is sometimes called transparent partnering, where facilitators or teachers drop the façade of semi-omniscience and try to figure out what is going on or what to do next, in full view of their charges. The exchange is bracing for the students observing it, because teachers don't usually reveal this kind of vulnerability in front of them. When this kind of shift in classroom dynamics takes place, students become interested and attentive, as these students did. The room went still.

"You're speaking in abstractions, telling them about ideas and sounds that they can't see or touch or care about. They need information to be concrete."
"I'm not sure I know what you mean. How could I do that?"
"How about having the voices be like Papa Bear, Mama Bear, and Baby Bear? I've got some stuffed bears right here . . ."

We were pretty good at imagining and performing the different bears' speaking and singing voices. As it turned out, the Bear Family loved to sing together with their different vocal ranges, and those ranges translated well in to the soprano, alto, tenor, and bass ranges of the singers in the chorus we were preparing to hear. The students' engaged response to the more physical (the bears have bodies and voices, and are present), narrative, and interpersonal approach (the bears have individual characters and relationships) immediately confirmed Ms. Lovano's insight that my abstractions needed to be concretized. The information I needed to convey took hold, thanks to Ms. Lovano's kind and efficient intervention.

The picture of a young teaching artist floundering in Ms. Lovano's class makes for an instructive disaster. Mistaken View, too much talking, lack of a good analogy, developmental inappropriateness, and failure to honor prior knowledge all make an appearance; it was a disaster by Design. My self-diagnostic question was "Was I *presenting* . . .," which revealed my View that my role was that of a presenter of information, instead of a designer of experiences, a View I now consider mistaken. Time spent on *presenting* is time taken away from the workshop participants' *Making & Doing*. It is easier to foster engagement (with a process or a work of art) by Making & Doing than by asking students to listen to the workshop leader talk. It can also be easier, and therefore tempting, for an artist to plan what they want to *say* than it is to design a Make and Do activity. Put simply, I was talking too much, motivated by my View that my talking was effective.

Better to talk less and do more. One measure I have for a successful workshop Design is how little I plan to say, and less is invariably better. I love a good lecture, but please don't ask me to deliver one. If I am speaking less, it means were are Making & Doing, that my prompts are concise and effective, and that the reflecting that is happening is the students', not mine. If an activity is designed well, the moments when teaching artist explanations are essential will be few and far between.

Another problem my floor-rolling critics helped me to identify involved developmental appropriateness. Seven-year-olds have a limited ability to think abstractly; I was presenting them with an abstract musical idea (identifying different vocal ranges). The mistake is a common one for teaching artists getting to know this age group. I was inexperienced, feeling my way into what would work. When teachers in the planning sessions would comment that an activity I was proposing "won't work with our children," I thought they were underestimating their children's' abilities (which reveals another weakness in my approach, that I was not making the best use of the expertise around me). A few teachers did underestimate their students, but they were right about the abstract thinking: the children were not developmentally able, that is, not *capable* of connecting strongly with or caring about an idea that wasn't narrative or concrete in some way. They may want to connect, but abstractions often fail to resonate with children. The disconnect trigger that I accidentally designed into the activity might have been avoided had I started with the students' prior knowledge. Even if the concert involved abstraction (for example, wordless or non-programmatic music, not uncommon), I could have used students' prior knowledge to help them make the connection between the known and the new.

OBSERVE THE EXISTING COMMUNITY

In 2010, I was asked to design and facilitate a new program for Carnegie Hall at Sing Sing Correctional Facility. Some of the men incarcerated there were already playing together in ensembles, and interacting informally with artists from Carnegie who went inside the walls to present concerts. The workshop proposal already approved by the New York State Department of Corrections outlined an eight-month, twenty-visit, two-concert residency. During this time, the men would "develop their musical abilities." The specific nuts and bolts of the workshop Design would be up to me.

I knew next to nothing about prisons and prison life. Without sitting down and making music with the men, I had no idea as to what the potentials of the situation were in terms of music, teaching, and learning, and little sense of how to predict or remove any impediments—no way of knowing how to Design a workshop. Manuel Bagorro, Weill Music Institute's program manager for Musical Connections at Sing Sing, understood this and agreed with the idea that my detailed workshop proposal would only be developed after meeting with the men, once I experienced how they responded to various challenges and opportunities. The initial session that resulted was a kind of interactive observation of an existing community of learners that I have come to think of as a *diagnostic session.*

On the appointed day, I entered the facility for the first time. A corrections officer escorted me to a room in the school where sixteen men had gathered, most with guitars or keyboards at hand. We warmed up with some whole-group rhythmic improvisations. Then I asked each of the men to play sponta-neous improvised duets with me (Figure 6.12).

In this activity, I assume a kind of naïveté in order to elicit the information I need to know. The invitation "OK, let's improvise together . . ." is at best very general and at worst problematically incomplete for a musician who wants to respond in a coherent way. I know that my overly broad invitation might elicit a) silence (meaning *I can't,* or *I don't know what to do*), b) some music (with the bold participant soldiering on without having set up any useful parameters, out of enthusiasm, or perhaps without regard for musical interaction or col-laboration), c) an already composed song or piece of music (i.e., *I don't want to improvise with you—here is something I have prepared*), or d) an intelligent question that reveals the state of the participants' existing knowledge, such as *What key are we in?* or *Should I play chords or lead?*

All of these responses are equally valuable because they reveal aspects of each participant's musicality, and something of their learning style, person-ality, and position in the local socio-musical hierarchy. A series of dialogues ensues as the men observe and applaud each other's efforts. A working mu-sical vocabulary quickly arises. We explore different kinds of textures, roles, tonalities, and other harmonic, rhythmic, or formal structures, or sometimes play it safer and invent a simple chord progression. I begin to know where

Diagnostic Session (10 minutes per participant)		
activity	steps	support
SPONTANEOUS DUET (10 min)	• Each student improvises a short duet with the teaching artist. • All discuss: *What just happened?*	Rather than overtly setting up each duet, relinquish control; wait for the musician to offer up whatever structure or idea that makes it possible to play together. Stay loose, and musically commit to whatever arises. Avoid atonality with beginners. Intermediate players may be able to do spontaneous two-part counterpoint.

FIGURE 6.12 Diagnostic Session Activity

these men are in their development as musicians, what they know and don't know, what they value, and it all comes out in our interaction.

Our active and engaged first session is fun, even joyful. The safe space we create becomes the basis upon which we build our community. As I more or less wordlessly get to know the men, they are getting to know me; I too am revealing aspects of my personality and musicality as I draw them out and respond to their ideas, as I notice and praise their choices (a form of *stealth reflection*—see page 117). These incarcerated men are already skilled readers of body language and spoken tone. I couldn't hide my feelings if I wanted to. But I don't want to: I am there to connect.

As we play together the men reveal a wide range of abilities, a yearning to express their ideas, and a hunger for learning and for beauty. At the end of the session, I ask the men to tell me what they want to learn. What they want, judging by the list they offer up, is a music conservatory education, everything from traditional harmony, arranging, orchestration, and music theory to contemporary songwriting and how to notate pop, funk, heavy metal, and R&B rhythms. They want to know everything.

With their desire to learn and their musical capabilities as revealed in the duet work clear in my mind, I design an ongoing atelier setting where new work, musical skill, and theoretical knowledge will develop simultaneously, with an emphasis on freedom and personal expression. Today the workshop is in its ninth year and has gained national media attention, as well as Carnegie Hall's strong support, and has grown to directly serve some forty men each year. Had I designed the Sing Sing workshop without a diagnostic session, I doubt it would have turned out so well.

In another kind of diagnostic session, I spent a day watching teachers work with their grade 2–5 students at a progressive public school on East 33rd Street in various nonmusical areas of study (math, ELA, visual arts), just prior to beginning a six-visit preparation workshop for a jazz performance at Lincoln Center. In their third grade classrooms, squirmy interlocutors were respectfully reminded, "Eyes on the speaker." Since everyone agreed that this was socially important, and that failing to do so was rude, students were not put off by the reminder. It felt good to remember, and to do. I adopted the phase, and used it to good effect. But second graders weren't familiar with the third graders' classroom social contracts. When I said "Eyes on the speaker" to a second grader, I received only a confused look. I can understand her bewilderment: in order to say "Eyes on the speaker" I myself had just a) interrupted the speaker and b) looked at someone other than the speaker, in effect adding to the very problem I was trying to fix. The second graders had their own shorthand: a teacher's saying "Magic Five" was understood by everyone to mean *please 1) sit down, 2) legs crossed, 3) hands in lap, 4) stop talking, and 5) put your eyes on me.* Like "Eyes on the Speaker," "Magic Five" wasn't demeaning, it was efficient and had the community-acknowledging quality of insider jargon.

The best teachers I observed that day were at once more rigorous and more playful than I had anticipated. I saw that students could be asked to work harder, do more, support their thinking, and follow guidelines without losing any pleasure in the process. These teachers provided clear and well-enforced rules and guidelines for the community. But they could also get profoundly silly once in a while without interrupting the learning. In fact their silliness fed the learning, because it embodied mutual trust: *There is space here for all of us to get silly, and I trust you to do so in a fun and appropriate way.* After my day of observation, I adopted the tone and some of the practices of the most effective teachers. I did not have those teachers' experience or insight, still less their ability to observe the micro-shifts in their classroom community's flow, but a day of observation was enough to allow me to begin imitating their rigorous yet playful tone.

A more interactive diagnostic session: men who participated in fatherhood groups at homeless shelters in the NYC area were invited to bring their children to Carnegie Hall for a family concert. The *existing community* met for weekly discussions at the shelter, men only, guided by a social worker, with the goal of becoming better dads. I was asked to create a forty-five-minute workshop activity for the group to prepare them for the concert experience. As the father of a twelve-year old, the opportunity to work with the men struck a chord in me: I identified with what they were trying to do in their weekly meetings, the direct way they were trying to improve their fathering skills, with their children's and spouse's benefit in mind. I planned to join the weekly Fatherhood Group discussion during its usual time slot, then facilitate the music workshop immediately afterward. When the group met, I was introduced and settled in with the idea of being a respectful and attentive guest. The discussion topic that evening was *discipline*. I joined the conversation and was sometimes dismayed by what I heard, though I tried not to show it. My claim that I did not hit my own child was openly disbelieved. Nevertheless, a mutually respectful and accommodating atmosphere prevailed. The men made me feel welcome. In those first forty-five minutes I made a transition from guest to community member, thanks to the willingness of the workshop participants to admit an outsider into their circle. The men's trust was key to the concert preparation workshop's being fruitful and fun. For a closer look at this workshop, see page 277, the *Fatherhood Family Concert Workshop*.

The positive effects my participation in the group discussion had on the music workshop interaction were *anticipated* and built in to the Design. What I did not anticipate was the way the discussion—which included many honest revelations about beliefs and motivations in the men's worlds—gave rise to a heightened sense of my responsibility to serve them and their families to the best of my ability. My sense of service took deeper root that night, grew over time, and contributed to my desire to write this book.

In your role as the Predictor and Remover of Impediments, take the measure of the community you will be working with: its nature, dynamics, and especially its potentials. If you can't schedule any diagnostic time, have a conversation with someone who already works with the students, a teacher or other leader. You may also be able to look at written work or art work from previous workshops to inform your sense of your participant's potentials. Notes from other teaching artists who have worked in that community can also tell you a lot. If none of these options is available, begin your first workshop with a community-establishing warm-up. What you learn in that short time can be a foundation for your Design.

MAKE THE LANGUAGE EXPERIENTIAL

The terminology you use during workshops can create or remove impediments. The musical terms *beat, rhythm, pulse, groove* may have unclear meanings or multiple, divergent meanings to any two people. *Ostinato, riff, vamp*, and *pattern* may mean the same thing or different things to any two musicians. Students will look to you to define artistic terms. Limit the number of words you use in a workshop by choosing a focused, functional set of terms to work with. Decide if you will say *melody* or *tune, harmony* or *chord*, according to what serves, then more or less abandon the other word, except if you need it momentarily to better define your chosen word. Your consistency should help everyone build a shared, accurate understanding of the language you use to describe the work. In her book *Variations on a Blue Guitar*, Maxine Greene reminds us that "*(as educators), we learn the appropriateness of specific vocabularies when talking about art and non-art and the inappropriateness of others. Even more important, we learn the degree of craftsmanship and care and discipline required for the making and interpretation of art forms.*" An art-specific term may be useful because it is efficient: it is easier to say *ombre* than to say *they way the color slowly fades into the other color as you move across the surface and ends up getting darker toward the bottom*. If you are getting a kinesthetic feel for the way ballet dancers move, knowing the French word *jeté* ("thrown"), may help you understand how to take the leap itself, the spirit in which it is undertaken, and something of the cultural antecedents of leaping *jeté*-style as opposed to any other way. To a Cajun musician, the wooden instrument on display is a *fiddle*; to the Paganini-playing recitalist it is probably a *violin*. An *ostinato* in a Steve Reich minimalist orchestra piece, a Rebirth Brass Band horn section's *shout chorus accompaniment riffs* and a Vijay Iyer *loop* all have different names, but share the basic quality of being *insistently repeated patterns of notes*. Words that are unfamiliar, rich, or otherwise interesting or ambiguous may be just the thing to spark your student's curiosity.

Sometimes the attempt to define an unfamiliar art-specific word leads down a wonderful rabbit-hole of derivations or resonances. If you use the word *polyphony* to talk about the Tallis frog pond analogy (page 85), you'll want to demonstrate what the roots *poly* (many) and *phony* (voice or voiced sound) mean, which may lead you down the road to *mono* (one) *phony* or even *hetero* (different) or *homo* (same) phony, musical terms describing the relationship of independent or concerted voices, or even *tele* (distant) *phone* and *mega* (great, mighty) *phone*. This flowering of *phonys* would be explored in the service of clarifying the original term. If you use the word *counterpoint* to describe Mendelsohn's Octet (page 86), you may end up side-tracked, asking students for all the *counter-* and *contra-* prefixed words they know (*contraband, contradict, contrary, counterinsurgency, countermand, counteract* . . .) in order to open up the meaning of the *counterpoint*. Such sidetracks into language may enhance your students' engagement, and the spontaneous pursuit helps to keep your classroom practice loose and responsive.

Whenever you can, make unfamiliar terms *experiential*. This requires your expertise and imagination. Translate concepts into kinesthetic or visual experiences as simply and directly as possible. Let's use the musical term *pitch* as an example. Pitch refers to the specific frequency of a sound, how high or low it seems, defined by a musical alphabet letter name or by the number of vibrations per second associated with that letter name. When the oboist provides the orchestra a pitch to tune to, it is an A 440, a note called "A" whose waveform vibrates 440 times per second. You might have the goal of your students being able to define *pitch*, or the term may simply come up unplanned-for during an activity; either starting point is valid for this scenario: your students just listened to the unaccompanied melody from the American Negro Spiritual song "Swing Low, Sweet Chariot," sung by a female soloist. You ask "What do you notice about this song?" and opportunities to connect vocabulary with direct experience come up:

> TA: What did you notice about the music we just heard?
>
> STUDENT: She was singing high.
>
> TA: Good. Let's investigate that idea. Please be my echo. . .
>
> (singing and raising/moving hands high, middle and low): High pitch, middle pitch, low pitch.
>
> STUDENTS (SINGING AND RAISING/MOVING HANDS HIGH, MIDDLE AND LOW): High pitch, middle pitch, low pitch.
>
> TA: (similarly) High high high, low low low, high-low, high-low. . .
>
> STUDENTS: (similarly) High high high, low low low, high-low, high-low. . .
>
> TA: (speaking) I'm going to sing some little melodies. Please raise your hand to tell me if you hear them as high, or low or mixed.

The teaching artists experiments with improvised melodies, tracking the students' abilities to differentiate pitch, leading them to more complex mixtures of high, middle, and low pitch, then reconnects with the song:

> TA: (speaking) Follow along with me. . .
> (singing the entire song while raising/moving hands) Swing low, sweet chariot . . . (speaking) What's happening with (or *Where do you hear. . .*) high, middle, and low pitches in this song?

Within a couple of interactive minutes, everyone learns that *pitch* is a quality that has characteristics of highness and lowness. The teaching artist rendered the quality noticed by the student in visual, kinesthetic, and aural modalities and brought the students back to the music, asking them to use *pitch* as a way to more carefully describe what they heard. The description might serve as the basis for analysis and interpretation (see "Describe, Analyze, Interpret," page 131. At first, "She was singing high." might have meant any number of things to your students. It's the kind of ambiguous, not-exactly-correct answer that can feel disappointing to a teaching artist (see "Honor Every Response," page 149. But also provides some realistic assessment: this is where the students are in their ability to listen and report what they observe. In every response, and especially in the questions they ask, students are revealing what they do or do not understand. Knowing this and having a sense of what to do with the information empowers teaching artists to honor every response, and makes it possible for them to stay in the moment with their students.

This Ain't Working, But It's Not Their Fault

Confidence and pride are tricky wardrobe pieces. The former is like the go-to, fashionable pair of pants you know you can pull off because of your experience, your swag. I am very confident in my ability to go into any learning context and get young folks dancing and creating work that either has a self-empowerment or social justice message. So when I embarked on a short in-school residency with high school students in a dance elective, I just knew they would be game to create a choreo-poem that explored how distal environmental and social events impact everyone regardless of geography. We would explore concepts of causality by using spoken word and choreography prompts to create a full-class collaborative piece. *This will be a breeze!* But the class wasn't engaged, and didn't respond to my invitations and prompts, and I became increasingly frustrated. As it turns out, I was wearing off-putting pride pants that blocked me from realizing my students had never had an experience that might prime them for peer collaboration or creating choreography. I redesigned the residency around my learning what the students were interested in, and my learning how to communicate with them individually and collectively. They would all write and perform, but to streamline the process and model more, I (not the group) would choreograph. I communicated with each student privately about their progress in personal check-in journals. We worked together to establish community accountability for actions and attitudes that held us back from the new shared goal. We still had some hurdles that come with high schoolers and first period attendance, but I am so grateful to have had my pride humbled and confidence reframed. Biggest takeaway: *What wasn't working was me conflating confidence with pride, and not making space for students' voices. Now I wear this understanding as the most essential garment in my practice.*—Aysha Little Upchurch, dance TA, Boston, MA

Chapter 7

Working with Teachers and Administrators

Teaching Artists as Professional Development Facilitators

The two toughest crowds I have ever worked with as a teaching artist both consisted entirely of professional educators. The first encounter was during an aesthetic education workshop for NYC-area school and district arts administrators, hosted by Lincoln Center Education at Juilliard, where every participant appeared to believe they had already seen or imagined anything I had to say or would ask them to do. Perhaps they had. But trying to form a functional container with thirty-five experienced, self-assured, professional container-formers was, at best, exhausting. They were more interested in critiquing and professionally developing the teaching artist at every step than they were in the work of art. Imagine a workshop where every time you issue an invitation or pose a question the participants avoid responding to the prompt, and instead delightedly start *critically dissecting* what you've just said in terms of its educational efficacy. Unforgettable.

The second was a group of junior high school teachers who had been gathered for a mandatory after-school professional development session, or PD. Five out of twenty teachers present walked in, avoided eye contact, and sat at the back of the room; two of them opened their newspapers, three simply sat side by side, folded their arms and closed their eyes (yes, they were all men). The remaining teachers were more or less present. It makes me laugh to remember it, but at the time I was quite daunted such a display of disregard from people that I had assumed were colleagues. I later learned (and this turns out to be fairly typical in spite of everyone's good intentions) that the teachers hadn't signed up for the workshop, and didn't have any idea who I was, who I represented, or what the PD might be about. They were required by contract to be present for forty-five minutes. Apparently their contract did not stipulate that they needed to be attentive or even awake. In this case my self-esteem and nerve held just firm enough for me to persevere. As I worked with group in the front, whose eyes were open, I occasionally addressed someone in the back, throwing out a line to see if I might draw them in. They came back at me with funny or sarcastic answers. As we continued this way, the work we were doing up front proved interesting enough that the newspapers became steadily less captivating. Eventually the fun that the more engaged teachers were having brought most of the back row around, and we all parted on friendly and respectful terms.

All teaching artists will at some point be asked to lead a program-related PD session for classroom teachers, most likely for whatever program they are hired to facilitate. In this chapter, we'll look at the three kinds of meetings teaching artists facilitate for our professional educator partners: planning sessions, post-workshop reviews, and professional development. The "Planning Session" section details what you'll need to do for a pre-workshop curriculum review or curriculum creation meeting. The "End-of-Unit Review" is a structured reflection, useful in situations where more extensive assessment tools are not yet in place. The "Collaboration Workshop PD" and "Structure and Freedom PD" are general-purpose PDs that build collegiality and have potential application in the teachers' non-arts classrooms. The "Structure and Freedom PD" in particular might be useful in many classroom contexts, or with students studying any work of art that involves improvisation; the activities it contains formed the basis for the jazz and world music units of study in Carnegie Hall's Global Exchange program. In the "Classroom Teacher Art-Making Video PD," teachers publish a video featuring themselves as art-makers. All of the workshops have been road-tested in urban and suburban schools, with classroom teachers from a variety of specialties.

In a typical planning session or professional development, you'll meet with a group of between two and forty teachers. Some of them will be in their first years of teaching, others grade- and subject-leaders, and some of them formidable masters and mentors. Each has her own style, passions, and varied interests in educational theory, research, and technique or practice. They take pride and pleasure in their work, long days and tired voices notwithstanding. *In a single session of forty-five or ninety minutes, what can a teaching artist offer that these professional colleagues might want or need?*

Before answering, let's consider the current zeitgeist. Teaching artists should be aware that our classroom teacher partners are under various pressures and constraints, as Allison Gulamhussein's introduction to the Center for Public Education's *Teaching the Teachers: Effective Professional Development in an Era of High Stakes Accountability* outlines: *"In the coming years, schools will be hit with a trio of potent reforms: teacher evaluations that will include student test scores, widespread adoption of higher academic standards, and the development of high stakes standardized tests aligned with these new standards . . ."* While working within local, state, federal, and funder guidelines, *"the real challenge schools face is how to create opportunities for teachers to grow and develop in their practice so that they, in turn, can help students grow and develop their knowledge and ability to think critically."*[1]

But delivering quality professional development to teachers remains problematic for many schools and institutions: *"In a recent study, researchers found that while 90 percent of teachers reported participating in professional development, most of those teachers also reported that it was totally useless (Darling-Hammond et al, 2009) . . . One-time workshops are the most prevalent model for delivering professional development. Yet workshops have an abysmal track record for changing teacher practice and student achievement. (Yoon et al, 2007)"*[2] I'd like to think that the 10 percent of professional developments that were deemed effected in the quoted study were facilitated by teaching artists. But let's return to the question: *In this environment, what do teaching artists have to offer?*

As Arts-in-Education partners and artist-facilitators providing professional development, teaching artists are in effect guests at the education table. We function as liaisons between the institutions that employ us and the schools with whom they partner. While we are ready to facilitate workshops and programs, few of us are equipped to deliver the catalysts for systemic change that Gulamhussein tells us is needed. And while classroom teachers are not entirely resistant to attending state-mandated professional development, they have already sat through a lot of unhelpful sessions, and many understandably regard any infringement on their dwindling preparation time skeptically. Our teacher partners already struggle to incorporate what they see as best practices in a system skewed toward assessment and away from teachers freely exercising their craft.

But in our role as occasional professional development providers, we have something valuable to offer. Teaching artists regularly practice key components of recent education reforms and standards that teachers are urged (or required) to embrace: incorporating students' prior knowledge, making learning social through collaboration and discussion, and engaging students in meaning making. These practices are hallmarks of our work. For example the constructivist-inspired View, Design, and Respond practices we've explored in this book have the potential to address at least four of the ten main findings of the Center for Public Education's research. Finding: *The Common Core standards focus on teaching for critical thinking, but research shows that most classroom instruction is weak in this area. Therefore, professional development needs to emphasize practices that will turn students into critical thinkers and problem solvers.* Critical thinking and problem solving are woven in to the Making & Doing in our ateliers. Finding: *Teachers' initial exposure to a concept should not be passive, but rather should engage teachers through varied approaches so they can participate actively in making sense of a new practice.* Our PDs, like our workshops, are as participatory and creative-generative as we can make them, and seek to make the most of teachers' expertise and willingness to experiment and grow. Finding: *Modeling has been found to be a highly effective way to introduce a new concept and help teachers understand a new practice.* Teaching artists model often, and, like classroom teachers, constantly cultivate modeling skills. Finding: *Support during implementation must address the dual roles of teachers as both technicians in researched-based practices, as well as intellectuals developing teaching innovations.* Teachers are often more familiar with constructivist theory than we are; there is intellectual muscle behind the way we practice that they will recognize.

Some PD sessions are brief, forty-five minutes or an hour designed to allow the classroom teachers and teaching artists a chance to get to know each other well enough to co-teach or at least share a classroom with some trust and confidence. Programs with a written curriculum may require a separate planning session for each unit of study, during which the work of art is studied and lesson plans reviewed, to make sure everyone involved understands the goals and means of the work. Less commonly, individual teachers or even whole schools agree to form a deeper relationship with a presenting institution, and to receive ongoing professional development. Such programs might involve workshops lasting as long as two or three weeks, as Lincoln Center Institute's summer session used to do. At that time, classroom teachers were viewed as qualified and prepared to work with a teaching artist only after the training.

Are classroom teachers and teaching artists different in any substantive way? We all make use of the Design Practices and Respond Principles explored in this book. And if there is any difference at all between an arts specialist in a school and a teaching artist, it is a matter of the school's expectations of each individual. But we develop different skill sets. Teaching artists spend more time making art, studying art and art-making, and in other ways living the artist's life than classroom teachers do. Our art-making practice allows us to embody *artistry* in a particular way. Artists have completed the three classic phases of apprenticeship: deep observation, skills acquisition, and experimentation. If we have completed the 10,000 required hours of work detailed by Malcolm Gladwell in *Outliers*, we are approaching or have attained mastery of our craft. Shaped by the roots of our artistic practice, teaching artists bring energy, ideas, and indeed a presence to the classroom that is different (not better) than that of classroom teachers, who have been shaped by a different set of experiences and disciplines.

Accomplished, active artists are rare birds in school contexts, in part because we have a different relationship with tradition and authority than the one usually encouraged by schools, and students are intrigued by this relationship. We enter the classroom not to impart information, but to invite students to take part in new creative experiences. We invite them to explore aspects of their human potential that may not otherwise receive much attention. Students' curiosity about us can open a door to interaction and collaboration, and help set up the conditions for a relationship that may be different from those that they have with their classroom teachers. For teaching artists who share a classroom with classroom teachers, we find that they value us for the intellectual and physical bravery we bring out in their students. They know that we can help certain struggling or quiet students to shine. Teachers tend to welcome the vitality and sense of adventure we bring to their community.

Most classroom teachers will welcome you as a colleague or honored guest, and value what you bring to their students—but a few will not. Don't be surprised if you do not connect well with all classroom teachers. When our teacher partners minimize, discount, or ignore our work, they may do so subtly (not attending planning and review sessions, arriving late, leaving early) or obviously (reading the paper while we teach; neglecting to complete any follow-up or reflection; avoiding any co-teaching). Perhaps teachers see themselves as more permanent members of the school community and the profession, and see teaching artists as occasional, less dedicated and less skilled practitioners. It is true that we are less permanent. And in terms of formal training in teaching technique, most of us are less skilled. Is the teaching artist/classroom teacher divide that we sometimes experience born of a professional antipathy, or a personal one? We are required to work as best we can with everyone on the team, including individual teachers and staff who feel or create a sense of opposition. It may not be possible to explain why an adversarial tone develops. A classroom teacher may feel threatened because they are being *observed* by a teaching artist. Most often, arts-phobic teachers avoid showing interest or modeling engagement (let alone risk-taking) because the art form at hand makes them feel inadequate or uncomfortable. This unfortunate dynamic arises with perhaps one out of ten teachers, and I'm sorry to report that in these situations I've only been able to bring about a positive resolution if we continued to collaborate in a multi-year program. Fair warning: you can break bread with and open-heartedly share personal life details with a classroom teacher, or favor a given teacher's class with extra time and resources, and lead energized, productive sessions with their students, and they may still strongly recommend that the school leadership team de-fund your program. Also, there are politics in any faculty that we are not (and probably do not want to be) privy too—that's natural enough. The problem comes when we unknowingly fall afoul of those politics. All these conflicts—profession, personal, political—are not something that anyone in Arts-in-Education really wants to talk about. Who would want to admit that not everyone works and plays well with all others? But we can admit the problem is there, do what we can to minimize its effect, and continue to work as best we can with the nine out of ten classroom teachers who kindly welcome us as a colleagues.

Ideally, the classroom teachers you work with will have self-selected to take part in your program, and will look forward to planning sessions and PDs and co-teaching with curiosity and a spirit of openness. My scary stories were caveats. Almost every classroom teacher you'll work with will be professional and ready to engage, even when they are at the tired end of the energy curve. They'll value you for your expertise, serious play, and the free exploration of ideas you bring to their students. As the busiest human beings on the planet, classroom teachers will notice and appreciate your taking the time to design planning, review, and PD sessions that are fun, have a clear purpose, and provide them with useful tools.

The Kids Are Watching

When I was new to the field, I was asked to work with a classroom teacher who was "burnt out." I said yes, thinking that partnering with an artist might be just the thing to reinvigorate her. But every day I witnessed her making derisive, even nasty remarks to and about her students. So the students resented the teacher. They perceived me as her ally, and therefore resented me. The classroom was toxic. To get projects built, I started pulling small groups out to work with me in the hall. We sculpted a 360° walk-through map after the teacher told the students "Maps mean nothing to you!" I stuck with the residency out of sheer stubbornness. In the end, we were able to complete our project. But I had been naïve, and possibly overconfident. I should have walked away from the partnership when I first understood that I couldn't be a "fix-all" arts solution to what was going wrong in that classroom. As guests in schools, we teaching artists want to say "yes" to requests, and hesitate to say "no." But we need to be vigilant and safeguard the quality of our work—and not just artistically. My takeaway: *As professionals partnering with educators, we have a right to healthy and positive working relationships, and a responsibility to safeguard those qualities. The kids are watching.*—Jeff Mather, visual arts, Atlanta, GA

Why I Love Working With Classroom Teachers

I was doing a drama integration residency with a fifth-grade teacher named Michele. She was a fully engaged partner teacher, and came to our planning sessions with enthusiasm and ideas. We designed a series of lessons using process drama and improvisation to explore topics in American history. We used a variety of strategies moving through World War I and the Twenties. For the Great Depression, we wanted to give the students the experience of living through the hard times. We designed and executed a lesson in which we played the parents of a farming family, and the students were all our children; we cycled them, seven or eight at a time, through a series of family dinners in which the family's fortunes and prospects spiraled downward. After each dinner, all the students, whether they had been in that particular improvisation or had simply watched from the outside, wrote a journal entry about the meal and the bad news. The format worked like a charm, and Michele played her role as the mother with conviction and pathos. The students' writing was detailed and insightful. Since then, I've developed a three-session residency around those lessons, incorporating period photos, music, primary source diary excerpts, and a video recording of all the students in character with simple costume pieces reading from their journals chronicling the downfall of an imagined Depression-era family. Now I bring the residency to several schools year after year—and I owe it all to Michele. My takeaway: *a good partner teacher can help me grow.*—Barry Stewart Mann, actor, storyteller, educator, Atlanta, GA

Planning Sessions

Planning Session: Curriculum Review (60 min.)

5 min.	welcome/personal connection
5 min.	active work-of-art-connected warm up
5 min.	veterans describe program (if applicable)
10 min.	look at and discuss work of art
25 min.	review existing curriculum
10 min.	Q&A

Planning Session: Curriculum Writing (90 min.)

5 min.	welcome/personal connection
10 min.	active work-of-art-connected warm up
5 min.	veterans describe program (if applicable)
20 min.	look at work of art
40 min.	create actual curriculum
10 min.	Q&A

During planning sessions for Preparation workshops, teaching artists and their classroom teacher partners meet to review an existing curriculum (Curriculum Review) or lay out a new one together (Curriculum Writing). In the field you'll find many variations in planning and partnering processes, ranging from units of study that are scripted to those that are completely teaching-artist-planned and taught without input from the classroom teacher, to units where all the work is co-planned and co-taught. This chapter walks you through basic Curriculum Review and Curriculum Writing planning sessions. A Planning Session Checklist is included at the end of the section.

If you are in a planning session for a Studio or Arts Integration workshop, you can still follow the outline for Preparation workshops, allowing for a shift of focus and perhaps authority. Preparation workshops focus on the *work of art* (as defined by the teaching artist and presenting or sponsoring institution). Studio workshops are all about the *art-making process* (also as defined by the teaching artist and presenting or sponsoring institution; the school has input when it chooses a program that suits its needs). Arts Integration workshops grow out of academic or curricular goals (as defined by the school); the role of the art-making is determined by classroom teachers and teaching artists in collaboration.

Before you begin a unit of study in a school, you'll ideally be meeting with all the teachers involved for a planning session. You are entering into a collaboration, in a space where you are a guest, so it is prudent to get to know your collaborators and hosts. They want to know you too, because they are giving their charges over to your care. If a teacher can't attend the planning session, a grade leader or program coordinator might pass on details of the meeting to the missing colleague. But much is lost in translation when you don't have face-to-face interaction with your partner teachers. If all the classroom teachers cannot be present at a scheduled time and place, instead of beginning with a handicap, make an effort to reschedule the planning session and get all the teachers in the room for the meeting. If that isn't possible, it may be a signal that the school's commitment to your program is weak, and you might watch for other signs of disconnectedness. Consider asking your sponsoring organization for support, perhaps in the form of a phone call between administrators. Most principals and classroom teachers are doing Arts-in-Education programs because they value them and genuinely want their students to benefit from the experience, and they know how important the shared planning is. Get your supervisor or administrator to give them a nudge.

The grade leaders or program coordinators designated to work with you are your best partners and allies. Their teaching and leadership skills and their genuine enthusiasm for the work lead them to these positions. They are tuned in to the general atmosphere in the school, and the health of the management/employee relationships you may find yourself observing. They also know their colleagues personally, their strengths, and the stresses they may be facing in school or at home. Grade leaders are the senior teachers at their grade level; they keep an eye on their grade level as though it were a discrete department within a company, supporting, sometimes mentoring. A program co-coordinator is anyone in the school who is the designated on-site person meant to handle logistics: schedules, space, materials, and any problems that come up. They are usually compensated for the time they spend ironing out details, so they are generally able to be more interactive and better prepared than the classroom teachers who are often not compensated to prepare for meetings with you. Sometimes neither the coordinator nor the teachers are compensated for the meetings in any way, hence the origin of the thirty-minute sandwich-in-hand lunch-time planning session.

The classroom teachers you meet with are experts in several areas that you are not: their students' capabilities and predilections, educational philosophy, theory, and practice, and subject-specific methods, to name a few. They have examined, evaluated, facilitated, and perhaps created whole curricula. Some teachers are arts-friendly, some arts-phobic. A few are accomplished artists. They appreciate that you, the teaching artist, have insight into the work of art that they lack, and skills and art-specific abilities that they want their students to experience. Since many of them are specialists themselves, they appreciate your specialty and what your skill makes possible. Although they have formidable skills of their own, they are also aware that they are working in your (the arts specialist's) area, and are dependent on you to guide both the collaboration and the work.

The sixty-minute Curriculum Review and the ninety-minute Curriculum Writing planning sessions outlined earlier at the beginning of this section are most effective when they are at the center of these *before, during,* and *after* steps:

BEFORE THE PLANNING SESSION

Get to Know the Work of Art

Become familiar with the work of art and/or curriculum; see the suggested Study Prompts on pages 214–218 for suggestions on what to look for. If you are going to be creating a curriculum, prepare some likely activities to share with the classroom teachers, and a couple of outlines for contrasting units of study.

Provide Materials for Study

Create or provide concise samples and excerpts from the work of art, and a selection of contextual materials, for your teacher partners to review. In the case of a pre-written curriculum, these materials should already be provided by the sponsoring institution.

Teachers Get to Know the Work of Art

Ask the grade-level coordinators or lead teachers to review the work of art/curriculum and any attendant contextual information *with their teachers in a scheduled meeting before the planning session.* Making this very specific request will mean that more teachers will actually take the time to do so, in part because these meetings are usually compensated. If your invitation is more general, as in, "Please try to look at this material," you'll find that teachers cannot find the time do so before the meeting. Asking is worth the effort: less-informed classroom teachers make less able partners.

Settle Logistics

Discuss the use of classroom spaces, which are available, how are they equipped. Confirm that the room you'll meet in for the planning session includes gear to lay back any video and audio you'll want to present. Finalize the schedule of all teaching artist visits before the planning session takes place. Clarifying schedules can take up an entire meeting, so make it clear that you don't want to do any scheduling during the planning meeting. Your coordinator should be able to provide teachers' names, specialties, grades, class, and room numbers on a list for your reference. Create a project-specific email list with the coordinator's help, and test the list with a *hello and RSVP* note to make sure it is functional. Begin the process of confirming the existence of (or creating of) class lists and nametags for the students. (See "Workshop Space, Time, and Resources" on page 219 for a detailed checklist).

DURING AND AFTER THE PLANNING SESSION

Welcome and Personal Connection

Take time to greet and make a small personal connection with your partner teachers. Eye contact, handshakes, nametags, and general conversations—as in any working relationship, these first interactions and impressions matter.

Active Work-of-Art-Connected Warm-Up

Present your View by embodying it. Become *a community of learners; make and do* in an impromptu *atelier setting*. Based on this activity, your classroom teacher partners will understand your approach, and something of your style and substance. As with any warm-up in any setting, make sure it is directly connected with the work of art. You may want to use a Preparation activity from one of the thumbnail curricula you created before the meeting, since the teachers are about to encounter the work of art.

Veterans Describe Program (if applicable)

If there are teachers in the meeting who have worked with you before, ask them to speak about the program. They already know what their colleagues want and need to know, and can guide the group toward whatever information is most vital to them from a classroom teacher perspective. You are inviting them to lead part of the meeting, and demonstrating that you value your partners' ideas and opinions—and planting seeds for healthy collaborations during the program.

Look at the Work of Art

Anyone teaching to a work of art benefits from having as direct as possible an experience with that work. Show video or audio excerpts. Guide some reflection, and return again to the work of art. Ideally the teachers have already spent time with the work of art. If they have not, don't skip this step. Many teachers and teaching artists leave the work of art too soon, assuming they "got it," that their contact has been significant enough to allow them to teach to it. Resist that sense of complacency. If the teachers have all viewed the work before, watch it again, together, commenting, pointing out what you notice as it happens. Model the kind of sustained attentiveness that you hope to engender in the entire community, teachers and students alike.

Review Curriculum (if you are working with an already-written curriculum)

Before teachers start paging through the written document, establish an overview of the work, your goals and means. Most curricula have a summary or overview page. If yours does not, make one for your own benefit, an elevator pitch version of the program. Once everyone has a sense of overall shared purpose, allow some reading time. If time allows, look through every lesson together. Summarize steps where the work is clear, and talk through other less clear activities word by word. If time seems short, focus on lessons for which the classroom teachers are responsible, and give the teaching artist lessons brief summaries that make any connections or dependencies between the two explicit. For example if classroom teachers need to make a mask in Lesson #2 so that you can create a dance for a masked character in teaching artist–led Lesson #3, make sure that necessity is understood.

Create Actual Curriculum (if you are writing a new curriculum)

This is where you collaboratively create your Design, or at least as much of your Design as you can in the time allowed. Depending on your personal approach, some steps will take place during the planning session with the teachers, and some afterward. Generative planning sessions can take such unpredictable turns that it is almost impossible to adhere to a schedule of steps. It is usually a wonderfully messy process. Use your knowledge of the work of art as a kind of compass. This will make decision-making easier, and make the meeting more efficient, especially if the discussion starts getting sidetracked. Stay connected with the work of art.

Q&A

Leave a little time at the end of the meeting to clarify how far you've come, and what you have decided and designed. Make a list of questions that still need answers, as well as any action steps that require follow-up. And just to be safe, refer to your planning session checklist (Figure 7.1) before you adjourn the meeting.

Planning Session Checklist

A) Before

☐ TA get to know the work of art / curricular goals

☐ TA provide materials for the team to study

☐ teachers get to know the work of art / art-making-process

☐ team settle logistics

B) During

☐ welcome and personal connection

☐ active work-of-art- or curricular goals-connected warm up

☐ veterans describe program (if applicable)

☐ look at and discuss work of art / curricular goals

☐ review existing curriculum / create new curriculum

☐ Q&A

C) After

☐ share notes and unit outline

FIGURE 7.1

Share Notes and Unit Outline

After the meeting, once you've typed up your new curriculum and/or meeting notes, send them to the team as a Word document attached to an email. You may also want to create a one-page précis PDF that tracks schedule, lesson titles, field trips, and so on. all in one place, so teachers can easily write all these items into their personal calendars without having to work through the entire curriculum document. Ask your coordinator to check the dates and times against the school schedule one last time.

End-of-Unit Reflection

End of Unit Reflection (55 min.)

5	warm-up
15	review student reflections and evidence of learning
15	open discussion: self-evaluation
15	invent improvements
5	journal/written response

After you and your partner teachers have completed a unit of study, you will almost always have a meeting to reflect on your work. These sessions are part debriefing, part celebration, and part diagnostic. During the meeting, unless you have identified other goals, spend more or less equal amounts of time on *evidence* (reviewing student reflections and evidence of learning), *discussion* (to compare workshop experiences and evaluate both the work and the collaboration) and *redesign* (inventing improvements to the Design based on your evidence and discussion).

The first order of business in the meeting is to examine student learning, anecdotally as teachers give their general impressions, or according to *evidence* of learning in some more concrete form such as student portfolio contents: reflections, drawings, journals, art-making artifacts. When portfolio items are shared amongst teaching artists, teachers, and hosting and sponsoring institutions, there is a natural temptation to cherry-pick, to show only those student work samples that are *outstanding*. Everyone involved wants to have their work and their students' work seen in the best possible light. The best evidence of student achievement would arguably be work that shows a high level of artistic accomplishment and creativity. And it is appropriate to share and celebrate our students' high-level achievements. But be realistic regarding how big a part of the picture these accomplishments represent. The downside of cherry-picking is the same as doing so for any other body of evidence: a blatantly biased sample gives you a skewed picture of what you are trying to examine, in this case evidence of student learning.

Show and enjoy outstanding examples, but whenever possible show the work of the entire class side by side with that of your star pupils. An accurate picture of student learning is a better tool for improving your future programs than an overly rosy one.

During *discussion*, you have an opportunity to compare experiences in the workshop: *What worked well? What didn't?* How you measure the success of a unit of study depends on how you designed it in the first place. If your Design included specific student learning outcomes, you'll want to see how your evidence of student learning lines up with those goals. If your Design centered on an Inquiry, you'll want to know how completely and deeply students are able to answer the Inquiry questions. If you worked with a focused vocabulary, you'll want to know how many students are fluent in their use of those art-form-specific terms. If your Design stressed self-expression or self-discovery, you'll want to examine what the students themselves report about their journey. During this evaluation, try to gain some understanding about the mechanics of your successes and less-than-successes. If something worked (or did not work), tease out why it did so.

Ideas for *redesign* will naturally percolate as evidence of student learning and classroom experiences are discussed. *A particular activity worked well for more students: Why was that so? Should that activity be expanded or lengthened in the next Design? If a worksheet bombed, should it be replaced?* In this part of the meeting, you'll be able to see some of your classroom teacher partners' teaching craft. Compare the classroom teachers' different workshop experiences, including their thoughts on your teacher/teaching artist collaboration. Draw on their expertise in development and instructional design. If you've had doubts about any part of your Design, especially your own technique, ask your colleagues what they think, and how it might be improved. Ask what they would change about the program if they had a chance to do it again. At the end of the meeting, leave a few minutes and provide blank paper for anonymous written reflections, to capture ideas that may have gone unvoiced during the discussion. If teachers are filling out official end-of-unit evaluations (online surveys are a handy way to do this), request copies of the completed pages from your sponsoring organization and read them as part of your own Design self-assessment. Privately written evaluations sometimes include observations that teachers are not willing to or did not have a chance to bring up in a public discussion.

What are reasonable expectations for student success? Measuring student success for an entire unit of study is almost impossible to do in a manner that any four educators will agree is valid. You can more easily measure student *engagement*, the necessary first step on the way to success, during a given activity. Here you can set your sights very high: it is possible to have nearly universal attention and engagement nearly all the time if your activity is developmentally appropriate and otherwise well-designed. Once students are engaged, the rough percentages of observable student success (meaning the activity you invited was completed) recur with surprising regularity:

In a typical class of twenty-five students...

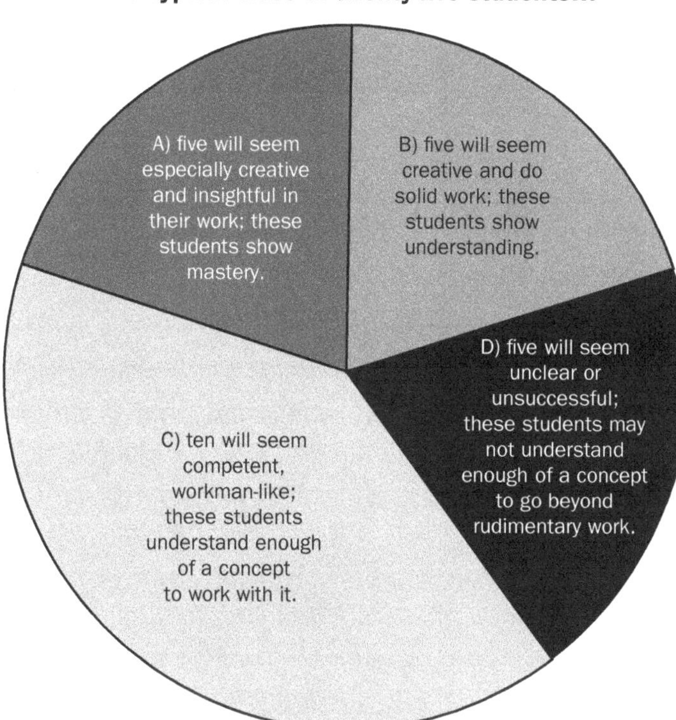

FIGURE 7.2 Observable student success in a typical class of twenty-five students

On any given day, about 20 percent of your students (A and B) will show a good if not excellent understanding of your inquiry, process, or concepts. Another 40 percent (C) will generally understand, but not *appear* as fluent as the top 40 percent (A and B). And 20 percent of your students (D), five out of every twenty-five, will *appear* to struggle or not follow your inquiry, process, or concepts to various degrees (Figure 7.2). The caveats here are important. *On any given day* might also be stated *during any given ten-minute interval*. Students' ability to engage with and complete an activity can fluctuate for many reasons. And that students may not *appear* to be as fluent does not suppose that they *are not* as fluent. We can't know what is happening inside our students' hearts and minds; assuming the contrary is unrealistic. That 20 percent of students struggle to various degrees doesn't implicate your Design or Response in any way. Think of that number as a more or less standard, perhaps unavoidable percentage of kids who will struggle. Students get tired, have problems at home, get sick, get hungry—all causes for distraction, inattention, lack of engagement.

These unscientific numbers are meant to help you set some reasonable professional goals. So many aspects of the classroom community you serve are beyond your control. As you assess your work, remember this, and be realistic as to your own expectations of yourself. For more on this, see "Thriving and Struggling" on page 167.

Rather than leaving your classroom teacher partners to their own devices as they prepare for the end-of-unit reflection, provide some simple materials to make the process easier. For the *Hello, Composers* program, a half-page suffices to remind them of the overall Design:

HELLO, COMPOSERS - End of Residency Reflection Support

Our inquiry: *How do composers work with improvisation, patterns, and layers to create new music for voices and instruments?* Our vocabulary: *improvise, composer, pattern, layers.*

Week-by-Week Program Outline:

1. Play along with Daniel and establish community, pattern, layers (glocks only)

2. Play along with Daniel and establish community, pattern, layers (add Noteflight)

3. Play along with Daniel and establish community, pattern, layers in Noteflight

4. Name Songs (model)

5. Name Songs (continue)

6. Name Songs (complete)

7. Layers (experiments)

8. Squiggle Scores (orchestrations using invented notation)

9. Celebration Prep: Choose, Edit, Orchestrate

10. Celebration

11. Reflection

Well in advance of any culminating events, request that teachers gather student responses to that event immediately afterward, as well as reflections on the rest of the residency. Suggest a couple of reflection methods, and remind them that their documentation will be shared with their colleagues:

HELLO, COMPOSERS end of residency invitation to reflect

Dear Teachers – Just a reminder to please take some time to help your students reflect on the residency and Celebration experiences. I'll ask you to share this work when we meet for our final classroom session after the Celebration Concerts, as well as at our teacher final reflection session. – sincerely, your TA

Student Reflection Examples:

– make a web

– describe an important or memorable moment from the concert in detail, and draw that moment

– create a list of superlatives

– my favorite music was… the most challenging thing for me this year… the most fun… the easiest… the biggest surprise.. I was confused when… I was confident and proud when… the thing I saw another student do that I loved was…

– our advice for composers of the future is…

FIGURE 7.3 Karen's reflections, PS54, NYC, 2018

The effect of front-loading all this preparation is to make the sixty minutes the teaching artist and classroom teacher team have together substantive and rewarding. The reflective process is already in full swing by the time the meeting begins. Everyone in attendance is familiar with at least some of the materials and is already formulating opinions and responses as they evaluate the evidence of student learning (Figures 7.3 and 7.4). The materials that are presented during the meeting have already been vetted and edited. There is an increased sense of focus and purpose: *We're not just going to drink coffee and tell stories—we have the materials we need to bring our professional skills to bear as we evaluate student learning and our own teaching practice.* Teaching artists' assessment methods are too casual for professional statisticians. But until we have experts in educational research backing us up, we have to be content with

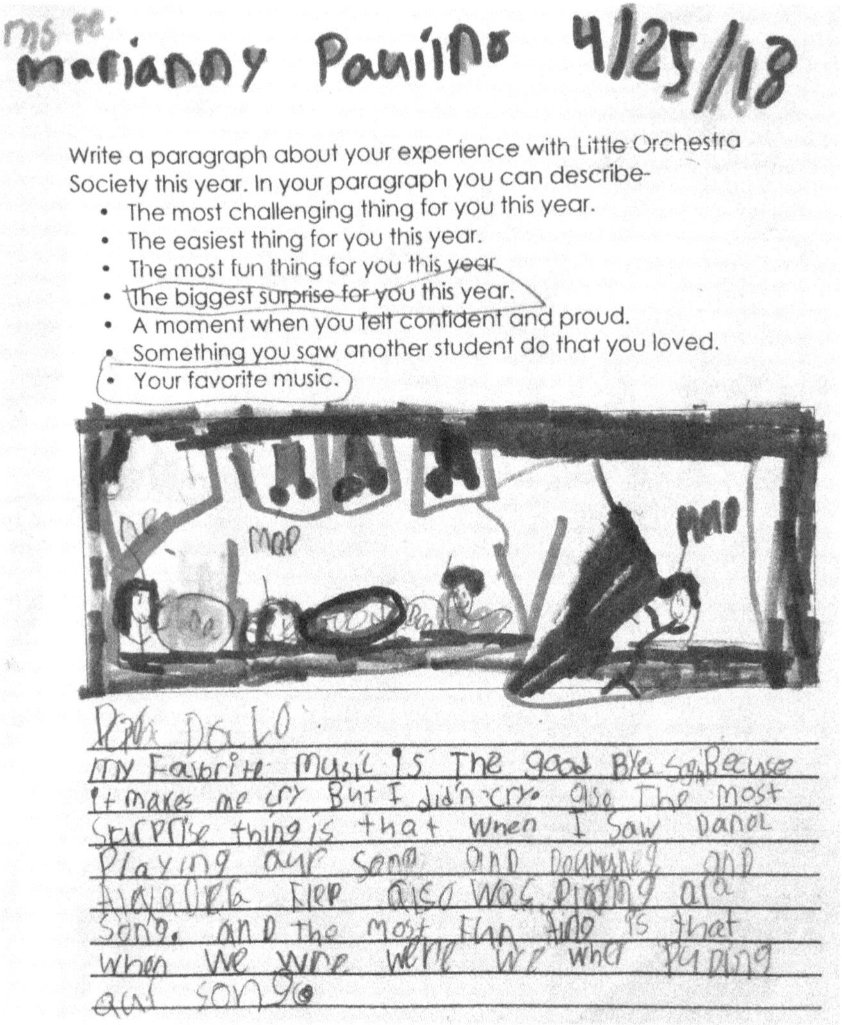

FIGURE 7.4 Marianny's reflections, PS54, NYC, 2018

our anecdotes, observations, soft evidence, and intuition as we reflect on an improve our Designs, according to our own lights.

You'll need a signed release form if your documenting photos and videos are going to be made accessible outside of your host's school or organization. Public display of images that include participants' faces is illegal without such a release, for many good reasons. Posting to any websites or social media without a release opens you and your sponsoring organization up to liabilities. If your host doesn't have an approved form, your sponsoring organization may. If not, don't take the responsibility and potential liability onto yourself. Suggest to them that they use the New York City Department of Education's

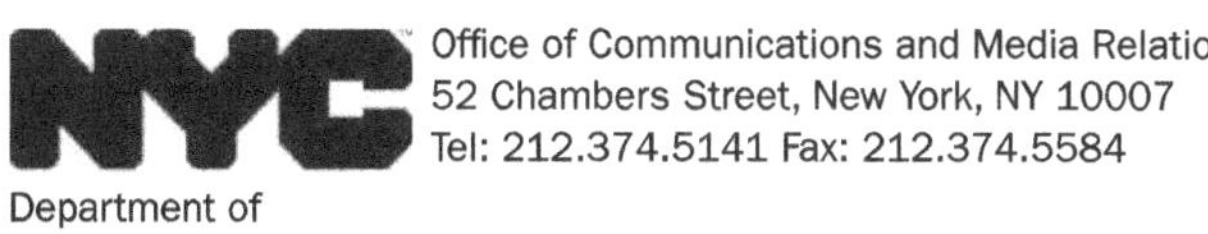

CONSENT TO PHOTOGRAPH, FILM, OR VIDEOTAPE A STUDENT FOR NON-PROFIT USE
(e.g. educational, public service, or health awareness purposes)

Student Name: _________________school: _______________________________

I hereby consent to the participation in interviews, the use of quotes, and the taking of photographs, movies or video tapes of the Student named above by_______________.
I also grant to__________________the right to edit, use, and reuse said products for non profit purposes including use in print, on the internet, and all other forms of media. I also hereby release the New York City Department of Education and its agents and employees from all claims, demands, and liabilities whatsoever in connection with the above.

Signature of Parent/Guardian (if Student is under 18):__________Date:__________

Address of Parent/Guardian: ____

OR

Signature of Student (if 18 or over):__________________Date:______________

Address of Student: ____

FIGURE 7.5 New York City Department of Education, *Consent Form*, accessed May 1, 2018

consent form as a model for creating their own (Figure 7.5).[3] It is pithy and available online in nine different languages.

Professional Development

In a single session of sixty or ninety minutes, what can a teaching artist offer that classroom teachers might want or need? If you are already teaching a preparation or studio workshop in a school, you'll likely be invited to lead some professional development, or PD. Most often the PD you lead will be program-related, connected with the work of art you'll be studying or the art-making processes you'll be doing. Schools may also invite you to lead a PD outside the auspices of an ongoing workshop; in that case you're free to invent an arts-related workshop. This section includes plans for and comments on three professional development workshops that are not connected with any particular curriculum or program: *Collaboration, Structure and Freedom*, and *Classroom Teacher Art-Making Video*. These PDs can be used as is, if they suit your needs and style, or as frameworks that allow you to place your own art-form-specific activities into the workshop structure.

PROFESSIONAL DEVELOPMENT WORKSHOP: COLLABORATION

Collaboration PD Workshop (60 min.)

10 min.	welcome/personal connection
15 min.	making shapes
20 min.	making pages
15 min.	reflect, connect, and extend

Where in your life are you a collaborator? What kinds of choices do you make that allow your collaborations flow more easily? Directly or indirectly, happily or kicking and screaming all the way, everyone collaborates. If you enjoy sharing a creative space and cooperatively solving problems, you might already collaborate as if it were second nature. Few people, however, take time to examine their approach to collaboration, or to develop their collaborative skills. This professional development is an active one-hour meditation on the nature of collaboration, and a chance for participants to develop an awareness of collaborative dynamics and perhaps some collaborative skills. Classroom teachers who participate in this workshop might easily adapt it for their own use with students.

Welcome/Personal Connection (10 min.)

Welcome and make a small personal connection with your participants: eye contact, handshakes, name tags, and general social conversations. Lead an active physical warm-up that gets everyone loose for Making Shapes.

Making Shapes (15 min.)

Invite small groups to collectively use their bodies and feet to create and define a series of shapes on the floor (straight line, candy cane, circle, square, rectangle, oval, triangle, star, blob). The group has to work out how to do it without a leader and without speaking to each other—no pointing, no bossing. The shapes called out by the TA get progressively more complex, culminating in a tableau or two: a Burger King cheeseburger, Coke and Biggie Fries; the entrance ramp to the Golden Gate Bridge during rush hour.

Making Pages (20 min.)

Pairs sit together and *take turns* making marks on paper. The TA calls out directions, a series of modifications to the process: short marks, longer marks, going with the flow of whatever partner number 1 does; working against partner number 1's flow; switching the order of who goes first. If you are making figurative drawings, switch to abstract, and visa versa. Each pair has to work it out without a leader and without speaking—no pointing, no bossing.

Two pairs share their pages with each other, and discuss: *Which pages attract your attention? What was the process that led to that page?*

Reflect, Connect, and Extend (15 min.)

Students post all the drawn pages on the wall, art-gallery style, so that they can be referred to during this next whole-group discussion. With their drawings at hand, students can better support their statements with evidence and examples from their own work.

- *In these Shapes and Pages activities, there are various levels of open-endedness. Rather than being told exactly what to do, you were invited into an unfamiliar process. All of you accepted the invitations. How did it feel to step into an unfamiliar process?*
- *Once you were in the process of making shapes or drawings, how did you know what to do next?* (draw out: individual decision-making strategies, intuition, noticing details, sense of play, responding to specific stimuli, etc.)
- *How did the presence of others—who were also deciding what to do—affect you?*
- *What kinds of choices made your collaborations flow more easily?*
- *Where in your life are you a collaborator?*
- *What kinds of choices do you make that allow your life collaborations flow more easily?*

PROFESSIONAL DEVELOPMENT WORKSHOP: STRUCTURE AND FREEDOM

Structure and Freedom PD Workshop (90 min.)

20	welcome and personal connection
20	structure and freedom in poetry
20	defining structure and freedom
30	structure and freedom in the (music, dance, visual art, plays) of _____

What are some of the characteristics of freedom?
What are some of the characteristics of structure?
Where do you have freedom in your life, and what do you do with it?
When do you find structure satisfying, and when is it frustrating?

In this workshop, we move through structure and freedom in poetry and our personal lives to set up a brief but actively analytical contact with a work of art. The workshop is a guided dialogue, where the community of learners is responsible for providing not just some but all the information that comes to light. The teaching artist invites the *Making & Doing*, setting up the final inquiry question: *What is the relationship between structure and freedom in [artist's name]'s work?* The workshop also embodies my pro-inquiry, anti-lecturing bias, with the teaching artist as instigator, rather than expert. Perhaps the main ingredient for the overall workshop's success is your own light touch. Since structure and freedom make for an interesting lens in many areas of study (creative writing, family relationships, sociology, history, politics, current events, all the fine and performing arts), classroom teachers who participate in this workshop can easily adapt it for their own use.

Welcome and Personal Connection with Active Warm-Up (20 min.)

Welcome and make a small personal connection with your participants: eye contact, handshakes, name tags, and general social conversations. Lead an active warm up, directly connected with the work of art. To transition into the workshop proper (the next four sections), provide a small frame: *[Artists name] is an expert at working with [musical, dramatic, visual, choreographic/spatial] structure and freedom. To get to know her/his work, we will need to become experts on structure and freedom.*

Structure and Meaning in Poetry (20 min.)

Brainstorm the structural elements in Robert Frost's "Nothing Gold Can Stay." Read the poem out loud (twice, different individual students) from a large-lettered copy on paper on the wall, with colored markers at hand:

> Nature's first green is gold,
> Her hardest hue to hold.
> Her early leaf's a flower;
> But only so an hour.
> Then leaf subsides to leaf.
> So Eden sank to grief,
> So dawn goes down to day.
> Nothing gold can stay.

Read aloud together, everyone choral style, focusing on and exaggerating the sounds of the words, and not focusing so much the words' meaning. Discuss, supporting ideas with evidence from the poem: *What structures did the poet choose to use? Out of all the possible poetic structures, why did Robert Frost choose these structures for this poem? Can you make any connections between the meaning of the poem and the structures the poet chose to use?*

During discussion, participants may notice these and many more technical characteristics: the poem consists of eight lines; the last word in each of the four couplets (or pairs of lines) rhymes; every line except the last has six syllables; the middle two lines of each quatrain start with a repeated word ("her," "so"); the poem uses alliteration ("her hardest hue to hold," "so dawn goes down to day"). Your participants' ability to go deep with "Nothing Gold Can Stay" may surprise you. Even after having taught the same workshop six or eight times, I found that every new group of teachers was able to add some new observation on Frost's structures. The final reflective prompt "Can you make any connections between the meaning of the poem and the structures the poet chose to use?" is a bit of a nested double question, asking participants to a) find personal meaning, then b) analyze the means used by the poet to evoke their own subjective responses. The invitation should yield some divergent thinking, perhaps along these lines: Frost's use of simple words makes it all feel more true; the steady, three-beat repeated rhythm points up the end rhymes and makes the concluding line feel inevitable when it finally lands; the use of "subside," "sank," and "goes down" all in a row in the second half makes the poem a real downer; the poem feels intense, compressed, because in a very short space, Frost links deterioration in nature and the biblical story of creation, with deterioration in our experience of everyday life.

Poet, teaching artist, and imagination activist Glenis Redmond suggests alternatives to Frost's "Nothing Gold Can Stay": "We Real Cool" by Gwendolyn Brooks, "Dream Deferred" or "I Loved My Friend" by Langston Hughes, "Won't You Come Celebrate" by Lucille Clifton, "Poetic Side" by Rita Dove, "Making History" by Marilyn Nelson, "Those Winter Sundays" by Robert Hayden, and for elementary school students "Fog" by Carl Sandburg, and "By Myself" or "Things" by Eloise Greenfield. Any short poem that has strong bones should work for this activity, for example Ms. Redmond's "Nerds Rule!"

> Nerds Rule!
> I'm a word nerd.
> I'm a reading freak.
>
> One day the Universe will be mine
> Understanding MC 2 like Einstein.
>
> Do you want to be large and in charge?
> Then, get yourself a library card.

Defining Structure and Freedom (20 min.)

Create loose working definitions of the terms "freedom" and "structure," the whole group filling in a wall-sized side-by-side chart (Figure 7.6): *What are some of the characteristics of freedom? What are some of the characteristics of structure? Is there any overlap or crossover in these two lists? How do you explain it?* Add arrows and alterations as needed.

structure	freedom

FIGURE 7.6 Structure and Freedom blank table

Journal individually, then discuss in pairs or as a group: *Where do you have freedom in your life, and what do you do with it? When do you find structure satisfying, and when is it frustrating?*

Structure and Freedom in (your art form, or work of art) (30 min.)

In this activity, choose an audio or video excerpt to be your work of art. Draw on the two previous activities and discussions as you consider structure and freedom in that work. As an artist you already know, and may be tempted to say, that in music, as in poetry, architecture, or dance, anything that repeats can be considered "structural." For example repeating rhythms, melodies, bass lines, fragments, chords—all of these elements create structure in music. Elements that are improvised, or spontaneously created, can be considered "free." But instead of being the expert who reveals aspects of structure and freedom in your chosen work of art, facilitate your students' discovering them.

Dance

Watch the chosen video excerpt. *Does the choreographer seem more interested in freedom or structure? What specifically about the music makes you say that?* Mirror (move along with) the dancer(s) in the video. *Which of these movements seem more structural? Which seem more free? What is the relationship between structure and freedom in [artist's name]'s work?*

Visual Art

Examine the chosen still image(s) or video excerpt. *Does the artist seem more interested in freedom or structure? What do you see that makes you say that?* Point out aspects of the work using words and gestures. *Which of aspects seem more structural? Which seem more free? What is the relationship between structure and freedom in [artist's name]'s work?*

Theater

Watch the chosen video excerpt. *Does the playwright or director seem more interested in freedom or structure? What do you see and hear that makes you say that?* Mirror (move and speak along with) the actor(s) in the video. *Which of these movements or words seem more structural? Which seem more free? What is the relationship between structure and freedom in [artist's name]'s work?*

Music

Listen to the chosen musical excerpt. *Do these musicians seem more interested in freedom or structure? What specifically about the music makes you say that?* Sing along with the structural layers of the musical excerpt. *Which of these individual layers of music sound more structural? Which sound more free? What is the relationship between structure and freedom in [artist's name]'s work?*

PROFESSIONAL DEVELOPMENT WORKSHOP: CLASSROOM TEACHER
ART-MAKING VIDEO

Classroom Teacher Art-Making Video Workshop PD (60 min. with teachers, 150 min. total)

30 min.	prepare models (pre-workshop)
10 min.	welcome/personal connection
10 min.	art-making scenarios
10 min.	screenplay
30 min.	shoot
60 min.	editing and sharing (post-workshop)

Do you remember the afternoon you spent with your early-teen friends and the audio recorder, making fake radio shows and news reports, or scatological commercials and song parodies, how you listened back and howled with pleasure at your own out-of-control, sassy inventiveness? That same spirit lives on in this workshop. The Design is loose, indicating steps in a process. The teaching artist sets up a filmmaking atelier, and invites the classroom teachers to create videos that model, illustrate, or otherwise work with (or play with) the content of a workshop that students will eventually experience. The video is edited, then shared with students and parents. The teaching artist facilitates and supports the work in whatever manner is needed at any given moment, sometimes operating the camera, other times joining in or coaching.

As long as what you capture on video is even tangentially connected with the students' art-making, it will work educationally. Anything from a straightforward teacher-performed improvisation of a serious nature to parodies, slapstick, or other comedic options are all good. Teacher participants will self-regulate, knowing that the work will be shared. If they are sure they won't be portrayed in an unflattering light, teachers will likely love having a chance to Make and Do and get goofy for a change. Many of them won't even mind a little unflattering light, because they know the value of fun in their classrooms and the rewards of going out on a silly limb from time to time. The students love seeing their teachers Making & Doing, especially in modes that are identical or at least parallel to their own creative work. A satisfying recognition comes about when students watch the final video: *hmm, my teacher does this process too—she is a student too—even uses the same tools and same terms as I do—and sometimes struggles, too—but she stays with it and something good and delightful happens . . . I think I can do that, too.*

The video planning, shooting, directing, and editing that this workshop calls for may be beyond your current facility with the medium. If so, consider adding some videographic skills to your teaching artist toolkit. You'll probably learn quickly, and after a couple of shoots be making thoughtful, decently-shot and edited video documentation. Final Cut Pro (FCP), AVS, Vegas, and the other high-end editors are nice, but take longer to learn; iMovie and applications like it are less powerful but more user-friendly. In a pinch, you can rely on in-camera edits (only shoot what you are sure you want, in the exact order you want it, then leave it that way). Also most smartphone photo apps allow you to shoot and edge-edit videos (remove any unwanted bits from the beginning or the end) right on the phone screen.

Present the teachers' work to them via email, then again to their students in class, with the teachers present. Your students love to watch their teachers (and themselves) at work and play—they will be your most dependable and enthusiastic audience. When they watch, it's more than fun because of the opportunities for reflection that the viewing makes possible. Whoever appears on screen, whatever the process, make the connection between the classroom teachers' video and the students' own art-making work explicit. Ask the viewers to think about the artistic and aesthetic choice the people on screen are making. And if they don't do so spontaneously, remind the viewers to give their teachers and classmates a big hand for being willing to take risks and share their work this way.

Your sponsoring institution may want to use your video in grant proposals as evidence of classroom practices or student learning. You may want to share the video on your own website or Facebook page. Make sure your sponsoring institution's photo and video release form has been distributed, signed by teachers, and collected before you start shooting, and confirm that personal posting is allowed before doing so.

Pre-Workshop

PREPARE MODELS (30 MIN.)

Before the meeting, get to know your curriculum or works of art. Define for yourself the basic creative activities involved. Invent different ways classroom teachers might perform these activities on camera that students might enjoy watching. For example, if students will be creating a mystery play, teachers might create a sock-puppet whodunit that involves choices similar to those their students will make (character, setting, plot, resolution). If students will be drumming, do some drumming, and plan to get the school principal and secretaries in for five minutes to do some drumming too. If students will be visiting an exhibit of Wayne Thiebaud paintings, teachers could narrate their own choices while they color in an uncolored line-drawing version of one of Thiebaud's ice cream cake or cupcake images. You may or may not use these ideas in the video shoot, but it is prudent to have some back-pocket plans in case your teachers have trouble generating ideas during the "generate scenarios" section of the main workshop.

Main Workshop

WELCOME/PERSONAL CONNECTION (10 MIN.)

Establish an easy-going, supportive atmosphere as you welcome and make a personal connection with your participants. Get a good vibe started, the way you would for any gathering of artists that you were responsible for. Eye contact, handshakes, name tags, and general conversations matter. If you are nervous or fiddling with a camera or shuffling paper and paint around instead of connecting, that nervous feeling can communicate itself to the participants. Instead, be present, confident, and attentive. If participants get the impression they will be listened to and their ideas will be honored, they'll have a much easier time being loose and creative during the shoot. The teaching artist is a director at this point, setting her actors up to do their best work once the camera starts rolling; the video shoot is the container you are responsible for establishing and maintaining.

GENERATE SCENARIOS (10 MIN.)

Confirm the focus of the students' workshop (Figure 7.7), then use 1-2-3 and A-B-C as jumping-off points. Brainstorm scenarios, toss around ideas for what you might shoot. Grab props and other needed items as they come up in discussion. Track which ideas have the most energy and delight built in. By the end of this brainstorming, each participant should have some intuitive, personal sense of which idea(s) they'd like to try.

GENERATE SCREENPLAYS (10 MIN.)

Teachers separate into small groups to plan and rehearse what their group will shoot. Groups might form around a shared interest in a scenario, or for other social reasons, but each group needs to agree on a scenario. At the end of ten

The three main Make and Do activities in the students' workshop are

1._______________ 2. _______________ 3. _______________

The three most important terms in the students' workshop are

A._______________ B. _______________ C. _______________

FIGURE 7.7 Reflection prompts to help generate video scenarios

minutes, each small group should have a rough screenplay in their minds. It can't be complicated: they only have ten minutes to develop and agree on the entire idea. The time limits keep the work simple, which in turn helps make it possible to shoot it quickly, on a first or second take.

SHOOT (30 MIN.)

Anything and everything can happen here. A minimally-planned shoot has to stay light on its feet, ready to honor whatever arises. As the facilitator of the workshop and the director of the film, you set the tone. You can keep the atmosphere playful by remaining playful yourself, regardless of how messy or crazy the shoot seems to become. Whoever is actually shooting video needs to be comfortable with a camera, and have some sensitivity to framing and light. When possible, the camera person should keep multiple teachers' faces in the shot, even when other action (puppet characters, instruments) is in the foreground. But in general avoid camera movement, except to re-frame. Smartphone video and sound are good enough, if you don't have a video camera. Rough edits and low production values are not a problem, but do make sure your camera's microphone is close enough to the action to record clear audio. If you have to perform, someone else may have to direct (or perhaps stage manage), that is, gather performers, confer with the camera person as to how they will shoot the action, get the performers to stop and start together, and decide whether to get another take or not.

TA Post-Workshop Follow-Up

TA EDIT AND SHARE VIDEO (60 MIN.)

This workshop requires a lot of follow-up: editing, adding titles and credits, packaging, and delivering the video in full-resolution and email-friendly compressed forms. Depending on how much watchable video your shoot produced, you'll need an hour—or much more—to edit. Most personal computer software packages come with basic video editing software, and it isn't difficult to put together a good-looking product. Shorter is better. Titles for sections can be fun. Remember to put all participants' names in the credits.

Chapter 8

Materials for Professional Teaching Artists

Teaching Artist Compensation 101

How can a teaching artist determine what constitutes a fair wage? What do our Arts-in-Education employers expect from us during different phases of the work? Let's look at teaching artist fee structures, and the actual work, contractual or hidden, required of us. We'll start out global, and get more specific as we go along.

Do you see your teaching artist work as a gig, or a calling? Musicians refer to almost any job as a gig, and I grew up using that word with the understanding that there was nothing mercenary about it, nothing worthy of disapprobation. Work that pays is a gig: my bass gig, my film score gig, my teaching gig. A calling is associated with a higher or more deeply felt, perhaps altruistic, purpose. Work that you take on according to an internal drive to do so may also be your calling: your calling to work with children or seniors, or to spread the gospel of dance, or to make a woodcut print without worrying about marketing it once it is made. For me, teaching artist work is both a gig and a calling. I appreciate, in fact depend on, the income that the work generates. At the same time, I want to be of genuine service to workshop participants in my care. I want to do good and meaningful work at a fair wage.

The organizations that sponsor your teaching artist gigs (museums, presenters, performance or exhibition venues, arts ensembles, government programs, or service organizations including homeless shelters, prisons, and schools) have already worked out what wage they can offer you, and what activity and proficiency they expect in return. You can't exactly bid a teaching artist gig the way you can a mural, or a recording session, or a set design for a play. The exception to this might be certain pilot programs where you and your sponsoring organization understand that there is going to be a lot of troubleshooting, program development, or curriculum writing involved; in that case the fee and work expectations may open up for discussion. But in most cases the fees are set and are not going to change. Ultimately that inflexibility is good for the organization, and good for you. They have to adhere to a budget to survive, and their survival means continued work for you and other teaching artists. When they are clear about what they can offer, you can determine if the fee versus work expected is fair.

Nationally you'll find a broad range of fees offered and work expected. For your actual teaching time (those minutes you are with students in a workshop or classroom), a rural program might offer $25 per hour, an urban presenter up to $90 per hour. Most teaching artist gigs fall somewhere in the middle. Some organizations provide and pay you to attend professional development, aka PD—but many offer a PD fee that is half of what they offer for teaching. One organization might pay lavishly for you to attend performances with your students, another doesn't even expect you to do so. You might or might not be given a travel stipend, money to cover state-mandated fingerprinting, or a materials budget. Some organizations pay for planning time or paperwork, or for assessment; others expect you to take care of those aspects of the work without having them explicitly represented in the fee structure.

Teaching artist fees are set, but there is no single determining factor by which you can measure their fairness. That's OK, you say; I am an artist and am pretty good at working with complexity and at least a dash of ambiguity. In 2018 the Teaching Artists Guild rolled out an online TA Pay Rate Calculator (Figure 8.1)[1], a "tool to help teaching artists to negotiate at least a minimum living wage" and "help hiring organizations advocate for funding to pay teaching artists a living wage." It works with any of 620 pre-defined metro areas.

A professional-level teaching artist, in a household with one dependent, working for a medium-sized organization in the San Diego area should negotiate (according to the calculator) for an annual pay rate of $150,268.15, or an hourly rate of $129.54. Those numbers reflect "the amount you would need to charge hourly to support yourself and any dependents . . . at a living wage," one that is "high enough to maintain a normal, sustainable standard of living." The Guild is "well aware that these rates may be currently inaccessible to many small (and even larger) organizations"; the Calculator is still in development. It's still a great tool for imagining and advocating for what teaching artists might be paid in an enlightened society that valued education and the arts. Until that society comes into being, you'll need to do your own pay rate calculation. To begin making that estimate, let's break our work down into its component activities, and total the resulting hours, using a Teaching Artist Fee Calculation Worksheet.

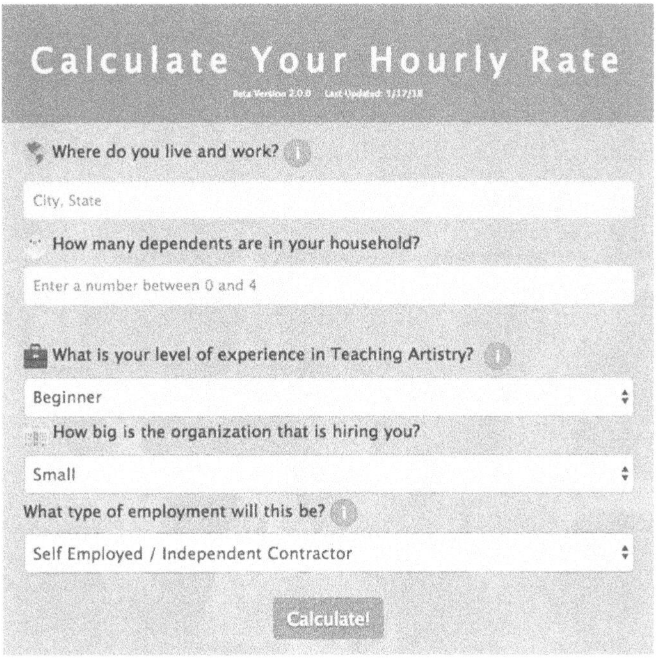

FIGURE 8.1 Teaching Artists Guild, interactive Pay Rate Calculator

Screen Shot from the Teaching Artist's Guild Pay Rate Calculator

THE TEACHING ARTIST FEE CALCULATION WORKSHEET

On the worksheet you'll find our work separated into a before, during, and after sequence: *Planning, Teaching* (your actual time with students), and *Follow-Up* (documentation, assessment). Each should be considered separately when working out the hours a teaching artist gig will actually require. The worksheet represents a formalization of something I've been doing informally for many years, when attempting to factor the many variables that arise into my estimates. It was beta-tested and modified at ITAC4, the Fourth International Teaching Artist Conference in September 2018 by a group of teaching artists (a mix of veterans and beginners). They judged it to be a useful, flexible, and fairly transparent tool, and I hope you also find it so. Let's look at the worksheet's *Estimating Planning Time, Teaching Time*, and *Follow-Up Time* sections separately, as well as other factors to consider when estimating your fee. You can refer to a filled-out worksheet (Figure 8.2), but a blank worksheet is also included on (Figure 8.3) as well as a downloadable PDF version (at www.DanielLevyMusic.com.)

TA Fee Calculation Worksheet

job offer description

work & time: 3 45-MIN WKSPS X 5 CLASSES   + ONE HOUR MUSEUM VISIT = 6 CLASSES

contractual fee: $35/CLASS   also note: 4TH GRADE

phase of work   X 17 $595

hours required

planning

curriculum provided ✓ 1

write-your-own curriculum .... —

familiar / (unfamiliar) work of art 5

(familiar) / unfamiliar students .... —

familiar / (unfamiliar) art medium 5

other .... —   2

planning subtotal

teaching   3 x 45 x 5 = 675 ÷ 60 = 11.25 + MUSEUM

time with students 12.25

set-up (15 MIN X 3 DAYS = 45 MIN) .... .75

clean-up .... (BY STUDENTS)

commute .... (4 HOURS N.A.)

other .... —   13

teaching subtotal

follow-up   EDIT LABEL + POST IN-CLASS JPGS

lesson plans .... —

documentation 1

assessment 5   1.5

follow-up subtotal

total fee $ 595 / total hours 16.5 = $ 36.06 / hour

FIGURE 8.2 TA Fee Calculation Worksheet (filled in)

TA Fee Calculation Worksheet

<u>job offer description</u>

work & time:____
_____

contractual fee:_____________________________ also note: ______________________________
_____

phase of work	**hours required**

planning

curriculum provided   _____________________

write-your-own curriculum   _____________________

familiar/unfamiliar work of art   _____________________

familiar/unfamiliar students   _____________________

familiar/unfamiliar art medium   _____________________

other   _____________________   _____________

                                                 planning subtotal

teaching

time with students   _____________________

set-up   _____________________

clean-up   _____________________

commute   _____________________

other   _____________________
____

                                                 teaching subtotal

follow-up

lesson plans   _____________________

documentation   _____________________

assessment   _____________________
____

                                                 follow-up subtotal

total fee $________ / total hours _________ = $________ / hour

---

FIGURE 8.3 TA Fee Calculation Worksheet (blank)

Estimating Planning Time

Your planning time is affected by the material support available (curriculum), and by your previous experience with the workshop type, art, and/or participants. If you find yourself handed a curriculum to follow, your planning time is reduced. You don't have to create a curriculum—just read one and internalize the goals and means it lays out well enough to use it effectively during your teaching. If you are invited to Design your own curriculum, you'll need to make a realistic estimate of the hours involved. Writing a lesson plan for a one-hour workshop takes me between two and four hours, especially if it is the first time I am teaching to that work of art or art-making process. It might take even longer if it is the first time I am with an unfamiliar age group, in part because I have to allow time for *rewriting* lessons as I learn to work with the class (if you think it will be easier to write lessons for fifth graders you've never worked with than for the college students you know well, please think again). Planning can take more time if I am writing a Preparation workshop because I have to take the time to get to know the work of art before I can teach to it. It can take less time if I am writing a Studio workshop that centers on making works of art in a medium that I've mastered.

Estimating Teaching Time

Teaching time seems simple enough at first glance: meeting with students from 11:00 to 11:45 adds up to forty-five minutes of teaching. But scheduling, commuting, set-up, and clean-up also factor in. Of course you'll want to avoid teaching four classes a day that are scheduled for the first two and last two periods of the day. And if you are only teaching three classes, you probably won't want a lunch break or a prep placed between any of them. No one will put you in this kind of situation on purpose, but it is best to address this during your initial discussions. For half days, ask that the three or four classes be clumped together without a break. Also confirm the actual class durations and passing times, so that you don't end up spending sixty minutes at the school for every forty-minute class you teach; that extra twenty minutes multiplied by six classes over an eight week residency becomes a lot of uncompensated time.

Do you factor in your commute? If you are traveling more than forty-five minutes one way, I believe you should. You don't want to commit to traveling an hour or more if you are teaching for less than the commute time. Exercise some caution regarding work time versus commute time, and let your program manager know whenever you have concerns about it. Younger and less-experienced teaching artists are often saddled with longer commutes than veterans.

Set-up and clean-up time should also factor in to your teaching time calculation. Anything over twenty minutes of combined set-up and clean-up time occurring daily is a factor to be considered. But as an example of an exception to my set up/clean up rule: one of my favorite music TA gigs required me to set up a venue for a final celebration concert. To do so, I spent three hours transforming a large empty classroom into an pro-audio and video equipped performance venue for 100 people, and another hour striking it all away. I even provided the actual audio (PA, mics, stands, cables, digital recorders) and video (computer, digital projector) gear. It all made for a beautiful event, but none of that time or those materials appeared in my fee agreement. I accepted this as fair because it was connected with a long residency whose weekly sessions required minimal set-up or clean-up.

Estimating Follow-Up Time

You'll find the Follow-Up requested by sponsoring organizations is as varied as the fees offered. You may be asked to assess your own work, your students' work, or your relationships with partners at the teaching location (classroom teachers, other staff). The assessment might be anecdotal (you reflect and respond with written notes, following a prompt sheet) or according to a rubric (you read, reflect, and fill in dots). The prompt-sheet style assessment is the most common. In addition to assessment, various kinds of documentation will be required. You may be asked to provide evidence of student work (photos, videos, actual physical artifacts). You will certainly be asked for lesson plans. Be careful to understand what the organization requires. A well-laid-out lesson plan form can be a wonderful support for your work. It might also be something of a time sink (where you watch hours go slipping down the drain), depending on the level of detail required, or the density of the organization-specific terminology used (each organization might use the terms *activity, exercise, workshop, session, class, lesson, unit of study, residency, plan, design, curriculum, pedagogy, goals, learning objectives,* and *big ideas* differently). Veteran teaching artists have developed their own style of written plans; some are idiosyncratic, written in a personal shorthand, and others are easy for any reader to follow. You sponsor will want to see the easy-to-follow kind. It can take a good deal of time and effort to create a document that serves both you and the reader. Beginning teaching artists might do themselves a favor by strictly adhering to whatever form the sponsor requires. In terms of follow-up, I also add (and don't consider as part of my billable time) a self-reflection where I assess every lesson plan and make notes on how to do it better "next time," if there is a next time. Doing so is an investment in my craft. I've become better at planning, and more free and responsive in teaching interactions, thanks to this uncompensated self-reflection.

The Planning Time and Teaching Time sections on the Teaching Artist Fee Calculation Worksheet each include a blank space for "other." This is a necessary catch-all category for those aspects of the work that are particular to a specific residency, but not needed for every residency: professional development (your facilitating, or attending), culminating events, mentoring, trips, gear, additional meetings, hiring subcontractors, commuting, security clearances, and for correctional facilities, allowing time for daily on-site searches and gate processing.

Other Factors in Estimating Your Fee

The working conditions also matter, particularly the nature of the workspace. The school may be able to provide materials that make the work easier or more fun (a closet full of Orff instruments, art supplies, a computer lab, a digital projector, a boom box), or at least make it possible for you not to have to schlep heavy bags of equipment from class to class. The school may be able to provide a space that is especially conducive to the work you want to do (a beautiful open space, Smart Board access, a real art room with a real sink, a dance studio with a sprung floor). This kind of accommodation can make a huge difference in the amount of preparation you do. Once you know you have a Smart Board or Internet access, many instructional doors open. For example: a document camera coupled with a projector or Smart Board allows you to project a piece of $8.5'' \times 11''$ student work as a 3-foot by 4-foot image for the entire class to see and discuss. If you bring in personal gear (speakers, projectors) or materials (paints, paper, costumes, photocopies) because neither the school nor your sponsoring organization provide them, does that affect your fee? Reimbursement is rare, and being paid any kind of rental fee for the gear you provide rarer still.

Work out these space and materials details up front as you negotiate your contract so that you begin with an informed understanding of the basic time and materials required. You'll always be working with limited time and materials; knowing these limits in detail strengthens every aspect of your program Design. Before the end of a workshop or residency, there will moments when you want to give a little more time to the work. Opportunities will come up, and for altruistic reasons you will want to honor them, and put in some extra effort that was never planned for and will never be acknowledged with a fee. Knowing that this will happen, be somewhat circumspect with your time and energy commitments at the beginning of the process. Artists almost invariably choose to go past the requirements into a sincere and generous gift of time and attention. To avoid burning out from giving too much, hold a little time in reserve.

The Association of Teaching Artists is a practitioner-led online forum. Their "Teaching Artist Wish List" is a compilation of the wishes of practitioners from all over the country. Many of the items on the list refer to compensation, which may say a lot about the current state and status of our profession:

Association of Teaching Artists TA Wish List[2]

To be compensated in a way that recognizes professionalism, education, and experience.

To be compensated for prep time, as other contract professions do (designers and therapists, for example).

To have work throughout the school year, not only the last 8 weeks.

To have teachers, administrators, and principals invest in long-term Arts-in-Education programs and not look for quick projects.

To have cultural organizations with Arts-in-Education programs recognize the professionalism of teaching artists and not continually pay the same rate year after year even though the teaching artists demonstrate excellence and mastery.

To have cultural organizations value teaching artists as integral to their mission and not rationalize that teaching artists can pay taxes, health insurance, and transportation on less than $50 an hour.

To not have to hustle for funding and residencies every year.

To not be held hostage to flavor-of-the-month pedagogies and emperors with no clothes on.

To be paid in a timely fashion.

To be able to work with teachers enrolled in certification programs in schools of education to foster the team-teaching collaborative environment with artists. There are great strides that need to be taken in teacher education to take advantage of the opportunity of Arts in Education and nourish it in a way that will allow for the optimal educational experience for the students.

To offer professional development to arts administrators who have forgotten the value of art, teaching artists, and what really goes into implementing Arts in Education: living wage fees, prep time, research, travel, and opportunities for reasonably priced health, disability, and liability insurance.

To educate cultural organizations and arts administrators with the message that they are there to support the teaching artist as well as the school.

To educate cultural organizations that push their programming instead of understanding the potential of Arts in Education for school reform and for the professional career of a teaching artist.

To provide professional development for community organizations who work with teaching artists on fees, teaching artists, program assessment.

To have funders meaningfully address the training, the lack of work, and how hard it is to earn a living as a teaching artist.

To have more connection with fellow teaching artists across the country.

Special Needs and Special Education

They were the best of classes, they were the worst of classes, the spring of hope and the winter of despair. Take a teaching artist out for a beer and ask her if she has any stories of students with IEPs (Individualized Education Programs) to tell, and you're likely to hear a tale of two classrooms, the best and the worst, sometimes in the same room on the same day. I look forward to working with these students because the depth of their engagement and the pleasure they take from process moves me. That positive anticipation is tinged with a measure of anxiety, because I still lack the tools that professional educators can bring to bear, so I may not serve these students well. I'm somewhere on a learning curve. A special education classroom asks more from a teaching artists than almost any other container. It is also the area where most of us have the least experience or training. But just as everyday disruptions and students' struggles with art-making processes need to be folded into our practice, so too do the experiences of students who struggle with physical, emotional, cognitive, and developmental disabilities. Depending on the robustness of their program, schools provide a combination of special education teachers (general education teachers who are also certified or licensed in this field), psychologists, guidance counselors, and resource specialists, and arts, behavioral, and occupational therapists to help meet these students' special needs—or as we might better put it, special rights. Working full-time in this field is a unique and demanding calling, and I find myself in awe of the professionals who devote their lives to serving these students.

Teaching artists aren't officially required to know anything about special education before entering a special ed classroom. Some arts presenters provide professional development for those of us working with special ed classes, and some suggest a short planning session with special ed co-teachers, which I believe is essential for success. Fortunately we don't need to be experts ourselves, because we'll be partnering with experts. But in order to work effectively in this setting, teaching artists need to know something about the ways special education students experience our work with them. And in order to collaborate effectively with the teachers, we need some insight into their professional View and teaching practice, and the places where our approaches might overlap or conflict. I am not a scholar in the special education field. What follows reflects my experience in the classroom, and my current idea of what it would have been helpful to have known sooner. I won't include any specific information about working with students who have severe or multiple disabilities, since I am not experienced in this area, but instead will focus on students, mainly children, in special ed and inclusion settings. I hope you can put this to good use in the working world.

Licensed psychologist and board certified dance/movement therapist Diane Duggan describes the prevailing self-image of special ed students as "I'm defective, I'm bad, I will fail." What a daunting place for a child to begin each day. "Their deepest secret is that they believe they are broken and will never be better. For many of these children, being bad, and getting the attention that comes with being bad, is better than feeling defective." Duggan "sees the good" in all of them, a View that guides her practice.

Autism, sensory, visual and hearing, orthopedic, learning disabilities, mental retardation, emotional disturbance, speech and language, traumatic brain injury, and other health impaired are the nine categories or types of disability used in New York State education regulations to describe students with disabilities. *Emotionally disturbed* appears in sixth place on the list, but is the most commonly used classification for the majority of special ed children.

Duggan advises teaching artists to see people classified as having emotional/behavioral disorders as "normal people twisted by the synergy of very adverse circumstances." It isn't a lack of grit or character development that causes these individuals to struggle. They have trust issues with peers and adults, problems with relationships, and experience inappropriate types of behavior or feelings under normal circumstances. They also experience a generally pervasive mood of unhappiness (which is appropriate: most of these children have many negative experiences every day) and a tendency to develop physical symptoms of fears. We all experience these things to some extent, but special education students experience them with greater frequency, intensity, and duration.

These negative experiences and conditions can accumulate and overwhelm a child, resulting in aggressive behavior. When a child lashes out (a fourth grader looks you in the eye and shouts "fuck you"), they discharge that negative energy, in an attempt to rid themselves of a painful or confusing experience. The psychological term is *displacement*, taking a feeling that has one object or origin and directing toward another person. When this happens, try to remember that you are in a therapeutic relationship with the student. Bring caring to your response or intervention, which may include ignoring the behavior or de-escalating the situation by backing down and deferring to the classroom teacher. Don't loom over the student, raise your voice, or approach quickly while making eye contact: these can be seen as aggressive or threatening. Don't fight back or go head to head. Instead, give them time and space: *You seem really upset . . . do you think you can handle staying in the classroom now? Or do you need a break?* Later on, after the moment passes, catch the child making a good choice and praise them.

Autism (or ASD, Autistic Spectrum Disorder) is the next most common special ed classification. Autism is known as a "spectrum" disorder because there is wide variation in the type and severity of symptoms people experience. According to the National Institute for Mental Health, ASD occurs in all ethnic, racial, and economic groups. Although ASD can be a lifelong disorder, treatments and services can improve a person's symptoms and ability to function. Students on the spectrum experience persistent deficits in social communication and interaction. They may struggle with social-emotional reciprocity, and often have trouble developing, maintaining, or understanding relationships. They may also engage in restrictive or repetitive patterns of behavior, insisting on sameness or returning to fixed interests. Many of these behaviors are anxiety-based or anxiety provoked. You can help calm students on the spectrum by using routines such as these:

Design Strategies To Reduce Anxiety
give warnings (in three minutes we're going to . . .)
use timers (a clock students can objectively observe)

embed improvisation within routines (routines are comforting)
use multiple modalities (especially words and pictures together)
favor kinesthetic learning
ritualize beginnings, endings, and transitions (routines are comforting)

If the special ed teachers you work with have a calming or centering ritual, learn it and join their community by asking students to teach you how to do it. If they do not have a calming ritual, or are open to learning a new one, try board certified dance/movement therapist Rena Kornblum's *Four Bs to Help Us Relax:*

BRAKES	press hands together
	(clap, and hold them together to catch the energy)
BREATHE	take a deep breath
	(thumbs on belly button, push against your hands as you breathe in)
BRAIN	gently place hands on forehead and say "I can be calm"
	(hands lightly on forehead)
BODY	give yourself a gentle hug and say "I feel calm"
	(hands on shoulders)[3]

If serving special ed students is of particular interest to you, you may want to look into Universal Design for Learning (UDL) and Positive Behavior Interventions and Supports (PBS/PBIS). The National Center on Universal Design for Learning website is a good place to start your reading. Positive Behavior Supports are specific preventive and responsive teaching practices, organized into three types: Universal (those that apply to all students in all settings), Targeted (those that apply to at-risk students who need extra help to succeed) and Intensive Individualized (for students with persistently challenging behaviors). Most of the planning and management techniques mentioned in this chapter make an appearance on the PBS practice continuum, including positively stated rules, routines, and acknowledging and praising students who are on task.

Some students receive a Functional Behavior Assessment (FBA) as part of Intensive Individualized Positive Behavior Supports. This is a diagnostic, a formal assessment used to get a clearer picture of a student's problem when other techniques prove ineffective. The basic reasoning used in the assessment is useful for teaching artists who wonder why a particular behavior is taking place: in a Functional Behavior Assessment all behavior is seen as *functional,* meaning that students always do things for a reason. Off-task, provocative or agitated behavior may feel dysfunctional for the teacher or other students, but is still functional for the child. This empowering insight should have implications for how we Respond. Functional Behavior Assessments focus on the student's needs or wants:

Four Needs or Wants that Motivate Students' Disruptive Behavior

a need to receive attention

a tangible need (wanting a pencil, or a CD, or a treat)

a sensory need (a strong need to feel, or stop feeling)

a need to escape (such as not wanting to answer or work).

Using the assessment, the teacher isolates the function that gives rise to the child's problematic behavior: *I want attention, so I shout and run away.* That done, the teacher is empowered to *not* reward the behavior: *I choose not to chase you when you shout and run,* since rewarding the behavior reinforces it. Once the reinforcement loop is stopped, it's possible to try other approaches. Teaching artists may never take part in a formal Functional Behavior Assessment, but it should prove helpful to remember that struggling, disruptive students are doing their best to pursue the things they need. Seeing behavior this way reflects a psychologist's approach: to deal with aggression, first identify with the aggressor.

Special ed teachers are showing children another way to be in the world, and you too become a special ed teacher when you enter their classrooms. The best special ed classroom teachers are masters at modeling basic goodness for students who need more goodness in their lives. Teaching artists can observe them, defer to them, and take a few pages from their book. During the brief extra planning meeting that you schedule with the special ed teacher, ask them how they see your classroom teacher and teaching artist roles and collaboration. Ask them what to do and what not to do, and also make clear what you hope they will do (participate) and not do (have a meeting with a staff member while you are teaching). Ask them how they define and deal with disruption, how they set up for potentially noisy, messy, or physically vigorous arts activities, how they handle students' emotional displacement.

The *Arts and Students with Disabilities Online Resource Compendium* (2017) should be of interest to teaching artists. Developed by the New York City Department of Education's Office of Arts and Special Projects, the web-based materials are designed to support general education arts teachers who are also teaching students with disabilities in inclusive classrooms. A diverse group of educators, administrators, and cultural partners, with and without disabilities, wrote and curated the documents, vetting the materials in order to provide useful and comprehensive resources. The informfrom presented "does not attempt to address the various theories or the historical, cultural, or political complexities of educating students with disabilities," but provides arts teachers with "practical tools that can immediately be utilized in the classroom to provide high standards and rigorous arts education to all students." The site provides separate documents and support of visual arts, music, theater, and dance. One item that repeats for all four disciplines on the *Online Resource Compendium* is Dr. Duggan's "How to Prevent Students from Engaging in Misbehavior in the Classroom," which suggests a preventative approach to classroom management. You'll find a more complete version of this list online, but here are the headings. These thoughtful classroom management techniques, many of which make appearances in the Design and Respond chapters of this book, are useful in any classroom or workshop, special ed or otherwise.

How to Prevent Students from Engaging in Misbehavior in the Classroom

Proximity Control
Planful Ignoring
Signals
Emotional Drain-Off
Humor
Help with Difficult Work
Diversion and Re-Direction
Support from Routines
Direct Appeal
Conflict Resolution outside the Visual Arts Room
Encouragement Rather Than Criticism
Anticipation Planning
Setting Limits
Time and Space to Comply
Affirm Positive Behavior
Ask, Don't Tell
Reprimand in Private[4]

Finally, a few caveats for teaching artists working with students with disabilities. The arts-based teaching and learning that teaching artists provide is genuinely healing and therapeutic, so you naturally want to keep as many children working within the group as possible. But when an individual child needs help, don't neglect the larger group; your primary responsibility is for the entire class. And don't feel you need to go it alone; reach out to the special education experts in the room for support. Before you enter the classroom, Design for student success by structuring a calm, purposeful, and clearly delineated learning environment, including careful use of space, simple (and minimal) transitions, and ritualized routines. When you teach, start with students where they are. Praise students' successes and the good and positive choices they make. If a child needs attention, try to fold them into the group: *David, can you start the warm-up please?* State rules simply and positively: *Always Barefoot*, rather than *No Shoes*. Use your physical presence as a kind of proximity control: move around, interact, and—without being threatening—move close to students who seem to be drifting away. Don't worry about what you can't control. Whatever techniques and approaches you employ during challenging moments, make sure you maintain your own peace and sanity, and work from that foundation.

Open and Ongoing Invitations

I worked with Sandor, a student who was diagnosed with autism, during two eight-week dance residencies. In Year 1, each class began with my saying hello, inviting him to participate, and pointing out his spot. He would not take off his jacket or backpack, and often was disengaged, sitting to the side and watching. Over the course of a few weeks, Sandor started to participate in the warm-up, and in the *across the floor* activities . . . but he only watched the final class performance. A year later, during our second residency, I continued to invite him to participate. He slowly grew more and more engaged in the class, making eye contact, using language on occasion. After our rehearsal for the Year 2 culminating performance the other teaching artist and I were sitting next to each other on the stage. Sandor came up to us and motioned for us to move over so he could sit between us. He took my hand and squeezed it while making eye contact (as if to say thank you) and then sat next to us smiling. During the final performance, his jacket and backpack were off, and he was right at the front of the group dancing with a big smile. Sandor's eye contact, use of language and touch, and smiling voluntary participation all indicated positive development—and all took place on his schedule, according to his own needs. My takeaway: *meet every student where they are in each moment, and extend ongoing invitations for students to participate, even when they seem disengaged or uninterested.*—Heather Bryce, dance, Vermont

---

Special Needs, Special Talents

I was at a library preparing for a storytelling program. A mother and her two sons had come in early, and we began to chat. The younger son, about six years old, was very engaging, and the mother urged him on. The older, about eight years old, sat quietly, with little affect. The program began, and I came to a point where I needed a volunteer to come up and, basically, mirror my movements. Both boys, right in the front row, raised their hands. The younger boy was effusive, and would certainly have done the part well. I knew the older boy was different—on the spectrum? I invited him up, and a look of terror came over his mother's face. Perhaps she was concerned about her son being humiliated, or about me being disappointed. But her son was superb, owing to his amazing capacity to focus, which is just what the mirroring activity required. After the program, the mother came up to thank me and tell me that her son had ASD (Autistic Spectrum Disorder). The following year she arranged for me to come and present at her sons' school for students on the spectrum. In my storytelling program with the first graders, a boy in the front row was fidgety, chattery, and mildly disruptive. When I needed a volunteer, I called him up. He quickly focused, settled into the role, and even took some leadership in helping me to tell the story. He truly shone. Then too, a teacher afterward came to inform me of his Asperger's, and to thank me for choosing him. My takeaway: *sometimes a student's liability is also his strength.*—Barry Stewart Mann, actor, storyteller, educator, Atlanta, GA

Frameworks, Outlines, and Blueprints

In your art-making, craft might be said to be any technique that enhances your ability to practice your art. Similarly, your teaching artist's craft is any technique (skill, ability, understanding) that makes it possible for you to do your best and most inspired work. In her introduction to *Steering the Craft—Exercises and Discussions on Story Writing for the Lone Navigator or the Mutinous Crew*, writer Ursula K. LeGuin beautifully traces a connection between craft and art. She's talking about writing, but what she is saying is just as true for our teaching artist practice:

> *Once we're keenly and clearly aware of (the) elements of our craft, we can use and practice them until—the point of all practice—we don't have to think about them consciously at all, because they have become skills. A skill is something you know how to do. Skill in writing frees you to write what you want to write. It may also show you what you want to write. Craft enables art. There's luck in art. There's the gift. You can't earn that. You can't deserve it. But you can learn skill, you can earn it. You can learn to deserve your gift. I'm not going to discuss writing as self-expression, as therapy, or as a spiritual adventure. It can be these things; but first of all—and in the end, too—it is an art, a craft, a making. To make something well is to give yourself to it, to seek wholeness, to follow spirit. To learn to make something well can take your whole life. It's worth it.[5]*

What is a teaching artist's craft? We have yet to arrive at any consensus. But we have succeeded in becoming an increasingly collegial and communicative profession. *The Teaching Artist's Journal* is a quarterly collection of essays and articles by teaching artists and arts administrators; the current back issues include over three hundred individual articles. Teaching artistry is also addressed by Jaffe, Barniskis, and Hackett-Cox's *Teaching Artist Handbook Volume I: Tools, Techniques, and Ideas to Help Any Artist Teach* ("a collection of essays, stories, lists, examples, ideas, techniques, and opinions"), and by David Wallace's *Reaching Out: A Musician's Guide to Interactive Performance*, as well as *The Reflexive Teaching Artist: Collected Wisdom from the Drama/Theatre Field*, edited by Dawson and Kelin (which explores "a series of foundational concepts, including intentionality, quality, artistic perspective, assessment, and praxis . . . (as it) examine(s) the practice of teaching in, through, and about drama and theater), and Eric Booth's *The Music Teaching Artist's Bible: Becoming a Virtuoso Educator*. These books and the journal present teaching artistry from different angles: an arts administrator's point of view, a student's point of view, a theoretical or technical point of view, and most often a teaching artist's own close-up point of view. These publications are evidence of a rich and passionate public dialogue about our work, a manifestation of a tremendous amount of experience and erudition. Familiarity with the ideas these writers present should be part of our basic training.

In this final section of *A Teaching Artist's Companion*, I've collected lists, frameworks, and approaches from the current writings on (or writings that I connect with) teaching artistry that I find especially inspiring or provocative. See what resonates for you. Use these to reflect on your own craft. If you'd like to do so within the context of View, Design, and Respond context, ask yourself:

Where does my View align with or differ from the View implied by this item?

How would this item manifest in terms of Design?

Which new ideas do I want to borrow and include in my own View or Design?

To what extent does my current program or approach address the areas emphasized in this item?

Which aspects of the item can I translate into a way to improve my View, Design, or Respond work?

HIVE CHICAGO—HOMAGO'S VIEW STATED IN THE FORM OF KEYWORDS

This delightful list of keywords has a jaunty feeling that reminds me how much fun it is to be working in this field. HOMAGO = Hang Out, Mess Around, Geek Out.

collaboration, collaborative
hang out
mess around
geek out
tips/feedback
cool
adult/street cred
drop in experimental making
creative support
new media traditional media like you've never seen it
exciting
free
youth
access to resources
connections
fun conversations

comfortable
autonomy
non-judgmental space
choice based
open
sharing ideas
media making mentoring
safe
nurturing without coddling
aesthetics
mentoring
risk taking[6]

NICK JAFFE'S "WHAT DOES GOOD TEACHING ARTIST WORK LOOK LIKE?"

Nick Jaffe is a Saint Paul, Minnesota–based musician, recording engineer, teaching artist, editor, former aircraft mechanic, ESL teacher, elementary school teacher, and audio engineer with a degree in history from Yale—perhaps a typical teaching artist bio. His beautifully compressed list from the *Teaching Artist Handbook—Volume I* invites us to take a global and relational view of the work we do. I especially appreciate his use of "seems" and "seems to . . .". We do our best to assess our processes and relationships, but we can't and don't know for sure. At best, in process, things "seem to be." Then again, in the end, with number five, the resulting work will speak for itself, through its qualities.

1 Students are making something that seems important to them.
2 The teaching artist seems to relate to the students as artists.
3 The students seem to relate to the teaching artist as an artist.
4 The students seem to relate to each other as artists.
5 The students were making good art, work that exhibited

variety
invention
power
development
wholeness[7]

ERIC BOOTH'S "LIST OF THE ELEMENTS OF THE ARTFORM OF TEACHING ARTISTRY"

Eric Booth isn't pulling any punches. He knows that successful teaching artists are doing most or all of this, almost all of the time. I re-read his list of elements from *The Music Teaching Artist's Bible*[8] when I need to hear a calm, clear voice reminding me what matters.

1. Placing a High Priority on Personal Relevance
2. Using Engagement Before Information
3. Tapping Competence
4. Knowing the Learners
5. Planning Backward
6. Planning Thoroughly
7. Never Forgetting Fun
8. Controlling the Classroom
9. Clarifying Instructions
10. Setting the Work Environment
11. Turning the Responsibility for the Learning over to the Learner
12. Practicing the Activities You Propose
13. Scaffolding—Step by Step
14. Remembering Reflection
15. Balancing the Focus on Process and Product
16. Separating Observation from Interpretation
17. Witnessing
18. Making Choices, and Noting Their Impact
19. Using High Quality Questions
20. Working with Classroom Teachers
19. Using Warm-Up Activities
20. Connections to the Curriculum
21. Planning Meetings with Teachers
22. Staying Fresh
23. The Law of 80 percent

ERIC BOOTH'S "AESTHETIC EDUCATION INCLUDES . . ."

Eric shared this list during a professional development I attended in the 1990s. I'm always impressed with his ability to clarify important ideas in a short time or small space. Here he holds a mirror up to Lincoln Center's emphasis on aesthetic education, as inspired by Maxine Greene. I remember my main take-away from the PD was Eric's insistence on *authentic work*, and his implied distain for any work that wasn't so. What does it mean to be *authentic*? Do our invitations to students open a door to a process that is authentically artistic, unpredictable, rewarding? This list—like a lot of Eric's writing—opens up any number of questions that stay open.

Aesthetic education includes . . .
yearning
engagement before information
inquiry based (open questions)
personal relevance

intrinsic motivation
tap competence
authentic work
entry point
reflection
balance between process and product

THREE AREAS OF TEACHING ARTIST MASTERY

Karen Erickson's way of looking at teaching artist practice is impressive in its completeness and practicality. She lays out the *abilities, skills,* and *knowledge* we are called to master in our *artistic, teaching,* and *business* practices.

1) Artistic Aspect
   Teaching artists should be accomplished artists in their fields.
   a) Ability or Skill:
      - Have formal training and/or years of experience in arts discipline or traditional arts practice.
      - Demonstrate professional practice: perform, exhibit, publish, maintain a healthy body of work as appropriate to the art form and cultural community.
      - Provide authentic model for power of artistic thinking, creating, perceiving, reflecting, and attending.
      - Take risks as an artist (model behavior).
      - Develop self-assessment/critique/evaluation skills.
      - Model flexibility and adaptability.
      - Possess artistic skills to deal with any situation that might arise.
      - Use components of art form to teach in new ways.
      - Transform passion for own art form and motivate participant to push their own aesthetic experience.
      - Synthesize and make connections.
   b) Knowledge Base:
      - Historical and societal context of own art form.
      - Wide range of materials and methods within art form.

2) Teaching Aspect
   TAs should provide expertise in teaching that includes organizational abilities, people management, knowledge of organizational systems (e.g., schools, prisons, park districts, etc.) ability to teach (to transfer knowledge to others governed by age, gender, physical, cultural, and brain development considerations), and knowledge about current trends in the organizational system into which they have been hired.

a) Ability or Skill
  - Collaborate with teachers, administrators, staff, students, parents, community.
  - Conduct a needs assessment in collaboration with the classroom teacher or site contact person.
  - Engage a roomful of people who have different abilities.
  - Teach across gender, age, race, and cultural boundaries.
  - Create successful sequential lessons that are developmentally appropriate.
  - Assess participant learning and evaluate overall program effectiveness.
  - Be flexible, assess progress and success of classroom in progress and make any necessary adjustments (in teaching style, materials, equipment, timing, sequencing, teacher/staff involvement).
  - Model behavior and best practices.
  - Access resources to support own teaching, e.g., people, organizations, and literature.
  - Use the arts to foster and build healthy self-esteem.
  - Share genuine affection for the audience/population that one is teaching.
  - To build community through art.

b) Knowledge Base:
  - Classroom management skills.
  - Multiple intelligence theory and its integration into teaching practice.
  - Current state curriculum standards and an ability to link them with teaching practice.
  - Developmental capabilities of their participants, and child development in general.

3) Business Aspect
  TAs should be able to operate with business acumen.
  a) Ability or Skill
  - Manage time and schedule effectively, not over-booking, ability to be on time.
  - Communicate: to talk with teachers, staff, administrators, parents; ability to follow up on conversations.
  - Manage an office: administrative skills, book-keeping.
  - Be organized and prepared.
  - Be professional in demeanor: respect for school/community space environment, materials, rules, schedule, and property.

- Use good presentation skills: using voice and body language to captivate audience.
- Be able to write workshop descriptions, promotional literature, and more: literary skills.
- Plan and promote own work as an artist-educator.
- Write grants and raise funds.

b) Knowledge Base:
- Understand how to access different communities and to facilitate meetings with a diverse group of people.
- Negotiation skills and working with contracts.[9]

CALARTS COMMUNITY ARTS PARTNERSHIP, "FIVE QUALITIES
OF SUCCESSFUL TEACHING ARTISTRY"

When coaching teaching artists, Glenna Avila, the Wallis Annenberg Artistic Director of the CalArts Community Arts Partnership, points out five qualities of our work—attentiveness, flexibility, authenticity, positivity, responsiveness—in the form of actionable verbs. I enjoy the way thinking about these qualities allows me to simply hop over questions of philosophy and technique, and access the power of our fundamental approaches, our basic attitudes and energies, to shape successful containers for teaching and learning.

Be Present

Give your full attention to your students. Listen carefully to what they have to say and respond to them in a clear and positive way. Be present in the moment with them. And of course, learn their names.

Be Flexible

Your class may be cancelled at the last minute due to shifting school schedules or other reasons. Students may be pulled out of your class, or are absent and are not there, missing important parts of your lesson or project. Any number of things can interfere with the best laid plans. Be flexible and nimble as you deal with the situations that arise in a forward-moving, problem-solving way.

Be Authentic

Be true to who you are, share your background, and share the artist part of yourself with your students. You are likely are the most famous artist they know, so be generous with them. Students, especially teens, can sniff out fakeness and snobbishness immediately. They greatly appreciate authenticity in all its forms.

Be Positive

Enter your class each day with a positive demeanor. Everyone wants to be around positivity, even seemingly bored, skeptical, or sullen teenagers. You have lots of information and skills to share with your students, so show them your passion for the arts. Your positive outlook can also rub off on hardworking classroom teachers and administrators.

Be Responsive

Respond to all the questions your students have. Find ways to make the arts activities relevant to them. Bring in culturally specific and culturally diverse materials to challenge them. To the best of your ability, be responsive to their individual needs. Learn as much as you can about their cognitive and social development, demographics, languages, and cultures, and design developmentally appropriate, culturally relevant curricula.[10]

SOCIAL JUSTICE ARTS EDUCATION AND CREATIVE YOUTH DEVELOPMENT

Teaching artists are asked to balance art-making, the study of works of art, art for art's sake, community-building and historical context with students' personal development. Social Justice Arts Education and Creative Youth Development priorities re-frame our work along the lines described in these samples from the field. For many of us, it's the right frame.

> Social Justice: *A vision for a society in which all people, of all social identities, are treated equitably . . . To work toward social justice, we must make the invisible visible.*—National Guild for Community Arts in Education Justice Working Group[11]

> Social Justice Arts Education: *Art that draws attention to, mobilizes action toward, or attempts to intervene in systems of inequality or injustice . . . As long as the process of making art offers participants a way to construct knowledge, critically analyze an idea, and take action in the world, then they are engaged in a practice of social justice art-making.*—Marit Dewhurst, "An Inevitable Question: Exploring the Defining Features of Social Justice Art Education" (*Journal of Art Education*, September 2010)[12]

> Creative Youth Development (CYD): *A recently coined term that organizes a longstanding community of practice that intentionally integrates the arts, sciences, and humanities with youth development principles, sparking young people's creativity and building critical learning and life skills that carry into adulthood.*—The National Guild for Community Arts in Education[13]

AU, BIGELOW, AND KARP'S SOCIALLY JUST CURRICULUM

In *Rethinking Our Classrooms: Teaching for Equity and Justice*, editors Wayne Au, Bill Bigelow, and Stan Karp begin with the premise that "schools and classrooms should be laboratories for a more just society than the one we live in now." Their introduction to the book presents this vision for a social justice classroom.

> A socially just curriculum and classroom practice must be . . .
> grounded in the lives of our students (rooted in children's needs and experiences)
> critical (the curriculum should equip students to talk back to the world)
> multicultural, anti-racist, pro-justice
> participatory, experiential
> hopeful, joyful, kind, visionary (children feel significant and cared about by the teacher and by each other)
> activist (students come to see themselves as truth-tellers and change-makers)
> academically rigorous
> culturally sensitive[14]

ARTS CORPS' SOCIAL JUSTICE FRAMEWORK FOR TEACHING

In Seattle, Arts Corps' staff and teaching artists meet regularly to address issues of racial and social justice. Executive director and veteran theater teaching artist James Miles makes the meetings a priority, knowing that "We cannot get certified in this work, nor will we be equipped after one training, but we will most effectively deepen this work through long-term organizational commitments." In their Social Justice Framework for Teaching, Arts Corps has developed an elegant and effective tool for self-reflection. Many of the practices described in *A Teaching Artist's Companion* appear in this framework with a social justice and creative youth development emphasis. This would be a good tool to use before beginning (or in the middle of) a curriculum Design, as a checklist for purpose and tone. I appreciate the way these questions call us to a higher level of intentionality.

> Social Justice Framework: a metaphor for classroom teaching
> 1. Look in the Mirror
> 2. Walk in the Door
> 3. Connect with Students
> 4. Build It together/Work It Out
> 5. Leave the Room

> Look in the Mirror: Self Knowledge
> *Who am I to myself? How do I appear to the world? What is my story?*
> *What brings me to art? What has brought me to teach?*
> *What is my story as it relates to race/class/gender/sexuality/culture?*
> *How have I experienced power? How have I experienced oppression?*
> *What makes me feel powerful? What makes me feel disempowered?*
> *What are my personal triggers? What are my teaching triggers?*

Walk in the Door: Classrooms and Institutions

What do I know about my teaching classroom? Where is the school? Who is in the room? How many people? What is the age group?

What is the socio-economic/gender/racial/cultural/ethnic/linguistic background

of this class?

Who am I co-teaching with? What context do both teachers and students have about me/my art form in their classroom? What is this classrooms culture?

What does the classroom look like? How are the seats arranged? Is there student work presented on the wall? Where are the students sitting? Who is sitting with whom?

What do I know about this institution? What is its history in the community? How does it receive funding? Who backs it? Who does not?

How does the institution determine who has access, feels supported, has opportunity, uses power, and who is ignored, punished, penalized?

Connect with Students: Communication and Facilitation

How do I create safety in this classroom with this particular group of young folks?

How can I use my experiences/knowledge to work with this demographic of young folks even if we are coming from different places?

Do these youth relate to the subject matter/connect with my art form?

What effective teaching tools do I use to bring my art form to life?

How do I unintentionally and intentionally create unequal and inequitable power dynamics? What youth do I like/relate to the most? Who receives my praise and how often? Whom do I send out of the class or punish? What do I do to prevent this?

Build It Together: Community and Conflict

What tools and teaching strategies do I use that honor student voice, perspective, and experience?

How do I actively make space for student empowerment and agency in my classroom?

What mechanisms does my classroom have for moderating conflict? Personal accountability?

How will I know if I am in the wrong? How do I make space for humbling moments? What classroom structures are built for young folks to bring these moments to my attention?

What structures are in place for young people to engage in deep dialogue and interrupt oppression amongst themselves?

How do I actively interrupt moments of oppression when class is in session? When oppression occurs within the administration of parents?

How will art act as an agent of liberation in this particular class and in this institution?

Leave the Room: Assessing Transformation

How do I evaluate the efficacy of my teaching through an SJ lens? What teaching methods do I keep? What do I need to build? What do I need to change?

How can I measure the level of student agency in the room?

Have I spoken out about inequitable/unequal/unjust situations I have witnessed: in the class, with the administration, to the youth?

Have I celebrated my students' achievements and individual lives?

Did my art have a liberating affect? How will I know this?[15]

THE CULTURAL ICEBERG

All educators would like to be better able to connect, observe, and respond during teaching and learning. Artist, educator, and activist Derrick Gay reminds us that our belief that "my reality is the only reality" impedes those activities. Gay urges us to have "more interaction with—and empathy for—each others' narratives, our stories, identities, use of language" in order to yield "a closer alignment between *what is* and our world view." One way to start is to become aware of cultural assumptions we make about ourselves and others. This graphic (Figure 8.4), inspired by anthropologist Edward T. Hall's 1976 "external/internal" iceberg graphic, is used by the Peace Corps, universities, and Arts-in-Education organizations to open up discussion of those assumptions. Some versions include the idea that the further down the iceberg one goes, the stronger one's emotional attachment. I like the way it works, and appreciate the density of reflection-provoking ideas it packs into a small space.

DREAMYARD'S ANTI-RACIST STATEMENT

Here is a window into the work being done at DreamYard in the Bronx, an institution where the underlying philosophy is wholly *embodied*. From the staff and programming level, through the documentation, outreach, architecture, and work displayed, down to and including the wording of the invitations that individual teaching artists craft for the *Invite–Work–Show* sequences of their workshop activities and the refreshments they offer to guests, their belief system is bracingly apparent.

Anti-Racist Statement

At the DreamYard Project, we commit to being an anti-racist organization. We lead with race because we operate in a country founded on the genocide of indigenous people, the enslavement of African people, and the oppression of countless others. We acknowledge the role this history plays in perpetuating inequity and dominant white culture.

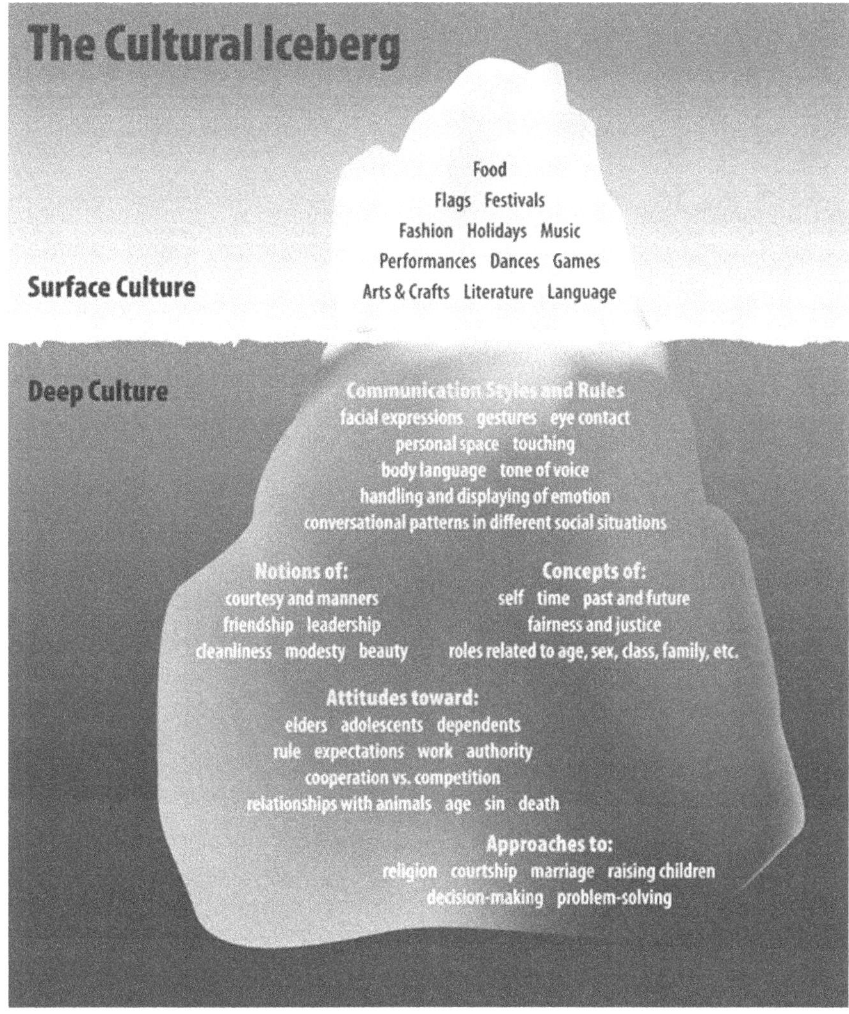

FIGURE 8.4 The Cultural Iceberg

We are intentionally building a path toward racial equity by:

- Challenging oppression and its intersections
- Using art and education as a platform to offer a hopeful vision of the future
- Identifying and uplifting the power and cultural assets that exist within our community of educators, artists, dreamers, young people, and life-long learners
- Encouraging the principles of justice, unity, equity, creativity, and joy
- Transforming policies, procedures, practices, and programs (for example: striving for transparency and equity in pay and compensation structures regardless of race, culture, gender, ethnicity, creed, etc.)

- Understanding our staff, community members, and partners are at different levels on the anti-racist continuum and embracing that we all have a place in this work

We invite you to join us on this journey.

THE ASSOCIATION OF TEACHING ARTISTS' BASIC CAPACITIES OF ALL TEACHING

The Association really is what its name suggests, a "practitioner-led network and community of practice that supports artists who work in education and community venues," now celebrating their twentieth year. If teaching artists ever formed a medieval-style guild, journeymen practitioners would need to show evidence of understanding or accomplishment in all these areas before being certified as Master TAs.

1. Understanding Your Art Form
    a. Knowledge of basic formal language
    b. Knowledge of trends, history, and styles of the discipline
    c. Knowledge of key practitioners of the discipline, both historical and contemporary
    d. Understanding of the creative process (e.g., inspiration, planning, developing an idea, using materials and techniques, expression)
2. Understanding Classroom Environment; Pedagogy, Human Development
    a. Process and product, the continuum in experiencing the arts
    b. Planning a lesson, including modeling, demonstration, differentiated instruction
    c. Time management
    d. Hallmarks of early childhood, middle elementary, junior high, and high school human development
    e. Curriculum unit and residency planning
    f. Classroom management
    g. Evaluation and assessment, strategies, and practices
3. Understanding the Collaborative Process; Working in a School Environment
    a. The residency planning process
    b. Working with administrator, teachers, and parents[16]

VISUAL THINKING STRATEGIES

This approach has deep roots, and is backed up by robust research and documentation. Developed with visual arts students in mind, it is well worth adapting to your own art form (as suggested earlier in "Use Open Questions," page 77). Start by substituting the appropriate words in the opening quote: *theatrical literacy is the ability to find meaning in theatrical works of art; musical literacy . . . dance literacy . . .*

In his 1997 article "Thoughts on Visual Literacy," the former education director of New York's Museum of Modern Art and co-creator of the Visual Thinking Strategies (VTS) curriculum Philip Yenawine describes visual literacy as "the ability to find meaning in imagery. It involves a set of skills ranging from simple identification (naming what one sees) to complex interpretation on contextual, metaphoric, and philosophical levels. Many aspects of cognition are called upon, such as personal association, questioning, speculating, analyzing, fact-finding, and categorizing. Objective understanding is the premise of much of this literacy, but subjective and affective aspects of knowing are equally important."

In VTS discussions, teachers support student growth by facilitating discussions of carefully selected works of visual art.

> Teachers are asked to use three open-ended questions:
>> What's going on in this picture?
>> What do you see that makes you say that?
>> What more can we find?
>
> Teachers follow up with three facilitation techniques:
>> Paraphrase comments neutrally
>> Point at the area being discussed
>> Linking and framing student comments
>
> Students are asked to:
>> Look carefully at works of art
>> Talk about what they observe
>> Back up their ideas with evidence
>> Listen to and consider the views of others
>> Discuss many possible interpretations[17]

A Teaching Artist's Companion Online Materials List

To download PDF versions of these materials, visit www.daniellevymusic.com

NOTES

Introduction

1. Chogyam Trungpa, *The Collected Works of Chogyam Trungpa: Volume Three: Cutting Through Spiritual Materialism; The Myth of Freedom; The Heart of the Buddha; Selected Writings* (Boston & London: Shambhala Publications, 2010), 252

Chapter 2

1. Patti Saraniero and Lisa Resnick "Constructivism: Actively Building Arts Education: A Brief Introduction to Constructivism and How Arts Educators Can Utilize It Effectively," from the Kennedy Center's ARTSEDGE website, 2018. https://artsedge. kennedy-center.org/educators/how-to/from-theory-to-practice/constructivism

Chapter 3

1. Daniel Levy, ed. Ava Lehrer and Larisa Gelman, *The Music of the Silk Road Curriculum Guide* (New York: 92Y School of the Arts, 2017), 21–22 https://www.92y.org/ 92StreetY/media/DOCUMENTS/Uptown/Misc/Fall_17/MISCurriculum2017_18.pdf

2. Daniel Levy, ed. Ava Lehrer and Larisa Gelman, *The Music of the Silk Road Student Music Journal* (New York: 92Y School of the Arts, 2017), 24–25, https://www.92y.org/ 92StreetY/media/DOCUMENTS/Uptown/Misc/Fall_17/MISJournal2017_18.pdf

3. James Alan Sturtevant, *You've Gotta Connect* (Chicago: World Book, 2014), 151

4. Jeremy Roschelle, "Learning in Interactive Environments: Prior Knowledge and New Experience," in *Public Institutions for Personal Learning: Establishing a Research Agenda*, ed. John Falk and Lynn Dierking (Washington DC: American Association of Museums, now American Alliance of Museums, 1995)

5. Matt Utterback, *Building and Activating Students' Prior Knowledge—It Is What They Know That Counts* (*North Clackamas Schools E-Newsletter*, September 2013)

6. Garvin Brod, Markus Werkle-Bergner, and Yee Lee Shing, "The Influence of Prior Knowledge on Memory: A Developmental Cognitive Neuroscience Perspective." *Frontiers in Behavioral Neuroscience*, 7 (2013): 139. PMC. April 19, 2018, https://www.ncbi.nlm.nih. gov/pmc/articles/PMC3792618/

7. Stephen Sondheim, "Another Hundred People," song lyric from *Company* (1970), courtesy of Round Hill Music https://roundhillmusic.com/. https://www.allmusicals.com/ lyrics/company/anotherhundredpeople.htm

8. Eric Booth, *The Music Teaching Artist's Bible* (2009), by permission of Oxford University Press, USA

9. *What Is VTS?* The Center for Creative Community at Commonweal, accessed May 1, 2018. http://ccc-commonweal.org/visual-thinking-strategies/

10. Adam Cohen, "An SAT Without Analogies Is Like: (A) A Confused Citizenry . . ." *New York Times*, March 13, 2005, https://www.nytimes.com/2005/03/13/opinion/an-sat-without-analogies-is-like-a-a-confused-citizenry.html

11. Howard Gardner, *The Unschooled Mind: How Children Think and How Schools Should Teach*, 2nd Edition (New York: Basic Books, 2011)

12. Barbara Solomon and Richard Felder, "Index of Learning Styles," accessed March 1, 2018, http://www4.ncsu.edu/unity/lockers/users/f/felder/public//Learning_Styles.html

13. Booth, *The Music Teaching Artist's Bible*, 27

14. Alex Ross, "Violent Vivaldi: *The Four Seasons* as Uneasy Listening," The *New Yorker (periodical)*, February 19, 2001, New York https://www.newyorker.com/magazine/2001/02/19/violent-vivaldi

15. John Dewey, *How We Think* (Boston: D.C. Heath & Co., 1910) https://archive.org/details/howwethink000838mbp

16. Jenny Moon, *Reflection in Learning and Professional Development: Theory and Practice* (New York, RoutledgeFalmer, 2004)

17. Graham Gibbs, *Learning by Doing: A Guide to Teaching and Learning Methods* (1988), reproduced with his permission by the Oxford Centre for Staff and Learning Development, Oxford Brookes University, Wheatley Campus, Wheatley, Oxford, UK. https://thoughtsmostlyaboutlearning.files.wordpress.com/2015/12/learning-by-doing-graham-gibbs.pdf

18. Peter Pappas, "A Taxonomy of Reflection: Critical Thinking For Students, Teachers, and Principals (Part 1)," from his blog *Copy/Paste*, accessed March 1, 2018, http://peterpappas.com/2010/01/taxonomy-reflection-critical-thinking-students-teachers-principals.html

19. David A. Kolb, *Experiential Learning: Experience as the Source of Learning and Development*, Vol. 1 (Englewood Cliffs, NJ: Prentice-Hall, 1981)

20. Saul A. McLeod, *Kolb—Learning Styles* (2017), accessed March 1, 2018, from www.simplypsychology.org/learning-kolb.html

21. Karen Barnstable, "Four Dimensions of Reflection," from her blog *Stable Transitions: A Journey of Learning*, accessed March 1, 2018, http://kbarnstable.wordpress.com/2009/12/15/22-questions-for-reflection/

22. Maxine Greene, *Variations on a Blue Guitar: The Lincoln Center Institute Lectures on Aesthetic Education* (New York: Teachers College Press, 2001)

23. Terry Barrett, *Criticizing Art: Understanding the Contemporary* (Mountain View, CA: Mayfield Publishing Company, now McGraw Hill, 1994) https://pdfs.semanticscholar.org/35f5/50763b8b83fd733914cdf719b6ae356cb1b4.pdf

24. Joyce Payne, "Teaching Students to Critique," *Kennedy Center ArtsEdge tipsheet*, accessed March 1, 2018, http://artsedge.kennedy-center.org/educators/how-to/tipsheets/student-critique.aspx

Chapter 4

1. Barry Boyce, "Ocean of Dharma," *Lions Roar*, April 4, 2017, accessed March 1, 2018, https://www.lionsroar.com/ocean-of-dharma-january-2012/

2. Ozgur Ozer, "Constructivism in Piaget and Vygotsky," *The Fountain*, 48 (October–December 2004) Blue Dome Press http://www.fountainmagazine.com/2004/issue-48-october-december-2004/CONSTRUCTIVISM-in-Piaget-and-Vygotsky

3. Roya Jafari Amineh and Hanieh Davatgari, "Review of Constructivism and Social Constructivism," *Journal of Social Sciences, Literature and Languages*, 1:1, 9–16, April 30, 2015, http://www.blue-ap.org/j/List/4/iss/volume%201%20(2015)/issue%2001/2.pdf

4. Rose Senior, "Learning With Laughter," *Guardian* (US Edition), December 5, 2007, accessed March 1, 2018, http://www.theguardian.com/education/2007/dec/05/tefl2

5. www.youthspeaks.org/methodology/ accessed May 28, 2019

6. Lois Hetland, Ellen Winner, Shirley Veenema, and Kimberly M. Sheridan, *Studio Thinking* (New York: Teachers College Press, 2007)

7. Bena Kallick and Art Costa, "What Are Habits of Mind?" *Institute for Habits of Mind*, accessed March 1, 2018, http://www.habitsofmindinstitute.org/wp-content/uploads/2015/08/Habits-of-Mind-w-icons-and-eduplanet.pdf

8. Lincoln Center Education's Capacities for Imaginative Learning aka Learning Framework provided courtesy of Lincoln Center for the Performing Arts, Inc. Copyright © 2017.

9. Jaffe, Barniskis and Cox, "14 Ideas About Classroom Management," *Teaching Artist Handbook*, Vol. 1 (Chicago: Columbia College Chicago Press, 2013), 84–90

10. Paul Tough, *How Children Succeed: Grit, Curiosity, and the Hidden Power of Character* (New York: Mariner Books, 2012)

11. Wendell Berry, "The Real Work," from *Standing by Words* (Berkeley, CA: Counterpoint Press, 1983)

12. Dena Rosenbloom, Mary Beth Williams, and Barbara E. Watkins, *Life After Trauma—A Workbook for Healing* (New York, NY: The Guilford Press, 1999)

13. James Garbarino, *Raising Children in a Socially Toxic Environment* (San Francisco: Jossey-Bass, 1995)

14. Shawn Ginwright, *Hope and Healing in Urban Education* (New York: Routledge, 2016), from his webpage for the book, accessed May 1, 2018, http://www.shawnginwright.com/books/

Chapter 5

1. Daniel Levy, *Musical Introduction Series Curriculum Guide 2012–2013* (New York: 92Y School of the Arts, 2012), 11, https://www.92y.org/92StreetY/media/DOCUMENTS/Uptown/Misc/Spring_14/MISCurriculumGuide2012-13.pdf

Chapter 6

1. Lincoln Center Education's Brainstorming Guide for Designing an LCE Instructional Unit provided courtesy of Lincoln Center for the Performing Arts, Inc. Copyright © 2017

2. Daniel Levy, *Musical Introduction Series Curriculum Guide 2012–2013* (New York: 92Y School of the Arts, 2012), 11, https://www.92y.org/92StreetY/media/DOCUMENTS/Uptown/Misc/Spring_14/MISCurriculumGuide2012-13.pdf

3. John Dewey, *Art as Experience* Copyright © 1934 by John Dewey (London: Berkley Publishing Group, 2005)

Chapter 7

1. Allison Gulamhussein, *Teaching the Teachers: Effective Professional Development in an Era of High Stakes Accountability,* Center for Public Education (2013), accessed May 1, 2018, http://www.centerforpubliceducation.org/research/teaching-teachers-effective-professional-development

2. Gulamhussein, *Teaching the Teachers*

3. New York City Department of Education, *Consent Form,* accessed May 1, 2018, http://schools.nyc.gov/NR/rdonlyres/2E974D18-2CA2-445D-8A0F-8AAE9B4EF238/88120/consent_form_revised35.pdf

Chapter 8

1. Teaching Artists Guild, interactive Pay Rate Calculator, accessed May 1, 2018, https://teachingartistsguild.org/pay-rate-calculator/

2. Association of Teaching Artists, Wish List, accessed May 1, 2018, https://www.teachingartists.com/TAwishlist.htm

3. Rena Kornblum, "Four Bs To Help Us Relax," from *Arts and Students with Disabilities Online Resource Compendium* New York City Department of Education's Office of Arts and Special Projects (2017), accessed May 1, 2018, https://www.weteachnyc.org/resources/collection/students-with-disabilities-online-resource-compendium/

4. Dr. Diane Duggan, "How to Prevent Students from Engaging in Misbehavior in the Classroom," from *Arts and Students with Disabilities Online Resource Compendium* New York City Department of Education's Office of Arts and Special Projects, accessed May 1, 2018, http://schools.nyc.gov/offices/teachlearn/arts/files/swd/Dance_SWD_intro-resources.pdf

5. Ursula K. LeGuin, *Steering the Craft—Exercises and Discussions on Story Writing for the Lone Navigator or the Mutinous Crew* (Portland, OR: Eighth Mountain Press, 1998)

6. Hive Chicago, HOMAGO'S View stated in the form of keywords, accessed May 1, 2018, https://issuu.com/yollocalli/docs/homagoguidebook

7. Nick Jaffe, "What Does Good Teaching Artist Work Look Like?" *The Teaching Artist Handbook, Vol. 1* (Chicago: Columbia College Chicago Press, 2013), 139

8. Eric Booth, *The Music Teaching Artist's Bible* (New York: Oxford University Press, 2009)

9. Karen Erickson (2009), "The Professional Life of Professional TAs," *Teaching Artist Journal*, 1:3, 172–177, DOI: 10.1207/S1541180XTAJ0103_08

10. Courtesy of Glenna Avila, the Wallis Annenberg Artistic Director of the CalArts Community Arts Partnership

11. National Guild for Community Arts In Education Justice Working Group. Author's notes, Philadelphia, 2016

12. Marit Dewhurst, "An Inevitable Question: Exploring the Defining Features of Social Justice Art Education," *Journal of Art Education*, 63:5, September 1, 2010, DOI:10.1080/00043125.2010.11519082

13. National Guild for Community Arts In Education Key Initiative, accessed May 1, 2018, http://www.nationalguild.org/Programs/Key-Initiatives/Creative-Youth-Development.aspx

14. Wayne Au, Stan Karp, and Bill Bigelow, *Rethinking Our Classrooms: Teaching for Equity and Justice* (introduction) (Milwaukee, WI: Rethinking Schools Ltd., 2007)

15. Arts Corp's Social Justice Framework for Teaching, created by Roberto Ascalon and Tina LaPadula, based on the contributions of team of Arts Corps; internal organizational document.

16. Association of Teaching Artists, *What Does a Teaching Artist Need To Know*, accessed May 1, 2018, https://www.teachingartists.com/TeachingAritstneedknow.htm

17. University of South Florida Academy for Teaching and Learning Excellence, *Visual Thinking Strategies*, accessed May 1, 2018, http://www.usf.edu/atle/teaching/visual-thinking-strategies.aspx

INDEX

9 780190 926168